COLUMBIA UNIVERSITY STUDIES IN ENGLISH
AND COMPARATIVE LITERATURE

THE GLOOMY EGOIST

THE GLOOMY EGOIST

MOODS AND THEMES OF MELANCHOLY
FROM GRAY TO KEATS

BY

ELEANOR M. SICKELS

Only the dreamer venoms all his days
Bearing more woe than all his sins deserve

1969

OCTAGON BOOKS
New York

TO

THE MEMORY OF
MY FATHER

Reprinted 1969
by special arrangement with Eleanor M. Sickels

OCTAGON BOOKS
A Division of Farrar, Straus & Giroux, Inc.
19 Union Square West
New York, N. Y. 10003

Library of Congress Catalog Card Number: 76-76008

Printed in U.S.A. by
NOBLE OFFSET PRINTERS, INC.
NEW YORK 3, N. Y.

FOREWORD

This study of melancholy poetry in the generations between Gray and Keats had its inception several years ago, at the time of the appearance of Professor Amy Reed's *Background of Gray's Elegy*. The original intention was simply to carry the history Professor Reed had so ably begun down to the closing years of the eighteenth century. But just as she had found it impossible to treat of the first half of the eighteenth century without delving deep into the seventeenth, so I soon found myself more and more involved in the ideas and output of the full-fledged romanticists of the early nineteenth century. It remains true, however, that the closer and more detailed research has been in the transition years, and that, if anything new be here presented, it is probably rather in the history of those years than in any radically unexpected interpretation of romanticism proper.

In the pursuit of this history, one other book has been so nearly indispensable as to call for a word of special acknowledgment. I refer to Professor R. D. Havens' exhaustive study of *The Influence of Milton on English Poetry*, the bibliographies of which have been especially helpful. Acknowledgment of various other aids in this corner and that of the field will be found both in the text and in the notes and bibliographies.

The initial suggestion of the subject came from Professor Ernest Hunter Wright of Columbia University, and the study has been carried forward from beginning to end with the invaluable aid of his scholarship and encouragement. A word of appreciation is due also to the helpful suggestions of Professor A. H. Thorndike, Professor Emory Neff, and Professor Hoxie Neale Fairchild. The routine of the work itself has been lightened by the sense of adventure along byways of the past, and not infrequently punctuated by amusement or delight. If even a little of these things be passed on to the reader, I shall think the labor spent not altogether in vain.

E. M. S.

New York
June, 1932

CONTENTS

Chapter I

COMPOUNDED OF MANY SIMPLES

Let these be well together blended—
Dodsley's your man—the poem's ended.
                                        —Anon.

Whoever has spent even half an hour dipping here and there into Burton's *Anatomy of Melancholy* has no need to be told that into a discussion of melancholy anything from Utopia to demonology may find its way. A more vague and amorphous subject, perhaps, it would be hard to find: no more can it now be successfully confined to literature, much less to a certain type of literature and that in a certain period and country, than it could in Burton's time to medicine; but rather it drifts off into metaphysics or sociology or psychological biography until one despairs of calling it back. Yet this disembodied quality of the subject is, from the point of view of the literary historian, its chief delight. For it always reaches out to touch life. Refusing to stay in preconceived literary pigeonholes, it continually lures one into the regions of philosophical speculation, tantalizes one with the fleeting aroma of a long-past social order, yields dissolving glimpses of living men and women. And though it is more often than not impossible or inadvisable to follow up its elusive suggestions, one would do ill to lose the consciousness that they are there.

I

In an attempt to bring to view any clear outlines in a subject like moods of melancholy, even limited to British poetry of the period 1740-1830, we are further confronted with an apparently hopeless confusion of categories and cross-categories, influences and cross-influences, definitions and counter-definitions, approached, to be sure, but scarcely surpassed in any other period or type of human activity on record. Who shall say with certainty whether a given melancholy landscape derives from the wind-swept hills of Ossian's wanderings, or the country beloved by St. Preux and Julie, or the Miltonic-Thomsonian tradition, or a gray autumn day in the poet's own countryside? Who shall decide whether a given poem is sincere sentiment or fashionable sentimentality? And what is melancholy? How is one to distinguish its nuances, the boundaries between its moods, the point where it merges into mere lack of levity on one frontier or into mental derangement on another? Nor is it always easy or even possible to tell how much of a poet's manner and substance is due to the literary fashions and philosophical ideas of the day, and how much to the state of his digestion, the encroachments of tuberculosis, the disposition of his grandfather, or the importunities of his creditors. Finally, the chronicler of modern literary modes, unless he is possessed of almost superhuman industry, is ever embarrassed by the practically unlimited amount of relevant material, and the chastening consciousness that his generalizations are based on incomplete data.

But if in the work of a given poet, or in the mass of the miscellaneous and anonymous verse of a group or collection, we endeavor to determine the attitude of the poet, and through him and his contemporaries, of the age, toward certain things which have been from time immemorial the objects of melancholy contemplation, a basis of discussion may be found, though our categories remain mercifully flexible and our definitions emerge but tentatively as we proceed. How then does our poet, or group of poets, feel and write about the mutability of things earthly? about death in its more personal and immediate aspects? about the sorrows of unhappy love? about the relation of external nature to melancholy moods in men? about the lamentable lot of man as a race and the very personal unhappiness of himself as an individual? It is my purpose, in attempting some answer to these questions as they apply to British poetry in the latter half of the eighteenth century and the first two or three decades of the nineteenth, to throw what light is possible upon the changing conceptions and expressions of melancholy between the time of the "Night Thoughts" and the "Elegy in a Country Churchyard" and the time of "Childe Harold's Pilgrimage" and the "Ode on Melancholy."

The change is, I believe, essentially from intellectual generalization and restrained sentiment to intensely imaginative subjectivity. This is certainly not a startlingly new idea, and will perhaps have been the first thought of the reader. I cry his patience, however, for there is more behind. On analysis this romantic melancholy may reveal itself to be more complex and multifarious than one would at first suspect, a thing whose roots and intricate affinities it may be of interest to explore. No attempt will be made here to trace actual literary reminiscences at all exhaustively, although to the special studies that have already been made in various corners of this vast field such items will be added as come in the way. But we may hope to trace at least some of the roots and phases of romantic melancholy back in uninterrupted historical development through the neglected minor verse of the latter half of the eighteenth century. Such a study ought to throw light from a new angle on the great figures at the beginning, and the greater figures at the end, of the period. We may hope also to gather along the way both amusement and delight, wherever our intellectual curiosity or our snobbish modernism may discover the one, or our esthetic eclecticism the other.

II

Of course when we talk of tracing a thing back, what we really mean to do is to go a sufficient distance back and trace it forward; and indeed there is so important a group of melancholy masterpieces at each end of our period that discovering what came of the earlier is only less interesting than analyzing the background of the later. The inevitable starting point of this double pursuit is the twelve-year period 1740-1752, which saw the publication of all the best mid-century melancholy verse except the elegies of Shenstone, which, although apparently written at that time, were not published until 1764.[1] in 1740 appeared Dyer's "Ruins of Rome," and in the same year young Joseph Warton composed his "Enthusiast" (published 1744). The year 1742 saw the publication of Hammond's "Love Elegies" (written however some years before) as well as of the revised version of Shenstone's "Schoolmistress," interesting, from our point of view, rather for the author than for itself. In the same year began to appear the greatest monument of mid-century melancholy (in point of bulk at least and possibly in point of influence), Young's "The Complaint, or Night Thoughts on Life, Death, and Immortality." The next year came Blair's "The Grave" (written in the 1730's). In 1747 was published the first collected edition of the "Night Thoughts," the "Odes" of Joseph Warton and of Collins, and Thomas Warton's "The Pleasures of Melancholy." In 1748 we have "The Castle of Indolence," Hervey's pseudo-poetic prose *Meditations among the Tombs,* and the first three volumes of Dodsley's *Collection of Poems by Several Hands,* containing among other things some of Shenstone's verse. Johnson's "Vanity of Human Wishes" appeared in Dodsley's *Preceptor* in 1749. By this time Gray's "Elegy" was doubtless written, but the delay in its appearance slips the culmination of the mid-century movement over into the 1750's: the "Elegy" was at last printed hastily in 1751 to forestall the piratical activities of *The Magazine of Magazines.* Aside from Parnell's "Night Piece on Death" (published posthumously in 1721), our list thus includes all the most important examples of the type as developed in the first half of the century.

Furthermore, there is a pause of nearly a decade after the appearance of the "Elegy" before any strong new current was set flowing in English poetry. To be sure the triumph of middle class sentimentalism in the novel, as embodied in Richardson, was already upon us.[2] But *La Nouvelle Héloise* was not to come until 1761, nor *Les Confessions* until 1781-1788; not until 1760 was Macpherson to set the poets to turning his "translations" into heroic couplets or communing with ghosts among the dark hills; the ballad revival was still in its infancy, with Percy's *Reliques* (1765) more than a decade in the future; and the German impulse did not become strong until after the publication of *Werther* in 1774. In poetry at least, the 1750's were a moment of pause. The neoclassic tradition was moribund, the true romantic tradition was unborn or, at most, still in unconscious infancy, and the precarious balance of disparate intellectual and emotional elements, of freedom and conventionality in technique and subject-matter, toward which such artists as Thomson, Shenstone, and Gray had been groping, was apparently capable for the moment of producing nothing more.

Between 1748 and 1758, Robert Dodsley, well known and influential as poet, dramatist, book-seller, publisher, and all-round man of letters, edited and published a six-volume *Collection of Poems by Several Hands,* by far the most popular and representative anthology of the middle decades of the century.[3] The first three volumes, as has been noted, appeared in 1748; the fourth followed in 1755, and the fifth and sixth in 1758. It may therefore help us to gain the proper mid-century point of view if we consider with what poetical moods of melancholy the ordinarily well-read reader of Dodsley's *Collection* must have been familiar.

III

The first thing that must be said after an examination of the six volumes from this point of view is that the total effect is not particularly melancholy. From among the "loose and fugitive pieces, some printed, others in manu-

script, which for forty or fifty years past have been thrown
into the world, and carelessly left to perish,"[4] those Dodsley has thought worthy of preservation are largely *jeux
d'esprit*, sprightly fables, didactic or panegyric epistles,
long philosophical, didactic, or descriptive poems in blank
verse or octosyllabics, and above all innumerable odes on
everything from spring to the people of Great Britain.
I have counted only between thirty and thirty-five selections which seem to me predominantly melancholy in
tone,[5] an average of less than six a volume. Mid-century
poets and poetasters, therefore, did not by any means all
worship at the shrine of Joseph Warton's "goddess of the
tearful eye."[6] The melancholy strain, also, is more notice-
able in the later volumes than in the earlier, so that one
suspects that the new impulse from the melancholy
masterpieces of the forties and early fifties has already
made itself felt. It is worth noting also that, barring the
Queen Anne men, the best-known writers whose work is
represented—Gray, Shenstone, Johnson, Dyer, Thomson,
Green, the Wartons, and others—all of them contributed
in one way or another to the melancholy material, which
thus takes on an importance out of proportion to its mere
bulk.

Our hypothetical reader, running through the first three
volumes of his *Collection* in 1748, would find many im-
portant poems which at least impinge on our subject: in
Volume I, Green's "Spleen," Johnson's "London," Dyer's
"Ruins of Rome," Collins' "How Sleep the Brave" and
"Ode to Evening"; in Volume II, Lyttelton's "Monody"
on his wife, Gray's "Ode on the Distant Prospect of Eton
College" and "Ode to Spring," and Richard West's

"Monody on the Death of Queen Caroline"; in Volume III, Thomson's "Ode to Solitude" and "Ode on an Aeolian Harp," Joseph Warton's "Enthusiast" and "Ode to Fancy." When he opened Volume IV in 1755, the first poem to strike his eye would be Gray's "Elegy Wrote in a Country Churchyard," most famous of all the melancholy poems of the century; the elegiac note would be echoed again and again as he read on, till he came upon the black despair of "The Vanity of Human Wishes," was called back to less terrible things by the very young Thomas Warton's lines on "The Pleasures of Melancholy," and closed the book on the graceful love melancholy of Shenstone's "Pastoral Ballad." If he completed his set in 1758, he would find in Volumes V and VI more Shenstone, and perhaps fifteen or sixteen other poems of lesser poets strongly echoing the elegiac strain or sounding the deeper note of "black" melancholy; and just before ending on the more vibrant tone of Gray's "Progress of Poesy" and "The Bard," he would come upon Mason's "Ode to Melancholy." In the six volumes, there are 16 poems called elegies, 3 definitely about our subject (Green's "The Spleen," Mason's "Ode," and Warton's "Pleasures"), 3 monodies, 7 other poems occasioned by the death of someone (not counting 3 laments over dead pets), besides a sufficient amount of calling Melancholy hither or bidding her hence with the usual liberal sprinkling of capital letters.

A good deal of caution must, however, be exercised in interpreting the statistics just given. The modern reader, in particular, nourished on Gray rather than on Tibullus and Ovid, will very probably be puzzled to know what the mid-eighteenth century meant by calling a poem an elegy. Dr. Johnson, in his *Dictionary* (1755),[7] gives three definitions: "a mournful song," "a funeral song," and a "short poem without points or turns," which last is especially indefinite. Prosodically, the term was in Latin literature associated with poems in alternating hexameters and pentameters. About the time of which we are writing, the term elegiac meter, as applied to English verse, was coming to mean the meter popularized in the elegies of Hammond, Shenstone, and Gray—the iambic pentameter with alternate rimes used in Gray's "Elegy." But this vernacular application, made over the protest of purists like Johnson,[8] was not yet a settled thing: not only is Lyttelton's translation from Tibullus[9] in heroic couplets, but so is the "Elegy in the Manner of Ovid"[10] by Hammond himself. It must be remembered also that none of Shenstone's elegies was published before 1764, and his carefully considered theory that English elegies should be in the new "elegiac stanza"[11] was consequently still known only to his immediate circle. In that circle, however, it must have been influential, and was doubtless of more weight than Hammond's example in influencing Shenstone's friend Jago's choice of the meter for his pleasant elegies on "The Goldfinches" and "The Blackbirds."[12] It may also have influenced Gray, though that is much more doubtful. As for the contents of an elegy, there was even less agreement. Shenstone[13] quotes Horace and Ovid to show that the word originally involved a "tender and querulous idea"; and shows how it was first applied to grief for the death of friends, then extended to the sorrows of love, and thence, with complete forgetfulness of the original meaning, to love in all its phases. It is Shenstone's hope to reclaim the form for melancholy, to exclude on the one hand the more joyous aspects of love, and to include on the other hand a variety of other subjects, over which elegy may throw its "melancholy stole." Since too, like a true son of his time, he believed that the "most important end of poetry is to encourage virtue," he goes on to tell us that "there is a truly virtuous pleasure connected with many pensive contemplations, which it is the province and excellency of elegy to enforce. This, by presenting suitable ideas, has discovered sweets in melancholy which we could not find in mirth; and has led us with success to the dusky urn, when we could draw no pleasure from the sparkling bowl."[14] This is the kind of elegy we have come to expect, and this kind is already to be found in Dodsley's *Collection* in Gray's famous poem and in at least one other piece, "The Robin, an Elegy,"[15] which, however, is in alternately riming tetrameters instead of the now orthodox stanza; perhaps we should include here also the two elegies of Jago already mentioned, although there is in them a hint of raillery. But there are also five love elegies,[16] only two or, at most, three of which are really melancholy in tone. Not one of the poems on the death of an individual is an elegy: they are monodies or odes or epistles or merely verses, and are fully as likely as not to be didactic or panegyric and not in the least mournful. There is on the other hand a satiric poem in couplets purporting to be a parody of Pope's "Eloïsa to Abelard" which yet calls itself an elegy.[17] Finally there is a series of six elegies by William Whitehead, dated between 1754 and 1756, presumably suggested by Gray if not by Shenstone, but scarcely coming within Shenstone's definition, and, to us, seeming elegiac only in choice of meter.[18] It is a question therefore just what our hypothetical mid-century reader would mean if he used the word elegiac, and we shall have to define it for ourselves.

For our purposes the word shall be applied approximately in Shenstone's sense, except that for convenience love melancholy must be separately treated. We shall take as our norm the mood of Gray's "Elegy," pensive rather than deeply mournful, penetrated with a love of quiet and solitude and philosophic musing. Its favorite themes are death and mutability. Its favorite haunts are ivied ruins and yew-shaded churchyards. It loves twilight and silence and the notes of the sweet bird that shuns the noise of folly. Its basis is an intellectual contemplation of the instability of life and of fame, and its emotion is vague and diffuse and on the whole not unpleasant. It is Gray's "white melancholy," which he describes as "a good easy sort of state,"[19] and of which Dyer wrote

How sweet thy diapason, Melancholy![20]

With this mood the reader of Dodsley was thoroughly familiar.

Neither what we have called the elegiac mood nor the other moods we shall discuss in this chapter should by any means be thought of as exclusively preromantic. On the contrary, they developed during the neo-classic period as an integral part of the neo-classic attitude and practice. The story of the growth of neo-classic melancholy during the first half of the eighteenth century, through the combined influence of Milton and the Latin classics working on the early seventeenth century conception of melancholy represented in Burton, may be read in Professor Amy Reed's indispensable study of *The Background of Gray's Elegy*,[21] to which any study of eighteenth century melancholy must be largely indebted. All the classic melancholy themes distinguished by Professor Reed[22]— the death theme, the retirement theme, and the complaint of life—are expressed or implied in Gray's poem. But since it is an elegy in a *churchyard* it is natural that the predominant theme should be death; and since it is not a funeral elegy but the expression of a generalized elegiac mood, it is natural that the theme should be death in its more general aspects, shorn of its intimate terrors and transmuted into a symbol of all that is unsubstantial in ambition and uncertain in mortality. Therefore it is easy to associate with this elegy and similar elegies such a descriptive-historical poem as Dyer's "Ruins of Rome":

> Fall'n, fall'n, a silent heap; her heroes all
> Sunk in their urns; behold the pride of pomp,
> The throne of nations fall'n; obscur'd in dust.
> Ev'n yet majestical; the solemn scene
> Elates the soul, while now the rising sun
> Flames on the ruins in the purer air
> Tow'ring aloft, upon the glitt'ring plain,
> Like broken rocks, a vast circumference;
> Rent palaces, crush'd columns, rifted moles,
> Fanes roll'd on fanes, and tombs on buried tombs.[23]

This fine passage is very near the beginning of Dyer's poem; some three hundred lines further on he moralizes the scene:

> So time ordains, who rolls the things of pride
> From dust to dust . . .[24]

Even closer to Gray are the well known lines from "Grongar Hill"—a poem, by the way, by no means elegiac in general tone:

> A little rule, a little sway,
> A sunbeam on a winter's day,
> Is all the proud and mighty have
> Between the cradle and the grave.[25]

Thus had the age learned to find "a truly virtuous pleasure" in contemplating the wrecks of time.

However much the expression of this mood may owe to the classics and other influences, Milton has set his seal upon it as he has upon so much eighteenth-century verse. Professor R. D. Havens, in his monumental study of *The Influence of Milton on English Poetry*,[26] while he traces the tremendous vogue of Milton's octosyllabics from its early beginning, through its high point in the 1730's and 1740's, and on through the century—leaving one with a feeling that scarcely an eighteenth-century poem escaped the influence of their author in one way or another—yet gives it as his opinion[27] that "Il Penseroso" had nothing to do with the rise of the "graveyard school." He reminds us that Milton's title means "the pensive man," not "the melancholy man," and that the love of gloom was well established before the Miltonic octosyllabics came into popularity. But as Professor Reed has shown,[28] the eighteenth century certainly identified pensiveness, however much in defiance of etymology, with the paler shades of elegiac melancholy. Indeed, the connection between melancholy and contemplation may be traced back through such writings as Burton's *Anatomy* at least as far as the history of the Melancholy Dane. Milton himself, although he calls his second mood pensive, nevertheless opens the poem by invoking "devinest Melancholy," whom he hails first as a "Goddess sage and holy" and then as a "pensive Nun!" and the poem ends

> These pleasures, Melancholy, give;
> And I with thee will choose to live.

As for the love of gloom, it undoubtedly was not due to Milton, but primarily to the type of religious melancholy to be discussed presently. Consequently the more dismal and probably the more characteristic moods of the so-called graveyard school bear little resemblance to that of "Il Penseroso"; but its lighter moods, such as that of Gray's "Elegy," and the corresponding moods of much melancholy verse having nothing to do with graveyards, approach rather closely to Milton's type of melancholy.

Then too, all the world borrowed from Milton, as Professor Havens has so amply shown, and the melancholy poets were far from being exceptions; often the poems in which they express their melancholy or describe the melancholy types echo Milton's phrases or imitate the meter and structure of his poems. In Dodsley's *Collection* there are echoes and imitations of Milton everywhere, and nowhere so much as in the elegiac verse. Here is a clear characterization of the penseroso type, from a poem avowedly in imitation of "Paradise Lost":

> The pensive spirit takes the lonely grove:
> Nightly he visits all the sylvan scenes,
> Where far remote, a melancholy moon
> Raising her head, serene and shorn of beams,

Throws here and there her glimmerings through the trees,
To make more awful darkness . . .[29]

Another poem, Francis Coventry's "Penshurst," is a med-
ley of "L'Allegro" and "Il Penseroso," and contains many
lines echoing the pensive note:

> With them in aged groves to walk,
> And lose my thoughts in artless talk . . .
>
> But chief of Virtue's lovely train,
> A pensive exile on the plain . . .
>
> Lead me to the green retreats,
> Guide me to the Muses' seats,
> Where ancient bards retirement chose,
> Or ancient lovers wept their woes . . .
>
> And evening saddening into night . . .
>
> In these transporting, solemn shades . . .
>
> Where Philomel at ev'ning chants . . .[30]

In John Gilbert Cooper's "Estimate of Life"[31] Dodsley
gives one of the numerous imitations of Milton's companion poems. The poem presents three views of life, the
Melancholy, the Cheerful, and the Moderate; but Cooper's Melancholy is Melpomene and not Penseroso, and the
influence of Milton is mostly in the form. In both phrasing and substance, parts of Thomas Cole's "The Grotto:
an Ode to Silence"[32] recall "Il Penseroso":

> Come, musing Silence, nor refuse to shed
> Thy sober influence o'er this darkling cell . . .

This sober contemplative mood, of which Dodsley would
yield plenty of other examples, the mid-century seemed

agreed to call melancholy, and it will be convenient for us to call it elegiac.

IV

It has been impossible to represent this elegiac mood properly without revealing how its treatment of the death theme shades into the other classic melancholy themes of complaint of life and retirement, and how a gentle melancholy has already associated itself with the nature poetry whose most distinguished early poet is Thomson. Professor Reed devotes a whole chapter to the development of the close relationship between melancholy and description. Not that all nature descriptions were melancholy, of course, but that a descriptive poem of any length almost inevitably contained passages of pensive wanderings in the moonlight or moral reflections on mortality such as the lines quoted above from "Grongar Hill"; and that on the other hand any poem, long or short, expressing a pensive or mournful mood, was more than likely to have a background of outdoor nature. Gray gives us the "lowing herd" and the beetle's "droning flight," Collins the "brawling springs" and "dim-discovered spires" of his "pensive Eve"; it is wandering "in cloudless nights" when "twinkle the streams" under the rays of the moon that Joseph Warton meets Philosophy and Wisdom; and the enthusiastic young Thomas Warton urges Contemplation, "queen sublime," to lead him

> to solemn glooms
> Congenial with my soul; to cheerless shades,
> To ruin'd seats, to twilight cells and bow'rs,
> Where thoughtful Melancholy loves to muse,
> Her fav'rite midnight haunts . . . [33]

Of this delight in evening or midnight, groves and streams, "twilight cells" and ruins, we shall have a great deal more to say in succeeding chapters; the more specifically sentimental element in it is the newer one—the men quoted were leaders in the more experimental poetry of their time —and it will change and increase.

On the classical side, the connection between melancholy and description grows partly from the praise of retirement and learned leisure, of withdrawal into country seclusion from the distractions and corruptions of the city and the court. It is an aristocratic and sophisticated sort of retirement: to which Lord Lyttelton could welcome the victor of Blenheim[34] and to which Lord Hervey could long to retire in the evening of his days.[35] Its pastoral simplicities, recommended to Delia by Hammond (in close imitation of Tibullus) aroused protest from Dr. Johnson's common sense;[36] and even Shenstone, chanting the praises of simplicity in his widely advertised and elaborately "natural" estate at the Leasowes, was hardly living a primitive life. However, one can indubitably get closer to nature at the Leasowes or at Penshurst than in London; and it was inevitable that a Thomson or a Dyer should arise to combine the classical love of retirement with an eye for the loveliness of hills and streams; and given the faintly pensive cast of the mood involved in giving up ambition and the bustling world to busy oneself about one's garden and library, the result might very well be what we find it in the "Elegy," "The Enthusiast," or Thomson's "Hymn on Solitude."

It is notable that the neo-classic devotion to Virtue is evident in all these poems: Gray moralizes the obscure lives of the peasants, Warton meets the lady Virtue in person toward the end of his poem, and Thomson opens his with the Miltonic invocation

> Hail, ever-pleasing Solitude!
> Companion of the wise and good![37]

Echoes of the controversy as to whether retirement, or for that matter melancholy in any form, was really virtuous, a controversy traced at length in Professor Reed's book, are clearly to be heard in our *Collection*. William Melmoth, in a poem dated 1735 and printed by Dodsley in Volume I,[38] carefully balances the respective advantages of the active and retired life, and comes to the conclusion that both are good to the man of virtue and judgment.

> Yet of the various tasks mankind employ,
> 'Tis sure the hardest, leisure to enjoy,

he remarks sensibly, and proceeds to show the necessity of a cheerful mind grounded in "conscious virtue" and an ability to fill the "vacant hour" with thought and reflections rather than with guilty imaginings and melancholy superstitions. Benjamin Hoadly, in "The Trophy,"[39] represents his Volunteer (Cantata I) as a youth enjoying a "calm retreat" in a shadowy forest, but called to serve his country. William Whitehead, who became poet laureate the year before the appearance of the last two volumes of the *Collection*, and who elsewhere also expressed his disapproval of too much withdrawal from the world, assures Mason in Volume VI[40] that he cannot avoid taking his place in the activity of the world. But the poets continued to like retirement, and increasingly to take their sorrows not only into the country but out of the library into the fields and woodlands.

The other neo-classic melancholy theme to which we have referred is the complaint of life. This may combine itself with a plaintive melancholy indistinguishable from what we have called the elegiac mood; or it may pile up the sorrows of life in order to present the consolations of religion and immortality, and thus connect itself with the religious melancholy to be discussed presently; or it may ally itself with satire and lash the follies and crimes of the age until melancholy is lost in anger; or it may resolve itself into that *tedium vitae* known to the earlier eighteenth century as spleen or vapors and to the later as ennui. Several of Gray's earlier odes, printed by Dodsley, are good examples of the elegiac type: the "Ode to Spring," the "Ode on a Distant Prospect of Eton College," and perhaps the sterner "Ode to Adversity."[41] A good example of the classical-religious type is to be found in the poem in Miltonic blank verse called "Pre-Existence,"[42] in the course of which Jehovah describes to the trembling followers of Lucifer and the other guilty chiefs, condemned to expiate their rebellion by becoming men, the scene of intellectual darkness, suffering, tyranny, war, and death, to which they are destined. A famous example of the complaint that is too robust and angry to be exactly melancholy may be found in either of Johnson's important poems printed by Dodsley, "London," or "The Vanity of Human Wishes."[43] The former seems to me to be purely satire, and although angry satire is as it were the reverse of melancholy's shield, we cannot treat it here. The later poem, however, has a deeper and less strident note, and seems to me a magnificent expression of the mood of black melancholy grounded on a reasoned complaint of life and gaining force by restraint:

> Yet hope not life from grief or danger free,
> Nor think the doom of man revers'd for thee . . .

> [Man] Hides from himself his state, and shuns to know
> That life protracted is protracted woe . . .

> Time hovers o'er, impatient to destroy,
> And shuts up all the passages of joy . . .

> Must helpless man, in ignorance sedate,
> Roll darkling down the torrent of his fate? . . .

Johnson's answer to the last query is of course a qualified no, since man may leave dark matters to heaven; thus this poem allies itself not only with the satirical type but with the religious as well. A more personal expression of the theme, with a curious anticipation of the Byronic notion of loneliness-in-the-crowd, is to be found in Lady Mary Wortley Montagu's fine lines "In Answer to a Lady Who Advised Retirement,"[44] which, incidentally, indicate neatly the relation between the complaint of life and the retirement theme:

> You little know the heart that you advise;
> I view this various scene with equal eyes:
> In crowded courts I find myself alone,
> And pay my worship to a nobler throne.
> Long since the value of this world I know,
> Pity the madness, and despise the show.
> Well as I can my tedious part I bear,
> And wait for my dismission without fear.
> Seldom I mark mankind's detested ways,

Not hearing censure, nor affecting praise;
And, unconcern'd, my future state I trust
To that sole Being, merciful and just.

This little poem would have done almost as well to illustrate *tedium vitae*, although it is too stoic to merit the equivocal appelation of spleen. The term spleen, which occurs again and again in Dodsley's pages, harks back to the conception of melancholy as a physical disease which finds its fullest exposition in Burton's *Anatomy of Melancholy* (1621). There were, however, two main types of spleen, stemming from the double meaning of the word as either captious anger or low spirits,[45] which dates back at least as far as Shakespeare. The first type, which, as noted above, is really the other side of melancholy's shield, would in its literary manifestation typically give rise to angry satire such as that of Swift; the second to such melancholy verse as that of Gray. This kind of spleen, or vapors, as it was often called, especially in women,[46] was very fashionable among the upper ranks of society. Pope elevates it into a goddess attended by Affectation for a handmaiden. The poets, pamphleteers, and periodical writers discuss it pro and con: Swift blames the English tendency to it on the climate; Addison tells us that it is frequent among men of studious and sedentary habits; Hughes represents a fashionable gentleman as threatening to drop it because every "heavy wretch" is taking it up.[47] But the classic treatment of the subject is the poem called "The Spleen" by Matthew Green, which the reader of Dodsley's *Collection* would find in the first volume.

This poem, which was first published after the author's death in 1737, seems to have been a favorite of Dodsley's, although Johnson claimed that it was "not poetry." The modern reader is likely to agree with the doctor rather than with the editor, but will find, as indeed Johnson did, that Green's sprightly Hudibrastics are amusing reading. Green is chiefly concerned with telling his friend—for, like so much early eighteenth-century verse, the poem is an epistle—how to avoid the spleen: it is almost an *Anatomy* in miniature:

> If I am right, your question lay,
> What course I take to drive away
> The day-mare Spleen, by whose false pleas
> Men prove mere suicides in ease;
> And how I do myself demean
> In stormy world to live serene.

His prescriptions are on the whole very like Burton's: good plain food, exercise, mirth—

> Laugh and be well. Monkeys have been
> Extreme good doctors for the Spleen;
> And kitten, if the humor hit,
> Has harlequin'd away the fit—

tragedy—

> We borrow joy by pitying woe—

comedy, music, books, coffee-house gossip, chats with fair women—all these are good. On the other hand, we must avoid dissenters' meetings—a point worth remembering presently—law suits, gaming, passion, reforming schemes, speculation, toadying to the great, and writing rimes. In discussing this last point he says that when he sees

> some poet pensive sit
> Fondly mistaking Spleen for Wit

he blesses his stars that he never knew such "whimsies"
—the current performance to the contrary notwithstand-
ing, it would appear. He turns to an admittedly ideal pre-
scription of delightful retirement; then, growing "more
serious," he warns his Memmius against enthusiasm and
superstition; queries as to immortality follow, and he toys
with a theory of pre-existence which reminds one of that
in the poem of that name previously mentioned:

> A stranger into life I'm come,
> Dying may be our going home,
> Transported here by angry Fate,
> The convicts of a prior state.

He closes by emphasizing the necessity of holding one's
passions in check and keeping Reason at the helm. All
in all, the poem is a sensible and pleasant representation
of the best neo-classical attitude.[49]

V

Besides the moods of melancholy which thus rang the
changes on the classical themes of death, retirement, and
the woes of life, combining them sometimes with Miltonic
elements, sometimes with the nascent sentimentalism,
sometimes with Thomsonian description, sometimes with
the old conception of melancholy as a disease, there is another type of melancholy, designedly excluded from discussion by Professor Reed but essential to our purpose,
which also combines classical and non-classical elements.
This is love melancholy. It was of course the staple of the
Latin elegies. It sent Lancelot and Ywain wandering mad
through the shadowy land of medieval romance. It filled

the sails of the Elizabethan sonnet with sighs, and breathed upon Duke Orsino like the sweet south. Its symptoms and treatment fill nearly a third of the vast bulk of Burton's *Anatomy of Melancholy*. It throws its "melancholy stole" over even the neo-classic couplets of Pope's "Eloïsa to Abelard." And, since during the romantic period its expression came to know distinction of neither race, age, sex, nor social status, it is requisite that we discover something of how our reader of Dodsley's *Collection* would be likely to expect the poets to treat of it.

There is only a modest amount of love melancholy in the *Collection,* and much of what there is sounds to us conventional, even perfunctory. There are numerous love songs in the six volumes, but if they touch the subject at all it is usually merely to make orthodox complaint of Phyllis' cruelty or enumerate Damon's orthodox woes. For most of the love poetry, whether song, elegy, or courtly compliment, makes use of the pastoral machinery. It is rather hard for the modern reader to believe in a love melancholy in which the lover represents himself as forgetting his flocks to wander under Cynthia's rays, or pictures a train of swains and shepherdesses strewing willow over his humble grave. Yet we are told that Shenstone, whose charming "Pastoral Ballad" (not at all like a real ballad, by the way) closes the fourth volume, was actually in love and actually jilted by his lady. The pastoral tradition was of course often carried over into the love elegy, especially when the model was Tibullus. Our reader of Dodsley is almost certain to have seen Hammond's love elegies, only one of which, and that not a typical one, appears in the *Collection.* If he had, he would perhaps have had his opinion to pass on the proposition later set forth by Johnson in his "Life of Hammond": "He that describes himself as a shepherd, and his Neaera or Delia as a shepherdess, and talks of goats and lambs, feels no passion. He that courts his mistress with Roman imagery deserves to lose her: for she may with good reason suspect his sincerity." Yet we are told that Hammond too was most desperately in love with at least one of the ladies to whom the elegies were addressed. There are three love elegies in the stanza of Gray and Hammond in the 1758 volumes of the *Collection;* they vary in mood from comparative cheerfulness to deepest woe, and in originality of appeal from regulation pastoral to a puzzling vague suggestion of "Corinna's Going a-Maying."[50] Lord Lyttelton's verses to his Lucy are graceful and give the appearance of sincerity; but then, his love was soon crowned with success and at least a little while of happiness. There seems to me to be more real unaffected anguish in an anonymous heroic couplet "Epistle to a Lady" in Volume II[51] than in all the elegies and pastorals in all six volumes.

Yet the love melancholy found in these poems is, when it occurs at all, usually at least theoretically subjective. I note only one example of the type of mournful love poem later to become so popular—the story of unhappy love. That example is, significantly enough, in the only poem included that belongs to the early ballad revival: Tickell's "Colin and Lucy."[52] Another of Tickell's poems included, "Kensington Garden,"[53] announces itself as a "melancholy tale," and is in fact a story of the sad fate of a royal changeling and his fairy princess, but its purpose seems to be rather to furnish a romantic account of the origin of the Garden than to celebrate unhappy love. To balance these more or less romantic peasants and fairies, we have several epistles in the manner of Ovid,[54] two of the four of which are complaints of deserted women. It is notable that this objective material takes more account of the fact that women as well as men suffer from love, and brings us to observe that practically none of the love poetry of any kind is by women. Lady Mary Wortley Montagu, to be sure, writes of it in "A Receipt to Cure the Vapours";[55] but it is only cynically to advise her correspondent to cease useless mourning for Damon dead, since

> Long ago the worms have eat him,

and take another lover, for, as she confides to her fellow-woman,

> Single, we have all the spleen.

It would, however, be wrong to leave "female virtue" in such company, and I hasten to add that the note of the new day is already sounded in the first of the 1758 volumes, with an adoring and obviously feminine tribute to that apostle of tearful sensibility, Samuel Richardson.[56] The lady in question invokes the gentle Muse of Shenstone to sing the "soul-harr'wing genius" of the creator of Pamela, of Clarissa ("martyr to our sex's glory"), and of their masculine counterpart, new style, Sir Charles Grandison. Here too, then, Dodsley, like the excellent editor he was, has included verse and ideas to appeal to both older and younger generations.

VI

One type of melancholy remains to be discussed: it has been left till the last because there is in it almost nothing of the classical, and because it is not quite adequately represented in Dodsley's miscellany. Yet anyone who would buy and read six volumes of fugitive verse could hardly fail to be familiar with Young's "The Complaint, or Night Thoughts on Life, Death, and Immortality," and would very probably know also Hervey's prose *Meditations among the Tombs* and Robert Blair's "The Grave," all of which appeared in the forties and were immediately popular. Hervey of course was out of the question for a verse anthology, and the "Night Thoughts" would have been excluded by their length if for no other reason. One would rather expect to find "The Grave" included, but it may not have appealed to Dodsley's anti-evangelical taste. The mood represented by these famous poems is a deep funereal gloom engendered by the contemplation of death in its more terrible and intimate aspects. It finds no "sweets" in looking on the "dusty urn," no pleasing diapason in the echoes from beyond the tomb. Or if it partakes at all of the nature of joy, it is the sadistic joy of the saints watching from Paradise the tortures of the damned, or, in milder and more earthly figure, of the sophisticated citizen applauding a tragedy by John Webster. Thus its distinguishing ingredient is fear, either real or assumed, and its literary technique characteristically makes free use of gratuitous horrors. Its whole spirit is opposed to classical restraint; its roots on the contrary are deep in religious fanaticism and inextricably bound up with the history of the Christian church. Burton classifies religious melancholy as a subdivision of love melancholy, and the erotic mysticism in much of the melancholy religious verse of Quarles, Flatman, Isaac Watts, or Elizabeth Rowe makes quite unnecessary an appeal to Freud to prove that, for much religious melancholy at least, his view is basically sound. But during the "peace of the Augustans" the erotic element was driven underground, and even the stern and melancholy doctrines of Calvin which had filled Puritan devotional verse with fear of hell and decorated broadside elegies with cypress boughs and death's heads,[57] were already being glozed over or explained away by the deistic and Shaftesburian clergy of the Establishment, and survived in their pristine vigor only among the dissenters. Nevertheless the tradition persisted, as has been shown by Professor Reed and others, and its gloomy musings and "mortuary landscapes" have given rise to the somewhat misleading term "graveyard school," which is likely to be applied indiscriminately to Parnell's grisly voice speaking "from among the bones," to Young's gloomy sermons, not propounded from a graveyard at all, or to Gray's gently philosophical generalizations, in a graveyard to be sure but haunted by no Calvinistic ghosts.

Our mid-century reader, at all events, had, we shall assume, read Young. He had read, then, nine long diatribes, each more extended than the last, written in a strangely ejaculatory blank verse and full of a gloomy religious excitement which to most modern readers seems rather hollow and whipt-up. He had been invited to share the personal grief of the poet over the almost simultaneous loss of three (more or less legendary) beloved relatives; had heard the pathetic tale (also more or less legendary) of the interment of perhaps the dearest of them, Narcissa, in a cruel and Catholic foreign land;[58] had listened to the poet's midnight musings on death and man and grief and immortality; had taken sides, perhaps, for or against the unfortunate Lorenzo, whom the poet implacably pursues through night after night with arguments against his infidelity and warnings of his impending damnation. The mood here is by no means gently elegiacal, but fiercely didactic and persistently personal. We are not invited to sigh softly over the ruins of the Roman forum or Sylvia's flower-strewn bier, but to remember hourly that, although "All men think all men mortal, but themselves,"[59] nevertheless the hour may strike for us personally and individually at any moment, and if we are not ready, how shall we meet the terrors of the Day of Wrath? Nor will it avail us to seek the Epicurean refuge: Young exerts all his powers, in Books VI and VII, to expound the familiar argument that the ills of this world argue the existence of another, and concludes pessimistically that not only happiness but virtue depend on belief in immortality, and that

> if man loses all, when life is lost,
> He lives a coward, or a fool expires.[60]

Whatever one may think of the ethics of this rather pusillanimous conclusion, it cannot be said to contribute to cheerfulness. There are, it should be added, very few "horrifics" in "Night Thoughts";[61] its dismal tone is due to the drift of the argument, to the personal confessions of grief, and to the solemnity of the midnight apostrophes to man and to death.

The important things in this mood, for our purpose, are its didacticism, the depth of its gloom, and its unabashed egoism. Each of these elements is natural to religious melancholy, and may be traced alone or in combination in the religious poetry of the seventeenth century and the early eighteenth. The last has usually been thought of as a harbinger of romanticism,[62] and in a sense it is that. The amount of actual introspection as against doctrine in the "Night Thoughts" may, however, be easily exaggerated, and it is too easy also to forget that emphasis on the worth of the individual is as essential an element in the Christian scheme of salvation as it is in the doctrine of original genius.[63] It is true that this last fact had been largely ignored by the regular clergy, of whom Young was one, during the early years of the century. Young's poem is avowedly a protest against the deistical doctrines of Pope's "Essay on Man." It thus allies itself with the individualistic movement in the Church, the most striking manifestation of which was Methodism, and is romantic in the same limited sense. The element of egoism is undoubtedly there; and it is associated with dismal meditations on death in the solitary night watches by the vague light of the moon.

To trace the influence of all this would be to anticipate. But before returning to Dodsley's miscellany, it will be best to say a word about the other important "graveyard" poem of the forties with which we have assumed our mid-century reader to be acquainted: Blair's "The Grave."[64] This is a poem between seven and eight hundred lines in length, written in a sinewy masculine blank verse which distinctly recalls the author's delight in Shakespeare.[65] The central idea is very close to that of the "Night Thoughts"—if the "Night Thoughts" may be said to have one central idea: that in the midst of life it behooves us to think on the tomb. There is then the same didactic purpose, though shorn of argument and mercifully condensed. But the whole is kept objective, although at one point, to be sure, the poet adjures his own soul to think how serious a thing it is to approach

That awful gulf no mortal e'er repass'd. (1.372)

For the most part we are presented, however, with a series of sharply etched pictures and characters—of the schoolboy fleeing the churchyard at night at some imagined sound, of the weeping widow seeking her husband's grave, of the doddering sexton cracking an obscene jest over his pot of ale; or, toward the end, direct apostrophe or moralizing concerning suicide, the incommunicativeness of the dead, the indiscriminate mixture of types and classes in the grave, or the doctrine of the resurrection. But, for our purpose, the most important element in this poem, once so popular but now fallen into undeserved neglect, is the wealth of macabre detail, the almost sadistic dwelling on sickness and corruption. This sort of treatment of the death theme had, during the early part of the century, been associated closely with the broadside elegies and other personal laments for the dead, especially among the dissenters,[66] and of course with Parnell's "Night Piece on Death" and such less well known poems as Broome's "Poem on Death."[67] In Blair, however, who, though a Scotchman, was no dissenter, and appears to have been naturally of a calm and sunny disposition,[68] the macabre element has, like his blank verse, an Elizabethan flavor. He has all the "horror" paraphernalia of his own century—the "sickly taper," the yew, skulls, coffins, worms, "night's foul bird," shrieking ghosts. Perhaps it is the Elizabethan phrasing rather than the idea which makes one hear, in such passages as follow, echoes of Shakespeare or Webster rather than of Parnell:[69]

Why this ado in earthing up a carcase
That's fallen into disgrace, and in the nostril
Smells horrible? . . . (11. 169-71)

Now tame and humble, like a child that's whipp'd
Shakes hands with dust, and calls the worm his kinsman . . .
(227-28)

Methinks I see thee with thy head low laid,
Whilst, surfeited upon thy damask cheek,
The high-fed worm, in lazy volumes roll'd,
Riots unscared . . . (224-27)

Oh! how his eyes stand out, and stare full ghastly!
While the distemper's rank and deadly venom
Shoots like a burning arrow 'cross his bowels,
And drinks his marrow up . . . (274-77)

. . . Human nature groans
Beneath a vassalage so vile and cruel,
And its vast body bleeds through every vein . . . (595-97)

. . . O great man-eater!
Whose every day is carnival, not sated yet!
Unheard-of epicure, without a fellow!
The veriest gluttons do not always cram;
Some intervals of abstinence are sought
To edge the appetite: Thou seekest none.
Methinks the countless swarms thou hast devour'd,

And thousands at each hour thou gobblest up,
This, less than this, might gorge thee to the full!
. . . .
As if diseases, massacres, and poison,
Famine, and war, were not thy caterers. (639-47, 652-53)

Of this strong wine also our reader of Dodsley may have
known the taste.

But even if he had not read "The Complaint" or "The
Grave," he would have found their disparate elements in
his *Collection.* As has been said, one of the ancestors of
Young's lugubrious confessions of personal bereavement
is the profusion of elegies, monodies, epitaphs, and other
verses on the deaths of individuals. Sometimes these are
merely formal panegyric of a departed patron or public
character. Sometimes they exist only to point a moral.
But sometimes they are honest expressions of the mood
of black melancholy natural to one truly bereaved. Examples of the first type in Dodsley are Richard West's
"Monody on the Death of Queen Caroline" (which contains a few lines reworked by Gray for his "Elegy") and
Mason's "Musaeus: A Monody to the Memory of Mr.
Pope;"[70] of the second the lines "On Seeing Archbishop
William's Monument in Carnarvonshire,"[71] which I spec-
ify because it does have at least a touch of the "graveyard" technique at the beginning; of the last Tickell's
well known couplets on the death of Addison (1719),
and Lyttelton's moving monody on his wife (1747).[72]
There is also the King of Prussia's "Ode to Death," translated by Johnson's friend Hawkesworth,[73] a somber poem
in which the King seems to apply the thoughts of Blair's
"Grave" to his own personal situation. One Dr. Ibbot, in

"A Fit of the Spleen,"[74] calls Hamlet into requisition to vent his black melancholy. An anonymous writer paraphrases Isaiah's description of the destruction of civilization in Miltonic blank verse, to the "direful dirges" of owls, cormorants, vultures, and ravens.[75] The mood and paraphernalia of the first eleven stanzas of Thomas Denton's "Immortality"[76] is so complete an amalgam of the thoughts, mannerisms, and even phrases of the melancholy poems of Blair, Young, Gray, and the Wartons that it must certainly have been written after all of them, and to discuss it would be an anticipation of what is to be said in the following chapters.

VII

It remains to note how, especially in the work of the Wartons, a large section of the melancholy poetry was already attaching itself to the infant Gothic revival. How natural this association was will be more fully expounded later; but one very simple reason for it will appear from these lines in Joseph Warton's "Ode to Fancy":

> Haste, Fancy, from these scenes of folly,
> To meet the matron Melancholy,
> Goddess of the tearful eye,
> That loves to fold her arms and sigh!
> Let us with silent footsteps go
> To charnels and the house of woe,
> To Gothic churches, vaults, and tombs,
> Where each sad night some virgin comes . . .[77]

The graveyard poet must go to the charnel house, and that is always hard by the Gothic church. Besides, most

English ruins are Gothic, and a ruin, whether his melancholy is black or white, the graveyard poet must have.

> Beneath yon ruin'd abbey's moss-grown piles
> Oft let me sit, at twilight hour of eve,

cries Thomas Warton[78]—where silence reigns

> Save the lone screech-owl's note, who builds his bow'r
> Amid the mould'ring caverns, dark and damp,

—or let him listen to "the taper'd choir" and solemn organ, as he sits

> Far in sequester'd iles of the deep dome,
> There lonesome listen to the sacred sounds,
> Which as they lengthen through the Gothic vaults,
> In hollow murmurs reach my ravish'd ear.

"The Pleasures of Melancholy," from which these lines are taken, was written in 1745, when the author was only seventeen. It is predominantly Miltonic, with versification after "Paradise Lost" and much of the phrasing and a little of the mood after "Il Penseroso." Remembering the master's

> storied windows richly dight,
> Casting a dim religious light,

we may discern his strong hand as another reason for the early association of melancholy and Gothicism.

We are to think then of our hypothetical mid-century reader as familiar, although of course probably not articulately so, with many themes and moods of melancholy and combinations thereof. He had heard much of the pensive joys of solitude and retirement, much of death and ruins, even something of death and corruption, much of the generally unsatisfactory nature of human life and the illusiveness of worldly pride and ambition. He knew white melancholy and black, melancholy neo-classical and religious, melancholy sincere and assumed, melancholy praised as the nurse of virtue and reviled as the enemy of society. He doubtless believed, or said he did, in hell. He undoubtedly knew what it was to suffer from the spleen. All this he found, with much else not to our purpose, expressed for him in the verse with which he was most familiar.

Naturally it is dangerous to make generalizations about this mass of verse as a whole. What is true of Gray, is palpably false of Young; what describes the Wartons will by no means apply to Blair. Something of a common element will, we may hope, appear as we proceed. For the present it is to be observed that, as melancholy poetry is a product of its age, so the things which melancholy poets have in common one with another will be the things characteristic of the age as a whole. In many ways the middle decades of the eighteenth century were a period of transition, even more truly than are most ages, although all ages must, in the nature of things, be transitional. At the same time, these decades have a flavor all their own. Like that of the reigns of Queen Anne and the first George, mid-century verse as a whole, perhaps especially mid-century melancholy verse, is essentially didactic. Almost all the verse we have been considering has strong didactic elements; this is true of Young, of Shenstone, of Gray, less true but not quite false of Collins and of the Wartons. Sometimes the didacticism is religious, sometimes moral, sometimes philosophical; but it is nearly always there. The appeal is therefore as much intellectual as emotional, and the poets delight in resounding generalizations and capitalized abstractions. But the mid-century output differs from the characteristic output of the Queen Anne men in that a vague emotionalism, sentimentalism if you will, has softened the edges of its intellectuality; Gray and Shenstone are excellent examples of this. Also that personal quality which had never been absent from the innumerable epistles, polite compliments, and death notices of the century, has sounded with a more somber note in the long-drawn griefs of Young, though this is not so typical as the pleasant unconvincing elegiacs of Shenstone. Even in Young there is a self-conscious and deliberate element. Behold me, he seems sometimes to say, how bereaved I am, how pious, how concerned for your soul's salvation. Blair's "Grave" is said to have been written, as though to persuade himself, when the author was young and personally untouched by the fear of death. Shenstone consciously set out to write elegies which should express the "truly virtuous pleasure" to be found in melancholy. Thomas Warton calls his earliest publication "The Pleasures of Melancholy," and tells us of the "elegance of soul refined" needed to appreciate those pleasures. Even Gray, as at least one eighteenth-century critic pointed out with needless acerbity,[79] seems deliberately to settle himself on a tombstone and start to meditate. The artificiality of the mid-century love melancholy has been noticed at some length. There is involved in these poems a certain intellectual detachment, combined with the indulgence of sentiment, which distinguishes them from the characteristic verse of the generations before and after them.

Before leaving the direct consideration of this literature to follow its influence until it merges into new influences and new modes of expression, it should be observed that melancholy in one mode or another furnished most of the poems of the middle decades of the eighteenth century which are still remembered. Their simple generalizations, their diffuse emotion, and it must be added their invariably consolatory conclusions, together with the exquisite form attained by some few of them, have raised them as an enduring monument of mid-century melancholy.

Chapter II

INVOCATION TO MELANCHOLY

Come, let us set our careful breasts,
Like Philomel, against the thorn.
                                        —*Hood*

Eighteenth-century melancholy continued to be a little self-conscious and to affect philosophy. The satirist Churchill was in 1761 already making fun of the fashion for melancholizing:

> If, in these hallowed times, when sober, sad,
> All gentlemen are melancholy mad,
> When 'tis not deemed so great a crime by half
> To violate a vestal as to laugh . . .[1]

One thinks immediately of the tremendous vogue of monody and funeral elegy: of how all through the latter half of the century, though in diminuendo as time went on, the poetry departments of the magazines and the poetical output of the publishers consisted in astonishing proportion of such outpourings; of how it was clearly considered almost disrespectful toward the dead for anyone even reasonably literate to let slip an opportunity for publishing in verse an account of the virtues of the deceased and the tears and religious resignation of the survivors. But grief in time of bereavement, however self-conscious, is rather a temporary anguish than a settled melancholy, and, at least in eighteenth-century England, usually seeks consolation in religion rather than in philosophy. So it will be impossible to treat this vast literature here for its own sake; examples of it must merely be used as convenient in other connections. The conscious fondness for melancholy found an abundance of more direct expression during the last fifty years of the eighteenth century, and built up another vast literature, largely imitative in nature, but leading directly to several excellent poems in the next period, even if we count Keats's "Ode on Melancholy" as owing but little to the tradition.

The philosophical basis of this literature, in so far as it is aware of any philosophy beyond a mere following of fashionable tradition, is in a belief that it is the part of wisdom and of virtue to seek a solitude filled with melancholy musings, and that in such invocation to melancholy lies the truest happiness of a sensitive spirit. To follow the poetic expression of this idea, particularly in relation to the Miltonic tradition and the neo-classic theory of contemplative retirement, is the business of this chapter.

I

The literary influences back of the poetry of deliberate melancholizing are those which had been operative in the earlier part of the century—primarily the classics and Milton—shot across with the newer semi-romantic influences of Gray, Shenstone, Collins, and the Wartons. The things for which the latter group stood will be followed in their various ramifications in later chapters. Here they concern us only as they worked upon the classic-Miltonic tradition. That tradition, embodied in innumerable odes to abstractions, and in reflective poems in heroic couplet, blank verse, or elegiac stanza, managed to keep a life of its own, never altogether swallowed up in sentimentalism or romanticism, until well into the nineteenth century. Thomas Love Peacock wrote his "Philosophy of Melancholy" in 1812; and the last of the Miltonic odes to melancholy that has been found (Motherwell's "Melancholye") did not appear until 1832.

Milton's procedure in "L'Allegro" and "Il Penseroso," it will be remembered, consists of several definite steps: he opens with a passage in alternating trimeter and pentameter with interwoven rimes, in which he bids hence the opposite of the desired quality; next, falling into his peculiar tripping octosyllabics, he invokes the desired quality, describing her appearance, giving her ancestry, and enumerating her allegorical attendants; lastly, he describes her haunts and the occupations of a day in her company, closing with a final promise of fealty if she will bring him these joys. Among the innumerable imitations of the octosyllabics which appeared during the period we are considering—Professor Havens lists four hundred eight between 1740 and 1820—by no means all have any connection with melancholy: they may be companion poems like the group cited above from Dodsley's *Collection*,[2] or the mood may be that of "L'Allegro," or the technique may be applied to something remote from the mood of either of the original poems. But a goodly number do reflect something of either the mood or the allegorical imagery of "Il Penseroso": and to this group must be added other poems or parts of poems not so clearly imitative of Milton. The result will be ample material on the appearance of the personified Melancholy, on her train of attendants, on her haunts and favored times and seasons, and on the pleasures of her society.

Milton describes his "Goddess sage and holy" as veiled in black to hide her too awful countenance, and invokes her:

> Come, pensive Nun, devout and pure,
> Sober, steadfast, and demure,
> All in a robe of darkest grain,
> Flowing with majestic train,
> And sable stole of cypress lawn
> Over thy decent shoulders drawn.
> Come, but keep thy wonted state,
> With even step, and musing gait,
> And looks commercing with the skies,
> Thy rapt soul sitting in thine eyes:
> There, held in holy passion still,
> Forget thyself to marble, till
> With a sad leaden downward cast
> Thou fix them on the earth as fast.[3]

Collins (1746) adds the appropriate touch of melancholy music:

> With Eyes up-rais'd, as one inspir'd,
> Pale Melancholy sate retir'd,
> And from her wild sequester's Seat,
> In Notes by Distance made more sweet,
> Pour'd thro' the mellow Horn her pensive Soul . . .[4]

Almost at the same time Joseph Warton was writing the description to which reference has already been made:

> Haste, Fancy, from the scenes of folly,
> To meet the matron Melancholy,

> Goddess of the tearful eye,
> That loves to fold her arms, and sigh . . .[5]

While the lilt of these octosyllabics and the phrasing of the first two lines quoted are indubitably Miltonic, the folded arms and the sigh sound more like Fletcher:

> Welcome, folded arms, and fixed eyes,
> A sigh that piercing mortifies,
> A look that's fasten'd to the ground,
> A tongue chained up, without a sound![6]

It would be interesting to believe that this pioneer of romanticism had in this matter also anticipated his age and gone back of Milton to the exquisite little Caroline lyric which has been thought to be Milton's source.

But poets of the forties, as indicated in the first chapter, did not always invoke melancholy, and when they bid her hence their portraits of her were naturally less flattering. For example, she appears among the six favorites of Disease in William Thompson's "Sickness":

> Next, in a low-brow'd cave, a little hell,
> A pensive hag, moping in darkness, sits
> Dolefully-sad: her eyes (so deadly dull!)
> Stare from their stonied sockets, widely wild;
> Forever bent on rusty knives, and ropes;
> On poignards, bows of poison, daggers red
> With clotted gore. A raven by her side
> Eternal croaks; her only mate Despair . . .[7]

And the cheerful Mary Leapor tells us of a fearful vision she had of passing through a region of night-shade, yew, cypress, and blasted firs, past a guard of Sickness, Poverty, Disappointment, and Error, and along dark haunted galleries to a subterranean cell,

> Where the sad Empress Melancholy reign'd;
> The musing Matron sat upon a Throne
> Of mould'ring Earth—her Footstool of the same;
> And for her canopy an aged Yew
> Spread o'er her Head its venerable Arms:
> Her careless Robe was of a sable Hue,
> And on her Shoulders flow'd her slighted Hair;
> Her Lips were clos'd with an eternal Silence;
> Her Arms were folded and her Head reclin'd . . .[8]

She is attended by Dejection and Despair, who are lugubriously described. The poet is much relieved when she can follow her guide to the regions of Chearfulness. The melancholy of these two poems is clearly of the black variety, and while it keeps some of the lineaments of the normal picture, it is colored with the tints of religious melancholy or Spenserian allegory. Both of these poems, it may be remarked in passing, are in blank verse, not octosyllabics, and the Miltonic influence is exerted primarily through the religious "Paradise Lost" rather than through the philosophical "Il Penseroso."

During the next sixty years Melancholy sat to many verbal painters, and a composite portrait made from their various impressions would not reveal any startlingly new elements. She is "Goddess of the downcast eye" (1786),[9] "Nymph retired and coy" (1787),[10] "Nymph of the pallid hue, and downcast eye" (1796),[11] "Nymph of pallid hue, and raven hair" (1801),[12] "Sweet matron of the pensive brow" (1792),[13] or, with a particularly low bow to Milton, "thou Goddess sage and holy, Sable-vested Melancholy" (1782).[14] Several poets mention her long tresses, which one ingenuously assures us are "black and brown."[15] Sometimes she is presented seated in contemplation, oftener walking musefully along as in Milton's poem. Her arms are folded and her look, as in "Il Penseroso," either bent on the heavens or fixed thoughtfully on the earth. Usually she is in tears.

> Come with sadly-plaintive sigh,
> With folded hands, and heav'n-ward eye;
> With streaming tears that ceaseless flow,
> And all the solemn suite of woe . . .[14]

The particular "Ode to Melancholy" from which both this and the "sable-vested Melancholy" above are quoted, was avowedly modeled on Fletcher, and between his aid and Milton's the poet has managed to produce a rather charming, if thoroughly derivative poem. It is further distinguished in being, as far as I have observed, the only one of the odes to melancholy (except the early ode by Broome) to be written as a funeral elegy. The details of the description, however, are not unique. Compare

> In her dusk-brown mantle clad
> See her walk sedate and sad,
> With folded arms, and tearful eyes,
> And breast upheav'd with frequent sighs . . .[16]

This is from an 1804 periodical. Or here is an earlier specimen, less reminiscent of Fletcher:

> Here Melancholy walks her nightly round,
> With haggard looks and wan; pale is her cheek
> As nightly mists that clothe the darksome side
> Of some hoar hill; gath'ring her tresses long
> From off the winds, she roves with measur'd step
> Along the grass-grown pavement, glancing oft
> An eye on heav'n, and heaving oft a sigh.[17]

Coleridge, in his early fragment on melancholy, introduces a slight innovation in imagining that the wandering nymph has "mused herself to sleep" among her favorite ivied ruins,

> Her folded arms wrapping her tattered pall.[18]

A rather darker, although still not altogether unsympathetic, description comprises the whole substance of a certain sixteen-line octosyllabic "Picture of Melancholy" (1806):

> Fly, O fly, from yonder cell,
> Where Melancholy loves to dwell.
> There she sits with moping air,
> Fix'd in dreadful deep despair,
> With folded arms, and body bent,
> On a human skull intent . . .[19]

In neither of these last two poems are there obvious borrowings from Milton,[20] but they clearly rest on the Miltonic tradition.

II

The orthodox procedure in an ode to melancholy is to follow the description of the goddess herself with an enumeration of her train of attendant abstractions and a more extended account of her reputed haunts. The attendants are very frequently omitted, but the staple of the odes is the description of the times, seasons, and landscapes beloved of the pensive nymph invoked. As for the times, there are for practical purposes only two—evening and midnight—although sometimes the poet can bear noonday if he is deep in some friendly shade. On the whole, evening is preferred for the milder shades of melancholy, midnight for the more dismal moods touched by personal dispair or by what Thomas Warton called "religious horror."[21] For the evening hour, the notes of Milton's melancholy bird are of course indispensable; and the evening lasts from soft twilight till a calm moon has risen. Not much is said by the ode writers about seasons,[22] and the association of melancholy with autumn and winter may be better discussed in another connection. But of the favored rural haunts—they are invariably rural—these poets have very definite ideas.

The haunts of melancholy seem to be of three sorts: mildly Miltonic, picturesquely romantic, and "horrifically" Gothic. Of course all three types frequently occur in the same poem; nor am I able to see any clear change of habit in this matter between the time when the Miltonic odes to melancholy became popular in the 1750's,[23] and the time of Keats. Differences there are, as we shall see, but not, I think, in the orthodox places for melancholy musing. For already in mid-century the "romantic" forest, desert, and precipice, have been added to the winding river and quiet grove; and even before Thomas Warton, Broome had written a Miltonic "Ode to Melancholy" (1723), which has much to do with black melancholy and with tombs. The poet then, having invoked his goddess, will usually either ask her a series of questions—whether thou comest from beetling precipice or somber vale or murmuring stream?—or bid her take him here or there—to gloomy forest, Libyan waste, or ruined tower. He is more than likely in this description, even if he has started off in an irregular meter, to fall naturally into tripping octosyllabics or into elegiac stanza, according to whether he is invoking the mountain nymph sweet liberty or meditating in some twilight churchyard or by some owl-haunted ruin. Thus these odes are the resultant of the impact on the Miltonic tradition of the melancholy verse of Gray, Collins, and the Wartons.

Most of the odes are written to invoke melancholy, not to bid her hence. Normally, therefore, the mood is that of "white melancholy," a sort of contemplative "joy in grief," although this Ossianic phrase is not found in any of those which I have seen. Such epithets and phrases as "sadly-soothing,"[24] "sweetly-sad,"[25] "mournful joy,"[26] "sadly-pleasing,"[27] "gloomy joy,"[28] "sad luxury of woe,"[28] occur and recur. There does here, however, seem to be some change as the century drew toward its close: more and more the basic mood of philosophical retirement and contemplation is colored by sensibility, with its emphasis on personal sorrows, whether of the poet or of those around him. And in the great odes of Keats and Hood, which conclude the series (barring the pleasant pseudo-Elizabethan "Melancholye" of Motherwell), this personal emphasis has sought and found a new philosophical basis, romantic rather than classic, and so little Miltonic that Professor Havens has included neither in his bibliography. Yet even here, particularly in the much less intense ode by Hood, there remains the characteristic quality of deliberate invocation, the tendency to make solitary melancholy musings the very basis of a considered attitude toward life—the systematic exploitation of melancholy which led the youthful Peacock to write a poem called "The Philosophy of Melancholy." For the illumination of these generalizations, it will be best briefly to analyze several representative odes in chronological order.

Two of the earliest of them, appearing within a few years after the publication of Gray's "Elegy," are in elegiac stanza, and are compounded almost equally of Milton and of Gray. The first of these, published anonymously in the *Scots Magazine* in February, 1756, opens with a typical Miltonic invocation:

> Come, sweet enthusiast, from the lonely vale,
>   Whence streams o'er all thy sadly-soothing lay;
> While Night sits list'ning to thy tender tale,
>   That melts the heart, and steals the soul away.[24]

The poet questions Melancholy of her "cool retreat" in "Afric's woods" or in "yon bowery grove," of her haunts in "Libya's trackless waste" or on "Andes' topmost mountain," in "some lone forest" where she listens to the strains of Philomel, or by some "rushing flood," or among the "bloomy landscape" by a stream. He calls upon her train—"Wan Sorrow, drooping her dejected head," "Calm Thought," and "pensive Solitude." It is evening, "Wisdom's soft transporting hour," and he depicts Wisdom herself musing by a stream. "O bear me," he cries, to some remote shade

> Where the lone warbler on the ear of Night
> Pours sweetly slow her melancholy note,

away from Tumult, Ambition, and all their train.

> Here let me mark, from human ken remote,
>   The crowds that land in Death's dark dismal dome,
> Here weigh th' events in cool impartial thought
>   That pass betwixt the cradle and the tomb.

Or let him

> tune the sweetly plaintive lyre
> Till all my melting soul dissolve in woe.

With that he swings into a close imitation of Gray's
"Elegy," with passages as near the original as this:

> The busts of grandeur, and the pomp of power,
>   Can these bid Sorrow's gushing tears subside,
> Can these avail in that tremendous hour
>   When Death's cold hand congeals the purple tide?

One would like to think that this anonymous poem was
written by John Ogilvie, and that the "Ode to Melancholy" which he later published with his "Day of Judgment"[29] was merely a later version; for certain it is that
long stretches of the two odes, including the stanza just
quoted, are identical. The "sweet enthusiast" has become
"queen of thought sublime," and "Hecla's cloud-wrapt
brow" and "Chili's boundless shade" are added to Libya
and the Andes. But the general effect even of the passages which differ in phrasing is not much different.

Elegiac meditations on death and mutability, such as
are to be discussed at more length in the next chapter,
play a large part also in Elizabeth Carter's "Ode to Melancholy,"[30] written in the sixties. Greek scholar that she
was, she affixed to this poem a motto from Sophocles.
The opening is Miltonic:

> Come Melancholy! silent Pow'r,
> Companion of my lonely Hour
>   To sober Thought confin'd:
> Thou sweetly-sad ideal Guest,
> In all thy soothing Charms confest,
>   Indulge my pensive Mind.
>   .   .   .   .

Thro' yon dark Grove of mournful Yews
With solitary Steps I muse,
    By thy Direction led:
Here, cold to Pleasure's tempting Forms,
Consociate with my Sister-worms,
    And mingle with the Dead.

The last two lines suddenly darken the picture, and we are not surprised that from here on Milton and his mood are forgotten, and the atmosphere is that of Hervey's *Meditations* and in general of the tradition of religious melancholy. And yet in her phrasing of this characteristically religious meditation, Miss Carter now and again echoes Gray, and though she has invoked "Midnight Horrors," she uses little of the more grisly paraphernalia of the tomb.

The seventies, an incredibly barren period, yield nothing even here. But a characteristic ode[31] from the later eighties strikes at once the note of the sentimental triumph:

Sister of soft-ey'd Pity, hail!
Say in what deep-sequester'd vale,
    Thy head upon thy hand reclin'd,
Sitt'st thou to watch the last faint gleams of light;
To mark the grey mists sail along the wind,
And shadows dim that veil the brow of night?
    Or 'neath some rock abrupt and steep,
    Hear'st thou the hoarse resounding deep,
        While from many a murky cloud,
Blue light'nings flash by fits . . .

Here we have the Miltonic invocation as well as passages of Miltonic octosyllabics, the apotheosis of Pity, the misty evening and resounding ocean so dear to early romanticism, even the blue lightnings of the Gothic school—though one wonders how they got into this particular recipe. In these surroundings, while the "glimmering landscape" fades as Gray would have it do, will the poet attend his goddess—

> And all the soul dissolv'd and fainting lie
> In Rapture's holy trance, and heav'nly ecstacy.

He trusts Melancholy will teach him peace of mind; but, mindful of the treacherous propensity of white melancholy to turn to black, he concludes with a prayer against Misfortune, Madness, and Despair.

The odes dating from the nineties include our single example of an "Ode to Melancholy"[32] devoted entirely to bidding it hence; this will more conveniently be considered later. One Mr. Hole has a long irregular ode[33] in which ruins and the transitoriness of "sublunary power" are again stressed, and the poet's melancholy fancy takes him on far flights as though in a blank verse descriptive poem, ranging with him from Palmyra to Egypt and thence to the primitive glooms of Canadian forests. He has traffic with Gothic ghosts, who rise around him as he strays at night among the catacombs. Then, his "late-distemper'd mind" tranquillized, he hastens to the orthodox promontory, where he sits and muses on the future and the past, swinging once more naturally into elegiac stanza as he had done when he was contemplating the ruins of Palmyra.[34] Less philosophizing and more sensibility on the other hand are found in the "Ode to Melancholy" which Ann Radcliffe ascribes to Emily in *The Mysteries of Udolpho*.[35] It begins:

> Spirit of love and sorrow—hail!
>   Thy solemn voice from far I hear,
> Mingling with ev'ning's dying gale:
>   Hail, with this sadly-pleasing tear!
> O! at this still, this lonely hour,
>   Thine own sweet hour of closing day,
> Awake thy lute, whose charming power
>   Shall call up Fancy to obey:
> To paint the wild romantic dream
>   That meets the Poet's musing eye,
> As on the bank of shadowy stream
>   He breathes to her the fervid sigh.

Let Melancholy lead her to pine woods (the pine comes to be almost as melancholy a tree as the yew or cypress), to the minster's "moon-lit aisles," to "the mountain's dusky head," to the "dark cliff" which bends over the waves while the "wild winds of Autumn sweep." This ode, as a matter of fact, in spite of the due presence of nearly all the elements of the old recipe, contrives to get farther away in spirit from the classic-Miltonic tradition we are following than any of the others with the exception of that shaped by the original genius of Keats.

Two more examples may be cited from about this time, which seems to be the most prolific period in the matter of odes to melancholy. In the first (written 1796),[36] the poet assures us:

> Thy pensive pleasures, gloomy joy,
> Had charms for me when but a boy,

and he still seeks Melancholy's "secret haunts to weep," lying in her "gloomy shade" to "wet the green turf as I cry." But the reader shall be spared more of this poet's maudlin octosyllabics. The other poem, by George Dyer (1801),[37] is better, and affords indeed an excellent illustration of the marriage of melancholizing and sensibility. After the opening invocation, the poet exclaims:

> How sacred gleams that form of speechless woe!
> And sacred are thy haunts, thou solitary maid!

These haunts are as of old the "willowy stream" and the nightingale-haunted wood, or, toward the end of the poem, "some lonely cell" furnished out with a death's head. But the description of the maid is all through much more tearful than Milton would have approved. She seems to Dyer to be a virgin "In life's young spring," carelessly clad, with floating hair—

> Thine eye now softly sad, now wildly bright,
> Bespeaks a lover dead, and thou canst love but one.

She is inspired by "Ovid's soft fictions," by "suffering ghosts," and the lines of "Pity's Bard" (Euripides—Dyer was a Greek scholar). Yet all the while she conceals in her own bosom secret wrongs "no pity can relieve":

> Thou hast a sigh for all; none heaves a sigh for thee!

It is at this point that he bids her, "Queen of Woe," haste to the lonely cell and the solemn death's-head, and

> As the spade sinks thy future grave-bed lower,
> I, too, will learn to die, sad pilgrim at thy tomb!

Yet in whatever form she may deign to appear, if only "soft Mercy dwell within" her breast, he will "make her sorrows" his. All of which makes a pretty enough set of verses, although it is not likely to leave one either philosophically uplifted or emotionally moved.

There are two poems on melancholy in the *Poetical Magazine* (1809-11). One[38] is merely a slight invocation to the "pensive nymph." The other, a more elaborate "Ode,"[39] begins with the statement that "If aught can raise the drooping heart" it is "heav'nly pensive Melancholy." Yet, after meditating with her on mutability on a hilltop at midnight, the poet pictures her in a churchyard, where she bends "O'er Beauty's early tomb" like a "picture of Despair." There are croaking ravens, and a storm, and mention of Melancholy sitting "on some high rock" over the sea with her sister Madness. If all this seems little calculated to raise a drooping spirit, the rest is more soothing. For in "some secluded cell" she will play her "magic shell," or, communing with her in a dark grove, the poet will

> Like Fingal's Bard, in lofty lays,
> Record the deeds of ancient days,
> And strike the Gothic lyre.

By 1810, it is clear, the goddess has become quite converted to romanticism.

What technical dexterity and a certain awareness of its own artificiality could still do with the old tradition, however, is amply shown in the fine "Ode to Melancholy" by Thomas Hood (1827).[40] There is no actual invocation of a personified abstraction here, and the octosyllabic lines are not rimed in pairs and have in their movement and phrasing as much suggestion of Fletcher as of Milton; but the conscious invoking of the mood of mild contemplative melancholy, the conscious use of the same natural symbols and the same recurring themes, make it clear that the poem belongs to the main stream of tendency we are following. There is nevertheless added, as has been said, a new depth of emotional perception, and a philosophic twist linking the poem in a manner to Keats's "Ode," which is not in the stream at all but a re-action against it, and which owes to its predecessors little more than its figure of Melancholy sitting veiled upon a throne.

Hood opens his poem with a frank avowal that his mood is to be artificially induced:

> Come, let us set our careful breasts,
> Like Philomel, against the thorn.

For, as he reminds us in the language of the Elizabethan revival, "there are dainty themes of grief" on which to think:

> True honour's dearth, affection's death,
> Neglectful pride, and cankering scorn,
> With all the piteous tales that tears
> Have water'd since the world was born.

There follows a passage of deliberate pathetic fallacy—

> For thus my gloomy phantasy
> Makes all things weep with me!

There is mention of "sweet nightingale," of "gloomy nooks," of "pensive shades for Melancholy":

> Mirth shall not win us back again,
> Whilst man is made of his own grave,
> And fairest clouds but gilded rain!

Follows a passage in the old *sic transit* theme, and even a meditation in a churchyard—we will think of Charon, he says,

> And for our table choose a tomb . . .

We have ravens, winding sheets, Death personified, yew-trees, and the question

> Is't not enough to vex our souls,
> And fill our eyes, that we have set
> Our love upon a rose's leaf,
> Our hearts upon a violet?

There is a rather long passage about the moon—

> The Moon! she is the source of sighs,
> The very face to make us sad . . .

Already he has introduced the reflection that "dark and bright will kiss." He closes with an elaboration of the doctrine:

> All things are touched with Melancholy,
> Born of the secret soul's mistrust,
> To feel her fair ethereal wings
> Weighed down with vile degraded dust;
> Even the bright extremes of joy
> Bring on conclusions of disgust,
> Like the sweet blossoms of the May,
> Whose fragrance ends in must.
> O give her, then, her tribute just,
> Her sighs and tears, and musings holy!
> There is no music in the life
> That sounds with idiot laughter solely;
> There's not a string attuned to mirth,
> But has its chord in Melancholy.

This perception of the mingled roots of joy and sorrow, of the eternal struggling of the soul (in a sense quite apart from that of orthodox religion) under the burden of dust, is one of the profoundest elements in romantic melancholy. The fact that an intense and personal development of it lies at the heart of Keats's "Ode on Melancholy" makes inappropriate any extended discussion of that poem in the present connection.

III

But the tradition of contemplative melancholy by no means depended on this particular series of odes for its perpetuation. Among the abstractions favored by the ode writers were many others besides melancholy itself which contributed to keep the tradition alive. For the attributes, haunts, and pleasures of Contemplation, Solitude, Silence, Retirement, Meditation, even Content and Health, often bear so striking a likeness to those of Melancholy that it becomes difficult to distinguish them. Nor is this altogether surprising in view of the identification, to which we have so often referred, of the milder shades of melancholy with mere pensiveness.

Consider the descriptive epithets applied to these various Miltonic nymphs. Contemplation is "lovely fair," "queen of pensive air," "calm Contemplation," "pensive sage."[41] Content is "meek-ey'd nymph . . . Sober, modest, and discreet."[42] Meditation is

> Sweet child of Reason! maid serene!
> With folded arms and pensive mien . . .[43]

Silence is "musing" and "sober."[44] Solitude, probably the most often practically identified with Melancholy, is "musing maid," arrayed in "robe of flowing black" and cypress wreath;[45] "pensive virgin," "sweet nun," and "Sister of peace and piety";[46] "silent matron . . . serious, caelestial";[47] "Parent of musing! sober matron";[48]

"Queen of sober thought";[49] "pensive" and the "nurse of thought."[50] Are not these attributes indistinguishable from those ascribed to the personifications of melancholy?

Or consider the places, times, and seasons, said to be beloved by these goddesses. Contemplation leads the poet at evening to her "rural bower," to wood and rivulet, to ploughman's cot, to "dusky lanes or shades," to meadows, promontories, or even to the churchyard.[51] Or she is to come in her "sable-sooted car" drawn by "two mournful turtles," and bear him to the place where she loves to roam, in the "deep dark solemn grove."[52] Or at "sober twilight," her "favorite hour," the poet would be with her on "moonlit seashore," in "pathless forest," by the "streamlet" in the "tranquil vale," or with her would trace some "ruin'd Abbey's hallowed rounds."[53] Or he will follow her from dawn to dawn as Milton did, through all her rural haunts, and at evening will muse with her by some "brawling rivulet" as he watches the "first glimpse of the eastern star," and the "distant sounds of pastoral lute" will invoke the "sober suit of dimmest darkness" and fit well with "sorrow's pensive spell"; there will be a distant curfew and an owl in a ruin quite in the manner of Gray, and the poet will sit on a tomb, again like Gray, and meditate in Miltonic octosyllabics on death, "deep wailing, ruin'd" maids, and the sorrows of life in general.[54] Content loves the "moss-grown cell," the "gloomy glade, the waving grove," the "mountain's rugged brow," as well as the "flow'ry vale."[55] Peace of Mind, too, loves to "walk at eve" by "murmuring streams," to view "with Contemplation's eye" the "headlong cataract," to haunt the "dark sequester'd wood" and "mossy grots."[56]

Health seeks not only the "daisied green" and "pearly grot," but, for some reason rather hard to fathom, also evening wanderings by "some tott'ring ivy'd tow'r" with owls, bats, ghosts, Philomel, the moon, and Contemplation.[57] Indolence wanders at the "silent noon of night" over "pathless wilds, and mountains drear" under the moon, or by gliding waters muses with Contemplation on the shortness and vanity of life.[58] As for Solitude, Joseph Warton consigns her to a "cavern low," with "bleak winds," a "hoarse, death-boding owl," the "wakeful howl" of a village mastiff, and a dim lamp casting "an awful gloom"—all of which is melancholy enough to border on the black variety.[59] Later writers are usually more cheerful, but still pensive. For Solitude too loves "groves and cooling shades" and "mossy banks of purling streams," communes with Nature, and abjures the vanities of life.[60] She even frequents the "churchyard walk."[61] She does not disdain the "moss-grown grove" or the "cloyster's mould'ring walls."[62] She wanders with Contemplation by "murmuring streams," through "darksome dells," in the "churchyard's gloom," to some lonely "mould'ring cell."[63] She delights in "shaggy woods," the "pebbly borders of the main," the "dew-spangled grot,"

> Where Meditation, like an Hermit pure,
> With bosom taught by mild philanthropy,
> In Silence mourns the miseries of Man![64]

It is all very confusing; or would be if we did not know that whichever of these pensive nymphs is being invoked, some at least of the others will probably be in her train.[65]

Lastly, consider the mood which dictates these nocturnal wanderings. Something of it has naturally been indicated by the haunts chosen and the descriptive epithets applied to them. A few more examples will suffice. Robert Lloyd speaks of

> The pensive pleasures, calm delights
> While Contemplation smooths her ruffled wings . . .

and is "all unwilling" to take his leave of Cynthia and "the pensive Muse" to mix "with the buzz of day."[66] "Y" (1783) wishes to be conducted by Solitude to Meditation in her "woodland wild," where he may hear "alluring notes of woe" and in that "calm recess" be blessed with "pensive pleasure."[67] "A Lady" (1778) in invoking Solitude, hails "peaceful shades," "awful silence," Philomel, and "th' involuntary tear," and calls to her breast "ever mild philosophy."[68] "Mr. H." speaks of the "faint desponding air" of Taste.[69] Southey (1792) talks of nursing "Reflection's sacred woe" and of the Ossianic "joy of grief."[70] As already hinted, the themes of contemplation are frequently the stock melancholy themes:

> To think, alas! how short, how vain,
> The rich man's boast! the poor man's woe! . . .[71]

> To muse upon the happier day
> When Hope would weave her visions gay . . .[70]

> We will muse on pensive lore
> Till the full soul brimming o'er,
> Shall in our upturn'd eyes appear,
> Embodied in a quivering tear . . .[72]

Thus over a surprisingly large proportion of this group of odes to abstractions lies the "sadly-pleasing" atmosphere dear to the devotee of melancholy.

Nor do the more "horrific" odes to Superstition, Despair, Fear, and Horror, lie altogether outside of our discussion. Already frequent reference has of necessity been made to the various stages or types of melancholy, and the insidiously gradual steps by which the black melancholy sometimes advances upon him who courts the white. Long ago, Burton had pointed out that the early stages of the disease are pleasurable:

Voluntary solitariness is that which is familiar with Melancholy, and gently brings on like a Siren, a shoeing-horn, or some Sphinx, to this irrevocable gulf, a primary cause Piso calls it; most pleasant it is at first, to such as are melancholy given, to lie in bed whole days, and keep their chambers, to walk alone in some solitary Grove, betwixt Wood and Water, by a Brook side, to meditate upon some delightsome and pleasant subject, which shall affect them most; *amabilis insania*, and *mentis gratissimus error*. A most incomparable delight it is so to melancholize . . .[73]

But he goes on to show, here and elsewhere, how the habit grows on one until one is unfit for any business, becomes a prey to *tedium vitae*, and may end in despair and madness. Although the conception of melancholy as a disease, except in the modern sense, was dying out,[74] the discerning poet could not fail to be aware that his favorite melancholy ranged in mood from a pleasing pensiveness to the madness of despair. As we have seen, it is when melancholy is conceived of as akin to despair that the poets describe it unsympathetically and bid it hence. Thus in a certain Miltonic ode "On Music,"[75] "dull-brow'd" Melancholy is told to

> creep away
> To weeping caverns, exil'd from the day,
>
> .   .   .   .
>
> Or go where endless horror dwells,
> To Bedlam walls, to Newgate cells . . .

Mary Robinson, as noted above, actually wrote a whole "Ode to Melancholy"[76] on the "hence" motif, calling Melancholy "Sorc'ress of the Cave profound," and banishing her to "native Chaos" with Frenzy and hopeless Love and her "haggard dam, Despair," or to some haunted churchyard amid ravens, murderers, "Horror's direful scream" and maidens strewing wreaths on lovers' graves under the "witching Yew." In another poem,[77] Mrs. Robinson, who frequently betrays the fear that her melancholy may deepen into despair, describes at length the progress from one extreme to the other, beginning with the familiar twilight wanderings by the "dreary monumental pile," following through horrible hallucinations on the bleak wintry heath, and ending with howling blast, a precipice over the wreck-strewn sea, and pale Melancholy leaping with a shriek to expire "in the bosom of Despair." An even more elaborate allegory to the same effect is presented by William Richardson, in a "vision" poem calculated to give friendly warning to a melancholy friend.[78]

The number of odes actually written to or on Despair, Superstition, Fear, and Horror—not to mention a sprinkling to Tragedy, Envy, Despondency, and kindred abstractions—is only less than the number to Melancholy, Contemplation, and Solitude. At one end of the series stand Collins' "Ode to Fear" and Joseph Warton's odes to Superstition and to Despair; at the other end Southey's "Ode to Horror" and Kirke White's address to the "genius of Horror and romantic awe."[79] Despair and Superstition are almost invariably bid hence, the former, however, sometimes only at the instigation of Religion or Patience and after a brief invoking of indifference or the oblivion of suicide.[80] Horror, on the other hand, is sometimes wooed, as in the ode by Southey,[81] who calls on her to do for him much the sort of thing usually expected of Melancholy—to take him to ruins, wastes, sea-cliffs, battlefields, and scenes of dark oppression. Neither is Fear always shunned, especially as it is so intimately associated with tragedy; Collins closes his "Ode to Fear" with the promise to dwell with her if she can but give him Shakespeare's cypress wreath.[82] The descriptions of these abstractions are full of "horrifics." Despair is "foul fiend" and "terrific Fiend, thou Monster fell,"[83] and is described with the grisly vividness of a Spenserian gargoyle: she may have, for instance, stony, staring eye-balls, foul blood-stained rags, "clotted hair," and a "cank'red breast" full of visible serpents.[84] Superstition, "demon accurst," is born of "ghastly Fear and darkest Midnight"

> Far in a blasted dale
> Mid Lapland woods and noisome wastes forlorn,

the haunts of evil witches, where in hellish darkness the blue flame is damped by infants' blood.[85] Much is said in the superstition-odes about convents and the Inquisition and "clanking chains" and "shrieking ghosts."[86] Their paraphernalia alone would link this whole group to the descriptions of black melancholy.

IV

Not infrequently the poet carefully differentiates between the two melancholies, and chooses the milder. Thus, at the beginning of our period, William Mason asks:

> Why lure me from these pale retreats?
> Why rob me of these pensive sweets?

but declares that he is not ready yet for wandering through "cloisters drear" to watch

> Thin shiv'ring ghosts from yawning charnels throng.

His "sober mind," he goes on,

> The fainter forms of sadness please;
> My sorrows are of softer kind.
> Thro' this still valley let 'me stray,
> Rapt in some strain of pensive Gray . . .[87]

Similarly an anonymous writer in the *Gentleman's Magazine*[88] says of Poetic Melancholy that he means

> Not her, of moping look, and haggard face
> That loves at home with Silence to abide,

but the Melancholy that is

> Child of serenity and sober sense . . .

A certain sonnet-writing Miss Locke, describing "The Visionary"[89] in Miltonic octosyllabics in the same journal, starts with "black congenial Night," "crumbling wall," Madness, Horror, Death, and Suicide wildly rolling his eyes amid foul vapours, bats, shrieking owls, and dancing Furies—discards all this (how could she else?) for mirthful day—and finally discards that too for "sacred, musing Melancholy" at "sober Eve," with Philomel, an "umbrageous grove," and

> meditation calm and holy,
> Becoming thee, O Melancholy.

Much more thoughtful and appealing is the analysis in the blank verse "Melancholy"[90] of the gently romantic "Barry Cornwall," written toward the close of our period:

> There is a mighty Spirit, known on earth
> By many names, tho' one alone becomes
> Its mystery, its beauty, and its power.
> It is not Fear,—'tis not the passive fear
> That sinks before the future, nor the dark
> Despondency that hangs upon the past:
> Not the soft spirit that doth bow to pain,
> Nor that which dreads itself, or slowly eats
> Like a dull canker till the heart decays.
> But in the meditative mind it lives,
> Sheltered, caressed, and yields a great return;
> And in the deep silent communion
> Which it holds ever with the poet's soul,
> Tempers, and doth befit him to obey
> High inspiration . . .

Grief, he goes on to tell us, may "sublime itself"

> until it seem
> Etherial, starry, speculative, wise.

Then comes Melancholy, like lovely morning after the storm.[91] It is usually this meditative melancholy which the poets desire, though most of them are too busy blindly following the "Il Penseroso" convention to be so articulate about it.

Sometimes, from the first, the moods are unconsciously confused; the spell of the artificial tradition is so strong that the poet slips from one set of symbols to the other without appearing to realize that he is confusing his recipes. This is most amusingly exemplified by a pair of parodies. The first is brief and may be given in full:

TO A GENTLEMAN, WHO DESIRED PROPER MATERIALS
FOR A MONODY[92]

Flowrets—wreaths—thy banks along—
Silent eve—th' accustom'd song—
Silver slipper'd—whilom—lore—
Druid—Paynim—mountain hoar—
Dulcet—eremite—what time—
("Excuse me—here I want a rhime.")
Black-brow'd night—Hark! scretch-owls sing!
Ebon car—and raven wing—
Charnel houses—lonely dells—
Glimmering tapers—dismal cells—
Hallow'd haunts—and horrid piles—
Roseate hues—and ghastly smiles—
Solemn fanes—and cypress bowers—
Thunder—storms—and tumbling towers—
    Let these be well together blended—
Dodsley's your man—the poem's ended.

The other composite parody is the "Ode to Horror" published in the *Student,* the spritely periodical edited in the early 1750's by Thomas Warton and Christopher Smart.[93] It bears the illuminating subtitle "In the Allegoric, Descriptive, Alliterative, Epithetical, Fantastic, Hyperbolical, and Diabolical Style of our Modern Odewrights, and Monody-mongers." It is so neat a take-off of the Wartons themselves, chief among many, that one is not surprised to learn that the quizzical young Thomas is suspected of having done it himself. It begins:

> O Goddess of the gloomy scene,
> Of shadowy shapes thou black-brow'd queen;
> Thy tresses dark with ivy crown'd,
> On yonder mould'ring abbey found;

and continues to enumerate indiscriminately charnels and pensive pilgrims, sheeted spectres and fairy-vales. Spenser is mentioned, and Éloise, and the pale midnight prisoner. Once more the goddess is invoked in orthodox style:

> O haste thee, mild Miltonic maid,
> From yonder yew's sequester'd shade . . .

One may be surprised at the adjective *mild* applied to Horror; but a few lines below she is "mother of the fire-clad thought,"

> Sprung from th' embrace of Taste and Night.

Then again she is all mild melancholy:

> O thou! whom wand'ring Warton saw,
> Amaz'd with more than youthful awe,
> As by the pale moon's glimm'ring gleam
> He mus'd his melancholy theme:
> O curfeu-loving goddess haste!
> O waft me, to some Scythian waste,
> Where, in Gothic solitude,
> Mid prospects most sublimely rude,
> Beneath a rough rock's gloomy chasm,
> Thy sister sits, Enthusiasm . . .

The first part of this passage clearly refers to "The Pleasures of Melancholy,"[94] but the last sounds more like

"The Enthusiast." Now if the faintly ecstatic mood of Joseph Warton's "Enthusiast" is thus to be ascribed to Horror, do we not already in 1751 have a somewhat scrambled tradition?

One "terrible example" of the way poetasters were still scrambling it a generation later must suffice: it is from an "Address to the Owl" by "T. T. S."[95] The writer hails the bird who delights to live and scream in ruins; to its haunts he often hastes

> at that lonely hour,
> What time the distant curfew tells
> The night-hags ope the deadly spells
> Of Sorcery's magic power,
> 'Midst lightning's glare, and thunder's roll,
> Whose terrors are accordant with my troubled soul.

> Then, ever dear to pensive melancholy,
> Joyful I list, thy dreary note resound
> From the mould'ring walls around,
> Vain monuments of folly . . .

and so on. The poet who could not only twist an English sentence into the shape of that last stanza, but could succeed in musing pensively on by-gone human folly amid night-hags and thunder-storms, surely should not have hesitated to sign his full name.

V

There were always, however, a goodly number to keep pure the mood associated with "Il Penseroso," or at least to keep it uncontaminated with either religious melancholy or Gothic horrors, although it was inevitably further affected as time went on by the growth of sensibility and of primitivism. Since at present our main business is with the lighter mood, space forbids further examination of the "horror material" in the odes. It will be more rewarding to take a hasty glance at the persistence of the neo-classic "retirement theme," concerning the popularity of which earlier in the century something was said in the preceding chapter.

Doubtless this classical hypothesis that the way to gain a chastened and pensive content is to abjure the world, by which is usually meant the court and the high society of the capital, and live in rural seclusion and "lettered ease," was during the second half of the century a dying tradition. Horace and Virgil had already been much diluted with the sentimentalism of Shenstone and the primitivism of the Wartons. Yet the tradition of philosophical retirement, generally linked to a mild melancholy, nevertheless persists in a recognizable degree of purity down to the next century. It is still strong in the fifties, in Dodsley's "Agriculture" (1754) for instance, in John Gilbert Cooper's "Epistles to the Great from Aristippus in Retirement" (1758), or in certain of Nathaniel Cotton's "Visions in Verse" (1751). It is implicit in much of the didactic and descriptive verse of later decades, although in the latter usually merging into the melancholy treatment of nature and thus lying outside our present discussion. Inscriptions for garden-seats, grottoes, and hermitages continued to be written and published, and to invoke Philosophy and "her loved sister Melancholy."[96] Practical indulgence in retirement continued occasionally to arouse ethical discussion. Bell, for example, published

(1790) in his *Fugitive Verse,* a pair of odes to ambition presenting opposite sides of the old controversy.[97] When Hannah More wrote her *Christian Morals* (1813), she was at pains to discuss the advantages and disadvantages of retirement, and to utter the warning that it is of no moral value if it brings no change "except from the idleness of tumult to that of ennui in one sex, and from levity to apathy in the other."[98] As for the incidental poetic praises of "sweet retirement's soothing shade,"[99] they grow less frequent after the sixties, and, as has been said, less purely Horatian, but they do not cease. The usually romantic Bowles, for example, writing in 1798, refers to "the blessings of retired munificence" and declares himself content with a "sequestered cottage" on the edge of the great estate, where he may mourn in solitude over Harriet's urn,

> scarce wishing to emerge
> Into the troubled ocean of that life,
> Where all is turbulance, and toil, and strife.[100]

Wordsworth and his friends constantly use the word retirement to describe their own retreat into the country.

Related themes persist or rise into popularity. Hermits have frequently figured as purveyors of philosophic wisdom since the days of Parsifal's sage advisor. The popularity of Parnell's didactic poem called "The Hermit" (published 1722), must have given an impulse to the use of this theme. Hermits appear not infrequently in preromantic verse, sometimes in connection with artificial hermitages, sometimes in a romantic ballad or vision setting, but always carrying the implication that their seclusion somehow gives them prerogatives of virtue and wisdom, naturally of a somewhat melancholy cast. They have usually sought retirement because of some great personal grief or because of the oppression of the woes of the world, and have in solitude gained a poised and chastened peace. Thomas Penrose's hermit (before 1779) sits high on a cliff, alone, and sees a vision of Joy, Hope, Grief, Anger, and other abstractions, until he calls on heaven to let Reason take the helm.[101] Thomas Dawson Laurence's hermit (1789), about whom he has written a recognition-and-restitution tale, soliloquizes in blank verse about "Dear Contemplation" and the lifting of his "pensive mind on high."[102] An anonymous "Hermit's Address" (1788) is even purer neo-classicism, with many pious sentiments about Virtue.[103] The theme was not abandoned by the romantic writers. Shelley, for instance, in "The Revolt of Islam," sends his philosophical hero to a hermit for comfort and instruction. John Wilson has an eight-page poem[104] about a hermit-sage whose holiness uplifted a whole peasant community and rescued a lovely glen reputed to be haunted.

Another related theme is the let-me-return-to-die motif, of which Goldsmith contributed the most influential example in the famous passage of "The Deserted Village" beginning "In all my wanderings round this world of care." He did not invent the theme, of course. It had been specifically enunciated in his own generation, for example, by no less a personage than Sir William Blackstone, whose "The Lawyer's Farewell to His Muse" (1764) ends with the wish that he may retire in old age to "the still, the rural cell" and, knowing that he has played his part, descend to the grave in peace.[105] After

Goldsmith, the theme recurs in certain poems probably influenced by "The Deserted Village," good examples being the closing passage of the precocious fragment on "Childhood"[106] by Kirke White, and the passage in John Struthers' "To Calder Water" which begins

> And after all my wanderings past,
> May I within thy vale at last . . .[107]

The same sentiment pervades Coleridge's lines "To the Reverend George Crabbe."[108] The whole spirit of the pastoral parts of "The Deserted Village" is a vaguely sentimentalized idealization of retirement, closer, however, to Shenstone than to Virgil or to Horace.

The tradition lingered in its purest form, probably, in the late progeny of Pomfret's "Choice," and in other short poems on content and on retirement itself. Dr. Johnson, it will be remembered, remarked in his "Life of Pomfret" that "perhaps no composition in our language has been oftener perused than Pomfret's 'Choice.' " It should not surprise us, therefore, to find minor poets still expressing "choices" and "wishes" fifty or seventy-five years after its publication. Take a series of variations on the latter topic in the *Gentleman's Magazine*. In April, 1746, one John Miller writes half a column of octosyllabics to the effect that he wants the usual cot "near some venerable wood," where he may walk and talk with God, and have Content as the "joint-tenant" of his "humble cell"; to which two writers reply in May, one assuring him in heroic couplet that his seeking Content is like Ixion's seeking to embrace a cloud, and the other reminding him that "Life is all a vain wish—like Corisca's fine ladle."[109]

In October, 1759, there is "The Wish," on the part of an anonymous Captain, for retirement *à deux;* it is answered in December by "Sylvia's Wish." In November, 1768, again there appears "A Lady's Wish," which is full of sensibility, and ascribes to cynicism the desire expressed by the men for retirement.

The odes to content are as numerous as the other odes to abstractions, and most of them carry on this tradition of retirement. Naturally, not all of them are melancholy; the wonder is that so many are. When Content is invoked as a goddess, she may have attributes and haunts comparable to those of Melancholy, as has been illustrated earlier in this chapter. When she is given a preference as to place of abode, it is usually, as in the wish-poems, in Arcadian retirement.[110] When content is rather a virtue recommended than a goddess invoked, there is the deep melancholy of affliction to be "harmonized"[111] into calm. Or the poet may emphasize the elusive quality of hope and the need of tempered desires and of resignation.

> I'm weary of the painful chase,
> Let others run this endless race,
> To catch a flying shade . . .[112]

advises one poet. And another:

> Keep peace and mild content within the line
> And to those limits every wish confine.[113]

And as a last example of the frequent connection of the content literature with melancholy may be cited a little poem "On Contentment" written by one Harriet Falconer at the mature age of fourteen, the last stanza of which is in obvious imitation of the "Elegy in a Country Church-yard":

> Perhaps in some sequester'd cottage laid,
> Contented Virtue like a flow'r unblown,
> Which if emerging from the humble shade,
> Might well have added lustre to a throne.[114]

There are also odes to retirement, and a good many miscellaneous poems carrying the word in their titles. Their mood varies from a didactic emphasis on virtue to a strain as elegiac as that of Gray's "Elegy." The connection with melancholy is illustrated near the beginning of the period by James Beattie's early poem, "Retirement" (1758):

> Ye cliffs, in hoary grandeur piled
>   High o'er the glimmering dale,
> Ye woods, along whose windings wild
>   Murmurs the solemn gale;
> Where Melancholy strays forlorn,
>   And Woe retires to weep,
> What time the wan Moon's yellow horn
>   Gleams on the western deep![115]

—in the eighties by William Bagshaw Stevens's "Retirement," said by a reviewer to be "the soliloquy of an old Penseroso,

>   smarting with the wrongs,
> And sated with the vanities of life,"[116]

—and in the nineties by the practical identification of retirement with meditation in an anonymous poem "On Retirement," with a succeeding enumeration of the haunts of Retirement which tallies closely with those of Melan-

choly and her sister goddesses.[117] The astonishing fecund-
ity of the tradition is illustrated, like that of the content-
ment-poems, by such juvenilia as the heroics in the pure
neo-classic strain contributed to the *European Magazine*
in May, 1787, by one "Master Drewitt, of the Grammar
School, in Plymouth, at the age of thirteen."[118] Late in
the century, there came to be a good many sonnets on retirement, but, like the descriptive poems, they are better
treated elsewhere. Early in the new century, Sir Egerton
Brydges published a long blank verse fragment on "Retirement" written in a deeply elegiac strain.[119]

The most interesting of these retirement poems is a
long poem by B. Fowler called "Philosophical Retirement," which appeared in the *London Magazine* for September, 1778, about midway in the preromantic period.[120]
It is definitely elegiac in tone. It bears a motto from
Thomson and is written in the stanza of Gray. "Philosophy the fair" is invoked as a "pensive queen." For her
the poet watches at evening by a "trembling rill"; there
are droning insects and lowing herds as in the "Elegy,"
as well as a "mild majestick moon" and a waterfall which
"in hollow murmurs roars."

> Night's solemn bird disconsolately plains
> From the lone abbey's ivy-vested wall;
> And sadly-pleasing Philomela's strains
> On the sooth'd ear in trilling accents fall.

After a bit more pure Gray of this sort, we are told that
in this peaceful seclusion the philosopher learns "to melt
at others' woes"—and the touch of sensibility serves to
introduce a long story of a bereaved friend. This story
in turn leads to a general "complaint of life," with enum-

eration of some of the woes which make the philosopher seek the shades of retirement with "divine Philosophy." There are a few stanzas then about the comforts of
religion, and the poet ends on a note of general humanitarian love of man and pity for his folly. It will be at
once perceived that this is by no means pure neo-classicism. In fact it might with reason be said that the poem
was one of the innumerable imitations of the "Elegy in
a Country Churchyard" to be discussed in the next chapter. The point in presenting it now is to illustrate two
things: the close connection between the "retirement
theme" and melancholy, and the insidious encroachments
during this period, of sensibility and humanitarianism on
material normally associated with the neo-classic tradition.

VI

Various other more or less elaborate didactic poems
carry on the tradition of deliberate contemplative melancholy. There is a group whose titles indicate direct imitation of "Il Penseroso," among which two at least bear Milton's title. The earlier of these,[121] written about 1745, bears
the first subtitle "An Evening's Contemplation in St. John's
Church-yard, Chester"—which immediately links it with
the "graveyard" material—and the second subtitle "A
Rhapsody," which well indicates its incoherent and discursive contents. It opens with a passage much more like
Fletcher than like Milton:

> Adieu, each modish Vanity,—adieu,
> The gorgeous glare of Dress, the brilliant Ball,
> The nightly Parties, the assembled *Route*,
> Adieu . . .

Leaving this "mummery absurd," the poet goes outside the walls to sit "among the letter'd tombs"; but for many pages his meditations are about the history and topography of Chester, the only melancholy material being some descriptions of ruins. These matters, however, lead him toward the close to a regular meditation on death and mutability. But this passage is much more like Young than like Milton. In fact, most of the Miltonic influence in the poem—outside the title—is rather from "Paradise Lost" than from "Il Penseroso."

The later poem, *Penseroso, or the Pensive Philosopher in his Solitudes*, published in 1771 by James Foot,[122] is much longer, and is definitely philosophical, or rather theological. The earlier pages of Book I, it is true, yield a perfect picture of the penseroso type:

> Oft his companions were
> The solemn birds of night, and deep in thought
> His nightly rounds he shapes . . .

Or the philosopher wanders amid the twilight sights and sounds of Gray's "Elegy" and stands

> Beneath the umbrage of an upland oak,
> Rapt into heav'nly thought . . .

In such a scene and mood

> The sage his meditations thus began.

It is not necessary, however, to follow these meditations, which fill the rest of Book I and all of the succeeding five Books; for they resolve themselves into a system of Christian apologetics, and do not concern us here.

There are various other pensive poems, mostly short, which borrow the suggestion for their titles from "Il Penseroso." "Il Meditante" (1752)[123] is in blank verse, and, after a descriptive opening which might be from an ode to melancholy except for the meter, it swings into a religious meditation in which the predominant Miltonic influence is not "Il Penseroso" but "Paradise Lost," as in the two blank verse *Penseroso* poems just discussed. At the other end of the preromantic period, however (1803), there is "Il Romito; or, the Hermit,"[124] which is in tripping octosyllabics in the best ode-tradition—with "Meditation, pensive maid," curfew, Gothic ruins, promontory, moon, tempest, a tomb, "dying tapers," yews, "the frequent sigh," "Ah! what avails . . .?", and a closing prayer for a dark and solitary grave.

More extensive is the group of poems on the "Pleasures" of this and that. These are almost all pensive. The series starts with Thomas Warton's "Pleasures of Melancholy" (1745),[125] and ranges through the pleasures of night, the mind, the poet, contemplation, and solitude, to the better known "Pleasures of Memory" (1792) by Rogers and "Pleasures of Hope" (1799) by Campbell. The other well-known poem of the group, Akenside's "Pleasures of the Imagination" (1744-1770), lies almost wholly outside of our purpose: it is full of Shaftesburian optimism, and never comes nearer melancholy than an occasional passage of diluted praise of retirement.

As for Warton's poem,[126] repeated reference has already been made to it, and all that remains is to give a brief connected summary in order that it may be seen as a whole. The poem opens, then, with an apostrophe to Con-

templation (ever, as we have seen, the sister of Melancholy):

> Mother of musings, Contemplation sage:
> Whose grotto stands upon the topmost rock
> Of Teneriff; 'mid the tempestuous night . . .

Thus early does Warton link contemplative melancholy
with the romantic love of mountains, to which he and
his brother contributed important beginnings. He goes
on to entreat his "queen sublime" to lead him to "solemn
glooms," "ruin'd seats," and "twilight cells," the "Fav'-
rite midnight haunts" of Melancholy. Let him sit musing beneath the ruins of an abbey at twilight, when the
"sullen, sacred silence" is broken only by the screech-
owl in the damp ivy-covered ruins. Or let him tread the
aisles in "religious horror." The mood deepens, one perceives, with the advancing night; for from "religious horror" we go, at "noon of night," to the regulation paraphernalia of black melancholy—the charnel house, the
"taper dim shedding a livid glare O'er the wan heaps,"
ghostly shapes. Or the poet awakes at midnight to reflect awfully that he awakes alone, and then falls asleep
again to dream of Britomart or of the Miltonic war in
heaven. Follow a passage in praise of winter, one pointing out the "elegance of soul refin'd" necessary for the
appreciation of the pleasures of melancholy, one in which
the poet invokes Night ("sister of ebon-sceptered Hec-
ate"), and one in which he essays a Thomsonian description of morning. He expresses a romantic preference for
the sorrows of Una rather than the adventures of Be-
linda: again pointing the way melancholy was to go, away

from spleen toward sensibility and the romantic *Heim-weh*. He glances at the pleasures of love melancholy, when pensive lovers pour out their sorrows to Philomela and "the pitying moon." Then he returns to the Gothic church, though this time to one not in ruins, and watches the "taper'd choir," and listens to the "many-sounding organ," losing himself, one imagines, in the melancholy ecstasy of the music as Shelley was to do after him. Then, close at Milton's heels, he goes to the tragedy. Then, wandering in the true manner of the descriptive poems, he tells us of a banished noble in Siberia, of a gazer on Athens, of the ruins of Persepolis. The poem closes with a final invocation to Melancholy and to Contemplation, which latter, he takes occasion to tell us, was reared by a Druid. Thus this youth of seventeen gathered into three hundred fifteen lines of blank verse most of the influences —Milton, Thomson, Young, Dyer—and all of the paraphernalia of the earlier melancholy tradition, and at the same time pointed out and himself influenced the way in which that tradition was later to develop.

Of the very minor poems of this group between "The Pleasures of Melancholy" and "The Pleasures of Memory," much less need be said. The main observation to be made of them is that, like the odes to abstractions, they tend to identify the attributes of melancholy and those of the qualities and occasions associated with it. "The Pleasures of the Night" (1747),[127] which is in blank verse, is largely religious in inspiration and owes a good deal to Young; but it has "melancholy joys," the blessings of "sweetly solemn" Meditation, and of course Philomela. "The Pleasures of the Mind" (1758)[128] is in octosyllabics, and has little of the melancholy paraphernalia except the "pleasing horror" of winter. "The Pleasures of Contemplation" (1768)[129] is again in blank verse and influenced by the "Night Thoughts." In its less didactic portions, however, it involves churchyards, ruins, night-birds, and "towering Fancy," quite as though it were an ode to melancholy. The pleasures of the poet[130] prove to be identical with those of melancholy and her associate nymphs: he wanders through various rural haunts, muses on Milton, Thomson, and Young, and contemplates the heavens.

There are several poems on "The Pleasures of Solitude." The earliest I have noted (1752) is a mere recipe poem in octosyllabics—"grot," "mossy cell," "hermit-like," "the vanity of life," "piles of mighty ruin," "With thee I'll live, with thee I'll die." It is followed in the same periodical number by a poem in heroics, called merely "Solitude," and the editor refers to "the different manner in which it [the theme] is treated by the ingenious authors." Yet the ingenuity seems to consist largely in saying identical things in not quite identical words.[131] A more elaborate treatment of the theme, in blank verse, is found in P. Courtier's "Pleasures of Solitude" (1796).[132] This poem reminds the reader by turns of Thomson, Milton, Young, Blair, and Gray. It would be easy to fill a page with summary and quotation from it, showing this indebtedness, but the repetition may be spared. Suffice it to say that it includes pensive communion with nature, a "beauteous victim of Deserted Love," a warning to sinners and atheists concerning the Last Day,[133] a meditation on ruins and the devastations of Time and Death, an invocation to Solitude as "friend of Virtue" and "nurse of Thought," and a concluding statement of the theme of the return to die in these lone retreats. It is, in short, fully in the tradition of contemplative melancholy. The remark may be made in passing that the artificial nature of this whole tradition is again pointed by the extreme youth of many of the writers involved: Courtier tells us that all the verse in his volume containing this poem was written before he was twenty. It is not meant to imply that youth is never melancholy, a statement which would be an obvious absurdity; but that young poets, being imitative, will express their melancholy in the orthodox manner, or, if it be fashionable, will imagine that they are melancholy whether they are or not.[134]

Samuel Rogers' poem "The Pleasures of Memory"[135] appeared four years before Courtier's book. It has many romantic affinities, and, like "The Deserted Village," to which it owes much besides the modified heroic couplet in which it is written, it is indeed a notable attempt to apply the classical technique to essentially romantic material. Thomas Warton had been able to discuss the pleasures of melancholy in a fairly impersonal manner. Now memory is a poignantly personal thing, and it is the lyric elements in both Goldsmith's poem and Rogers' which catch for us something of that poignancy. But Goldsmith had in the eye of his idealizing memory an actual village and actual people, and has been able to give us unforgettable pictures of them. Rogers on the other hand, much less of a poet to begin with, has cumbered himself with the obligation to be general and philosophical. The result is that the first few pages of his poem, in which he imagines himself returning to his native place and indulging in the mournful joy of remembering the happy past, are by far the most appealing; the succeeding sections of Part I, in which he attempts to illustrate the pleasures of memory[136] by tales of mournful exiles and returned travellers, and by the fascination of historic scenes and of portraits, do not wear so well.

Part II is more purely didactic, and is full of the pensive imagery and mild sorrow of the Miltonic tradition, considerably modified by sentimentalism. After a generalizing passage about Reason, Hope, Fancy, and Virtue, the theme is illustrated by the pensive memories of a nun and of a slave; by the ministrations of sleep; by the soothing memories even of madness. The poet goes on:

> Nor yet to pleasing objects are confin'd
> The silent feasts of the reflecting mind.
> Danger and death a dread delight inspire . . .[137]

and he adds examples and details to illuminate this sentiment; the passage has echoes of Gray and mention of Shenstone, and a metaphor from a ruined Gothic tower. Then, like Thomas Warton in "The Pleasures of Melancholy," he warns us that "these pure joys the world can never know."[138] Follows praise of twilight, and then a long idyllic love story involving a lyric about Memory and "her sister Solitude"[139] and ending with the bereaved lover wandering alone in the "shadowy grove"[140] in rapt communion with the memory of his beloved. The poet even ventures, next, to imagine the pleasures of memory among the dead. The poem ends with an address to a lamented brother, and a final invocation to Memory as mistress of Place and Time and the friend of Virtue.

Clearly in its sentimental nostalgia for the past this poem belongs with the writings of the minor romantics; but as clearly in its elaborate generalization, and often in its metrical technique and its diction, it belongs also with the tradition of neo-classic philosophical melancholy.

Thomas Campbell's "Pleasures of Hope" (1799),[141] also in heroics, is naturally less mournful than Rogers' poem by virtue of its purposely contrary subject. Yet, inasmuch as hope, too, involves something unattainable at the moment and is frequently invoked to give strength in some all but intolerable present suffering, an extended treatment of the theme would inevitably have at least in part a melancholy coloring. Thus Part I is concerned chiefly with the consolations of hope in situations of danger and distress, and with hope of the future improvement of human society as a comfort in the face of contemporary oppression, war, and general suffering. Here Campbell's intense passion for political liberty asserts itself, and there is a long passage of melancholy enthusiasm for Kosciusco and the tragedy of Poland. Part II is somewhat more cheerful in tone. Yet into the hopes and joys of domestic affection comes bereavement; and the discussion of death is made hopeful only by assumption of immortality and an incidental tirade against disbelievers in it. Thus this latest poem in our series, like "The Pleasures of Memory" immensely popular in its day, may be fairly reckoned as at least partly in the melancholy tradition.

But the most important of all these didactic poems for an understanding of how the classic-Miltonic tradition was perpetuated into the romantic period is Thomas Love Peacock's "The Philosophy of Melancholy." Although it was not reprinted between the original edition in 1812 and the Halliford edition of Peacock's *Works* in 1927,[142] this is not at all a bad poem of its genre, and furnishes, furthermore, an excellent analysis of the philosophical basis of melancholy. Peacock, being not only a scholar but a man of vigorous and original intellect, had clearly put actual thought into the matter; and the fact that he later found his true avenue of expression in joyous satire by no means invalidates the sincerity of the more conventionally solemn philosophy of his early youth. This youthful philosophy found full and elaborate expression in the poem in question, which is furnished with a general analysis, with separate longer analyses and Greek and Latin mottoes[143] for each of the four parts, and with lengthy and learned notes. The effect of these easy couplets is much less romantic, certainly much less sentimental, than that of Rogers' poem, or even Campbell's. There is no introspection; what personal matter there is merely furnishes a handy illustration for objective statement and has to do with nothing more intimate than Welsh scenery and a vague reference to the romance the poet found in the Welsh mountains. There are, to be sure, as would be inevitable in the author of *Maid Marian* and the lover of Jane Gryffydh, romantic elements; but the spirit is on the whole much nearer to Gray than to Byron.

Part I has to do largely with melancholy as reflected in the natural cycles of change in nature, and with melancholy joy in natural scenes; it lies closer to the literature we have been following than any other part of the poem. An opening description of the cycle of the seasons and the triumphs of "all-conquering time" leads to the familiar thought that man knows no second spring. The poet asks why the muse loves "the melancholy lay":

> Why joys the bard, in autumn's closing day,
> To watch the yellow leaves, that round him sail,
> And hear a spirit moan in every gale?
> To seek, beneath the moon, at midnight hour,
> The ivied abbey, and the mouldering tower,
> And, while the wakening echoes hail his tread,
> In fancy hold communion with the dead?[144]

The answer is that frivolous gaiety does not prepare for adversity. Therefore:

> Oh melancholy! blue-eyed maid divine!
> Thy fading woods, thy twilight walks, be mine!
> No sudden change thy pensive voteries feel . . .[145]

But a careful differentiation must be made between "the misanthropic gloom" of the cloister and the pure and virtuous melancholy of the "comprehensive mind," the "sentient heart," and the "intrepid hand." There follow examples: Zoroaster, Piso in the academic groves, Germanicus surveying a battlefield, Petrarch, Tasso—a list showing characteristic catholicity of choice. With vague echoes of Gray's "Elegy"—

> Far from the scenes the wretched vulgar prize,
> Thy cedar-groves, and cypress-bowers, arise . . .[146]

—he launches into what is probably the best passage poetically of the poem, a description of the wild mountain scenery of Wales. This passage includes praise of winter, of "the music of the plaintive surge" of ocean, and of "the mossy convent's crumbling pile." The book concludes with a picture of the exiled Marius contemplating the ruins of Carthage.

Part II shows how all the arts follow in the "pensive train" of melancholy—a sufficiently Miltonic figure and a sufficiently melancholy theme. The poet illustrates this, as to painting, by Claude and Salvator; as to music, by the plaintive strains of Arcadian bards, and the soft sounds of a lute over a mountain lake at twilight; and as to poetry, by a long array of names, including Homer, Sophocles, and Shakespeare. The most romantic passage of the poem follows: the poet points out the connection between melancholy and romance, not only with the Gothic novels clearly in mind but with mention of names —including that of *The Mysteries of Udolpho*. The section concludes with a pathetic and romantic tale of lovers fleeing from a tyrranical father through the mountains in the midst of a storm, and dying in each others' arms under a thundering avalanche.

This story of unhappy lovers, so favored a theme of the melancholy muse, leads naturally, at the beginning of Part III, to the sorrowful joys of mutual love:

> Blest is the sigh, the answering sigh endears;
> And sweet the solace of commingling tears . . .[147]

This passage involves the indirect reference to Peacock's Welsh romance[148] which was mentioned above. From the sorrows of the beloved the melancholy philosopher turns to those of humanity in general, and we have the inevitable widow, the almost inevitable tribute to the philanthropic Howard, an African story, and the apostrophe:

> These are thy triumphs, sacred nymph of tears!
> These the blest wreathes thy lonely myrtle rears![149]

This is followed by a passage a little like the opening of "The Pleasures of Memory," about the "churchyard grass that shrouds his earliest friends" and the memory of the dead in general. The section concludes with the rather distressing story of the hermit—there had to be a hermit—who dwelt beside a tree which grew from the urn of a beloved father.

The last Part is ethical and metaphysical. We have the insistence on the value of vicissitude as a nurse of virtue, especially the virtue of courage. Lengthy examples are given of the latter, notably the Norse legend of Odin. The concluding exhortation begins:

> And shall the savage faith, by phrensy taught,
> Nerve the wild spirit with all-conquering thought,
> While polished man, by sacred science led,
> Shrinks in the blast, and bends his weary head?[150]

The poet bids the mourner remember that "heaven is wronged, when virtue feels despair." The poem ends with a deistic hymn to the Creator.

Thus we have here, in the very midst of the romantic triumph, a restatement of the objective and reasoned philosophy of melancholy. It involves the Miltonic apostrophe, much about the haunts and even the train of the goddess, a warning against despair and superstition coupled with praise of mild melancholy as a nurse of virtue and humanity—all presented in heroic couplets, and, although softened, not greatly sentimentalized. Furthermore, most of the themes of melancholy, the treatment of which we shall be following through the succeeding chapters, are here gathered together: mutability, unhappy love, the melancholy aspects of nature, the sufferings of humanity. Even the theme of Gothic horror is hinted at in the passage on melancholy and romance, and referred to obliquely in the warnings against superstition and despair. Only the purely romantic theme of the unhappiness of genius is absent. The poem for that very reason stands at the end of the old tradition rather than in the midst of the new.

CHAPTER III

SIC TRANSIT GLORIA MUNDI

Methought a voice, severe and strange
Whispered of fate, and time, and change.
—*Peacock*

One of the favorite themes of the poet in melancholy mood has always been mutability. Thus we have inevitably found the semi-Miltonic literature of philosophical melancholy full of meditations on the conquering power of time, the instability of human fame, the indiscriminateness and inevitability of death. The glory of earth passes. Palmyra is no more, and the jackals wander in her ruins; the mighty baron who once ruled this very spot is gathered to his fathers and the owl shrieks from the ruins of his castle hold. Death sits in wait for us one and all, and who shall say whether the bones crumbling in state in Westminster Abbey lie easier than those beneath this rural churchyard stone? It is right that we should sit in this place of graves or by this noble ruin, to meditate on these things. The verse of the latter half of the eighteenth century and the early years of the nineteenth echoes and reëchoes this strain. To follow the theme outside the formal literature of melancholy may give some idea of how fully and with what implications our forebears took it to their hearts.

I

It goes without saying that the greatest eighteenth-century expression of this theme is the "Elegy in a Country 'Churchyard" by Thomas Gray (1751). As has already been said, this famous poem gathers into itself most of the elements of the earlier melancholy tradition, and adds to them the flavor of Gray's own sensibility and gentle humanity. That it left its own indelible impress on the development of the tradition has been illustrated by unavoidable references in the odes and didactic poems. But naturally the influence was greatest in the elegy itself; so great was it, in fact, that we have agreed to use the adjective elegiac as identical with the mood of Gray's poem. This is not to imply that Gray must take sole responsibility for all the churchyard yews, moping owls, and philosophical ruins of the latter half of the century; enough has already been said to guard against such an exaggeration. But it remains true that if it had not been for the famous "Elegy," late-eighteenth-century meditations on time, death, and human glory would indubitably have been different in technique and fewer in number.

No poem in the English language has been more quoted, parodied, imitated, translated, and generally talked about than "An Elegy Written in a Country Churchyard." Gray's bibliographer, C. S. Northup,[1] lists 205 appearances of the poem in the original English between 1751 and 1830, 126 in the 49 years before 1800 and 79 in the 30 years after. Of these items, 105 represent publications alone or with other works by Gray, and an even 100, anthologies and editions with certain other famous poems, notably Blair's "The Grave," in combination with which the "Elegy" appears no less than 17 times in the period cited. The peak of popularity as reflected in reprinting came between 1790 and 1810, which two decades yield 67 items, almost equally divided between them. Naturally the majority of these editions were issued from London; but Edinburgh, Boston, and Paris are well represented, the last by some 9 editions, and scattered items range Europe and America from Wilmington, Delaware, to Verona and Hamburg. Furthermore, before 1830 the "Elegy" had been translated into 11 languages: there were 30 versions in French, 19 in Latin, 14 in Italian, 13 in German, 8 in Greek, 4 in Spanish, and 1 each in Hebrew, Hungarian, Portugese, Russian, and Welsh.

Parodies and imitations and verbal echoes meet the investigator on every hand. Professor Northrup lists parodies and imitations ranging in date from 1753 to 1916, 166 items in all, of which 106 occur before 1830. On the basis of his list the crest of this wave would seem to have come in the sixties, which alone yield 25 items. After that the number per decade varies within remarkably narrow limits—between 10 and 17—with no sign whatever of any gradual falling off. Although I have run across a good many poems not on this list which seem to me to owe as much to Gray as some on it, I think that these figures are not misleading until after 1800 or perhaps 1810. After that the number of parodies and avowed imitations does not fall off, but I hear fewer fleeting echoes in the fugitive verse. It could scarcely be otherwise than that the quiet philosophizings of Gray should be drowned out by the multitudinous voices of triumphant romanticism. Yet the poem has been an abiding influence on British poetry, and it will be worth while to analyze the crop of imitations and parodies in relation to the development of the melancholy tradition.

First a word about the form. The popularity of the "Elegy in a Country Churchyard," backed by the much less impressive success of Shenstone's and Hammond's elegies, almost at once caused its stanza form to become associated in the public consciousness with elegiac emotion of one sort or another. During the latter half of the eighteenth century, although not, I think, after the romantic triumph, poems elegiac in mood are somewhat more likely than not to be written in this stanza.[2] I am not prepared to offer statistics on this point, nor are they perhaps especially needed: it is a general expectation on the part of the observant reader which is in question. The general expectation of the use of this stanza and this mood in poems called elegies is also increased. But the association of a pensive-melancholy mood with Gray's quatrain, and particularly of Gray's quatrain with the term elegy, is not nearly as universal as the modern reader might anticipate. For example, consider the treatment of elegy in the 1804 volume of the *Poetical Register, and Repository of Fugitive Poetry,* which ought to be fairly representative of the situation shortly before the waning of the greatest vogue of Gray's poem. The reason for choosing this particular volume for analysis is that it contains a reprint of one of Professor Northup's items, the parody beginning

> St. Paul's proclaims the solemn midnight hour,
> The weary cit slow turns the master key . . .

There are five other poems in the elegiac quatrain,[3] three of which are definitely elegiac in mood, but not one of which is called an elegy. One of the poems is Anna Seward's "Grenville and Julia," which is a melancholy enough tale, being a paraphrase of Vincent Bourne's Latin version of Mallet's "William and Margaret"; but it is not elegiac in the sense in which Gray is elegiac, and the movement of the stanza is a world away from that of the "Elegy."[4] Of the other four poems, one is an epitaph, dated 1796, melancholy but metrically imperfect. One is Mrs. leNoir's poem called "The Fond Wife, to her Husband at Sea," which is a pathetic love elegy of absence, notable chiefly for its obvious sincerity and for its transference of the machinery of complaint from the man to the woman. The other two are a set of unsigned "Stanzas" more full of sensibility than of melancholy, and some pensive lines about "The Robin Red-Breast" by a Mrs. Witlen. On the other hand, the volume contains two funeral and two love elegies definitely so called, besides three translations from the elegies of Propertius, all of them melancholy and not one of them in Gray's stanza, although two or three show traces of his influence in idea or in phrase.[5] It is more nearly true, then, to say that Gray's stanza is usually elegiac than to say that elegies or poems in what we have called the elegiac mood are usually written in that stanza.

II

No poem, of course, may be considered a definite imitation of Gray's "Elegy" which is not in the same meter. Within this obvious limit, the poems we are to consider range all the way from line-by-line parody to original meditation whose debt to Gray does not go beyond a fleeting verbal reminiscence or perhaps the hint for subject or mood.[6]

The parodies, of which there are some 29 nearly or quite stanza by stanza and some 13 less complete, are for the most part not really in the elegiac mood at all. It would be surprising if they were. The "Elegy" is not at all difficult to parody, and what more natural than to turn it to the uses of political and social satire, occasional description, or schoolboy nonsense? The tune once caught, what easier than to ring the changes on the opening line?

> The curfew tolls the hour of closing gates . . .
> Retirement's Hour proclaims the tolling Bell . . .
> The shrill bell rings the knell of "Curtain rise" . . .
> The courts are shut—departed every judge . . .
> Gazettes now toll the melancholy knell . . .
> Great Tom now sounds the close of busy day . . .
> Now sinks the hum confus'd of busy care . . .
> The clock proclaims the welcome dinner hour . . .
> The watchman drawls the hour of dawning day . . .
> The ev'ning gun declares the day is spent . . .
> The turnkey rings the bell for shutting out . . .

These are merely samples, the opening lines of representative parodies, dating from 1753 to 1821, and having to do respectively with university life, a nunnery, a theater, Westminster Hall, St. Stephen's Chapel, a London churchyard, Poet's Corner, a Christmas dinner, walking home at dawn after a ball, a military camp, and a prison.[7] As one reads on, one may still occasionally find amusement or sting in some clever twist of a familiar phrase:

Full many a rogue is born to cheat unseen,
And dies unhang'd for want of better care . . .

And leaves the town to tumult and to me . . .

Approach and read (none else will read) the play,
    If not, the epilogue may do as well . . .

Full many a Castlereagh, with hands yet clean . . .

The short insolvent annals of the debtor . . .[8]

But such fugitive wit is more entertaining in small quantities than in the gross, and the reader shall be spared further delvings in these particular burial mounds. Doubtless many of us have at one time or another attempted to parody Gray's "Elegy" ourselves, without thinking it incumbent on us to publish the *tour de force* which resulted.

Although most of the parodies are humorous or satiric rather than melancholy, it is not always easy at this distance of time to decide how seriously certain of them are meant to be taken. There is a Grub Street elegy, for instance,[9] the satire of which strikes one as of the grim variety turned desperately on itself. There is a parody satirizing an unsuccessful opera,[10] which bewilders the reader by ending in a self-epitaph on the poet, who turns out to be a neglected curate very proud of the fact that he will die with no dread of "the horrors of a Taylor's hell." Besides others on the border line, there are six or eight that seem to be completely serious in intent and strongly elegiac in tone. Edward Jerningham's "The Nunnery"[11] is called an imitation, but is really a fairly close parody, applying the ideas and turns of thought and phrase of the original to the nuns; the last and more personal part presents the poet hopelessly in love with a nun, and, as he departs from the country, leaving a "Letter" to take the place of the "Epitaph." An elegy written in King's Bench Prison "by a Minor,"[12] though an only slightly imperfect parody in form, is full of humanitarianism and self-pity: one hears of "hard-hearted pride," of the "dull complaint of the imprisoned poor," and of the heart-broken poet's hope that "the tender fair" will "drop a tear upon his early Tomb." There are two parodies concerned with military encampments and

> The simple annals of a private man.[13]

In each the unknown soldier is celebrated in gently elegiac mood and without a trace of satire. It is interesting to note that when serious imitation takes the form of parody, it is very frequently the humanitarian aspect of Gray's poem which is stressed.[14]

III

The looser imitations are after all more important. In these, however, neither the humanitarian element[15] nor the incidental influence of that delight in twilight and the quiet beauty of the English countryside which lies over the "Elegy" like a benediction,[16] can be dwelt on here.[17] The main direction of the influence of the "Elegy" on the melancholy tradition was undoubtedly toward an increase of meditations on the general theme of death and mutability.

> Each in his narrow cell for ever laid . . .

> No more shall rouse them from their lowly bed . . .

The paths of glory lead but to the grave . . .

Can storied urn or animated bust
Back to its mansion call the fleeting breath? . . .

Perhaps in this neglected spot is laid . . .

Yet ev'n these bones from insult to protect
Some frail memorial still erected nigh . . .

Ev'n from the tomb the voice of Nature cries . . .

Slow thro' the church-yard path we saw him born . . .[18]

Sic transit gloria mundi. It is Professor Reed's "death theme" in its gentler aspects. On its philosophical side it is closely akin to the love of the past which was becoming increasingly manifest as the century advanced, to the discovery of that nostalgic delight in antique art and primitive customs and the vague aura of legend and tradition hanging over monuments of human glory or human mortality which gave us finally "Childe Harold's Pilgrimage." It is akin to the intense contemplation of time and of death as such which gave us finally Shelley's lines (in an adaptation of Gray's stanza) on "Mutability," beginning

> We are as clouds that veil the midnight moon,

and ending

> Nought may endure but Mutability.[19]

In the romantic treatment of this theme an important, although usually deep-buried, element is undoubtedly Gray's "Elegy."

It is probable that Gray is ultimately responsible for

the greater number of the meditations in churchyards written during the seventy-five or eighty years after the appearance of his "Elegy," whether these meditations are couched in his stanza form or not, although it would be rash to call them all conscious imitations. Young, it will be remembered, did not actually go to the place of graves; the direct influence of Blair and Hervey may usually be detected by the more strongly religious cast of the meditations. The closely associated group of meditations by a single tomb admits more readily the contributary influence of the funeral-elegy literature as well as the Ossianic element to be discussed presently; but a few poems of this group show clear reminiscences of Gray. Another closely associated group is that of the meditations among the tombs in a church, usually Westminster Abbey; but the poetical habit of moralizing in the latter place owes much also to Addison's paper on Westminster Abbey in the *Spectator*.[20] In Professor Northup's list there are four meditations in churchyards,[21] four meditations by single tombs,[22] and four meditations in Westminster Abbey,[23] ranging in date from the 1760's to the early 1800's. I think we may safely add several other examples of the churchyard type.

For instance, Suzanna Blamire has such a meditation (1766),[24] which is surely close enough to Gray to be called an imitation. Her "pensive mind" contemplates the lessons in mortality to be learned from seeing cattle graze unreproved among the obliterated inscriptions:

> Then what is honour?—what is wealth or fame?
> Since the possessor waits the common doom!

The conclusion is a prayer that contemplating immortality may enable her to overcome "aversion to the body's doom." There is a churchyard meditation in elegiac quatrain,[25] also, among the verses (1791) of John Learmont, a minister of the Scottish Kirk:

> The village clock had struck the midnight hour;
>   The moon was set;—and no translucent ray
> Did o'er the night its cheary influence pour,
>   When thro' the churchyard's mound I took my way.

He meditates quite in the orthodox manner on death's inevitability and indiscriminateness, sometimes recalling Gray, sometimes, by the religious cast of his thought, rather Hervey or Blair.

The *Gentleman's Magazine,* which seems to have published practically all the verses submitted to it, and therefore is more revealing of fashions than rewarding to a search for quality, published, between 1772 and 1790, three churchyard meditations in elegiac stanza not mentioned by Professor Northup. The earliest (August, 1772), "Stanzas, Written in a Country Churchyard in Ireland, on the Death of an affectionate Parent," by J. Ferrar, recalls Gray in title, stanza, and mood, although not very clearly in diction. "A Walk in the Parish Church of Chelmsford," signed W. S. (January, 1783), is a hodgepodge of Gray's meter, Milton's phrases, and Gray's and Hervey's ideas:

> In these lone walks, these melancholy isles,
>   Where ever-musing Silence holds her sway . . .
>
> Hence, far away, ye vanities profane,
>   Fantastic reveries, and themes unholy!

> Come to my aid, with all thy pensive train,
> In sombre pomp, O sainted Melancholy . . .

Again, an "Elegy written amongst the Tombs" (September, 1790) presents more than a column of warmed-over sentiments from Gray. There is another "Elegy" with an almost identical title twenty years later in the *Poetical Magazine*.[26] It is presented as the "maiden production of an unlettered Muse," but clearly the Muse was not too "unlettered" to know Gray, Hervey, and Young. In the *Suffolk Garland* (1818), too, there are elegiac stanzas on "The Churchyard, St. Edmund's Bury," which yield the line

> Far from the busy croud, and noise of courts,[27]

and remind one alternately of Gray and Shenstone.

More interesting because by a better poet are the elegiac stanzas by George Darley called "Soliloquy among the Tombs, written in Beddington Churchyard,"[28] which, though on the whole a very loose imitation, come sometimes as near paraphrase as

> Gone, where the proud are lowly as the meek,

or

> Where Wealth is stripped as bare as wretchedness.

His descriptive images include a "stumbling beetle" and a "moody owl" in the "ivy-woven cowl" of the turret of a "gray Abbey." And yet, if it were not for the stanza, Darley's images of his "new kindred of the tomb," and of dead Beauty weeping for her "strange unloveliness," would remind us more of Blair, or rather of the Elizabethans, whom Darley loved even better than Blair did.

There are various other meditations in churchyards which are not in Gray's stanza and may or may not owe their inception to Gray. William Julius Mickle has one in blank verse called "A Night Piece" (1761);[29] the choice of meter may be due to Young or Blair or may be a natural accident, but the placing of the scene in "an old churchyard (now the principal street of the city of Edinburgh)" and the moonlight meditations on the indiscriminateness of death and the transitoriness of fame suggest the contributory influence of Gray. There is a similar fusion of Gray and Young in "The Churchyard," by a "youth of eighteen," two columns of Miltonic blank verse which appeared in the *Universal Magazine* for July, 1780. It ends in a moral couplet:

> Power, Wealth, and Beauty are a short-liv'd trust,
> 'Tis Virtue only blossoms in the dust.

Kirke White too meditates in blank verse in "Wilford Churchyard,"[30] but here the idea is more after Goldsmith's lines about the hope of returning home to die than after Gray. Still, he writes

> Yet nature speaks within the human bosom,
> And, spite of reason, bids it look beyond
> His narrow verge of being, and provide
> A decent residence for its clayey shell,
> Endear'd to it by time,

—which is the sentiment of Gray's

> Yet ev'n these bones from insult to protect
> Some frail memorial still erected nigh . . .

Bernard Barton, the gentle Quaker versifier who was a

friend of Lamb, has a poem called "The Grave" (1824),[31] which begins

> I love to muse, when none are nigh,
>   Where yew-tree branches wave,
> And hear the winds, with softest sigh,
>   Sweep o'er the grassy grave.

He has also two poems about Great Bealings Church-yard,[32] one of which was probably written before 1830. Even Byron and Shelley in early youth wrote each a churchyard meditation. Byron's,[33] like White's, reflects longing for burial in some particular spot, but it has the phrase "narrow cell" used by Gray, as well as the general conception of a churchyard as a place for meditation; Byron says he actually used to go to the Harrow churchyard at twilight for that purpose. Shelley's[34] has more of Collins than of Gray in the descriptive details, and more of Shelley than of Collins, but it may owe its name to Gray.

This poem of Shelley's ends on a note combining Gray's pensiveness with romantic introspection:

> Thus solemnised and softened, death is mild
> And terrorless as this serenest night:
> Here could I hope, like some inquiring child
> Sporting on graves, that death did hide from human sight
> Sweet secrets, or beside its breathless sleep
> That loveliest dreams perpetual watch did keep.

Usually in the later poems of this group the personal note is stronger than here. The poet does not avoid the pronoun "I," and very often lets it be clear that he is thinking more of his own death, usually thought of as imminent,

than of death in general. This is true of Byron's poem
of course, of Darley's, of Kirke White's, and, for a further example, this time not visibly beholden to Gray, of
Sir Samuel Egerton Brydges' sonnet "Written in the
Churchyard of Orleton":

> I come to keep my vigil on the ground,
> Where I, too, soon at peace with you shall be![35]

Besides the poets who, as Churchill worded it as early
as 1763,

> Along the church-way path complain with Gray,[36]

there was a fairly numerous company who did their complaining by some picturesque and probably Gothic ruin,
usually the ruin of an abbey. Professor Northup has six
such meditations among the ruins,[37] all but one of which
are by ruined abbeys, besides one by a monastery not yet
wrecked by time.[38] There is no ruin in Gray's poem, since
the "ivy-mantled tow'r" is doubtless that of the parish
church whence the poet heard the curfew. But obviously,
even without the suggestion of the ivy and the "moping
owl," even without the example of the Warton brothers
and the impulse of reviving interest in things Gothic, a
mouldering ruin is almost as natural a scene for elegiac
thoughts as a place of graves. And many of the poems
about ruins, especially in the fifties and sixties, are clearly inspired by Gray:

> Ah! what avail'd th' alliance of a throne?
> The pomp of titles what, or pow'r rever'd?

asks John Langhorne in 1756;[39] and in 1796 Edward
Hamley is still musing on the indiscriminate anonymity
of the tombs of Netley Abbey:

> Alas! whate'er their virtues or their crimes,
>> 'Tis all in blank oblivion buried deep . . .[40]

The most interesting in some ways of these imitations with a background of Gothic ruins is John Cunningham's "Elegy on a Pile of Ruins" (1761).[41] The whole tradition is here. The poet, from the conventional hill, sees the ruins of an abbey and of a castle, close by a tumbling rivulet, and overgrown with nettles and night-shade. There Contemplation

> Sits musing on a monumental stone,
>> And points to the memento at her feet.

At dusk the poet seats himself by her "sequester'd side," and, himself contemplating the ruins, muses on the ravages of Time:

> Inexorably calm, with silent pace
>> Here Time has pass'd—What ruin marks his way! . . .

But, in pity, Time has bound up the tottering towers with the ivy; and the pillared pile is a lovely haunt for Meditation. Follow the usual meditation on the indiscriminate mixture in the grave, mention of the inevitable ravens, rooks, lizards, and bats, and then several stanzas closely after Gray:

> Can the deep statesman skill'd in great design,
>> Protract, but for a day, precarious breath?
> Or the tun'd follower of the sacred Nine
>> Soothe, with his melody, insatiate Death!

And so on, till we come to the usual moral conclusion: let Luxury and Pride come hither

And from the moral prospect learn how vain
The wish, the sighs for sublunary things!

Chatterton too has an imitation (1769),[42] in which he mentions "dusky Contemplation" and the "darksome ruins of some sacred cell." The latest of these abbey-meditations in elegiac stanza of which I know is Byron's poem on Newstead Abbey, which begins

Newstead! fast-falling, once-resplendent dome![43]

It has in it little if anything of Gray.

As for the diffused influence of the "Elegy" hinted at by direct reference or fleeting verbal reminiscences of image or phrase, both in elegiac stanza and outside of it, it is far wider than any such list of imitations as we have been considering can indicate. In the *Gentleman's Magazine* alone, for instance, between 1762 and 1798, I have noted some nineteen poems not listed by Professor Northup which yield verbal reminiscences as strong to my ear as some in the "imitations." At least three of these, besides the three mentioned above as being elegiac meditations in a place of graves, may well be considered out-and-out imitations. The earliest is, appropriately, an elegy on Shenstone.[44] It begins

Clad in a sable pall, now frowns the sky,

and contains phrasing and ideas as close to Gray as this:

Full many a flow'ret blushing to the sun
That scents the sweetness of the eastern morn,
Inglorious oft its little life does run
Nor once the bosom of the fair adorn.

Or this, in which the poet has nearly but not quite as hard a time with his grammar:

> How many Shakespears have there liv'd alone
> And Drydens, thankless in their poorer day!
> And many a pensive Gray we've seen, unknown,
> Who to the world has still refus'd his lay.

In 1796 there is an elegy on the death of Burns,[45] obviously suggested by Grays' celebration of unknown geniuses who "pine unfed amid the dreary waste." Again, in December, 1797, W. Hamilton Reid manages almost to paraphrase parts of the "Elegy" in his stanzas on "Evening." For the rest, the movement of Gray's line, the mood, the turn of phrase, meet one on every side:

> Oh! pay to him,—the tribute of a tear . . .[46]

> Far from the madding crowd's ignoble strife
> Unbless'd with learning's scientific ray . . .[47]

> Should proud Ambition sleep beneath the tomb
> Of pomp, and state, to catch the public eye . . .[48]

> The plowman hies him o'er the wither'd plain . . .[49]

> Homeward the ploughman drove his weary team . . .[50]

> Say, can bright Beauty's magic powers save
> Its lov'd possessor from the loathsome tomb?
> Or, while Ambition's colours round us wave,
> Can we escape the inevitable doom?[51]

These extracts, by no means all which might be cited, are all from poems in elegiac stanza in the same periodical.

Outside the realm of fugitive periodical literature, the echoes are almost as insistent. Shortly after the appearance of the "Elegy," the blind poet Blacklock writes:

What summer-breeze, on swiftest pinions borne,
From fate's relentless hand its prey can save?
What sun in Death's dark regions wake the morn,
Or warm the cold recesses of the grave?[52]

In the 1780's Henry Headley writes:

The frowns of Censure and the smiles of Praise,
And all that Fortune and that Fate decree . . .[53]

Thomas Penrose is continually echoing Gray:

Where, low in earth—ah! never more to rise,
Unnoticed, unregarded, and unknown,
Full many a shrouded student sleeping lies,
O'er whom still weeps the monumental stone . . .

Full many a gallant youth untimely fell . . .

No tinkling fold, no curfew's parting knell . . .[54]

In 1824 Bernard Barton writes:

I ask no storied urn, no marble bust . . .[55]

These random extracts are all from poems in elegiac
stanza which are not on the list of imitations. If we turn
to other meters we are lost in the superfluity of the material.

IV

But in spite of the far-reaching influence of Gray, which
can be only vaguely suggested by such extracts and references as have been given, it would be impossible to understand the literary background of the elegiac passages
in "Childe Harold," or indeed in any romantic poem,
without noting other and more purely romantic streams
of influence. Chief among these is Macpherson's *Ossian*.

It makes little difference for our purpose that the prose-poems published by James Macpherson during the 1760's[56] as translations from the third century Gaelic bard Ossian, are now all but universally admitted to have been original productions, which used the floating Ossianic ballads of the Highlands only to twist their stories and falsify their spirit. Whether or not the old Celtic bards saw life through an elegiac haze was not for the moment important for the development of English literary history. The fact that Macpherson—himself a cheerful enough soul—caused his Ossian so to see it was on the other hand of immense significance. It was of significance in that the vast success of Macpherson's fraud gave indication that he had correctly gauged the public taste, not only in ministering to its growing interest in the past and the primitive, but also in clothing that interest in romantic sentiment and mild melancholy. It was of significance also in that the books are in themselves important as a literary event, and, above all, in that they exercised an influence direct and indirect far beyond their not inconsiderable deserts.

The elegiac tone of the poems is due partly, of course, to the nature of the stories told. They are one and all tales of war and death. These pages are as "full of laments as the Book of Job"[57]—which is, incidentally, one of Macpherson's models. The warriors fall in battle in the bloom of youth, or survive to a forlorn and sightless old age. The maidens follow their lovers to war and die by the sword, or fall expiring on the bodies of their lovers brought dead from the field. Ghosts lean from the clouds to warn men that their end is near. Ossian, unsteady with

length of days, puts out his hand to feel the tomb of Fingal his sire, and lifts his blind eyes toward the cloud-
chariots of his friends of other days. And the play is
played out against a backdrop of the bleakest and most
melancholy landscapes of the Highlands and the Hebrides.

Yet the *Iliad* is as full of battles and deaths in battle
as is *Fingal,* without having gained the reputation of being elegiac. Also, Gaelic scholars assure us that, aside
from the specifically elegiac funeral poetry, the old Celtic
ballads abound with joy in life and lust for battle. The
tales of blighted love are, to be sure, mostly Macpherson's
own invention. Of them, and of his melancholy landscapes,
more later.[58] But the general condition of insecurity and
constant warfare depicted in the stories is no invention
of any poet, ancient or modern. What Macpherson has
done is to dwell upon it, to sentimentalize it, to return
again and again to the theme of death and mutability
until there is scarcely a page on which its shadow is not
felt as presage or retrospect if not as present in actuality.

Frequently the theme is explicit enough:

We shall pass away like a dream . . . Our names may be heard
in song. What avails it when our strength hath ceased? . . .[59]

The valiant fall, O Fingal! the feeble remain on the hills! How
many heroes have passed away, in the days of Morni! . . .[60]

This is thy narrow dwelling, Erragon; this thy narrow house:
the sound of thy shells has been long forgot in Sora. Thy shield
is become dark in thy hall. Erragon, king of ships! chief of distant
Sora! how hast thou fallen on our mountains? How is the
mighty low? . . .[61]

I have seen the walls of Balclutha, but they were desolate . . .

The thistle shook, there, its lonely head: the moss whistled to the wind. The fox looked out from the windows, the rank grass of the wall waved around its head. Desolate is the dwelling of Moina, silence is in the house of her fathers . . . They have but fallen before us: for, one day, we must fall . . .[62]

O thou that rollest above, round as the shield of my fathers! Whence are thy beams, O sun! thy everlasting light? . . . But thou art perhaps, like me, for a season; thy years will have an end . . .[63]

The people are like the waves of ocean: like the leaves of woody Morven, they pass away in the rustling blast, and other leaves lift their green heads on high . . .[64]

To such general laments over mutability might be added innumerable personal lamentations over a forlorn old age, innumerable bardic elegies, innumerable passages about ghosts, and innumerable incidental phrases or references.

Much of the continuity of the elegiac tone is due to a series of melancholy phrases which recur from poem to poem like musical motifs: "a tale of the times of old!"[65] "the days of other years,"[66] "the voice of past times,"[67] "the voice of years that are gone,"[68] "tales of other times."[69] Two of these clichés in particular, both of which seem to be Macpherson's own, strike the attention and stay in the memory. The first is the strange phrase "the dark-brown years," which occurs repeatedly,[70] and seems, in spite of its essential meaninglessness, to carry something of the autumnal mood of regret that hangs over the poems. The other, usually applied to some tale of other days, is "the joy of grief."[71] This is the most famous phrase of all, and must have struck deeply into the consciousness of Macpherson's contemporaries, as it occurs frequently for many decades following the appearance of the Ossianic poems.[72] Once, in "Temora,"[73] the two phrases are used together: "The joy of grief belongs to Ossian, amidst his dark-brown years."

These elegiac clichés are reinforced by a systematic and indeed monotonous use of melancholy similes and epithets. Warriors are likened to clouds of mist[74] or "two dark clouds that are the chariots of ghosts,"[75] or, when they move together, to "a gloomy ridge."[76] They advance "gloomy, dark" as the "dark shades of autumn."[77] They fight "like the contending of ghosts in a gloomy storm."[78] The favorite adjectives are dim, dusky, gray, blasted, echoing, particularly brown, gloomy, and, above all, dark. The warring heroes are gloomy, and the battle, and the foe.[79] Not only the heath, the hinds of the mountains, and the hair of the heroes, but the field of battle, the faces of the warriors, the night, the waves of ocean, even, as we have seen, the years themselves, are brown, usually dark-brown.[80] Dark-brown is the usual epithet for the warriors' shields.[81] The first element of this compound appears with monotonous frequency and in all sorts of unexpected combinations. For instance, the adjective, or its related noun, verb, or adverb, is used singly or in compounds seventeen times in the first brief Duan of "Cath-Loda," the first poem in the Sharp Edition.[82] Besides the normal uses of the adjective—which are nevertheless abnormally frequent—we have it applied to the soul, the moon, heroes (including Cuthullin), silence, wounds, troops in war, blood, bucklers and helmets, faces, autumn, old age, a tribe and its chief, a ghost, tears, war.[83] The incessant winds that whistle through Fingal's beard and drive the cloud-chariots of the ghosts are usually described as dark.[84] The moon is nearly always darkened.[85] Men stand darkly, or darken with wrath or fear or sorrow, sometimes for days together.[86] They advance darkly to battle.[87] They darken in their strength.[88] Death is dark on the spear, or seems "dark-wandering" over the face.[89] We hear of a "blast of darkness," of "words dark like the songs of old," of "darkness blown back" on the soul, of the "dark tumbling of death," of how "sadness darkens in his hall."[90] Many compounds appear: dark-rolling (clouds, sea, stream, years), dark-skirted (night, heath, clouds), dark-bosomed (ships), dark-eddying (winds, streams), dark-bending (ghost), dark-winding (bards in procession), dark-striding (hero), dark-heaving or dark-bounding (ocean), darklywinded (stream—the compound is here a verb).[91] Illustrations of these varying uses could be multiplied indefinitely. Sometimes the darks come several to a paragraph or even to a sentence: "The heroes flew like two dark clouds: two dark clouds that are the chariots of ghosts; when air's dark children . . ."; "On their dim shields they darkly leaned: their spears are forward through night. Shrill sounds the blast of darkness in Starno's floating beard. . . ."[92]

Yet even if we added to these details a more complete study of the melancholy treatment of nature and the Ossianic ghost-lore than we have time for here, we should still not have all the secret of the Ossianic melancholy. Something of the residue undoubtedly lies in the rhythms of these strange prose-poems. That much of the elegiac effect is due to Macpherson's measured prose is indicated by a perusal of the various versifications which were one tribute to the popularity of the tales. Bruno Schnabel, in his study of the influence of Ossian in England,[93] lists twenty-three versifications of parts of the Ossianic literature between 1760 and 1830, grouped rather heavily in the years 1760-1785 and 1805-1830.[94] Of the four metrical versions of "Fingal" which I have seen, two are in heroic couplet and two in blank verse.[95] All the authors seem to make an effort to reproduce Macpherson's epithets, although the impression is given that the blank verse writers do it somewhat more faithfully.[96] Yet the effect is distinctly more elegiac in blank verse than in couplet; and the original is by far the most elegiac of all. In George Hervey's version (1814) may be seen the effects of various meters, for he has put into practice the knowledge of old popular verse and of metrics in general won by the romantic movement, and gives us the straight narrative passages in an easy couplet, the episodes in ballad stanzas, and the other songs of the bards in various irregular meters. The result is a pleasing and intelligent version—from which the brooding elegiac atmosphere has almost altogether evaporated. A minor stroke of genius in this version is the turning of Cuthullin's lament (Book III) over his defeat into elegiac stanza, with strong verbal reminiscences of Gray.

The effectiveness of this last expedient leads one to wonder why the elegiac stanza was not oftener employed in these versifications. One of the most successful attemps to retain the melancholy tone of a minor Ossianic poem is an anonymous version in this meter of Number V of the original Fragments. It ends:

They died, whom Memory long alive shall keep;
   And here, beneath this mountain tomb, alone,
At rest, the lovely pair together sleep;
   While the green moss devours the mould'ring stone.[97]

There seem to be only two or three other examples of the use of this stanza in the versifications.[98] Soame Jenyns, John Logan, Anna Seward, and even Byron, all versified passages in the unsympathetic couplet.[99] Coleridge's early versification of two passages in "Berrathon" are in two different modified ballad stanzas.[100] But the poetic prose of the original remains the most elegiac medium, whether or not it is otherwise the best.

This conviction is reinforced by a reading of the imitations of Macpherson which purported to be more translations from the Gaelic. It would be easy to quote passage after passage from these forgeries which the reader casually familiar with Macpherson's style would mistake for Macpherson's. They are one and all strongly elegiac, and reproduce with varying success the epithets and rhythms and characteristic motifs of Macpherson's prose. The first of the series, by John Clark,[101] appeared in 1778. In 1780 John Smith published his so-called *Galic Antiquities*,[102] which must have gained some popularity, since Paul Van Teighem says that in France they became indistinguishable in influence from Macpherson's own work.[103] Another extensive forgery appeared in 1787, in Germany, from the pen of an exiled Scot, the Freiherr von Harold.[104] This group of prose-poems is interesting chiefly in that it makes a determined attempt to repair the conspicuous lack of religious consolations in the complainings of Macpherson's Ossian:[105] the ancient bard is converted to

Christianity and, although he complains almost as much as ever, he trusts his final destiny and that of the world to an oddly deistic creator. Chatterton's forged imitations, in the guise of prose-poems "translated from the Saxon"[106] are, on the other hand, scarcely melancholy at all, but use the rhythms and some of the imagery of the original for the more legitimately primitive emotions of joy in life and lust for battle.

Most, though not all, of the other imitations are melancholy. Two of those listed by Schnabel are by Blake— "Visions of the Daughters of Albion" (1793) and "The Song of Los" (1795). That Blake's long irregular lines with basic heptameter movement are partly built on the rhythms of Macpherson's prose, and that the suggestion for some of his bizarre names may have come from the same source, has been long recognized. But the upward straining of Blake's philosophical imagination is so intense that it would be futile to speak of his prophetic poems as displaying Ossianic melancholy. On the other hand, Sir Egerton Brydges' "Six Bards" (1784)[107] has the familiar refrain

> But we return from night no more . . .

Coleridge's imitation[108] (1790) is a sad little tale of dead lovers. "Gorthmund, A Tale in the Manner of Ossian" (1800), from Southey's *Annual Anthology*,[109] which is written in a combination of blank verse and lyric measures, keeps the elegiac tone very well, especially in the bardic lament with which it closes. So too do the bardic song and the concluding funeral lament in Frank Sayers' "Moina" (about 1790),[110] which are obvious imitations, the former in blank verse, the latter in irregular unrimed lines. Of the imitations of Ossianic prose by Bruce (about 1766),[111] and Byron (1806),[112] the latter is fairly elegiac, but the former sounds more like one of Macpherson's models, "The Song of Solomon." There is an amusing take-off in *Probationary Odes* (1787)[113]—two take-offs, in fact—one in Ossianic prose, and one in Ossianic prose cut into lengths and printed as what we should now call free verse. The latter particularly is full of ghosts and exclamation marks:

> I behold thee, O King!
> I behold thee sitting on mist!!!

And so on.

V

Little conception, however, is gained of the immense leavening influence of Macpherson's work on English literature by a study merely of the direct imitations. It is true that the heated controversy over the authenticity of the material tended to divert attention from its intrinsic merits and demerits, and was a contributing cause to the fact that Macpherson's reputation was greater on the continent, especially in Germany,[114] than at home. Yet not only are Chatterton, Bruce, Logan, Jenyns, Anna Seward, Kirke White, Bowles, Southey, Thomas Moore, James Montgomery, Campbell, and a host of forgotten writers, beholden to the pseudo-Ossianic literature for melancholy inspiration or imagery, but so also are Blake, Coleridge, Scott, and Byron—poets high on our literary honor roll.[115] The epithets, rhythms, and sentiments of Macpherson echo and reëcho through English verse, from the lowest to the highest, only less persistently than do those of

Gray. Robert Couper, Scottish physician and poetaster, talks in person with Ossian and Malvina, who recline on their clouds above his head.[116] Colonel Alexander Dow of the Indian Service fills his Tartar and Egyptian melodramas with "darken'd" fate and storm-tossed ghosts.[117] The youthful Lord Byron hears the "hollow winds whistle" through the ruinous hall of his fathers, and adds a motto from *Ossian* to emphasize the borrowings.[118] "Pity struck the chords and tuned the Ossianic lyre,"[119] and the "plaintive strain"[120] of Macpherson's "drunken prose"[121] was adopted, like Hervey's, into English verse.

Where is the King of Songs? He sleeps in death:

. . . .

Hush'd is the storm of war, and hush'd is Ossian's breath.

. . . .

Dark is the poet's eye—but shines his name,
As, mid obstructing clouds, still gleams the solar flame.[122]

It gleams still, but dark, by reason of the clouds of Macpherson's vague regret for time and death and change.

Although there are not many ruins in the Ossianic poems, even as there are none at all in Gray, this influence too is felt on the ruin-literature. Not only their strongly elegiac tone, of which we have been speaking, but the very fact that they purported to be the recovered treasure of a vanished and unfamiliar past, would contribute to this result. Bruce (1766) compares the "strange sounds and music wild" which shepherds are said to hear on Lochleven to the ghostly warnings of Ossian's "untouch'd harp," and then launches into a fine description of the old Castle in lines reminiscent of "Carthon."[123] Others besides Byron remembered Ossian at their ruinous ancestral seats:

Campbell (1800) hushes his "dark spirit" among the "wind-shaken weeds" about the home of his forefathers.[124] Brydges (1807) hears the moan of ghosts "along the dark'ning forest" at the "poor deserted solitary dome" of his nativity.[125]

This last poem has also possible touches of Gray. But the fusing of the two influences is better seen in John Whitehouse's "Elegy, written near the Ruins of a Nunnery" (1787), from which a description of Melancholy has already been quoted.[126] The poem begins:

> Wand'ring in pensive mood beside the skirts
> Of this dark forest, visions, such as old
> Poetic eyes have seen, around me dawn:
> But who is he, whose daring hand shall wake
> The lyre's bold numbers to the solemn voice
> That paus'd but now between the hollow blast?
> Low is the bard of ancient days . . .

A note explains that the last phrase refers to Ossian. But not more than four lines below we hear that "meek twilight" comes "with pilgrim feet, and beckons . . . her shadowy train" as in the Miltonic odes. Then there is a touch of the horrific—"pale Desolation," "red-ey'd Horror," and "the whirlwinds' rapid wing"—quickly followed by the *sic transit* motif—"How chang'd the scene," "fall'n is the fretted vault." Next we have the description of Melancholy on her "nightly round"; then a description of the life of the nuns, with the usual anti-monastic bias, and, in conclusion, a long *sic transit* passage. This last describes "gaunt Ruin grinning o'er the wreck," the fond inscriptions slowly effaced by "Time's oblivious hand,"

and Reflection weeping amid the "moss-grown piles," which are haunted by bats, owls, and "pale spectres." A later example of fusion is "Abbey-Ruins," an imitation of Gray's "Elegy," in the *Poetical Magazine* (1810).[127] It is full of Solitude and Contemplation, phrases like "Ah what is grandeur?" and descriptive details after Gray; yet into the midst of it, while the poet is wandering in the Abbey graveyard, is dropt a stanza about the "mist-robed spirits of the vale," which the poet definitely refers in a note to Ossian.

V

But all that has been said of it in connection with the influence of Gray and of Macpherson can have given scarcely an inkling of the abundance of the literature of ruins, or of its constant stress on the theme of mutability. The growing interest in Gothic architecture, the awakening delight in England's past, the romantic curiosity about the chivalric and monastic life of the Middle Ages, the sentimental tendency to dwell on death and decay—all contributed to swell the volume of the traditional stream. Already in 1757 we hear that, following the New Style, my lord, who has one three-hundred-year-old ruin, will "soon build one three hundred years older than that."[128] Mason, in his "English Garden" (1772) advises a ruin for the perfect garden.[129] One gathers that a poetic youth liked a ruin to meditate by.[130] A poet could scarcely see a half-fallen castle or a moss-grown priory without immediately inditing an elegy or a sonnet. Every abbey in the land must have appeared in print at least once, and some, notably Netley Abbey, many times, even in the verse which has come down to us.[131] Nor did Tintern Abbey have to wait to be celebrated by Wordsworth.[132] Most of this material is negligible as literature. But occasionally one comes on something wherein the old sentiments and phrases have been touched, if only lightly, with poetic fire. Such are Henry Headley's couplets on the "Ruins of Bromhold Priory,"[133] or Charlotte Smith's on "St. Monica."[134] On the other hand, occasionally one stumbles on a perfect recipe poem, like an anonymous "Ode to Time" in the *Universal Magazine* for April, 1797. This concoction is in Miltonic octosyllabics, and opens with a Miltonic invocation:

> All-conquering power! who sit'st elate,
> Where human grandeur yields to fate . . .

It has an "aged abbey's hoary pile" after Gray, with

> Mould'ring vault, and long-drawn aisle,
> Along whose venerable walls
> The melancholy ivy crawls . . .

It then presents the ruins of Rome and the triumph of Time over Ambition, Beauty, even "nature's self" at the last awful day. So strong is the tradition here presented that one is not surprised to find so comparatively fine a poet as Darley, in the full flush of the romantic triumph, writing in "The Palace of Ruin"[135] a vivid picture of "grim Ruin sitting in thought alone" on a crumbling pile, and by a listless swing of his iron sceptre prostrating art and man before "the tyrant son of Time."

More and more, too, the poets went abroad in body or in spirit, and mused on the ruined cities of the ancient world. The romantic imagination was fired by the fallen splendor of Italy, and of course particularly of Rome. An anonymous writer meditates on mutability at nightfall in the "desert, solitary wild" about the ruins of Ocriculum.[136] Robert Merry, of Della Cruscan fame, is moved by a "Distant Prospect of Rome," and adjures Pride to gaze here and see that all sublunary things are "shadowy as the way-worn traveler's dream."[137] Even Samuel Rogers turns from his historical anecdotes and sober descriptions long enough to reflect, in the Roman Forum, that

> The very dust we tread, stirs as with life.[138]

Or the lure of the East calls the poets, and they write of Babylon,[139] or—and she is the greatest favorite of all—of Palmyra. The blank desolation of this desert scene, with its prowling jackals and pitiless blazing sun, seems to have fascinated the imagination even before Volney's famous meditation and vision at Palmyra in *The Ruins of Empire* (1791). Passing references neglected, there is, for example, a blank verse piece (1760) called "On reading an account of the ruins of Palmyra,"[140] with a peroration beginning

> Such are thy works, Oh Time! all must decay,
> This world itself to other scenes give way . . .

Thomas Love Peacock, who seems in youth to have been almost obsessed with the mutability theme, wrote (1806) a rather admirable rhapsody on "Palmyra," with erudite notes including references to both Ossian and Volney; later (1812) he worked it over so completely that he produced what amounts to a new poem, briefer and more restrained. One suspects Volney to have been chief inspiration for the whole, but Milton, Gray, and Ossian all contributed; the opening of the second version in particular has closely-mingled echoes of all three.[141] The Oxford Prize Poems from 1818 to 1830 are full of elegiac ruins: "The Coliseum" (1818), "Palmyra" (1822), "Stonehenge" (1823), "Pompeii" (1827).[142] But these last are after "Childe Harold."

One "Ode to Time" has already been quoted. That indefatigable ode-writer, John Ogilvie, also wrote such an ode (1759).[143] He presents Time in person sitting on a "solitary spire" (by which he apparently means the turret of an old castle), surrounded by the orthodox elegiac landscape—"murmuring flood," "lonely dale," a moon "list'ning" to a "melancholy tale," "wilds where heav'n-rapt Fancy roves," "sky-crown'd hills," "solemn groves," "low-brow'd vaults," "gloomy cells," caves, ghost-haunted and ivy-crowned tower—of course all this at midnight. The ode then wanders off to Palmyra, Persepolis, Rome, the pyramids, over all of whom Time

> Slowly shakes the flowing sand.

Toward the end of our period the technique has become more lyric and the form less stereotyped; but the age-old sentiment has not changed much, as expressed for example in "Time's Song" (1826)[144] by Winthrop Mackworth Praed, in which the question is "Who will chain my flight?" and the answer is, of course, Not war nor grief nor pleasure, not glory nor genius nor love. We too must bow to Time, as Praed reiterates two years later:

We too, we too must fall;
A few brief years to labour and to bear;—
Then comes the sexton, and the old trite tale,
"We were!"[145]

Yet between these chronological extremes most of the poets who write specifically of Time take pains to tell us that Virtue conquers Time at last; that, in truth, Time itself must one day pass away. Thus not only in verses about watches,[146] in admonitions to "the fair," in casual references, but in many of the poems about the Last Day we have meditations on mutability or reflections on ruins ending in moral or religious preachment. In fact, the most extensive of the poems actually *about* Time, those by Kirke White and by Robert Pollok,[147] are really Last Day poems. Of these, there is much more mutability and less dogmatic religion, in the poem by White. This melancholy and unfortunate young poet, whose work shows deep impress of Milton, Gray, and Macpherson, was, like the youthful Peacock and with much more personal conviction, obsessed with the idea of death and change. The long blank verse poem on "Time" remains a fragment, but Southey tells us that White returned to it again and again and took none of his literary ventures more seriously.

VI

The ruin and mutability passages in "Childe Harold" are, then, part of a well-developed and continuous tradition, as are also, though somewhat less completely, Shelley's lyrics on Time, Death, and Mutability. Something has already been said of the inspiration Byron drew in early youth from Gray and particularly from the Ossianic poems.[148] The direct influence naturally waned with the full awakening of Byron's strong individual genius; yet assuredly the literary habits of three generations continued partly to determine the modes in which that genius expressed itself. He will single out the same creatures of the ruins for mention—the bat, the owl, the dog;[149] or mention (inevitably perhaps) the same cypress and ivy.[150] He rephrases the same truisms:

> That little urn saith more than thousand Homilies . . .
> Their very graves are gone, and what are they? . . .
> Behold the Imperial Mount! 'tis thus the Mighty falls . . .
> Assyria—Greece—Rome—Carthage—what are they? . . .
> The Glory and the Nothing of a Name . . .[151]

"Out upon Time!" he cries, as many before him had cried in less striking phrase, for Time ever leaves us only "enough of the past for the future to grieve."[152] As he tells us elsewhere, he had

> stood upon Achilles' tomb,
> And heard Troy doubted; Time will doubt of Rome.[153]

Doubtless the vast popularity of "Childe Harold" was due in large part to Byron's genius for expressing magnificently what others had striven but feebly to express.

Yet of course it was by no means only the splendor of the descriptions and the eloquence of the truisms which endeared the Childe to his readers. It was primarily the revelation of a darkly dramatic and romantically sensitive personality—that "pageant of his bleeding heart" of which Arnold has written. The full implications of the Byronic gloom we are not yet ready to seek. Its inter-

penetration of the poet's treatment of mutability is, however, the most striking characteristic of these passages.
We are never allowed to forget that it is Childe Harold
(i.e. George Gordon, Lord Byron) who "stands upon this
place of skulls,"[154] "to meditate amongst decay. . . . A ruin
amidst ruins."[155] He pauses at that "long explored but still
exhaustless mine Of Contemplation," the ruined Coliseum,
to apostrophize Time, but cannot forbear offering his own
"ruins of years" among Time's "mightier offerings."[156] He
asks, amid the ruins of Rome,

> What are our woes and sufferance? Come and see
> The cypress—hear the owl . . .[157]

But as all the world knows, the question seemed ever to
him not a rhetorical one but one craving an answer at
length. Thus from the generalizations of Gray, made only
vaguely personal by the introduction of the lonely poet
whom Melancholy had marked for her own—through Ossian's personal lamentations for dead friends and a "dark
and unlovely" old age, veiled only by the pretense of translation—we come to the gloomy introspection of the soul
to whom time, change, and death carry above all a naked-
ly personal and individual implication.[158]

And yet this is not the whole of the romantic attitude.
The contemplative generalizations do survive in Byron;
in Shelley they frequently remain central, are deepened
by his introspection, made vividly incandescent by the
flame of his personality, rather than merely contributing
to the illumination of it. Shelley was profoundly and
mournfully conscious of the flux of things. He wrote, for
instance, four poems on "Death" (besides a juvenile "Dia-

logue" between Death and a Mortal),[159] two poems on "Mutability,"[160] and one on "Time."[161] Perhaps the most magnificent of all expressions in English of the theme *sic transit gloria mundi* is his sonnet[162] concerning that Ozymandias, "King of Kings," around whose grandiloquent and broken inscription

> The lone and level sands stretch far away.

That ability to teach without preaching, to say everything while seeming to say nothing, which was one of the chief rediscoveries of the great romantic poets, here gives enduring defense against the very power it celebrates. Shelley wrote elsewhere[161] of the "Ocean of Time" whose waters are "brackish with the salt of human tears," and asked

> Who shall set forth on thee,
> Unfathomable Sea?

He did set forth on it, in adventurous philosophical bark, and came to think of life and death and change and even time itself as strange veils over the reality of things, which shall one day be torn aside, that Earth may rejoice in new beauty and Man at last be free:

> Nor yet exempt, tho' ruling them like slaves,
> From chance, and death, and mutability,
> The clogs of that which else might oversoar
> The loftiest star of unascended heaven,
> Pinnacled dim in the intense inane.[163]

If the romanticist could have thought always thus triumphantly of death and time there would have remained small room for the melancholy contemplation of mutability. But, as we know, not even Shelley's theoretical optimism could save him from too frequent shipwreck on the "unfathomable Sea":

> Oh, cease! must hate and death return?
>   Cease! must men kill and die?
> Cease! drain not to its dregs the urn
>   Of bitter prophecy.
> The world is weary of the past,
> Oh, might it die or rest at last![164]

Chapter IV

KING DEATH

Then round with the health of Death, round with the health
Of Death the bony, Death the great, round, round.
Empty yourselves, all cups, unto the health
Of great King Death!

—Beddoes

The melancholy inherent in the contemplation of time
and mutability is normally a chastened and not unpleasing
mood, compounded of philosophy and sentiment—a mood
whose diapason seemed to Dyer "sweet," which was described by Gray as "white," which even in Byron, whenever he can separate it from his own tragedy, partakes
as much of grandeur as of pathos. But once let the death
theme present itself in its more intimate relationship with
the individual, let it clothe itself in religious terrors, or
work in the imagination with its grisly details of pain
and corruption, and the emotional-philosophical mood we
have been discussing is at once shattered. We are not here
concerned, be it repeated, with the occasional despondency
of bereavement, nor in this particular connection with the
temperamental melancholy arising out of an individual
premonition of death.[1] It is a question of the death theme
regarded still with an attempt at generalization, but now
applied specifically to human beings as such, and dressed
in all the terrors which religion, science, or superstition
have seen or imagined for the King of Terrors. And since

it has ever been fabled that Death leads us to judgment,
there is inevitably involved also the theme of Sin, who, as
Milton assures us, is daughter and paramour of Satan and
mother of Death.

This is black melancholy. Its human affinities are with
despair and madness, its literary affinities with the "horrendous" and the macabre. When it is sincere and subjective, it is a natural aspect of the religious melancholy partially analyzed in our first chapter in connection with
Young and Blair, and its essential ingredients are the
sense of sin and the fear of punishment; or it expresses
itself in a morbid preoccupation with the physical and
psychological details of crime and death, as in Beddoes
and occasionally in Shelley. When it is cultivated objec-
tively, or rather dramatically, and for its own sake, it
feeds on realistic horrors and outworn half-believed-in superstitions—in a word, on terror-romanticism. Always its
preoccupations are guilt, and fear, and death.

I

In its more specifically religious manifestations it may
be studied in the progeny of the "Night Thoughts" and
"The Grave," and in the other gloomy meditations on
death and judgment which continued to express Christian
pessimism throughout our period, in the very teeth of neo-
classic optimism and romantic meliorism. The "Night
Thoughts" as a whole had run through some fifteen editions before their author's death in 1765, and held their
popularity throughout the remainder of the century. John
Wesley had to pay damages to Dodsley for infringement
of copyright because he published (1743) long extracts

from them for the edification of his followers. Burke is said to have known a large part of them by heart.[2] Preachers made use of their eloquence, and poets plundered their aphorisms. References to Young, poems about Young, and the certainty or suspicion of his influence are very frequent until the close of the century, although not so frequent after the opening of the new. Abroad, the poem was translated into twelve languages before 1844, and had deeply impressed itself on continental literature, above all on the growth of German romanticism. The discontented ecclesiastical recluse of Welwyn, during the last twenty years of his long life and after his death, became to all Europe a pious legend—the high priest of solitude, night, and tombs.[3]

Comparatively brief imitations of "Night Thoughts" are not wanting, especially in the decades 1750-1770, although they seem to be much less numerous than those of Gray's "Elegy."[4] Pieces on night or death which are not in Gray's stanza and which are religious in spirit, are pretty sure to owe something to Young, although Blair and Hervey and even Parnell may also have contributed. Thus Nathaniel Cotton has a poem in octosyllabics significantly called "The Night Piece"—note the definite article.[5] It is primarily a hymn of renunciation, of resolution on religious grounds to forego

> the sparkling bowl,
> And mirth, the poison of the soul,

in favor of "instructive solitude." It is gloomy in tone, and makes use of melancholy paraphernalia, including "the prophetic raven," "solemn darkness," and even "silent spectres." John Cunningham's "Night Piece" (1762)[6] is in a sort of ballad stanza, and concerns his musings on the tomb when driven to shelter by a storm when on his nocturnal wanderings. As has already been indicated in the discussion of her "Ode to Melancholy," Elizabeth Carter's midnight meditations (and there are many of them) characteristically take a gloomy religious turn; so it is not surprising that her "Night Piece,"[7] though written in heroic couplet, should remind one of Young. But sometimes there is a clear attempt at imitation. Such is "A Midnight Piece" in the *Scots Magazine* (1756),[8] which catches remarkably well Young's ejaculatory style in blank verse, retails with a sympathetic pessimism the various horrid, sinful things which go on by night, and ends with a warning which might be by the master himself:

> Yet the muse
> One hint *must* drop: If awful midnight this,
> How sad, from this to plunge in midnight deeper!

There was even out-and-out parody:

> What's life?—what's death? thus coveted and fear'd?—
> Life is a fleeting shadow—death's no more:—
> Death's a dark lantern; life a candle's end,
> Stuck in a save-all, soon to end in stench—
> Foh! death's a privy; life the alley green
> That leads to 't . . .
>
> . . . .
>
> And yet, Lorenzo, if considered right,
> A life of labour, is a life of ease!
> Pain is true joy, and Want is luxury!
>
> . . . .

Would you be merry?—seek some charnel-house
Where death inhabits, give a ball to death,
A doom's-day ball, and lead up Holben's *(sic)* dance . . .[9]

I would call attention here especially to the passage about
the dance of death. For, although, as has been said, Young
does not even meditate in a churchyard, much less revel
in the Gothic details of the charnel house, others of the
"graveyard school" did so, and thus helped to prepare
the way not only for terror-romanticism but also for
"Death's Jest Book."

It would be a thankless and not particularly rewarding
task to attempt completely to disentangle the influences of
Young, Hervey, and Blair. To begin with, they influenced
each other: Young's "Last Day" seems to have influenced
"The Grave," "The Grave" to have influenced the later
books of "Night Thoughts," and both Young and Blair
to have influenced Hervey.[10] As has been illustrated both
in the preceding paragraphs and in the discussion of the
influence of Gray's "Elegy," most meditations on death
which are primarily religious in tone owe something to the
mingled tradition of the three, sometimes helped out by
Gray. When the poet in religious mood meditates in a
place of graves, or when he indulges in macabre details,
one suspects at least a strong contributory influence of
Hervey[11] or Blair—probably both. Müller finds echoes of
Blair in Nathaniel Cotton, William Thompson (who also
has a tribute to Young),[12] the Wartons, Collins, Gray,
Cunningham, Beattie, Burns, and Robert Pollok (author
of *The Course of Time,* of which more later).[13] On the
continent, Hervey figures as a pale satellite of Young;

Blair was never translated into French, although he had
some slight vogue in Germany.

Next to the masters of whom we have been speaking, the
most famous eighteenth-century poet of death was Bishop
Porteus, whose somber blank verse meditation won the
Seatonian Prize for 1759.[14] It doubtless owes something to
all the others, and Milton besides; at all events it fitted
snugly into the tradition and became in its turn a trans-
mitter of it. The gloomy bishop opens his poem by describing his search for Death in the silent watches of the night:

> Friend to the wretch, whom ev'ry friend forsakes,
> I woo thee, Death! In fancy's fairy paths
> Let the gay songsters rove, and gently trill
> The strain of empty joy.—Life and its joys
> I leave to those that prize them.—At this hour,
> This solemn hour, when Silence rules the world,
> And wearied Nature makes a gen'ral pause!
> Wrapt in Night's sable robe, through cloisters drear,
> And charnels pale, tenanted by a throng
> Of meagre phantoms shooting cross my path
> With silent glance, I seek the shadowy vale
> Of Death!—Deep in a murky cove's recess,
> Lav'd by Oblivion's listless stream, and fenc'd
> By shelving rocks, and intermingled horrors
> Of yew' (sic) and cypress' shade, from all intrusion
> Of busy noon-tide beam, the monarch sits
> In unsubstantial majesty enthron'd.
> At his right hand, nearest himself in place,
> And frightfulness of form, his parent Sin
> With fatal industry and cruel care
> Busies herself in pointing all his stings,
> And tipping every shaft with venom drawn

From her infernal store; around him rang'd
In terrific array, and strange diversity
Of uncouth shapes, stand his dread Ministers . . .

The ministers in question are Old Age, Fever, Consumption, Palsy, Gout, and their brethren, all waiting to

rush forth to execute his purpose,
And scatter desolation o'er the earth.

Obviously this passage, like so much of the religious poetry of death and judgment, owes a great deal to "Paradise Lost." That there are also debts to Young and Blair, and possibly a trace of Spenserian grotesque, is probable also. The passage is an excellent example of the confluence of all such literary currents.

Porteus goes on to assure us that God is not responsible for all this, but man only, first for the fact of death in consequence of the Fall, then by continued wickedness for the suffering of disease and early death—which last was unknown in early days, when everyone lived a pastoral existence for a thousand years or so. Our woes are due to Envy, Ambition with war in its train, and Luxury, which kills its ten thousands to the thousands killed by war. Worst of all, one gathers—and here the poet joins a well-nigh unanimous chorus—is suicide. "Hold, rash Man," he cries, and consider that no matter how miserable you may be here, in hell you will be more miserable yet. Better to live and repent, for the day of vengeance will come soon enough as it is. The poet ends with a prayer on his own behalf for a peaceful and pious death.

Various aspects of this melancholy picture are underlined in the numerous meditations on death scattered through the fugitive verse. A writer with neo-classic affinities writes in the *London Magazine* (1748)[15] a column of couplets "On the Universality and Impartiality of Death," with a motto from Horace and the concluding moral that Virtue conquers Time. Nathaniel Cotton devotes the last of his "Visions in Verse," "for the entertainment and instruction of younger minds," (1751)[16] to "Death," and points the moral that Religion can turn the fiend into a beautiful angel. Charles Emily (about 1763) meditates among the tombs somewhat in the manner of Hervey; he includes a description of the regulation list of maladies, among which, by the way, he places "Self-wasting Melancholy, black as night."[17] An anonymous writer in the *Gentleman's Magazine* (1765)[18] warns a lady who had wished for sudden death that no one is good enough to die without time for repentance and pious preparation. Plain speaking on the corruption of the flesh as a symbol of the democracy of the tomb is the whole point of an epigram on "Human Pride" in the *Scots Magazine* (1772).[19] Its conclusion that

> The real difference in mortals' fate,
> Is, that his Highness stinks in greater state

is akin to that implied in the well-known lines in Byron's "Vision of Judgment" concerning the gorgeous coffin of George III:

> It seemed the mockery of hell to fold
> The rottenness of eighty years in gold.[20]

Ann Yearsley, the poetical milkwoman who was for a time Hannah More's protégée, has a poem, published in 1785 but "written when very young,"[21] in which she deliberately

sets out to take the advice of Young and the rest, and
face the thought and certainty of death, however repulsive
to her youth. She determines to "make the drear regions
of the tomb" her choice, and imagines herself interrogating
a "sad spectre" leaning over "yon misty tomb" as to the
dwellings of the dead. When she receives for answer only
the assurance that she must one day herself feel the pangs
of death, she bids the "poor Ghost" farewell, and re-
nounces "vain Pleasure," calling on God to help her to use
her youth well. Poor "Lactilla" was not learned enough to
be deeply versed in any poetic tradition; yet "Ecclesi-
astes," "Night Thoughts," and her own religious upbring-
ing are more than enough to explain this and other of her
melancholy poems. Practically altogether derivative,
doubtless, is such a concoction as a certain "Extempore on
Death" (1787) by the same fourteen-year-old Harriet Falconer whom we found in Chapter III paraphrasing Gray's
"Elegy." The present performance[22] begins:

> O cruel Death, thou fatal canker-worm,
> Which on the damask cheek of Beauty prey'st;
> With thee the slave and sovereign too are one . . .

and so on for some twelve lines of blank verse. On such
fare were the children of our period nursed!

Perhaps as good a way as any to survey the state of this
particular tradition at the close of the century is to look
into the first number of Roach's *Beauties of the Poets of
Great Britain* (1793). Here we first come upon a frontispiece depicting a sentimental female mourner at a grave,
entitled "Eliza's Tomb" and carrying a quotation from
Young. Then follows a whole series of "Tombstone lec-

tures." The first of these is an imitation of Gray's "Elegy"
—"Evening Reflections Written in Westminster Abbey";[23]
then comes a passage from Addison's *Spectator* essay on
Westminster Abbey (Number 26); then Henry Moore's
"Night Thoughts among the Tombs." This last, which
dates from 1758, has not unnaturally been called an imitation of Young;[24] but the motto is from Hervey, the
meter is heroic couplet, and the sentiments are perhaps
even closer to Hervey and Blair than to those of the poem
from which the title is borrowed. The poet seems to have
descended, like Hervey, to the vault, for he speaks of a
horrible skull, which may once have been a belle "as fair
as you." Like Blair, he wonders why the dead do not
answer our questions. He almost faints with terror at the
vision of a fantastic dance of spectres, but pulls himself
together and begins, like Hervey, to moralize on this tomb
and that, imagining the occupant from the inscription.
The poem is furnished with footnotes from Shakespeare,
Young, and the Bible. This effort is followed by "The
Rich Man's Dream; or, Death Levels All," a variant on
the theme of the poem called "Human Pride" mentioned
above. It ends with the poor man's telling the rich

> *That* is thy rotting place, and *this* is mine.
> *Pride was not made for Man.*

There are a motto from Job and footnotes from Young.
The group is closed by reprints of "The Grave" and the
"Elegy in A Country Churchyard."

Nor did the didactic-religious poems on death and the
grave altogether cease with the romantic triumph. James
Montgomery's poem called "The Grave" (1806)[25] is a

visible example of the conflict between a characteristic romantic attitude toward death and the orthodox religious attitude. It starts out in the romantic mood of longing for the rest of death—a mood which we shall meet again later on. But almost at once the poet hears a strange sound, and the Grave speaks, to utter gloomy warnings against suicide in the old religious tradition. Among the points made is that if it is guilt that causes the poet to long for death, it would be much wiser (as Proteus, among others, had said before) to live on and repent and thus escape the pangs of hell.

An extremely interesting specimen of this genre, Robert Montgomery's "Death," appeared in 1828, at the very close of our period.[26] This blank verse poem by the favorite Evangelical poet of the period, runs to thirty or thirty-five pages, and is a curious amalgam of the Young-Blair-Porteus tradition with the newer influences of sentimentalism and of Wordsworth and the younger romanticists. It opens rather like a faint echo of Porteus, touched possibly by memories of *Vathek:*

> Throned in a vault where sleep departed kings,
> Behold the Tyrant of the World! . . .

The ministers who "do his deadly will" include Murder, Madness, Melancholy ("with a downward brow"), Intemperance, Anger, Terror, Consumption ("in beautiful decay"), War, Pestilence, Famine. We have the regulation meditation on the indiscriminateness of death, illustrated by the death of a king. There is a slight touch of the macabre in the passage which follows, on our fear of dying "To be the flesh-worm's feast." Yet like a true roman-

tic, the poet has felt the "sweet oppression" of the thought
of death, when pacing some aisle to "own the eloquence of
tombs" or when "Sublimely musing by the sounding deep."
He has often looked on a bright assemblage of youth, and
suddenly

> Death, as with a viewless wand,
> Has touch'd the scene, and witch'd it to a tomb!

—which is a touch almost worthy of Poe. Not a moment,
he goes on to say, is free from death's "grinning o'er The
new-dug graves."

All this is introductory. The body of the poem is taken
up by a series of visions of "dark tragedies of death." A
shipwreck is described, and the passing of a beautiful and
joyous child. Three pages are devoted to the piously sentimental tale of an erring and repentant girl, who nurses her
remorse in retirement, serving the poor, and meditating in
the village churchyard on mortality or by her window on
the lessons of the starry heavens.[27] Even more romantic
is the next vision: that of a high-souled and ambitious
genius, a true *belle âme,* who is crushed by the cruel world.
The description of how his growing soul drew inspiration
from nature is couched in words so close to "Tintern Abbey" that Montgomery felt impelled in a note to disavow
having read that poem before he wrote his own; and the
fate of the youth might almost be an idealized version of
that of Keats:

> The path of glory is a path of fire
> To feeling hearts, all gifted though they be,
> And martyrs to the genius they adore;
> The wear of passion, and the waste of thought,

> The glow of inspiration, and the gloom
> That like a death-shade clouds the brightest hour,—
> And that fierce rack on which a faithless world
> Will make thee writhe—all these ennerving pangs,
> With agonies that mock the use of words,
> Thou canst not bear—thy temple is a tomb![28]

The next vision is of a pestilence. Then there is an af-
fianced maid who dies of that most romantic feminine ail-
ment, consumption, departing "as gently as delicious
sound" and lying in death as "beautiful as an embodied
dream." If this passage carries a faint aroma of Shelley,
the account of the deaths of two political prisoners (following a very brief description of a battle) is surely after
Byron. The last picture, of a betrayed girl sunk to shame
and dead on a London doorstep, itself sentimentally romantic, is imbedded in a description of a London night
somewhat like that quoted a few pages back as an imitation of Young.

There is a long peroration, including of course a reference to "That glorious day, when Death himself shall
die!"—but mostly about the poet himself. Again like a
true romantic, he is, it seems, already old at twenty, and
looks back on his boyhood days "with mournful joy." He
has been nourished (like Wordsworth) on Nature, and
(again like Wordsworth) does not wish to outlive his re-
sponse to her. And he ends his poem not on his subject at
all, but on his own high ambition to embody his worship
of Nature and of Heaven in "deathless verse." Thus the
initial melancholy of the poem, and with it the fear of
death and hell, is swallowed up in romantic sentiment, nature worship, and subjectivity.

II

But an account of these religious poems on death would be utterly inadequate without some words about the collateral line of poems on the Day of Judgment. The late seventeenth and early eighteenth centuries had seen a long series of poems on this subject—by Flatman, Roscommon, Watts, Pomfret, and the American, Michael Wigglesworth.[29] Among Young's first publications (1714) had been a rather lurid account in couplets of "The Last Day." Several important poetic treatments of the theme appeared in the 1750's and 1760's. Then the subject seems to have merged for the most part with the treatments of death, night, and other melancholy religious subjects. But just at the close of our period appeared the most pretentious treatment of all, Pollok's *Course of Time,* as well as related poems on Heaven, Hell, and Satan, by the same Robert Montgomery whom we have been discussing.

The earlier group begins with the popular poems called "The Day of Judgment" written in 1757 for the Seatonian prize—R. Glynn's, which won the award, and George Bally's, which was published in *Musae Seatonianae* as though it had been a close contender.[30] Both are in blank verse, and show some influence from "Paradise Lost." The prize-winner opens with a pseudo-Miltonic apostrophe— "Thy justice, heav'nly King! . . . I sing advent'rous . . ." and closes with a prayer that God in His righteous wrath will "midst the wreck of worlds, remember man!" It is a thoroughly innocuous poem: one cannot help feeling that the poet had been too "advent'rous," and maliciously attributing the award of the prize to the passage which tact-

fully enrolls Seaton amid the redeemed! Bally's poem is
perhaps a shade easier to remember. After the description
of the death of Death and Time, one is asked to picture
one's own soul at the bar of justice:

> Pallid, aghast, and trembling for thy doom,
> Heav'n op'ning all her joys, her torments Hell.

Well will it be for us if some grateful widow or orphan
greets us from the throng—a prophecy which leads the
reader to consider the inevitability and ubiquity of widows
in this verse, and to reflect on the essentially aristocratic
nature of eighteenth-century ethics, which invariably
single out charity in its narrower sense as the first of virtues. There is the usual amusing description of the bodily
resurrection—

> From the four winds, by voice divine compell'd,
> Thick swarming atoms thro' the clouded air
> Precipitate their flight . . .

The dead, rising, "moult corruption." As is usual in these
descriptions, the dead know by instinct whether they are
saved or damned, and the arrival of the Messiah does little
more than confirm the judgment and pronounce the sentence. In his discription of both the saved and the lost,
Bally makes a vague unorthodox suggestion of some "proportion" in the award; but he lets it remain vague.

About the same time appeared John Oglivie's "Day of
Judgment"[31]—although he tells us that he had written it
out in a first draft at the age of seventeen. This is in heroic
couplet. It is admittedly endebted to both Milton and
Young. Surprisingly, it is not horrific; rather it is suffused
with a mild melancholy which leads the poet to moralize,
as in his "Ode to Melancholy," on the ruins of Palmyra

and Persepolis, and to represent his guardian angel as paraphrasing Gray:

> Say where, vain mortal! now the pomp of state?
> The pride of kings, the triumphs of the great?
>
> . . . .
>
> Hope's flatt'ring wish, Ambition's tow'ring aim?
> The boast of Grandeur, and the wreaths of Fame?

He even spends more space on the blessed than on the condemned—a most unorthodox procedure. Much more lurid and ruthless is the blank verse picture of the final judgment (1767)[32] over the polishing of which the unfortunate Michael Bruce spent the last days of his short life. This account bristles with Calvinistic horrors. Even Chatterton, as a child of ten (1762), and before he had learned to be more or less of a free-thinker, wrote a lyric fragment "On the Last Epiphany, or Christ Coming to Judgment."[33]

Between Bruce's "The Last Day" and Pollok's *The Course of Time,* there seems to be little except fragments and incidental or semi-lyric treatments of the subject. A brave contributor to the *Town and Country Magazine* (1775)[34] tries to describe the Judgment scene in an ode; but after depicting the thunders and terrestrial ruins, his "soul recoils" at the point when the Judge is about to pass sentence on the wicked, and he dares not survey the rest. No such scruples withhold Richard Lee, a very minor writer on religious subjects, from writing (1794) exultingly in his tripping doggerel stanzas of how

> Guilty Souls emerge from Tophet,
>   Join their rising Dust again,
> Curse the Union, and prove it
>   Highly aggravates their Pain.[35]

To this general period also belongs the long blank verse
fragment on "Time" by Kirke White, to which reference
was made in the preceding chapter. But most of this poem,
as there remarked, is rather after Gray than after Young;
the poet does not get to the Last Day until line 512, and
almost at once the hiatuses become frequent, and the fragment soon peters out. One gets the idea that the terror of
God's vengeance was not a congenial subject to the young
poet, although he does describe in phrases with a not un-
worthy Miltonic ring how

> The wicked shall be driven to their abode,
> Down the imitigable gulf, to wail
> And gnash their teeth in endless agony.[36]

The most elaborate treatment I know for these years
is Samuel Elsdale's "Death, Judgment, Heaven, and Hell"
(1810).[37] This poem, which is in couplets, is an attempt
to combine the death-poem and Last Day types. The author's meditation on the universality of death has some
timely details about crooked workhouse wardens and godless schoolmasters, and the judgment scene contains a
satisfying catalogue of the damned, beginning with atheists and ending with suicides. The various temporal
agonies which have won bliss for the martyrs are described as well as the eternal agonies of the lost. Toward
the end of our period, on the other hand, appeared a night-
mare-vision of the Last Day[38] which carries much the
deepest feeling of *lyric* religious terror of any of the poems
I have seen. The poet, John Clare, actually dreams that
he himself is among the damned, and feels himself sinking
into fathomless abysses of horror:

Sad boil'd the billows of that burning sea,
And Fate's sad yellings dismal seem'd to be;
Blue roll'd its waves with horror uncontroll'd,
And its live wrecks of souls dash'd howling as they roll'd.

None of the other poems in this series gives one the same sense of truly personal, if temporary, religious melancholy.

Of Robert Pollok, promising young Scotch theologian and author, who died of consumption at the age of twenty-nine, we are told that when composing at home, he used to go out to a neighboring farm and sit under a clump of trees within sound of a tiny waterfall, and that this sound and the voice of the wind in the firs "awakened emotions, to which may be ascribed a portion of that enthusiasm which infused animation and wildness into his cherished melancholy."[39] Yet if he too was touched with romantic enthusiasm and nature worship as well as romantic melancholy, these things have not remodelled his treatment of theological themes as we saw them remodelling Robert Montgomery's. His *magnum opus, The Course of Time* (1827), is a well-nigh interminable theological dissertation in ten books of pseudo-Miltonic blank verse, written with something of the gloomy religiosity of "Night Thoughts," but much more objective. Its approach to romanticism would seem to be rather one of opposition. There is a suggestion that a poet who substitutes melancholy and introspection for the championship of morality runs grave risk of damnation; and a rather long passage which obviously refers to Byron, describes how all his genius and fame could not save him from dying of wretchedness born of wickedness and pride. It is only fair

to add in this connection that Robert Montgomery too
was accused of consigning Byron to hell.[40]

No sufficient purpose would be served by a detailed
summary of Pollok's poem. The general plan is this: two
new arrivals in Heaven—long after the death of Time and
the destruction of our world—seek out a celestial hermit,[41]
who was once on earth also a hermit and a sage, and persuade him to explain to them some strange and terrible
sights they have seen on their journey thither; this he does
at length by rehearsing the story of man and his world,
stressing the final judgment and the fate of the wicked.
The poet dwells on the horrors of his theological system
with a ruthlessness approaching sadism.

He has a certain power in the horrible. Here is his picture of the Undying Worm, a sort of living symbol "traced
in fire" seen by the enquiring spirits on the walls of hell:

> Of worm or serpent kind it something looked,
> But monstrous, with a thousand snaky heads,
> Eyed each with double orbs of glaring wrath;
> And with as many tails, that twisted out
> In horrid revolution, tipped with stings;
> And all its mouths, that wide and darkly gaped,
> And breathed most poisonous breath, had each a sting,
> Forked and long, and venomous, and sharp;
> And, in its writhings infinite, it grasped
> Malignantly what seemed a heart, swollen, black,
> And quivering with torture most intense;
> And still the heart, with anguish throbbing high,
> Made effort to escape, but could not; for,
> Howe'er it turned—and oft it vainly turned—
> These complicated foldings held it fast.

And still the monstrous beast with sting of head
Or tail transpierced it, bleeding evermore.[42]

If that particular nightmare has direct literary ancestors, they are not, I think, in any of the verse we have been discussing. It is otherwise with Pollok's description of Death, embodied in an apostrophe to that insatiate tyrant at the moment of his fall; this passage is surely due to Blair, although the disciple pushes the figure of Death as feeding upon human flesh to even more horrible lengths.[43] Thus this late poem on the Day of Judgment serves also to illustrate the persistence of the line of gloomy religious poems on death.

III

Now, as Sir Leslie Stephen has remarked, "We are not melancholy because we believe in Hell, but we believe in Hell because we are melancholy."[44] But like most truths, this dictum needs to be hedged about with reservations and explanations. In the present connection it leads one to speak of the apparent complacence of most of these writers in the face of the terrible doctrine they preach. There is comparatively little pity for the damned. To be sure, we found Bally tentatively advancing the idea of "proportionate" punishment, and our anonymous ode-writer as well as the kindly Kirke White withdrawing at the edge of the pit. Even Pollok once—once only—allows his heavenly narrator to drop "a serious tear" for the folly of the lost.[45] But on the whole the poets keep a certain personal detachment; one never feels, with the single exception cited, that they are actually in terror for themselves, and as for the others—justice must be done. Young's early poem on the Last Day, to be sure, contains a long and convincing argument on behalf of the condemned (put into their own mouths); but it is cavalierly dismissed, and in the later "Night Thoughts," Young explicitly says that only the existence of Heaven and hell makes virtue either possible or reasonable. Thus the melancholy belief in eternal punishment for the vast majority of the race presents itself as a rational solution of life's mysteries, and contemplation of it may even hold, as we have seen, an element of sadistic exultation.

There were of course dissenting voices, even among those who gave the subject literary expression. The Wesleys certainly believed in hell. But they were no Calvinists; and Charles Wesley wrote a whole series of poems, mostly in the two issues of *Hymns on God's Everlasting Love* (1741 and 1756)[46] fulminating against the diabolical ideas of those who say that grace is reserved by predestination for a few elect. He goes so far indeed as to say that he can conceive no sin worse than belief in the "horrible decree," since it denies the fundamental character of God as love.[47] Certainly the horror of everlasting punishment had struck home to him, and a yearning to save from it others as well as himself is suffused through his hymns as through his life. This intensity of belief, and his recurrent strugglings with a conviction of sin and a yearning doubt of salvation, fill much of Wesley's autobiographical and some of his general poetry with a real religious melancholy. True, the doubt and suffering and temptation are presented to us as swallowed up in victory and love—but they are there.[48]

Indeed, when we speak of the eighteenth century as

lacking in a sense of sin and a fear of God and consequently in true religious melancholy, we are forgetting, not only
the vast popularity of the literature we have been discussing, but the whole intense and turbulent world of Methodism, and of the parallel Evangelical movement within
the Church itself. A picture of the times is strangely incomplete without the girl whom John Wesley found raving
and crying out "I am damned, damned; lost for ever! . . .
I am damned that you may be saved," and calling on the
"good devil" to come and dash her brains out;[49] or without the parishioners whom the preaching of Cowper's
friend, John Newton, is said to have driven insane. It is
true that comparatively few of the enthusiasts were articulate as far as literature is concerned. Yet with all its
didacticism and pious pose, there is assuredly a core of
sincere religious melancholy in "Night Thoughts," and
probably in some of the other death and Last Day poems.
There is a touch of it in Elizabeth Carter, as we have
seen. One almost seventeenth-century cry of agony was
uttered (about 1767) by Walter Harte,[50] although Harte's
anguish was rather from the sufferings of life than from
the pangs of sin. Still, in spite of all we have said, the
field, as far as literature is concerned, is comparatively
barren.[51] Byrom, the facile versifier of William Law's
ideas, utters a characteristic caution against religious
despair:

> Despair is a cowardly thing,
>   And the spirit suggesting it bad;
> In spite of my sins I will sing,
>   That mercy is still to be had.[52]

As for Johnson, it was part of his sturdy philosophy to

keep as much as possible to himself his doctrinal pessimism and his temperamental fear of death.

Of course there was William Cowper. Cowper must remain one of the great examples of religious melancholy, and of religious melancholy grounded in conviction of sin and fear of hell. We shall probably never be quite sure how far Sir Leslie Stephen's dictum applies to him: how far this theology caused his melancholy and occasional madness, and how far the melancholy and madness were inherent in his temperament and physique and merely found expression in his theological obsession. Yet it is difficult for a modern reader to study Cowper's autobiographical fragment and his letters, and the records of his life, without a growing conviction that the tenets of Calvanism as presented to Cowper's sensitive mind by his various ill-chosen spiritual advisors, particularly the Reverend Mr. John Newton, nourished and fed his melancholy and were a principal ingredient of his periods of insanity.[53] Whatever its origin, Cowper's melancholy was of course definitely pathological. Yet modern psychology tends to emphasize the likeness in kind of most phenomena of insanity to those of the normal mind, differentiating them by intensity rather than by intrinsic distinctness. And even if this were not so, Cowper is too important a literary figure in our period to be passed by.

The core of Cowper's melancholy, as all the world knows, was a terrible and implacable conviction of damnation. In his *Memoir*,[54] written shortly after he emerged (1765) from his first serious derangement, he tells us of his early sins and follies, heaping blame upon himself far beyond the warrant of the probable facts, as Bunyan had done before him. The familiar story of the public examination which he did not dare to take becomes the chronicle of God's merciful chastisement of a soul self-convicted of the murderous wish for the death of another; the pitiful and futile attempts to bring himself to the actual deed of suicide are told of with shuddering horror; and horror grips the reader also at the description of the culmination of Cowper's remorse in the conviction that he had committed the unpardonable sin. At last one day he felt a "sense of burning" at his heart— "an earnest of those eternal flames which would soon receive" him. He lay down "howling with horror." And thus his brother found him—to be greeted by the mournful word which recurs like a somber chord throughout the rest of Cowper's life: "Oh Brother, I am damned!" It is true that after his cure and conversion, the black genius was for some years exorcised. But after the 1773 attack, apparently brought on by too strenuous a discipleship of the Evangelical and emotional Newton, it returned, never again to be altogether absent from the poet's mind. His thoughts, he wrote to Newton in 1781,[55] were on the things of the spirit; "but the tallest fellow and the loudest among them all is he who is continually crying with a loud voice, '*Actum est de te; periisti!*'" Instead of lifting as the end approached, the cloud grew heavier, and when he was dying, he begged his friends not to talk to him of salvation. "I feel," he told them, "unutterable despair."

Most of Cowper's poetry, including the didactic pieces in the first volume (1782), "The Task" (1785), and the translations of Homer, were undertaken frankly as an escape from brooding, a method, like his carpentry, his sketching, his hare-raising, of laying the spectre. Moreover, Cowper's personal despair never in the least shook his piety, and, however hopeless he might be for himself, he always desired to help others by his writings, although, as he mournfully wrote to Newton,[56] it was "raising a scaffold before a house that others are to live in, and not I." The prevailing tone of his verse, therefore, is didactic rather than lyric, and not particularly melancholy. Yet sometimes his conversational style allows of a sudden confidential revelation, and at long intervals he expressed his hurt in a lyric cry.

The nearest approach to melancholy in the earlier verse is a series of rather stilted poems evidently inspired by his disappointed love for his cousin Theodora Cowper. Then one stumbles suddenly on those "appalling sapphics" written in the very midst of the 1763 attack:

> Hatred and vengeance,—my eternal portion
> Scarce can endure delay of execution,—
> Wait with impatient readiness to seize my
>   Soul in a moment.
>
> Damned below Judas; more abhorred than he was,
> Who for a few pence sold his holy Master!
> Twice-betrayed Jesus me, the last delinquent,
>   Deems the profanest.
>
> Man disavows, and Deity disowns me,
> Hell might afford my miseries a shelter;
> Therefore, Hell keeps her ever-hungry mouths all
>   Bolted against me.
>
> Hard lot! encompassed with a thousand dangers;

> Weary, faint, trembling with a thousand terrors,
> I'm called, if vanquished! to receive a sentence
>   Worse than Abiram's.
>
> Him the vindicative rod of angry Justice
> Sent quick and howling to the centre headlong;
> I, fed with judgment, in a fleshly tomb, am
>   Buried above ground.[57]

No one surely can read these terrible lines even at this distance of time without a shudder. There is in them the stark power of utter conviction. The only thing in Cowper's verse which approaches them in strength of despair is his last original poem, written thirty-six years later—the much better-known "Castaway." This poem is built on the figure of shipwreck, which Cowper had made use of at least twice before in the same connection,[58] to symbolize his own parlous case:

> We perished each alone:
> But I beneath a rougher sea,
> And whelmed in deeper gulfs than he.[59]

Between these chronological extremes there are various oblique references. The "Olney Hymns" were written during the interval of happy faith between the first and second seizures, and, although they are naturally full of Calvinistic self-abasement and protestations of sinfulness, not one ends on a note of despair. I should say that there is less religious melancholy in them than in the hymns of Charles Wesley. But in "Conversation," from the 1782 volume, Cowper remarks sadly that

> The Christian in whose soul, though now distressed,
> Lives the dear thought of joys he once possessed,

will not dare to "seem to boast a fire he does not feel."[60]
In "Retirement," in the course of the rather long discussion of melancholy which our acquaintance with this subject would lead us to expect, he speaks of how God may in
a moment jar loose ten thousand strings of the harp that
is man, and none but He can put them again in tune.[61]
There are one or two other lyrics, and the famous "strick-
en deer" passage in "The Task."[62] The sorrow of the last-
named passage is not, however, so much for the poet himself as for the wicked and unseeing world.

This brings us to remark that Cowper, sensitive and
gentle soul that he was, seems now and again—although
not nearly so often as one would expect—to have been
touched with pity for others than himself whom he considered lost. Later in this same passage he cries that he
feels his heart "Dissolve in pity." He wrote to Newton[63]
that he supposed both infants and virtuous heathen saved,
and he presents the same argument in verse in "Truth."[64]
Made charitable, he says, by the deathbed conversion of
of his beloved brother, he believed that many saw the light
at the very door of death. And as for the rest, he regarded
them with a sort of mournful sternness. He thought no
sight more melancholy, he once wrote to William Unwin,[65]
than a crowd of godless gentry, for the ultimate salvation
of *all* of whom "the Scripture gives no encouragement to
the warmest charity to hope."

IV

But usually, at least among the articulate of the
eighteenth century, it is not the people who really believe

in hell who are troubled over it. The Quaker poet John
Scott (died 1783) may end a melancholy meditation on
the woes of life by asking

> Say, will Religion clear this gloom,
> And point to bliss beyond the tomb!
> Yes, haply for her chosen train;
> The rest, they say, severe decrees ordain
> To realms of endless night and everlasting pain![66]

But he hastens to add a note: "The author does not give
these as his own sentiments, but merely such as the
gloomy moment described might naturally suggest. That
the above dreadful idea is adopted by a large body of
Christians is sufficient to authorize its admission into a
poem professing to paint the dark side of things." More
than a generation later (1822) Byron sardonically wonders if he may not be quite alone in the "unpopular" and
"blasphemous" wish that all may be saved—even George
III.[67] But it is matter of common knowledge that during
our period—whether by reason of the advances of ration-
alism, of worldliness, or of sentimentalism—the preaching of "hell-fire and brimstone" fell off a good deal, even
in Scotland; and as for the literate laity, they quietly
stopped talking about hell, even, one is constrained to
think, very seriously believing in it. It was not that they
became atheists or even out-and-out deists: one of the
perpetual astonishments of the browser in this literature
is the proportion of the poets and poetasters who were
clergymen;[68] and the women, without exception so far as
I know, were all pious. But softer manners and more humane sensibility taught most people to romanticize death

and to think more pitifully of human frailty—and man has ever made God in his own image.

Yet the intensity of belief and emotion which we have lost for ourselves we not infrequently seek to regain through vicarious experience—nor are fear, remorse, and despair by any means exceptions to this rule. This might be done the more shamelessly in the period we are studying because of the growing ideal of sensibility with its tendency to sentimentalism,[69] which frankly cultivates emotion for its own sake. And here was the whole world of the bygone Age of Faith being opened up by scholars and antiquaries; a world in which religious terror was by no means confined to a far-distant *dies irae,* but was a very present reality, compounded of strange asceticisms and secret ecclesiastical lusts, of ghost-lore, necromancy, and contracts with the Devil. This world arose on the imagination, furthermore, against a background of those ruined castles and abbeys, those twilight churchyards and midnight charnels, already connected in life and in literature with religious musing and half-superstitious fears. What wonder that religious terror, dying out as a living subjective force in most breasts, should flame anew in the vicarious terrorism of "Gothic" romance?

That such a psychological connection between religious and romantic terror is not altogether fanciful is indicated by the early association of the "graveyard" mood and paraphernalia with the Gothic. We found this association already illustrated in "The Pleasures of Melancholy," "The Enthusiast," and other selections in Dodsley's *Collection;* and the suggestion was then made that the mere propinquity of the graveyard to the Gothic church, and the Gothic connotations of ruins, might help to account for it.

But what country churchyard but has its ghostly or
Satanic legends? What charnel house but holds the possibility, nay the probability, of superstitious as well as religious terrors? What monastic ruin but may suggest to a
poet not only philosophical reflections on the power of
time, but all the strange and passionate and teeming life
that once peopled it? And what easier than to pass from
horrified Protestant meditations on that ancient life, such
as were not infrequent in the ruin-elegies, to a fascinated
analysis of its romantic crimes and austerities and the
half-forgotten beliefs on which it rested?

As for the connection between superstitious beliefs and
black melancholy, the odes to superstition have hinted at
it. According to Churchill, Credulity is "the child of Folly,
Begot on cloister'd Melancholy."[70] According to Anna
Seward, "grim Superstition" is "Demon of the Night," before whose "baseless terror" she prays she may not resign
her peace.[71] Henry Headley, in his "Invocation to Melancholy," tells of standing aghast under the moon by Superstition's antique shrines.[72] John Gilbert Cooper had
thought of a convent as the kingdom of "frozen chastity
and Horrour" and of "Melancholy, daughter of Despair,"[73] and in "The Power of Harmony" (1745) had associated black melancholy, superstition, guilt, and death
together as fit frequenters of a funereal place of cypress,
poison yews, and ruined tombs.[74] It needs only the change
of attitude already partly accomplished in Headley and
others, from pious horror or complacent superiority to
imaginative or even morbid sympathy, to give us *The
Monk* or *The Italian*, with their correspondent poetic phenomena.

Indeed the elements which terror-romanticism took

from the medieval revival were the very elements which it had in common with black religious melancholy. It took the backgrounds of dim cathedrals, midnight churchyards, ghastly charnel houses, and gloomy monastic ruins. It took the death theme, and embroidered it with all the terrors of physical corruption and spectral visitation. It took the theme of sin, and added domestic and exotic demonology, age-old tales of contracts with Satan, and the expiatory sufferings of the Wandering Jew. And out of the theme of sin, which is never far from the theme of death, it built its arch-types—the criminal monk, the tyrant, the strong dark hero inwardly consumed by remorse.[75] It is not suggested, of course, that the graveyard verse was solely responsible for the elements of black melancholy in the Gothic tales or in the Byronic hero-type; but that there is a real connection, and that it has deep psychological as well as accidentally literary roots, I am convinced is true.

Some idea of the extent to which the graveyard hor-rifics, largely inherited, as has been said, from seventeenth-century religious melancholy, and further popularized by the mid-century masterpieces of black melancholy, were disseminated through eighteenth-century verse waiting to be assimilated by the Gothic revival, must already have been gained in the course of the discussions of the odes and the elegies. That this material came to be thought of as an essential ingredient of the poetic education may be in-ferred from a passage in Beattie's account of the growth of his Edwin's soul:

> Then would he dream of graves, and corses pale,
> And ghosts that to the charnel-dungeon throng,
> And drag a length of clanking chain, and wail,

Till silenced by the owl's terrific song,
Or blast that shrieks by fits the shuddering aisles along.[76]

Illustrations of the incidental occurrence of the mood or the paraphernalia might be given *ad infinitum*. But space presses.

One or two striking examples of the fusion of the grave-yard and Gothic material toward the close of the century, we must, however, examine. One of these is an "Ode to Fantasy" (1798),[77] by the scholar and traveller, John Leyden. The ode was "written during an attack of ague" and is in consequence sufficiently dismal. In Miltonic octo-syllabics, the sick man cries avaunt to the singing lark and cheerful village throngs, and imagines himself in succession watching a funeral, sitting at midnight on the haunted grave of a suicide, listening to lost and wailing ghosts by a winter torrent, working lonely spells on St. John's Eve, watching all night by the tortured bed of a dying murderer, braving horrid spectres in some Gothic hall, voyaging over far enchanted deeps, whirling through the air with the fairies, and then—suddenly—witnessing the resurrection of the dead and hearing their shrieks of despair.

The other example, but two years earlier in date, is much more elaborate. When Coleridge and Southey first planned "Joan of Arc," the poem was fitted with allegorical trappings, which Southey later removed. The longest allegorical interlude, however, he made into a separate poem, which he later published under the title of "The Vision of the Maid of Orleans."[78] It is a dream-allegory or vision-poem in three books, the first of which is introduction in graveyard-Gothic style, the second a miniature

Purgatorio, and the third a miniature *Paradiso.* While practically worthless as poetry, it is thus an amalgam of literary and philosophical influences—Spenser, Dante, Milton, the melancholy tradition white and black, and the thought of the French Revolution and the rationalists being all distinctly discernible.

Falling to sleep at Orleans in somber mood because of her fore-knowledge of her tragic death, Joan dreams that she goes across a moor

> Barren, and wide, and drear, and desolate,

through a tempestuous night under a Miltonic moon which intermittently makes "the moving darkness visible." She comes to a stagnant water, and steps into a boat driven by a moaning melancholy wind and guided by a wan and hollow-cheeked female figure whose half-hid breast is gnawn by serpents (like that of the allegorical figure of Despair in James Scott's ode). There are bats and ravens and a "hollow blast." Joan leaps to shore at last, to find the orthodox ruin surrounded by "dark yew" and "melancholy cypress" and mounds of half-demolished graves. Moonlight filters through the "fretted windows." Within, fearfully following a wavering blue light, she comes upon an old man, sitting on a mouldering monument half covered with "wither'd yew-leaves and earth-mouldering bones." It is Despair.

> The tomb-fires on his face
> Shed a blue light; his face was of the hue
> Of death; his limbs were mantled in a shroud.

As he welcomes her and leads her further into the ruins,

the descriptive details are those of the ruin-literature, but darkened, as is usual in the Gothic tales, by midnight, tempest, and superstitious terror. The moon looks through the broken roof, there is ivy about the dismantled columns, there are mutilated sacred statues and fallen crucifixes—

> Meanwhile overhead
> Roar'd the loud blast, and from the tower the owl
> Scream'd as the tempest shook her secret nest.

Despair drags the Maid into the charnel house, and in that dank and fetid air, amid the gruesome "fragments of the dead," he repeatedly tempts her to suicide. When even the vision of the livid corpse of her dead lover cannot move her virtue or her logic, he puts her in a coffin and she is dragged towards the bowels of the earth by ghouls, past troops of their brethren feasting on the dead. In the vast "dome of death" to which they bring her, she sees the Fates (originally classical), and Superstition (perhaps originally Spenserian, certainly rather Gothic). But buoyed up by her eighteenth century arguments, even then she will not strike. This closes Book I.

At this point all the terror paraphernalia of the first vision vanishes, exorcised, one gathers, by the steady virtue of the Maid. Theodore, the beloved, appears to her in the guise of an angel, and is her Virgil throughout this book and her Beatrice throughout the third. Book II is particularly interesting as an illustration of that humanizing of the idea of punishment suggested above. For it is not really an Inferno at all, but a Purgatorio, since none of the punishment need be everlasting if the afflicted soul will repent and be cleansed. The descriptions are an odd melange of Dante, Spenser, *Vathek,* and the French Revolution. Two characteristic types of punishment, proportioned and fitted to the crime, may be given: lewd poets (so early did the future laureate put morals above art!) lie like rotting corpses until their works shall cease to lead men astray on earth; and in a Hall of Glory reminiscent of *Vathek,*[79] ambitious kings sit with burning crowns on their brows until men shall realize the wickedness of royal ambition and "form one brotherhood" (the future laureate, though moral, was still a radical). Book III, after *Paradiso,* need not detain us here. It is full of Arcadian love in distant stars and the sort of social philosophy we are more used to finding in Shelley.[80]

V

This poem of Southey's, besides giving a further idea of the paraphernalia of the literature we are studying, and serving as an example of the blending of religious and romantic themes, may stand also as an illustration of the complexity of currents and cross-currents with which we have to do. In truth, the streams which fed the river were very many. So many aspects of the movements which contributed to the satanic and the macabre in romanticism lie outside of our purpose, and so often the satanic and the macabre themselves are dissociated from melancholy, that it will happily be possible to be very brief. Yet something must be said of the most important of these newer influences.

We may speak first of the ballad revival. Macpherson's *Ossian* had been partly based on Highland ballads. But it took over little of the popular superstitious material; Macpherson's ghosts are after all pale and watery beings, completely stripped of terror, and ministering rather to that vague elegiac atmosphere of which we have spoken than to even a temporary black melancholy. To the popularity of the Ossianic poems is probably traceable the romantic partiality for meteors as a sign of terror—meteors are extraordinarily plentiful in *Ossian*—and also something of the partiality for whirlwinds and blasted heaths and tempestuous nights. But when Percy's *Reliques* (1765) and the various other collections containing folk poetry had made available the ballads themselves (or only slightly "refined" versions of them) there was turned into the stream of English poetry a torrent of new terror material —primitive fears and superstitions, witches and bleeding ghosts and haunted glens and palpable fiends, not excluding Satan himself. These things, being originally to a great extent the outgrowth of religious fear, may naturally be added to the churchyard paraphernalia, or the old paraphernalia may fit easily into the descriptions of ballad situations.

Thus in William Mickle's "Cumnor Hall"[81] we have bell, raven, and howling dog, plus the eerie suggestion of an "aerial voice" and the mystic medieval "thrice":

> The death-bell thrice was heard to ring,
>   An aerial voice was heard to call,
> And thrice the raven flapp'd its wing
>   Around the towers of Cumnor Hall.
>
> The mastiff howls at village door . . .

This is a fairly early specimen (about 1777). What could be done with much the same sort of material in a ballad-

like tale by a great romantic genius may be seen in
"Christabel." In the famous and exquisite opening of this
poem, the atmosphere of faerie is built up of such familiar
elements as a clock striking midnight, hooting owls, a
mastiff, the suggested legend of a shrouded ghost, and
a chilly moonlit night; and what would the tale itself be
without its medieval witch-doctrines and its superstitious
omens and marvels? Professor Lowes has taught us to see
in "The Ancient Mariner" the apotheosis rather of the
Renaissance voyage-books and of treatises on occult lore
than of the ballad revival.[82] But the form and movement at least were borrowed from the ballads. It is worth
remembering too that there were in the original draft
two or three stanzas, later omitted, which described the
figures on the phantom ship quite in the graveyard style.
The reader should at this point also be reminded of "La
Belle Dame Sans Merci."

Nor did the demonic and macabre elements in popular
tradition lack more authentic imitators. All the Scotch
poets who busied themselves collecting the traditional material tried their hands now and again at imitation. Burns's
were mostly songs, and when he used the supernatural
in "Tam O'Shanter" it was for humorous effect. Scott
used native and imported themes indiscriminately in
his early ballads and "tales of wonder." The influence
of the German is discernible in the technique of the
first native piece, "Glenfinlas" (1799),[83] wherein
the simple tale of the seduction of a young hunter by a
fiend masquerading as a fair maiden is tricked out in
all the Gothic paraphernalia of chill death-damps, danc-

ing corpse-lights, and loud bursts of ghastly laughter amid howling whirlwinds and a shower of bleeding human fragments. The "Eve of St. John" (1799), also written for *Tales of Wonder,* concerns a rendezvous with a murdered man, and the "sable score" of his burning fingers left on door and wrist when he comes to warn his lady and his murderer (her husband) of the consequences of sinful lust and bloody deeds.[84] The fragment called "The Shepherd's Tale" (1799) is apparently a legend of border warfare; it has an enchanted cavern in the bowels of the earth—a very popular folk-motif as we have already seen—and a whole army of knights in enchanted slumber.[85] "Cadyow Castle" (1801) is a tale of border revenge, but has no supernatural machinery.[86] Scott used ballad themes often enough later, and his work with ballads has been credited with inspiring all his long tales. In several of these he makes effective use of the macabre traditional material: he uses the legends of the sorcerer Michael Scott in "The Lay of the Last Minstrel," the eerie prophetic visions of the Hermit Monk in "The Lady of the Lake," and a glen popularly supposed to be haunted in "Rokeby." The fearful scenes in the convent vaults in "Marmion," like the conception of the hero in the same tale, are closer to the main Gothic tradition.

Scott's associates in ballad-collecting, John Leyden and James Hogg, and his follower, William Motherwell, all wrote ballads attaining a fearful and gloomy tone by the use of native superstitions. The best of Leyden's ballads is "The Elfin King."[87] It makes fine and restrained use of the macabre:

And the windlestrae, so limber and grey,
　　Did shiver beneath the tread
Of the courser's feet, as they rushed to meet
　　The morrice of the dead.

　　　.　　.　　.　　.　　.　　.　　.

Then Sir Geoffry grew pale as he quaffed the ale,
　　And cold as the corpse of clay;
And with horny beak the ravens did shriek,
　　And fluttered o'er their prey.

　　　.　　.　　.　　.　　.　　.　　.

With panting breast as he forward pressed,
　　He trod on a mangled head;
And the skull did scream, and the voice did seem
　　The voice of his mother dead . . .

As for the Ettrick Shepherd, he was at the height of his
by no means despicable powers as soon as he started to
write about the popular superstitions of his native land. He
was not a gloomy person, and his taste ran fully as much
to humorous[88] or pleasant use of the supernatural as to
the grim and grisly. Doubtless his finest poem is "Kil-
meny,"[89] the Thirteenth Bard's Song from the "Queen's
Wake" (1813); it catches with exquisite grace an eerie
and estatic supernaturalism. But there are macabre passages in two or three of the other bardic tales from the
"Queen's Wake," and those among the best: in "The
Abbot M'Kinnon,"[90] which tells how, in retribution for
ecclesiastical wickedness, St. Columba sank the Abbot's
ship off the shore of the Isle of Staffa, whereon is the Cave
of Fingal; and in "The Fate of Macgregor,"[91] which is
told by a bard who has listened to a Spectre's Cradle Song
far in the midnight mountains, and which itself concerns

a man carried off by an avenging spectre in a "barge of hell." Hogg has also a ballad based on "The Twa Corbies,"[92] and macabre traditional tales about a murdered pedlar whose little finger bone bled to reveal the doer of the deed,[93] about a criminal priest who, to feed his lust, made a contract with the fiend,[94] and about the murder of the pious mother of a famous warlock by a rout of witches gathered at midnight in a church.[95] No wonder, when it had so inspired his muse, that Hogg wrote a poem to defend superstition against its detractors![96] Motherwell, too, sometimes treats such themes of unnatural crime and death: the "dark Syr Hew" meets a horrible and supernatural death for parricide; a girl finds she has unwittingly married "the Ettin stark" who "rules the Realms of Fear"; a woman who has murdered her lover is dragged to a watery grave by his outraged ghost.[97] The best of these ballads and bardic tales manage to effect a dismal and eerie atmosphere by means of a certain naïve simplicity, and use the paraphernalia of terror with restraint.

Not so the more specifically "Gothic" tales. In them mingle the influence of the lurid melodramatic terrorism from Germany and that of the native graveyard-Gothic tradition. To speak of the Gothic school in England is to think of the novelists—Walpole, Clara Reeve, Ann Radcliffe, M. G. Lewis, Maturin—and it is true that Gothic tales in verse are for the most part but pale reflections of the movement in prose. Yet a brief reference to them is essential.

The classics of the type are M. G. Lewis' *Tales of Terror* (1799) and *Tales of Wonder* (1801), to which

Leyden and Scott both contributed. Reference has already been made to Scott's share in these volumes,[98] and perhaps little more need be said of it. In most of the tales, especially Lewis' own, there is really little left of melancholy, black or white. There is rather a lusty delight in superstitious horrors alternating with wild parodying of the same tales seriously presented a few pages back.[99] An excellent idea of Lewis' conception of romance may be gained by reading the Prologue of his *Castle Spectre* (1797). Therein Romance is described as the "moon-struck child of genius and of woe," a "lovely maniac" who haunts new-opened graves and tempestuous headlands, and is frequently seen fleeing in trembling terror

> As if from murderous swords of following fiends she fled![100]

Others besides "Monk" Lewis—from the Della Cruscans to Joanna Baillie—told tales in verse about this fearful maid.[101] The very youthful verse of Shelley—to say nothing of those queer concoctions, his schoolboy novels—is Gothic in the extreme. He (or perhaps it was his sister Elizabeth) even plagiarized a whole poem of Lewis' for the *Original Poetry of Victor and Cazire*.[102]

Next to the novel, the drama produced the best examples of the Gothic school. Some of these dramas are in prose, some in verse. Walpole's somber blank verse tragedy of *The Mysterious Mother* (1768), played out against the "haunted castle" background, reintroduces into English tragedy the Renaissance motif of incest, afterwards so popular with the romantics, especially Byron and Shelley. Besides the prose *Castle Spectre*, Lewis wrote several blank verse tragedies, none quite so Gothic as the prose piece, but all more or less in the tradition. Joanna Baillie, in *De Montfort* (1798), written to exemplify the passion of hate, paints, with all the accoutrements of midnight, murder, and religious terror, a gloomy and remorse-gnawn hero somewhat like those later made familiar by Byron. Maturin's *Bertram* (1816), which is reminiscent of both Lewis' *Adelgitha* and Schiller's *Die Räuber,* was mercilessly and justly analysed by Coleridge in *Biographia Literaria.* Yet there are Gothic features in Coleridge's own *Remorse* (1797-1813). Byron's *Werner* (1822) is a Gothic melodrama with strong German affinities. Dramatic poetry, however, is not our primary concern, and mere mention of this line of Gothic melodramas will have to suffice.

What all this meant in the development of the Byronic hero-type has been entertainly set forth by Eino Railo in his study of *The Haunted Castle.* He shows how the tyrant-type which appears in *The Castle of Otranto* gradually took to itself some of the physical characteristics of the hero-type and even the latter's essential nobility; how the center of interest shifted to the struggles within his own dark soul, and the tragedy became his rather than his victim's—a terrible tragedy of remorse. There was influence from without, of course: from Germany the terror tales, the specious melodrama of Kotzebue, the noble and heroic villain of *Die Räuber;* from France the gloomy heroes of Chateaubriand. But the roots were deep in the home soil: in the old preoccupation with death and charnels, with guilt and the consequences thereof; in the medieval revival, with its emphasis on the mysterious, the unconventional, the sinister; in the new humanitarianism,

which would not refuse sympathy even to criminals. So the
type foreshadowed by Walpole, Lewis, Ann Radcliffe,
Joanna Baillie, and Scott (especially in Marmion), and
brought into melodramatic celebrity by Byron, is more a
national than an international product.

The element in the Byronic hero which concerns us
here is the taint of sin which always clings to him. For it
is this sinister or satanic quality which has affinity with
the religious themes of death and retribution. Byron was
not the first to be of opinion that there is no suffering so
terrible as that of remorse,[103] and the theme appears
here and there in the fugitive verse,[104] as well as in novel
and drama. The ennobling of the criminal of course represents a moral revolt. The distinctive quality in the attitude toward sin represented by the satanic school is the
incompleteness of this moral revolt. Byron hated the tenets
of Calvinism under which he had been educated, but was
never able entirely to cast them off; he distrusted also
and defied contemporary moral dicta, but never altogether
ceased to believe in them. He knew the suffering of remorse, therefore, but never the submission of repentance.
And his heroes, like their creator, one and all from Childe
Harold to Cain, feel the beaks of the vultures that prey
on "self-condemning bosoms," and gnash their teeth in
"impenitent remorse."[105] They defy conventional morality,
then, without on the one hand denying it, or on the other
hand fully justifying their defiance. The attitude is to be
distinguished from that, for instance, of Southey's heroes,
who (except Roderick, whose is a story of bitter penitence
and abundant penance) do not defy conventional morality
at all;[106] and from that of Shelley's heroes, who defy it

and glory in their defiance. An unresolved paradox is of course a fruitful source of melancholy; and in truth the element of impenitent remorse lies close to the core of the Byronic type of romantic melancholy, to which we must later return.

Mention was made a moment ago of Southey's heroes. A word is due to the exotic themes of death, madness, and sorcery which their creator was chief among the poets in importing from the Orient. Contemporaries were tremendously impressed by the pretentious and somber eloquence of "Thalaba, the Destroyer" (1801) and "The Curse of Kehama" (1810). "Thalaba" is a tale of missioned vengeance, and "Kehama" a tale of world-towering, indeed super-mundane, ambition, ending in catastrophe and eternal punishment. Both are full of the lurid supernaturalism of the East, superimposed on a groundwork of Gothicism.[107] Space fails to enumerate their ghastly wonders: demonic prophecies in a sorcerers' cavern from the severed head of a new-born infant, madness in a place of tombs, descent into an abyss of flame—a curse of inextinguishable fire upon an innocent head, a supernatural struggle in a ruined city at the depths of ocean, an invasion of hell itself by a mortal sorcerer who only after temporary triumph receives his grisly and everylasting reward.[108] Southey contrives to make these gloomy poems moral and even pious in spite of their infidel origin, by the simple expedient of temporarily adopting the attitude which he attributes to the devotees of whatever religion he is depicting. The hero always fights on the side of the gods, and the whole story takes on a religious tone.[109]

Thomas Moore, whose natural genius was humorous

or sentimental, nevertheless dabbled also in the Oriental. The result was the popular "Lalla Rookh" (1817). One of the tales in this collection, "The Veiled Prophet of Khorassan," is compounded of murder, rape, and most horrible death, and contains a very Gothic passage in which the villain forces the heroine to swear fealty to him by the "bluish death-light" of corpses in a charnel house.[110] Another of the tales, "The Fire-Worshippers," ends with universal death by battle or suicide; it is gloomily romantic somewhat in Byron's vein, although the dark and mysterious hero has nothing in particular to be remorseful about. Incidental influence from these tales or from the prose *Vathek* may or may not serve a melancholy purpose.

VI

One more of the contributory currents remains to be mentioned; and it will bring us back to the death theme as such. Most of the paraphernalia of horror has ever been at home in tragedy. Toward the beginning of our period (1758), Robert Dodsley had written an ode to "Melpomene,"[111] in which he describes the various horrible sights of tragedy as he sees them in a sort of vision. It is rather in the spirit of the odes to horror, and contains an interesting bit of background in the graveyard tradition: "Behind yon mouldering tower with ivy crowned . . . " In truth the influence of England's greatest tragic writer had never been dead in the melancholy literature of his countrymen. Henry Headley used the famous passage about melancholy from *As You Like It* as a fitting motto to his own "Invocation to Melancholy," which is itself "compounded of many simples."[112] Blair, as has been said, modeled the versification of "The Grave" on that of Shakespeare's dramas. But not only did the admiration for Shakespeare increase as the century advanced, but the questing enthusiasm for the past soon restored knowledge also of the post-Elizabethan writers of the "decadence"— of the terrible and morbid imaginings of Ford and Webster and Tourneur. The Elizabethan revival,[113] then, must also be reckoned with, in an endeavor to understand the literary antecedents of some of the macabre poetry of the romantic period.

Perhaps it was what we have called the Elizabethan quality in Blair, joined with the intense religious imagination, which prompted William Blake to make a series of illustrations for "The Grave," including a watercolor of the Last Judgment. For the strength of Blake's own religious imagination, as we know also from "The Everlasting Gospel" (written about 1810),[114] did not shrink before either death or judgment. Nor did his literary imagination shrink from an occasional grotesque. In the early *Poetical Sketches* (1783) there is even a sort of tale of terror (written of course before any of Lewis'), though it is told in strange rhythms that no one but Blake would have thought of, and is garnished with unexpected echoes of "The Song of Solomon."[115] There also is the exquisite Elizabethan "Mad Song."[116] Later, one comes upon a venomed metaphor of hate[117] or the figure of a serpent "Vomiting his poison out" at an altar on the bread and wine;[118] or one is dropped without warning from the mild loveliness of the first part of "The Book of Thel" to the "dolours and lamentations," grave-plots and affrighted tremblings of Thel's visit to the regions under the earth.[119]

Blake's optimism was by no means without its under tones of horror and fear.

It is not suggested that Blake's use of grotesques was imitative of the Elizabethans, although their influence is clearly discernible in his early lyrics. Yet there is a certain kinship of spirit in these sudden descents of a strong and essentially joyous genius into the regions of death and terror. Somewhat similar descents are a marked characteristic of the intense and mystical spirit of Shelley. Shelley's recurring use of scorpions, of serpents, especially of poison, as figures of speech, his occasional dwelling on the details of death and corruption as in the third part of "The Sensitive Plant," his pitiless descriptions, as in "The Revolt of Islam," of plague and slaughter and physical torture,[120] certainly have deeper roots than a boyish delight in Gothic horrors. Rather they arise, as do Blake's, out of the very intensity of imaginative perception.

Thomas Lovell Beddoes was a great admirer of Shelley, one of those in fact who were concerned with the publication of his posthumous poems. But he was even closer to the Elizabethans. It has been well said that he was not an imitator but an Elizabethan born out of time. If that be true, however, he was spiritually akin rather to Tourneur than to Shakespeare. For he was all his life obsessed by the thought of death. The fact that he was, like his somewhat celebrated father, a physician, doubtless fed this obsession, through too constant contact with diseased and dying bodies and too intimate knowledge of the scientific details of death and corruption. His life was full outwardly of color and adventure and inwardly of tragedy and frustration. If he did not in the end commit suicide, it was only because in this also he was frustrated.[121] In his writing, from first to last, from "The Brides' Tragedy" (1822) to the last revisions of "Death's Jest Book" (published posthumously in 1851) he had always been the analyst and devotee of death. And like the Elizabethan and Jacobean dramatists whom he so lovingly studied, he pictured death surrounded by his ministers, pain, and cruel violence, and remorse.

It is almost impossible in brief summary to give a true idea of the ubiquity of the death theme in Beddoes' poetry. A mere roster of titles may carry conviction: "The Boding Dreams," "Love's Last Messages," "The Ghosts' Moonshine," "From the German" (which ends with a murder), "The Phantom Wooer," "A Dirge," "Another Dirge," "Bridal Serenade," "Dirge and Hymeneal"—I copy without omission the titles on pages 346 to 355 in the *Muses' Library* edition. The only completed drama, "The Brides' Tragedy," is an orgy of unnatural murder and frenzied remorse and horrible death. "Death's Jest Book," which was blocked out during the last decade of our period[122] and patiently worked over during the last twenty-five years of its author's life, is undoubtedly the most astonishing *danse macabre* in English literature. Yet impossible as it is as drama and morbid as it is in its preoccupation with crime and death, the strength and suppleness of its neo-Elizabethan blank verse and the exquisite and eerie music of its lyrics make it the finest artistic expression of the theme we have been following.

Beddoes regarded death with no religious solemnity like Young's or Blair's. Neither did he regard it with the somewhat sentimental regret or longing which we shall

find in some of the romantic and preromantic poets. The
nearest approach to the latter attitude is his habit of presenting it as an insidious wooer:

> A ghost, that loved a lady fair,
> Ever in the starry air
>   Of midnight at her pillow stood;
> And with a sweetness skies above
> The luring words of human love,
>   Her soul the phantom wooed.
> Sweet and sweet is their poisoned note,
> The little snakes of silver throat,
> In mossy skulls that nest and lie,
> Ever singing "die, oh! die!"[123]

So the ghost of Wolfram wooes Sibylla in "Death's Jest
Book," and then checks himself, crying

> Snake Death,
> Sweet as the cowslip's honey is thy whisper . . .[124]

It is as though the serpent again tempted Eve.

But the most striking characteristic of Beddoes' attitude toward death is its disrespectful familiarity. He
shrinks before the King no more than he romanticizes him.
He writes of him with a sort of savage glorification and
sardonic mirth. Like Tourneur in *The Atheist's Tragedy*,
he places the principal scenes of his play among the tombs
by a ruined cathedral at night. There the conspirators
meet, there the African slave raises the ghost of the murdered Wolfram, there secret foes meet and banquet at
midnight with the ghost acting as court fool, there the
revenger is murdered and the Duke is carried off living
into the tomb. These midnight revels are enlivened by the

famous macabre lyrics and ballads about the abortion squatting on a toadstool, the feasting of Harpagus on the flesh of his own son, and "Old Adam, the carrion crow."[125] Isbrand, the revenger and usurper who at first masquerades as court jester, calls death "brother King and Fool."[126] "I will yield Death the crown of folly," he cries earlier in the play. "Let him wear the cap, let him toll the bells; he shall be our new court-fool; and, when the world is old and dead, the thin wit shall find the angel's record of man's works and deeds, and write with a lipless grin on the innocent first page for a title, 'Here begins Death's Jest-Book.' "[127] And twice during the play,[128] to point the jest, the painted figures of the dance of death on the wall of the cloisters come to life and dance and banquet in the moonlight.

The *danse macabre* was not new in English literature any more than in art. It was a subject naturally suggested by the medieval and Renaissance revivals, and most congenial to Gothic writers or others with a penchant for eerie horrors. Lewis has one (1799), not quite in earnest, with a significant motto from *Othello:* "On Horror's head horrors accumulate."[129] Kirke White has something very similar—a dance of consumptives, in a fragment from an unfinished "eccentric drama" (about 1803). The dance is followed by a colloquy between the goddesses of Consumption and Melancholy, in which Melancholy makes use of all the churchyard paraphernalia from ravens to charnel-houses.[130] Even Scott was moved to write a "Dance of Death" (1815).[131] It grew out of his poem on "The Field of Waterloo," and makes use of the Scandanavian fable of spirits who foredoom the slain. They whirl in tempest

over the head of a lonely sentinel the night before the
battle, singing a wild song with the refrain

> Wheel the wild dance
> While lightnings glance
>   And thunders rattle loud,
> And call the brave
> To bloody grave,
>   To sleep without a shroud.

In this same year appeared the elaborate *English Dance of
Death,* plates by Rowlandson with accompanying doggerel rimes by the versatile William Combe. The tone of
most of these verses (and the same is true, as a matter
of fact, of the plates) is rather heartless, even at times
flippant, and it is with some surprise that the reader
comes at the end of the second volume on a lugubrious and
deeply pious meditation after the manner of Young, called
"Time, Death, and Eternity, A Night Thought."[132] The
most macabre of the verses are those describing "The
Vision of Skulls,"[133] a dream-visit to the catacombs, wherein Death appears in person to show the dreamer where
a space is left for his own skull; and "The Churchyard
Debate"[134]—a friendly conference among the tombs of a
lawyer, a doctor, a parson, a sexton, and Death.

But it is with Beddoes' dance of death that we would
leave the discussion of this theme. It has this in common
with the best treatment by the religious writers with whom
we started out: it is no mere titillation of a morbid desire
for vicarious horrors, but arises from a bitter intensity
of personal conviction. It has this in common with the
treatment by the Gothic writers and other purveyors of

the various romantic revivals: it is expressed in a technique and spirit deep-rooted in the English past, medieval and Renaissance. "Death's Jest Book" could not by any possibility have been conceived or brought to birth a century earlier. Even two centuries earlier something of its symbolism and its disillusion (born of the sophistication of two hundred years of scientific, philosophical, and literary development) would have been out of place. It is a thing unique in itself and quite personal to the writer; and yet it belongs nowhere but at the close of the romantic period.

CHAPTER V

BLIGHTED ROSES

Love's words are writ on rose-leaves, but with tears.
—L. E. L.

The philosophic and the religious-Gothic are but two
of the many moods in which romanticism looks at pain
and change and death. Within both these moods we have
watched the steady increase of the emotional element, the
shift of emphasis from philosophical or religious doctrine
to emotional realization, ranging in accordance with the
genius of the writer from high poetic inspiration to maudlin sentimentality or factitious horrifics. In the mood which
we are now to study, that of love melancholy, this increase
of emotional content is the fact of paramount importance.
The study indeed resolves itself into an analysis of the
growth of sensibility, and along with sensibility inevitably
of the growth of the literary power and importance of
women. Not that the love poetry came to be chiefly written
by women, but that it came more and more to be written
for them, and hence to reveal an increasing consciousness
of their point of view. And that, given the current ideal
of womanhood, could not fail to mean an immensely more
sentimental attitude toward love; nor, given the current
conception of sentiment, could such a shift of attitude fail
to increase the volume of sighs and tears, pitiful death
and general unhappiness, to be found in the poetry of
love.

I

The forms of love-poetry most popular in mid-century were those sponsored by Hammond and Shenstone, the elegy and the pastoral. On the whole, they suited the mid-century genius very well. They were safely grounded in classical tradition, yet allowed personal emotion to be expressed in a guarded and as it were pseudonymous manner. Their conventions allowed full play to the fashionable pleasure in mild rural landscapes and an idealized version of country life. No one expected them to be intense, or brilliant, or anything but skillfully turned and graceful and full of refined sensibility. Both forms were immensely popular in the third quarter of the century, and did not die out till the elegy was swallowed up in romantic love lyric and the pastoral in the realistic tale of rural life.

The love elegy is a form so completely extinct at the present time that many a young modern has grown up, received his education at one of our best universities, and been graduated with a major in English, without suspecting that it was ever naturalized on English soil, much less that on the lower levels of literature it flourished prodigiously for more than two generations. That it did flourish, a glance into almost any of the anthologies or periodical files of the latter half of the eighteenth century is ample proof. The peak of activity, if one may judge by the later volumes of Dodsley's miscellany, *The Poetical Calendar* (1763),[1] and the files of such a popular periodical as the *Gentleman's Magazine,* came in the fifties and sixties, as it did in the allied imitations of Gray. Around 1760 there was a veritable rage among poetasters for writing love elegies after Hammond and pastorals after Shenstone.

Even when the fashion had begun to wane, new elegies, some more, some less imitative, constantly appear; constantly also appear new translations of Tibullus and of Ovid, once in a while of Propertius. Bell devotes a whole volume of his anthology to reprints of *Elegies Moral, Descriptive and Amatory* (1789). There are five or six love elegies in Polwhele's *Poems Chiefly by Gentlemen of Devonshire and Cornwall* (1792). As has been already remarked, there are two original love elegies, besides translations of Propertius, in *The Poetical Register* for 1804. As late as 1809-11 the *Poetical Magazine* published some five new love elegies. With all this activity, however, the form has never managed to lift itself into the upper regions of English literature. No new Tibullus or Ovid arose, no Shakespeare or Sidney to stamp the foreign form, as that of the sonnet has been stamped, with native genius. But, weak and artificial as the English love elegy was and remained, it has a certain historical importance as a purveyor of eighteenth-century love melancholy.

The characteristic meter is that which we have called the elegiac quatrain. All but two (and those by the same author) of the eleven love elegies in the Bell anthology are in this stanza. Since Hammond's imitations of Tibullus had become the English classics of the form, this use of his stanza was to be expected, especially when strengthened by the immense popularity of Gray's "Elegy" and the milder vogue of Shenstone's elegies. Elegies continued occasionally, however, to be written in heroic couplet, especially if the model were Ovid or Propertius instead of Tibullus. Hammond himself had used the couplet for his translations of Ovid. Now and again, too, an elegy would

be written in the iambic tetrameter stanza we usually associate with the ballad. That about exhausts the meters[2]
used in love poems definitely called elegies.

The mood is characteristically melancholy, though by no
means always so. The melancholy will vary from the pensive pleasure of contemplating retired simplicity and obscurity with Delia to the black despair that ends or
threatens to end in suicide. Various motifs recur with monotonous regularity. There is the invitation motif: Damon, it is true, is no foppish beau to tread the mazes of
the dance, nor has he great wealth of flocks and fields; yet
if only Sylvia will prefer him, how happy they can be
in rural simplicity, and how sweetly some future bard
may hymn their faithful loves![3] There is the absence
motif: the accepted lover has sustained "four tedious days
of absence" and must somehow get through four more;[4]
or malignant fate has torn the lover from his beloved, and
he vows eternal constancy of heart and lyre till the welcome coming of death.[5] There is the fickleness motif: Cynthia has moved to town and now scorns her rustic swain,
who droops like a lily in a "blighting gale";[6] or Daphne
has changed and left Damon to warn the other swains
against the wiles of woman, and, pining away to an early
death, to write his own epitaph:

> His heart then sunk beneath the storm,
>   (Sad meed of unexampled truth)
> And sorrow, like an envious worm,
>   Devour'd the blossom of his youth.[7]

This last is only one aspect of the old motif of the cruel
mistress, which is in one form or another the chief staple of

these elegies. Usually, however, the lover is humble and
self-effacing. He will never forget his love; but though she
doom his "trembling breast to sad despair,"[8] he will bow
to her will. If he is "too humbly fearful of th' all-ruling
power"[9] to commit suicide in despair, he will endeavor
patiently

> To walk beneath the burden of my woes,
>   Or sink in death, nor at my fate repine.[10]

He almost always does or expects to do the latter. His only
request is that his cruel lady may drop a tear on his early
tomb. Sometimes, indeed, he is represented, in those comparatively infrequent elegies written in the third person, as
actually taking his own life. On an evening practically
identical with the one on which Gray wrote his "Elegy,"
Philander may bewail Daphne's faithlessness, and then,
under the now risen moon, call thrice on Daphne, and,
weeping, plunge headlong "into the rapid tide."[11] Or "at
midnight's solemn hour," amid "lightnings red," the despairing shepherd may soliloquize and die, to be found in
the morning by a pitying comrade, who raises his monument and epitaph.[12] More often, however, the lover is
found mourning over the tomb of his dead beloved; in this
large group, the love elegy merges into the ubiquitous
funeral elegy type.

The two suicide-poems quoted are called "pastoral elegies." This is by no means an unusual term, and serves
to emphasis the pastoral nature of much, perhaps most,
of the material. It is a trick caught from the Latin elegists,
strengthened by the example of Hammond and Shenstone,
and fitting nicely into the classic-sentimental glorification

of simplicity and rural retirement with which Shenstone's name and muse are so intimately connected. Sometimes the pastoral trappings scarcely go beyond the conventional names—Cynthia, Daphne, Sylvia, Damon, Philander, Thyrsis—or an occasional "swain" or "humble cot." Sometimes there are flocks and crooks and shepherds and all the rest. Habitually there is the affectation of rusticity and simplicity: even Horace Walpole talks of his "rustic hands."[13] There was, however, much less of this sort of thing as time went on.

Another type of paraphernalia early crept into the love elegies and either existed side by side with the pastoral or displaced it. This was the graveyard-Gothic type, of which so much was said in the preceding chapter. The youthful Chatterton wanders at dusk to the "gloomy cloister's lengthening way" and wishes the ruin would fall on him.[14] An anonymous lover wanders with Despair at "dead night" to "the churchyard's horrors," and, amid "fearful echoes," leans his head on "some cold stone," or "throws his body on the ground."[15] As late as 1810, "J.G." roams alone "Thro' the dark woodland's melancholy shade"—"the victim of Despair," with cold sweat coursing down his "ghastly cheek."[16] But the most indefatigable of these midnight wanderers, James Graeme, wrote while love elegies were still decidedly in style (around 1770). He died at the age of twenty-three of tuberculosis, and it is probable that ill health was as powerful as unrequited love in fixing the melancholy tone of his verse. At all events, his elegies usually represent him as wandering mournfully by some "time-struck turret" or "where wild woods thicken and where waters flow."[17] to complain to the moon of his "unmingled misery of mind."[18] He has much to say about ghosts and howlets, but is incapable of keeping his mind off his own grief—as when he ludicrously closes a description of the ruins of an old castle by blurting out the real reason for his nocturnal visit to them:

> The death of theatres scarce could break my rest . . .
> From love, from love my nightly wandering springs! . . .[19]

Repeatedly he prophesies for himself an early death—too truly, as the event proved, although disappointed love may not have been responsible for it. There are no pastoral trappings in these outpourings, which doubtless lack more in poetic inspiration than in sincerity.[20]

But on the whole, as has been said, the form was artificial. It tended, too, to become sentimental. Too much sensibility is responsible not only for such things as the drooping lily in Bishop Percy's elegy quoted above, but for the tearful haze through which the lover in Anna Barbauld's "Delia"[21] contemplates the happy life he expects to live with his beloved in "meek Simplicity," while she tends "each bruised plant" in the garden "with tender hand" and, reading of the wicked and suffering world, drops "a gentle tear." The artificiality of this particular elegy is emphasized by the adoption of the conventional male point of view by the female writer. As early as 1750 the irrepressible *Student*—which itself published two or three love elegies—wrote maliciously:

> I've wonder'd which, when poets sing
> Transporting Delia's praise,

> They most endeavor to attain,
> The *Lady* or the *Bays*.[22]

In 1799 there was ample warrant for Southey's Abel Shufflebottom "Love Elegies" in his *Annual Anthology*[23] —amusing parodies full of wild hyperbole, capital letters, italics, and cant phrases. Yet the Della Cruscan tribe do not seem to have favored the formal elegy more than the sonnet or the epistle as an amatory vehicle,[24] and probably Southey's satire was aimed at love poetry in general rather than at the elegies alone.

The poems called "pastoral elegies" or "elegiac pastorals," as well as the pure pastorals, are usually written in the third person, and are in various meters and on miscellaneous subjects. Naturally many are concerned with unhappy love. They follow much the same conventions as the elegies and present much the same sentiments and situations. Two of those called "pastoral elegies," ending in love-suicide, have been quoted. Often the grieving lover, who could only threaten to die when the poem was in the first person, actually droops into the grave. In these poems the predominant native influence is Shenstone rather than Hammond. Occasionally one finds a pastoral candidly imitated from him: a late example is "The Shepherd's Complaint," from the *Poetical Magazine,* which is full of disappointed love and the praise of simple living in some "anchorite's cell."[25] But even in the pastorals called "elegies" or "elegiac" some unexpected twist may swing the form outside the circle of love verse altogether;[26] and on the whole the pastorals, though full of sensibility,[27] are far from giving the impression of being so uniformly melancholy as the elegies. Furthermore, their main line of development was probably not toward romantic lyric at all, but rather toward the semi-realistic or realistic rural tale—Southey's early eclogues, Wordsworth's idylls, Crabbe's tales. Since these stories, although often enough mournful in tone, are not more concerned with love than with other human interest and emotions, they do not directly concern us here.[28]

II

But neither Hammond nor Shenstone, much less Tibullus or Ovid, ranks very high in the literary Olympus of the newer love poetry. Its gods were Rousseau and Richardson and Sterne and the young Goethe who wrote *Die Leiden des Jungen Werthers*. Thus melancholy poetry stands again for a time, as in the matter of the Gothic tales, in the shadow of the novel. I have found little direct mention of Richardson in the fugitive verse,[29] though his spirit is everywhere. There are tributes to Sterne, notably in the aptly-named *Sentimental Magazine*,[30] and many to Rousseau's Julie, and above all, to Werther and his Charlotte.

La Nouvelle Héloise appeared in 1761, and became at once the subject of eulogy and animadversion on both sides of the channel. In "The Wreath of Fashion, or, the Art of Sentimental Poetry," which seems to have been written sometime late in the sixties,[31] Richard Tickell presents the unexpected proposition that too much sentimental literature has made of the contemporary maiden a "fair Stoic," and lays the blame squarely on Rousseau:

> Deep in Rousseau, her purer thoughts approve
> The Metaphysics of Platonic Love . . .

Evidently he believes that it was not the earlier and more passionate part of this "wicked" novel which made the deepest impress on the feminine mind. Anna Seward, too, surprises us by speaking of the heroine of her "Louisa" (1782) as "unfashionably enthusiastic, and unfashionably tender." But Rousseau's influence was certainly for tenderness in literature if not in life. Part of this same "Louisa" is avowedly after passages in *La Nouvelle Héloise*.[32] When Serena, in Hayley's "Triumphs of Temper" (1781), visits the delectable realm of Sensibility, part of the entertainment consists in Rousseau's coming to the assembly from earth and reading his account of the death of Julie. Serena's guide has to draw her away by main force.[33] Yet it was certainly not only the virtuous end of *Julie* over which the fair ones wept: as witness the gentle reproof administered by Edward Lovibond to a feminine friend found reading the book with tears:

> What, though descending as the dews of morn,
>   On misery's sighs your tear of virtue waits;
> Forget the fallen Julia! You were born
>   For heart expanding joys and smiling fates.[34]

At least one English verse romance—William Russell's *Julia, a Poetical Romance* (1774)—was definitely founded on *La Nouvelle Héloise*.

As for *Werther*, it raised no question of a "fallen" heroine; its great moral heresy was of course the suicide of the hero; and the number of the poetical tears shed over this suicide's tomb are some measure of the sentimental triumph. The story was published in 1774, but did not reach England until 1779, and then in a censored and sentimentalized version.[35] Eugene Oswald, in his bibliography of *Goethe in England and America,* lists six editions of this translation, and eight other versions, some of which went through various editions, all before 1810. The fascination of the characters and the theme produced various continuations and expansions in prose. The passage in Werther's first letter about a girl who loved him and whom he had not been able to love in return, gave the hint for an anonymous moralist to provide an "antidote" for the "dangerous poison" of the argument for suicide by presenting this Eleanora as a female Werther withheld by religion from seeking her own death.[36] Another anonymous book, *The Letters of Charlotte, during her Connexion with Werter* (1786), was immensely popular and was translated into French, German, and Swedish. Frederick Reynolds, then (1786) at the beginning of his career as a popular dramatist, turned Goethe's story to account in what must be one of the worst of all blank verse tragedies.[37]

Nor were the non-dramatic poets silent. Amelia Pickering published (1788), with a huge list of subscribers, a series of letters from Werther and from Charlotte, written in elegiac stanza and furnished with a motto from Hammond.[38] Alexander Thomson, Charlotte Smith, and Anna Seward all have series of sonnets honoring the "wretched suicide."[39] In another poem, Anna Seward exhorts the reader to judge mercifully of this "wretched victim of a baneful flame."[40] Mary Robinson, visiting Germany in 1786, lavishes her usual number of capitals and italics on

his tomb. Thither she will go at balmy eve to weep;
thither, "Led by soft Sympathy," will the "love-lorn
maid" repair with "trickling tear":

So from the mournful CHARLOTTE's dark-orb'd lids[41]
   The sainted tear of pitying VIRTUE flows . . .
AND HEAV'N'S OWN INCENSE [will] CONSECRATE THE SHRINE.[42]

Various writers, named or unnamed, had been singing the
same tune for the previous year or two in that hospitable
home of sentiment, the *Gentleman's Magazine*. We ac-
company Charlotte as she weeps at Werther's grave and
hopes to meet him once more in heaven.[43] The following
month we have a description of the tomb, and of Sorrow
pleading in tears with Justice for mercy on the dead lover's
deed.[44] Even the breast-bow given to Werther by his beloved does not escape poetical celebration a few months
later.[45] Della Crusca himself, high priest of the temple
of sentimentalism, wrote an elegy celebrating this "isolated Being," this "Man of Woe," and actually defending
his suicide.[46] Meanwhile the popular actress, Mrs. Kennedy, was amusing audiences by singing a tripping popular song about "The Sorrows of Werter."[47]

Now, as everyone knows, this glorification of tearful
emotion was no new thing in the seventies and eighties. It
was not even new in mid-century, when we observed its
manifestation here and there in Dodsley's *Collection*. It
had existed as a concomitant phenomenon, a sort of safety-
valve in the very midst of the neo-classic triumph—in the
comedies of Cibber and of Steele, in the domestic tragedy
of Lillo, in the essays of Steele and even occasionally of
Addison, in the "Eloïsa" of Pope himself. Its rise and

triumph is bound up with the increasing economic and literary importance of the bourgeoisie, with the philosophical optimism associated with the name of Shaftesbury, with the conception of the essential goodness of the human heart implied not only in Shaftesbury's system but in the ideal of the "noble savage" and in primitivism in general. When the great bourgeois sentimentalist, Richardson, had set the whole feminine world a-weeping, and gained the suffrage of Johnson himself; when the bourgeois philosopher and novelist, Rousseau, had set all Europe talking of his theory of the priority of feeling to reason, of the innate goodness of the "natural man," of the sorrows and gentle faults and surpassing virtues of his immortal lovers, and of his own erratic and supremely sentimental personality; when Macpherson had thrown the "melancholy stole" of his vague sorrow over the adventures of Fingal and Agendecca, Oscar and Malvina; when Goethe, temporarily under the spell of Rousseau and *Ossian,* had swollen the stream with Werther's tears:—when all this and much more which we have no space to mention had come to pass, is it any wonder that the characteristic products of the *Zeitgeist* in the third quarter of the century were *A Sentimental Journey* and *The Man of Feeling?*

III

A general discussion of the manifestations of this movement in poetry would take us too far afield—would start us, in fact, upon another book. Some of the ways in which melancholy verse was affected have already been indicated; others will appear later. But as the impact of sentimentalism was most devastating on the poetry of love, it will be worth while at this point to consider for a moment the ideal which sentimentalism presented.

The word is taken to mean the doctrine or practice of cultivating—and expressing—the emotions for their own sake. Sensibility is the name ordinarily given to the personal ideal embodying this practice. That is not to say that a genuine intensity of sensual and emotional experience both personal and vicarious may not exist quite apart from the suggestion of pose implied in the word sentimentalism. But in actuality, this true sensibility is the attribute for the most part only of saints and of poets; and for all their sermons and verses, most of the people we have been talking about were of course of neither the one class nor the other. When sensibility becomes the fashion, it must perforce become self-conscious, and partake of the nature of sentimentalism.

The qualities of the man of sensibility are too well known to require extended analysis. He is exquisitely attuned to the slightest touch of joy or pain either in himself or in another. He is capable of swooning with joy or dying of a broken heart, of rejoicing in the good fortune of a rival or weeping over a sad tale from the antipodes or the death of a pet mouse.[48] If poetically inclined—as he usually is—he may write love elegies, not only about Negroes,[49] whom he does not understand, but even about a turtle-dove who dies of a broken heart,[50] or a nightingale who has lost her mate.[51] He is capable of ending a long and serious monody on a dead goldfinch with a query as to the possibility of birds' having immortal souls.[52] He will write an elegy or a sonnet to Pity,[53] or an "Ode to the Nymph of the Fountain of Tears";[54] he will celebrate the

"patient meekness" of the willow ("last resource of suf-
f'ring love"),[55] or indite a sonnet to a tear—"Ah! lus-
trous gem, bright emblem of the heart"[56]—or to a sigh—
"sweet breath of love";[57] or he will drop "one pitying
tear" over a late-blooming rose.[58] Whatever it may prove
as to the rights of the old quarrel between the optimists
and the pessimists, it is indubitably true that the Man of
Feeling finds it easier to savor to the full his own grief
than his own joy, easier to enter into the woes of others
than into their happiness—with the result that sentimental
literature is predominantly melancholy in tone.

An interesting side-light is thrown on this matter by the
poetical controversy which followed Frances Greville's
"Prayer for Indifference" (written about 1753). This
poem, deservedly one of the best-known bits of fugitive
verse of the period, is an impassioned cry for relief from
the pain of living and loving:

> Nor ease, nor peace, that heart can know,
> That like the needle true,
> Turns at the touch of joy or woe,
> But, turning, trembles too.
>
> .   .   .   .
>
> Then take this treacherous sense of mine,
> Which dooms me still to smart;
> Which pleasure can to pain refine,
> To pain new pangs impart.
>
> .   .   .   .
>
> And what of life remains for me,
> I'll pass in sober ease.
> Half-pleased, contented I will be,
> Content but half to please.[59]

The very intensity of this prayer is clear enough indication that it would not be answered—that probably in her heart of hearts Mrs. Greville did not for more than a rebellious moment want it to be answered. But very many of her contemporaries and their poetic successors took it quite literally, and reproached the writer for her repudiation of sensibility. There were echoes of her attitude, to be sure: as in Anne Yearsley's invocation "To Indifference," which begins:

> Indifference come! thy torpid juices shed
> On my keen sense: plunge deep my wounded heart,
> In thickest apathy . . .[60]

To Mrs. Yearsley, too, it seems that sensibility brings more suffering than joy: "To Sensibility, what is not bliss Is Woe." Some counsel a *via media*. A particularly mediocre "Prize Poem" (1798)[61] on the question concludes oracularly that

> Who feels too *little* is a fool,
> Who feels too *much* runs mad.

Mrs. Tighe's Psyche (1805) has to be rescued from both Spleen and Indifference.[62] But for the most part the voice of the two generations following Mrs. Greville's outburst was against her.

There were a goodly number of direct repudiations of indifference, some with mention made of the "Prayer." Cowper reproached the author in some early verses saturated with sensibility.[63] Another answer appeared in *The Poetical Calendar* (1763), which had previously published Mrs. Greville's poem: it flatly contradicts the melancholy theory that sensibility refines pleasure to pain and intensifies pain to agony:

> Thou pleasure canst from pain refine,
> To joys new joys impart.[64]

Whether or not the first part of this statement is true of genuine poetic sensibility, it certainly is true of the sentimental type which delights in vicarious weeping. Lady Carlyle published (1771) an "Answer to Mrs. Greville's Ode to Oberon" (which "Ode" is identical with the "Prayer to Indifference"), in which she declares that

> No grain of cold *indifference*
> Was ever yet allied to *sense,*

and, further, that Mrs. Greville is "doom'd to please," since it is "the lot of beauty."[65] Mary Sewell declares (1803) that to praise Indifference argues a "dismal vacancy of heart."[66] "An Ode to Indifference" or "to Apathy" often turns out to be on the hence motif.[67] A "Dialogue" between Sensibility and Indifference[68] is likely to end in the complete triumph of the former.

Hannah More, who certainly was no trifler either with life or with the Muse, defended "Sensibility"[69] at length (1782) in an epistle to the Hon. Mrs. Boscawen, one of the Blue Stocking circle. She takes issue at once with Mrs. Greville's thesis that sensibility is more awake to pain than to joy. As for the vulgar, "who ne'er have felt a sorrow but their own,"

> They never know, in all their coarser bliss
> The sacred rapture of a pain like this.

She is of opinion that Mrs. Greville would in reality refuse the "inglorious peace" she begged. Would Mrs. Boscawen, for example, wish she had no children because something might happen to them?[70] "Sweet Sensibility" is a "secret pow'r" whose "subtle essence" eludes the snares of affectation and the "chains of definition." It is a "keen delight," an "unprompted moral," a "sudden sense of right":

> Eager to serve, the cause perhaps untried,
> But always apt to chuse the suff'ring side!

She warns the reader then against a mere affectation of sensibility which "weeps o'er Werther while her children starve," and declares that "one genuine deed" performed for Love, "sole source of Charity," is "more dear" than "all thy touching page, perverted Sterne." The best domain of all for sensibility is the home. She then pays tribute in conclusion to the exquisite sensibility of Gray's "Elegy" and to that of "Serena's poet," William Hayley. This poem is notable as emphasizing the close alliance between sensibility and charity, religion, and melancholy, and, in particular, the identification of it as the peculiar province of woman.

As for the sonnets, odes, and miscellaneous poems addressed to Sensibility and her humanitarian sisters, Sympathy, Humanity, Benevolence, and the rest, their name is legion. The tearful nymph is almost always invoked, almost never bid hence.[71] A large proportion of these poems would be of more importance to a study of humanitarianism than to this of melancholy. Others interest only by the fact of their existence and of their somewhat lacrymose tone. One little invocation to Sensibility (1795) must, however, be quoted, in order to show how thoroughly the goddess might be adopted into the sisterhood of Melancholy, Contemplation, Solitude, and their attendant abstractions:

SENSIBILITY[72]

Nymph of the glist'ning eye, I know thee well;
　The jarring world is not thy favor'd sphere,
Thy silent tears alone thy sorrows tell;
　Thy sighs responsive to the gales I hear.
Thou liv'st to weep, the giddy world will say,
　By moss-grown tow'rs, or by the lucid stream,
To melt and sigh thy pensive soul away,
　While musing in the yellow moon-light beam.
When slander's secret whispers buzz around;
　Or rude reproof, or Envy speeds her dart,
Thy nerves strait quiver with the mortal wound,
　Bleeds ev'ry pore, and faints thy aching heart.
The tearful eye, the mantled cheek are thine,
　The pointed anguish throbbing at the heart,
The thrill of rapture, ecstasy divine,
　Which Angels to their favor'd Saints impart.
Then fly to Solitude's deep-russet shade,
　Where zephyrs gently wave the roseate bow'r:
The lute's soft swell, that dies along the glade,
　May sooth the sadness of the midnight hour.
With fancy trip the mountain's shaggy brow,
　And view the silver ocean's briny wave:
Which dashes restless on the rocks below,
　Or tends the sea-nymph to her coral cave.

Remove some of the enthusiasm and a very small portion of the tears, and this might do very well for one of the later pictures of Melancholy. Sensibility has the same characteristics, haunts, and diversions, it is clear, as has Melancholy herself.

This latter fact is especially evident in the most elaborate poem I have seen which deals explicitly with sensibility—David Carey's "Visions of Sensibility" (1811),[73] a long rhapsodic production in two parts, written in the softened heroics favored by the romanticists. The note of mild sentimental melancholy is struck in the opening lines:

> Why falls the tear for Beauty's faded bloom
> Where flowery garlands deck yon Virgin tomb?
> Why mourns the heart when sad and far away
> The lov'd companions of Life's happier day,
> Whose presence taught her vernal scenes to shine,
> Whose image lives in every soften'd line?
> Why throbs the breast with feeling's softest glow
> To share the bliss that Nature's charms bestow;
> While Fancy pictures in romantic mood
> The heaven of joy that waits the wise and good?
> 'Tis Love's soft power, 'tis Friendship, Taste refin'd,
> Prompts each fond thought, and sways the gentle mind.

The poet has a vision of the inspired bard, whose "wild harp rings to his impetuous hand" while he "Throws on the winds the deeds of other years."[74] Such a harp is the human heart wakened by the touch of Feeling:

> So quick the essenced spirit mounts on high
> At thy command, O! Sensibility![75]

But, although the subject is thus proposed, there is a long invocation to Nature, in the romantically melancholy manner which had arisen out of the Thomson-Warton-Ossian tradition,[76] before at last the poet cries

> Child of the feeling heart! awake! arise!
> The Muse invites thee wheresoe'er she flies;[77]

and, presently, "her wild music trembles from the strings," and at last the Visions are begun.

We have no space to examine them in detail. The general impression gained from the vague kaleidoscope that follows is a sad one. There is reference to the legend of the Nightingale and the Rose, a description of a caravan lost in the desert, a long passage about slavery in the West Indies, several pages of sad love stories (to some of which we shall return later), a shipwreck with its attendant "domestic affection and anxiety."[78] The first part concludes with an apostrophe to Sensibility as "Queen of the human heart!" In the course of the second part, the poet weeps poetical tears over Tasso, Homer, and Burns, over the "musing melancholy" of a convent, over tyrannous pride, bereavement, and delusive joys in general. He concludes with a long hymn to nature and nature's God, which nevertheless includes such melancholy matters as a "complaint of life" and a passage on the pathos of old age.

In the argument to his poem, Carey remarks that women "feel the pleasure arising from the contemplation of a beautiful prospect more acutely than men," and in the passage to which the Argument refers he says to them:

> And the wild warbling lyre that sings of thee
> Murmurs of love and Sensibility.[79]

Hannah More, it will be remembered, particularly addressed her poem on Sensibility to Mrs. Boscawen and other Blues. Indeed, even if it were not matter of common knowledge that the triumph of Sensibility in the eighteenth century was intimately associated with the rise

of women in social and literary importance, the reader of
this chapter must by now have been struck by the predominant femininity of the writers and points of view presented. It may be well for us to remind ourselves of the
causes and circumstances of this phenomenon, and to consider how it helped to turn the main force of the tide of
sentimental melancholy into the poetry of love.

In 1792 Mary Wollstonecraft wrote:

How women are to exist in that state where there is neither
marrying nor giving in marriage, we are not told. For though
moralists have agreed that the tenor of life seems to prove that
man is prepared by various circumstances for a future state,
they constantly concur in advising *woman* only to provide for
the present. Gentleness, docility, and spaniel-like affection are,
on this ground, consistently recommended as the cardinal virtues of the sex; and, disregarding the arbitrary economy of
nature, one writer has declared that it is masculine for a woman
to be melancholy. She was created to be the toy of man, his
rattle, and it must jingle in his ears whenever, discarding reason, he chooses to be amused.[80]

It was not that the author of *The Rights of Woman*—
whom her self-righteous contemporaries called an "unsex'd female" and a "fearful example" of infection from
"the Gallic mania"[81]—by any means wished to do away
with the affections. But she repeatedly protests against
masculine assumption of a monopoly of reason.[82] The implication of the unnamed author's remark about the mas-
culinity of melancholy would be two-fold: first, of course,
that it is selfish in a woman—though not in a man—to
be melancholy, because social obligations call for cheerfulness; and second, that melancholy is a prerogative of

reason—and hence of man alone. Considering the latter
aspect of the proposition first, we may remark that a
philosophical melancholy, such as that of Milton in "Il
Penseroso," of Gray in the great "Elegy," even of Peacock in "The Philosophy of Melancholy," is indubitably
based on a reasoned contemplation of life, and definitely
involves the faculty of philosophical generalization. No
woman, certainly, had produced a literary masterpiece of
this sort of melancholy; even among the fugitive pieces
we considered in our second and third chapters feminine
contributions are very few, and most of those that do occur are of the type most strongly touched by either sensibility or religion. Judging by the literature then, women
did not indulge in philosopical melancholy: whether they
are actually incapable of it, or whether the pressure of a
social ideal rather than a lack of reasoning power is ultimately responsible, is a problem rather for psychologists
and social historians than for chroniclers of literature.
Certainly Mary Wollstonecraft would have laid it rather
to the social ideal involved in our first implication: in
another passage she lays the domination which sentiment
has over women to the fact that they are almost never
alone.[83]

But if a reasoned philosophical melancholy was for-
bidden by society to women, "sweet sensibility" came to
be more and more a prime ingredient of the feminine ideal.
Ample evidence has been presented to indicate that sensibility leads directly to another kind of melancholy—a
melancholy having very little to do with reason or philosophy, but everything to do with romantic love, family affection, benevolence, and religion. Now since all these

latter things were popularly supposed to be the special realm of womanhood, it was inevitable that the great body of literate women—from an occasional singing milk-woman like Ann Yearsley to Mrs. Montagu herself, the "Queen of the Blues,"—from Hester (Thrale) Piozzi, the early patroness of the Della Cruscans, to "L. E. L.," the "mystery of the [eighteen] thirties"—should with re-markable unanimity move in the central current of senti-mental melancholy.

On the whole, the men seem to have relished it. Al-ready in 1755 we find a "little miss" commended in verse for her "sweet softness" when she bursts into tears "upon reading the Ballad of the Babes in the Wood."[84] Con-tinually the "fair" are admonished to "cherish Pity's soft tear,"[85] for "sweet Beauty's soul" is sensibility.[86] One brief "Song"[87] is perhaps worth quoting in full:

> O seek not to repress the sigh,
> Nor check the tear that drowns the eye!
> These love-fraught eyes seem more divine
> When the slow drops o'er Pity's shrine
> From pearly sources graceful flow,
> To bathe the bruised heart of Woe;
> And lovely is the bosom's swell,
> Whose quick, tumultuous heavings tell,
> That softest sympathy is there,
> And Laura's good as she is fair!

The soft flattery continued into the next century: the tear of Beauty which "from sympathy flows, To Manhood shall ever be dear";[88] for

> When Man has shut the door unkind
> On Pity, Earth's divinest guest,

> The Wanderer never fails to find
> A sweet abode in Woman's breast.[89]

And most of the women agreed. Woman, says Anna Seward, is

> Designed for peace, and soft delights,
> For tender love, and pity mild[90]

—and for delicate swoonings and melting tears.

But the sort of woman—especially the sort of young girl—who resulted from taking all this too literally did not, of course, escape satire. Hannah More castigates her in *Strictures on the Modern System of Female Education* (1799),[91] Jane Austen laughs at her in *Northanger Abbey* (written in the late 1790's), Maria Edgeworth amusingly shows her the absurdity of her romantic notions in "Angelina" (1801).[92] There is a neat satirical picture of her in *The Poetical Register* for 1803:

> Behold the sentimental Lady's mind,
> With flimsy novels, like a band-box lin'd.
>
> .   .   .   .
>
> No common feelings in her bosom reign,
> Eternal trance of pleasure, or of pain:
>
> .   .   .   .
>
> Lord! with what scorn she marks the vulgar crew,
> That rest in common-sense, like me and you! . . .[93]

Sentiment seems to this writer a "strange affected thing . . . Cloak'd in the specious garb of good and fair."

Now of course what the sentimental young lady read about in her endless novels, what she wept over in her poetry, what she sought above all things in life, was love. Her tears fell easily, to be sure, for worthy poverty, and if she chanced to be financially able—and otherwise she would scarcely be able to afford much indulgence in sentimentality—she might expend much of her time and tenderness in private charity. Also she had a very high notion of filial duty and family affection in general, and we often find her sensibility squandered without stint on domestic woes. But, after all, the only thing she was trained for—as Mary Wollstonecraft somewhat bitterly observed—was love and marriage. On that all the preparation of her girlhood converged, on that she staked her whole happiness, keeping nothing back,[94] in the shadow of that she would live out the whole remainder of her life. If she failed to find marriage at all, she was something of a derelict, unless, like Elizabeth Carter or Anna Seward or Jane Austen, she could command respect by a talent to the exercise of which the social barriers were not quite insuperable. What wonder that her sensibility fed on pictures of pale romantic heroes and lovelorn damsels, and her sentimental melancholy on tales of blighted love and broken hearts?

And so, after a sufficiently long digression, we are back again with our original subject.

IV

The feminization of lyric love melancholy was by no means complete. The lyrics become more and more penetrated with sensibility and show increasing awareness of the woman's point of view, but they continue for the most part to be written about, or at least by, men. Neither preromantic nor romantic poetry had an Elizabeth Barrett Browning to pour into it, under a transparent disguise, the intensity of a great passion; much less did it have an Edna St. Vincent Millay frankly and exquisitely to confess the tragedies of many broken loves. The time was not yet ripe for such candid subjective admission by women of their common humanity. There are exceptions of a sort. An occasional anonymous or pseudonymous lyric or sonnet of unrequited feminine love finds its way into the magazines.[95] Also several of the women in the Della Cruscan coterie, notably "Anna Matilda" (Hannah Cowley) and "Laura Maria" (our old acquaintance, Mary Robinson), wrote subjective love lyrics, and Mary Robinson's sonnet sequence on Sappho is probably the best verse she ever wrote. In the later eighties the London papers were full of poetical flirtations—"Della Crusca" and "Anna Matilda," "Arley" and "Eliza," "Benedict" and "Melissa," "Arno" and "Julia" (another name for Laura Maria). But on the upper levels of literature, the women have little to show.

A word is, however, due to the Della Cruscan episode, already several times mentioned in passing, for it is in itself amusing, and it was not without its importance in the growth of sentimentality, and also in the spread of the Italian influence so strongly felt by later romanticism.[96] In Florence during 1784 a group of temporary expatriates from England fell into the habit of gathering for literary conversation at the home of Mrs. Piozzi (Johnson's Mrs. Thrale). In 1785 they printed a small volume of their verse, consisting largely of mutual panegyric; it was edited by the officious William Parsons, and provided with a modest enough prose preface by Mrs. Piozzi. The book never reached a second edition.[97] But meanwhile many of the verses had appeared in London newspapers, and when the members drifted back to London—they were all there again by the end of 1787—they were astonished to find themselves famous. Approbation went to the heads of most of them, and they began to believe themselves great poets. Followers flocked about them. Henceforth for several years the public prints were deluged with their high-flown absurdities, signed by fanciful names—Della Crusca, Anna Matilda, Laura Maria, Julia, Reuben, Cesario, Benedict, Arley, Edwin, Yenda, the Bard.[98] Robert Merry, the most nearly a poet of the group, as well as on occasion one of the worst offenders against literary taste, was by far the most popular, and gave his name to his associates.[99] The *World,* and its successors, the *New World* and the *Oracle,* were their particular organs, although other papers, including the *Gentleman's Magazine,* were also hospitable. In the *World* appeared the exchange of sentimental love-epistles, alluded to above, between Merry and Mrs. Cowley, who was at that time a sprightly widow as well as a notable writer of sentimental dramas. The public watched this exchange with high delight, and the infection spread, until, in Gifford's well-known phrase, "from one end of the kingdom to the other, all was nonsense and Della Crusca."[100] Selections from this verse were published in 1789 under the title of *Poetry of the World;* in later editions the book was expanded and renamed *The British Album.* A decided damper was put on the enthusiasm by the ill-starred interview which Bell, editor of the *Oracle,* is supposed to have engineered in order to bring the enamoured Della Crusca and Anna Matilda (who had never met) into each other's

bodily presence at last. Merry, who was something of a
gay young blade, apparently did not relish the discovery
that the "enchanting maid" whom he had sworn he in-
stinctively knew so well,[101] was a middle-aged widow some
twelve years his senior.[102] At all events, he wrote a poem
called "The Interview," in which he gallantly laid the
parting to the lady's sense of duty (duty to what or
whom?—her husband was dead); and, in spite of protests from his erstwhile goddess, washed his hands of the
matter. A second check came with the publication of Gifford's venomous and damning satire, *The Baviad* (1791).
Although there was no lack of replies to Gifford, the public had already begun to recover its common sense even
before the publication of *The Baviad*, and *The Maviad*
(1795) merely conpleted the work of deflation.[103]

The bearing of all this on lyric love melancholy can be
made clear only by suffering a few extracts. The influence
of Italian love melancholy is indicated in the love-poems
in *The Florence Miscellany*. Parsons pays tribute to
Petrarch[104] in a poem built on the idea that lyric power
comes only from suffering. Merry writes a mournful
Italian serenade, probably the most attractive poem in the
volume.[105] *The British Album* contains, besides much other
matter, two series of exchanges between Merry and Hannah Cowley, interrupted during a trip of the former on
the continent.

Only intermittently is the feminine side of the correspondence at all melancholy. Normally, while Della
Crusca is affecting the conventional self-abasing misery,
Anna Matilda is all enraptured adoration. For a while
she drives him to frenzy by espousing the cause of In-

difference—going so far as to call Sensibility a "SAVAGE
UNTAM'D" who "smiles to drink our tears" and sinks her
"FANG" into the heart.[106] But when he has left England
—ostensibly in true lover-like despair—she is all tears.
Her violently jealous letter to him after he has rashly
offered (under the name of Leonardo) to help Laura
"drink oblivion to her woes,"[107] is too angry to be truly
melancholy.

But whether Anna Matilda rages or adores, Della
Crusca languishes. And whatever Anna Matilda may lack
as a purveyor of feminine pathos is more than atoned for
by Laura's mellifluous lamentations. The reader gathers
that Love has dealt very hardly with these two. Della
Crusca writes to Anna Matilda in the stanza of Hammond's elegies, of how he was musing at sunset "with
folded arms" (for all the world like a picture of Melancholy) on the shore of ocean:

> When thy sweet numbers caught my yielded ear,
> Bourne on the bosom of the flutt'ring gale,
> They struck my heart—and roused me to a tear.

For he thinks of his youth wasted in folly and of what
might have been. If only he had known her then—

> *Thy Minstrel* then might have escap'd Despair.

As it is, he whose "proudest boast" is "but an idle song"
is not even worthy to die for her the death of a soldier,
over whose "honour'd corse" the gales

> Waft the moist fragrance of the weeping rose.[108]

He defies, nay even wooes, the power of Death, for

> has not SORROW chose to dwell

> Within my hot heart's central cell;
> And are not Hope's weak visions o'er,
> Can Love, or Rapture teach me more?[109]

His beloved has met his adoration with Indifference: he'll write no more, and if some stray verse of his should be saved from the wreck of time by its association with hers, let it merely

> Say, that the wretched victim long endur'd,
> Pains which are seldom felt, and never cur'd.[110]

She has written an angry farewell because of his ill-advised letter to Laura: he will run mad unless she withdraws her curse:

> O rash severe decree! my madd'ning brain
> Cannot the pond'rous agony sustain,
> But forth I rush, as varying Frenzy leads . . .

And in the end he will die forlornly in some lonely spot. Nay more, angry goddess, till the hard sentence is withdrawn, "THY DELLA CRUSCA WRITES NO MORE."[111]

Meanwhile, poor Laura, who had been the innocent cause of Anna Matilda's fury, had troubles of her own. Della Crusca's letter had been occasioned by her reproachful farewell "To Him Who Will Understand It," on leaving England "to drink oblivion to my woes."[112] But she surpassed herself in "luxury of woe" when, with the grand gesture of a tragedy queen, she wrote to Anna Matilda to disclaim any designs on the affection of Della Crusca, who kindles only to Anna's lyre: only let her spread her "cheerless couch" in some "craggy cell" among the screech-owls, "lunar dew," nightshade, and "baneful Yew," where she may "breathe a strain forlorn,"

And like a ling'ring wintry morn,
Pale and with chilling rays appear,
Cold glimm'ring thro' a chrystal tear.[113]

The curious reader may find much more about Mrs. Robinson's chronically broken heart by turning the pages of her collected poems.

There are love-sonnets in *The British Album* also, a whole series of them, by Benedict—who languishes in Melissa's absence, and whose heart is convulsed by "tender spasms" when he sees her—who no longer finds joy in spring nor in his "artless rhyme" but craves from his cruel beloved only a tear

To dew the wither'd sod that marks my grave![114]

But as for the Della Cruscan style, with its pretentious affectation, its inept epithets, and its hyperbolical sensibility, it has long enough tried the reader's patience. And as for the sonnet form, it will be best discussed in the next chapter. For the sonnet revival as a whole owes more to Milton than to either the Italians or the Elizabethans.[115] Nevertheless it should be said that the growing interest in Italian literature did bring with it translation and imitation of Petrarch, and Milton never had undisturbed sovereignty over the sonnet; and although Shakespeare's sonnets were not admired during the eighteenth century, by the time Keats came to write, it was neither to Milton nor the Italians that he turned, but rather to the Elizabethans, whose variant of the Italian form he came to feel was more tractably handled in English. Keats's love sonnets, however, are essentially original and deeply personal: they give us glimpses of his own intense and tu-

multous passion. Yet among them, only the "bright star"
sonnet stands in the company of his greatest work.[116]

Romantic love lyrics in any meter, especially melancholy ones, are always in danger of a too luscious sentimentality. Moore's do not escape it, nor many of those
of the minor lyrists, nor is it avoided with complete con-
sistency even by Byron and Shelley. The measure of success on the negative side is the purging away of turgid
diction and artistic or personal insincerity; on the posi-
tive side it is of course the lyric genius of the writer. It
need scarcely be added that the line between legitimate
sentiment or passion, and illegitimate extravagance and
sentimentality, such as we have attributed to the Della
Cruscans, is a vague and tenuous one drawn largely by
individual taste. It must not be forgotten, above all, that
the romantic lyrics owe much of their frail loveliness and
charm to an immense advance in technique—to a freedom and variety of music and a metrical dexterity which
was the crowning achievement of a long line of obscure
experimentation, in which even the lowly Della Cruscans
had their part.

The themes of these lyrics are not greatly changed—
how should they be? The lover still grieves over unrequited passion, absence, bereavement, or lack of stead-
fastness. The last is a recurring theme particularly with
Moore, whose acute sense of the swift fading of youth
and habitual elegiac attitude toward the past lend it special poignancy. Though they usually vow eternal truth,
these later poets do not so often as the elegists represent
themselves as dying of their love.[117] Moore's sad love lyrics
are songs, graceful bits of mellifluous sentiment ill able to

sustain an air of deep tragedy. The few which Wordsworth wrote breathe an air of quiet sorrow. Byron would
have scorned to admit that a woman could break his heart,
and even into the exquisite "When We Two Parted"
creeps a bit of his defiance. Shelley's are the most intense, the most sincere, and the loveliest of the romantic
love lyrics. The questing idealism which made Shelley
once say that he must in a previous existence have been
in love with Antigone—which embodied the ideal in
woman's love in "Alastor" and built up the soaring exul-
tations of "Epipsychidion"—finds a voice of yearning in
the famous lyric metaphor of the moth and the star, the
night and the morrow.[118] And the reaction of pain and
disillusion is unforgettably expressed in the "Lines: When
the Lamp is Shattered":

> O Love! who bewailest
> The frailty of all things here,
>   Why choose ye the frailest
> For your cradle, your home, and your bier?[119]

This is neither unfeeling cynicism nor blind idealism, and
there is of course nothing like it in the eighteenth century.

A most interesting aspect of love melancholy in romantic lyrics is the proportion of it which is dramatic
rather than subjective. If the women were slow to follow
Mary Robinson's lead and express their own love melancholy, the men were not slow to do it for them. Besides
writing many lyrics with a masculine point of view which
is obviously dramatic,[120] they fell into the habit of writing lyric monologues for love-lorn women. The writers of
Scots peasant verse—Burns,[121] Hogg, Tannahill, Mother-

well—have many charming and plaintive lyrics supposed
to express the sentiments of lasses whose lovers have
marched (or more usually sailed) away to war. One
woman stands on the shore and reproaches the "cauldrife
wave" which rolls on regardless of hearts that are break-
ing.[122] Another feels the keen wind that blows "o'er the
braes o' Gleniffer," driving the "caul' sleety cloud . . .
along the bleak mountain," and remembers mournfully
how bonnie were the "wild flowers o' simmer" when her
love was called away.[123] Another cries:

O, wae be to the orders that marched my luve awa',
    And wae to the cruel cause that gars my tears doun fa' . . .[124]

Then, too, there are songs of grief over a lover or husband dead, usually in battle.[125] Or perhaps the maiden's
love is unrequited, or, more probably, she has been jilted,
or seduced and deserted by a faithless lover:

> O, wae's me for the hour, Willie,
>   When we thegither met,—
> O, wae's me for the time, Willie,
>   That our first tryst was set![126]

Often—and this is true not only of the lyrics inspired by
folk-poetry but even oftener of more sophisticated romantic verse—the neglected one is pining away to an
early death:

> Oh, tell ye not my lover,
> Lest he perchance should sorrow at the tale,
>   That from the time we parted
>   My cheek grew pale . . .[127]

> Now lock my chamber door, father,

> And say you left me sleeping;
> But never tell my step-mother
> Of all this bitter weeping . . .[128]

Despair over the faithlessness of a lover is a favored subject with Motherwell[129] and Procter.[130]

Indeed the kinship of love and beauty with death became almost an obsession. Juxtaposition of dirge and hymeneal may underline this contrast and kinship. Beddoes has a "Bridal Serenade" which ends

> I'll bless thee dying at thy door,[131]

and a "Dirge and Hymeneal supposed to be sung as the Funeral and Wedding Processions Cross each other at the Church Door";[132] Procter has a "Bridal Dirge."[133] Oftener the poet mourns over a sort of generalized grave of youth and beauty.

> Unhappy has the traveller been
> Who, where the languid flow'rets wave,
> The glitt'ring tears of morn has seen
> On beauty's grave![134]

Mary Robinson had cried. Darley has a frail and rather lovely little poem in the form of an epitaph, called "The Maiden's Grave":

> Here in a little cave,
> the prettiest nook of this most grassy vale,
> all amid lilies pale,
> that turn
> their heads into my little vault and mourn—
> Stranger! I have made my grave . . .[135]

All but one of Beddoes' half dozen miscellaneous dirges

(outside the dramas) are for young maidens.[136] The gentle
tears of Barry Cornwall are continually bedewing the untimely grave of loveliness.[137] There is no story—only a
generalized emotion—in Motherwell's little dirge over the
grave of lovers too early dead:

> Ding dong! ding dong!
> The church bells loom
> Above the tomb
> Where true loves meet.
> Ding dong! Ding dong!
> How sad and sweet![138]

"How sad and sweet"! Poe's belief that there is nothing
in the whole world so poetical as the death of a young
and beautiful woman (he might have added, except possibly the death of a pair of young and beautiful lovers)
is rooted deep in English romanticism.

V

The unexpected objectivity of much of this poetry of
unhappy love may prepare us for the overwhelming volume and importance of the narrative verse on the subject. There are innumerable little poems in lyric measures
presenting one of the situations of which we have been
speaking—unrequited love, the deserted and broken-
hearted girl, the dying lover of either sex—of which it is
difficult to decide whether they are more nearly lyric or
narrative. In this group the influence of the ballads is
very strong. Another large group consists of poems of
varying length which are clearly revisions or imitations
of the ballads. The long descriptive and didactic poems

which continued to be written continued also to be embellished by sad love stories. The long narrative poems made popular by Scott and Byron and written by almost all the romanticists are to a surprising extent occupied wholly or in part by various themes of love melancholy. In contrast to romantic novels, romantic love-stories in verse typically end in tragedy, usually in the death of one or both of the lovers. It will be observed that when it came to telling *stories* of unhappy love, the women were as industrious as the men; and that the men, on the other hand, tended to emphasize the feminine point of view and to be as sentimental as the women. It will be simpler and less repetitious to follow certain characteristic themes of this mass of narrative and semi-narrative verse, rather than to examine the various types of poem separately.

Unrequited love, that staple of the elegies and other lyrics, is not, even for the semi-lyric group, a favored subject. This might be accounted for either by the faint implication of imperfection, which the poet would rather throw on some subordinate character than on his hero or heroine, or by the lack of incident normal to such a situation. Yet little incident is necessary to the briefer ballad-like type, and one may go mad or die of a broken heart as well for unrequited love as for desertion[139] or bereavement. There are of course instances of this plot. The unfortunate one is sometimes the man, oftener the woman. Perhaps the lover scorned merely

> Associates with the midnight shadows drear;
> And, sighing to the lonely taper, pours
> His sadly tortur'd heart into the page.[140]

But sometimes he dies of a broken heart. Scott, unexpectedly enough, has an excellent example of the hero who slowly fades from hopeless love: for young Wilfrid (in "Rokeby") is presented as too sympathetic and important a character to be less than at least a joint hero of the tale. Or the lover may seek death on the field of battle, especially if the story belongs to the medieval revival:

> He scorned to weep, he scorned to sigh,
>   Heigho! the Wind and Rain;
> But like a true knight he could die,—
>   Ah, well-a-day! Life's vain.[141]

A woman, being denied this last recourse, usually pines away to an early grave.[142]

Much more popular is the plot of lovers separated by cruel fate—or rather, as usually happens, by cruel parents. Sometimes these tales come out happily at long last; sometimes the lovers meet only in death; sometimes they part to meet no more. A reasonably early example of the type in which the tragedy is temporary is Anna Seward's "Louisa" (1782),[143] already referred to. This poem has to do with the sufferings of Eugenio and Louisa, when the former is forced, in order to save his father from ruin, to marry an heiress. The epistolary form, some of the high-flown sentiment, and the descriptions of the night-wanderings of the despairing lovers in this poem are all reminiscent of *La Nouvelle Héloise,* although the descriptions also betray the influence of *Ossian.* The ending is sufficiently sentimental: the heiress conveniently dies of dissipation, and all meet around her deathbed in a shower of forgiving tears. If this tale is after Rousseau, a nearly contemporary story of almost fatally high-

minded lovers who finally reap the reward of virtue—
Thomas Whalley's *Edwy and Edilda*[144]—stems from the
medieval revival. It is in a ballad measure, and has to do
with the faithful loves of a poor shepherd and a nobleman's daughter in the time of Egbert. It is very badly
written and very sentimental, and yields some amusingly
Della Cruscan descriptive bits: the soul of the humble
Edwy has "open'd at the tender touch of sensibility";
when Edilda hears of her father's recent danger, "Her
pulse decay'd" and "the pearly sorrows flow." Another
and later example of this type, George Croly's "Sebastian"
(about 1820),[145] reveals the exotic influences from Spain
and the Orient. This "Spanish Tale" has all the expected
elements save the tyrannical father: a girl hides her hopeless love in a convent; later, when her lover is again free,
she runs away and follows him in disguise, singing wild
sad Moorish airs on her harp and fainting in his arms,
but fleeing again when his love is awakened; at length, in
a garden, he overhears her broken-hearted soliloquy of
love and repentance and despair. Unexpectedly to the
reader, she does not die in his arms; on the contrary, a
dispensation is obtained from the Pope and all is merry
as a wedding bell. The story is told from the point of view
of the melancholy and tantalized lover, and contains various quotable phrases descriptive of this romantic hero-
type:

> The melting, melancholy gaze above
> Show'd that the heart within was made for love . . .

> His face, so sad, so pale, so beautiful,
> Fix'd on the moon . . .

He lean's his folded arms and high pale brow
Against the casement's side. The light below
Fell, snowlike, thick, on palace-roofs and spires:
" 'Twas a vain world." He cast his eye above,
And gave the musings way . . .[146]

Sometimes the lovers meet at last, but only to taste the bitterness of death. Such a tale is Motherwell's "Clerke Richard and Maid Margaret,"[147] which tells of how, after parting in hate and anger, these two met once again to die in each other's arms. Such also is the fate of the lovers in Darley's much longer "Sorrows of Hope."[148] In this melancholy and somewhat sentimental tale appears also a variant of the theme, so frequent in *Ossian*, of a girl attending her lover as a page or youthful male companion.[149] In Darley's poem the two, parted by family tyranny, do not meet till after long years of despairing wanderings, and then do not recognize each other—so has suffering wrought upon them—until the heroine lies dying from a wound inflicted by the hero's wicked brother.

But oftenest it happens that the parting is final. Perhaps the girl goes into a convent: the fascination of monasticism for the romanticists has already been remarked. Whether this or some other unsurmountable barrier arises between them, one or both of the lovers will usually die of heart-break. There is a love story of this type (without the convent—the date is too early for that detail) embedded in Falconer's "Shipwreck" (1762-64).[150] Palemon is sent away by a ruthless father to prevent his marrying beneath him. When he perishes in the wreck, still cherishing Anna's picture, his friend Arion seeks his home with his last message, only to find that not only has

Anna gone a "lovely victim to the tomb," but the stern
father himself is about to die of remorse. Another rather
early story of this type is inserted in a descriptive ode in
the *London Magazine* (1770);[151] here both lovers die.
The same catastrophe closes Mallet's mournful ballad of
"Edwin and Emma" (1760).[152]

Among the earlier stories of this type which use the
convent material is T. P. Robinson's *Jessy* (1785),[153]
said, like so many of these tales, to be founded on fact.
It is the monologue of a girl forced by her father to give
up her lover and take the vows of a nun. This she has
just done, and feels dead to all things, even God. At the
end she cries

> Then hail ye glooms, ye silent horrors hail! . . .

But the contemplation of the accumulated horrors she
conjures up is the last stroke, and she sinks into the swoon
of death. The churchyard-Gothic element is strong also in
a "ballad" (1790) called "The Convent,"[154] which tells of
a nun and her lover trying vainly to find each other in
the vaults of a convent, and of her slow death by starva-
tion and despair.

Wordsworth, haunted, it has been surmised, by memories of Annette Vallon and her little daughter, put into
blank verse (1805) a tragic story of this type, also said
to be founded on fact.[155] After a period of periodic separa-
tions, suffering, and on Vaudracour's part, manslaughter
and imprisonment, Julia, it will be remembered, is forced
to enter a convent; Vaudracour retires to the wilderness
with the child, and, when it dies, goes mad. The convent
figures also in the dénouement of Felicia Hemans' "Tale
of the Secret Tribunal" (1819),[156] a gloomy pseudo-

Byronic story in which the separation of the lovers is less stressed than the filial devotion of the heroine, who insists on following her guilty and hunted father into exile. When he has finally fallen at the avenging hand of his long-lost son, fair Ella retires to a convent, whither the hero, Ulric, follows her—just in time to see her "features brightly pale" hidden beneath the "impenitrable veil." Mary Robinson has a tale with an even more dramatic conclusion. Anselmo, after several years spent as a hermit because his cruel family has separated him from his lady, finally wanders forth to find her, only to chance on her funeral in a convent. He dies on the spot from shock.[157] Campbell has a small ballad-like poem (1820) about how a false report of the death of "the brave Roland" drove his lady into a convent, and of how he, returning home just too late, dwelt near the cloister till she died, then sought his own death in battle.[158] Letitia Landon tells the same legend, with variations and at more length, in "Roland's Tower"; the variations, calculated to heighten the sentimentality of the plot, include a daily signal from the imprisoned nun, and the expiring of the lover on his lady's tomb.[159] Another of her tales of this particular group—practically all her innumerable stories concern love-tragedies of some sort—is "The Wreath," a pseudo-Moorish tale of lovers who renounce each other because of the difference in their religions. He died in battle, but she—

> She died as dies a breath of song
> Borne on the wind of evening along;
> She fell as falls the rose in spring.
> The fairest are most perishing.[160]

—which would seem to present the extreme type of sentimental heroine and sentimental love melancholy in a nutshell.

In Byron's contributions to this type, it is always the woman who cannot survive the separation. The most appealing of these unfortunate heroines, Haidée (in "Don Juan"),[161] has so much spirit that one is a little resentful of her finding it so much harder to forget than did her lover. But Byron's treatment of love (in fiction, that is, not in life) was frequently conventionally sentimental—witness the mellifluous sentimentality of the nightingale-and-rose passage at the conclusion of "The Bride of Abydos"—and even in "Don Juan" he can pause to ask:

> Oh, Love! what is it in this world of ours
> Which makes it fatal to be loved? Ah why
> With cypress branches hast thou wreathed thy bowers,
> And made thy best interpreter a sigh?[162]

Sometimes the lovers perish together, usually by drowning.[163] One of the sad love-stories in Carey's "Visions of Sensibility" is about how Juliet and Antonio were drowned in each other's arms, and how the "Maids of Ocean" strewed over them "ambrosial sweets, and tears," and lamentations.[164] Campbell's "Lord Ullin's Daughter" (1804) is a good example of the ballad type in this group. It is a spirited telling of how the lady eloped with her true love, how, fleeing from the hot pursuit, they persuaded the ferryman to row them over Lochgyle in the midst of a raging storm, and how the remorseful father reached the shore just in time to see them perish.[165] A similar story, in which the catastrophe is due to an avalanche, occurs, as has been previously noted, in Peacock's "Philosophy of Melancholy." Southey has a variant (1798) ending in double suicide to escape capture by the tyrannous father.[166]

But much more frequently in these tales—as in life—one lover is left to mourn the other. In romantic poetry there are, it would seem, only three possible courses open to the bereaved one: he or she may die of a broken heart, go mad, or commit suicide. Various instances have already been cited of a man's actually dying of heart-break because of unrequited or thwarted love, even if we discount the protestations of despairing lovers in lyric form. That it should happen occasionally also for bereavement is to be expected. The thing does occur in actuality at times, of course, [167] and all that the sentimental romanticists did was to multiply and idealize instances. Such tragedies, attributed to the loss (usually sudden and violent) of the beloved, are chronicled now and then all through the latter half of the eighteenth century, though they seem to fall off after about 1805. Sometimes the shock kills the mourner at once; sometimes he lingers for weeks or months before he succumbs. Both George Keate's descriptive poem on *The Alps* (1763)[168] and Grainger's exposition of "The Sugar Cane" (1764)[169] are diversified by such tales. In the former the bride is overwhelmed by an avalanche, in the latter struck by lightning; in each, as Grainger expressed it, when the bridegroom had looked upon the ruin of his happiness,

> He sigh'd, he swoon'd, look'd up, and died away.

Often, especially in the poems imitated from the ballads,

the beloved's death is by the violence of man, and in at
least one instance (1798),[170] baffled vengeance contributes
to the lover's decline. In one story noted (1770), the
bride's death seems to be due to her too great sensibility,
as she dies in her lover's arms at the altar, apparently of
pure joy; he follows her before the day is out, and they
are buried in one grave.[171] Two or three of this group
noted, show strong influence from *Ossian:* one by Kirke
White (about 1800)[172] is the lyric monologue of a lover
dying on the "verdant grave" of the lost one; one by
Robert Couper (1804)[173] represents the dead lover's ghost
as leaning from an Ossianic cloud to tell his mournful
story.

Men only occasionally go mad for love in romantic
story. It is with a distinct shock of surprise that the reader
realizes that such a little poem as the octosyllabics on
"Madness" in the *European Magazine* for April, 1787,[174]
refers to a *man* seeking his lost love, and not to a woman.
Much the most interesting romantic study of insanity in
a mournful love story seems to me to be Bryan Waller
Procter's "Marcian Colonna" (1820).[175] This poem, based
on an Italian legend, is, within the limits of its period and
type, an honest analysis of intermittent melancholia, and
of the terrible suffering it brought upon the patient himself and upon the woman he loved. In the end it drives
him to murder her in order to prevent her over-conscien-
tous return to a hated husband, whom they had supposed
to be dead. This poem also contains a characteristic romantic diatribe against monasticism, apropos of Marcian's
involuntary detention as a youth in a monastary.

Nor are there many instances of suicide on the part of

bereaved lovers, in spite of Werther. For that matter, not a bereavement but a separation occasioned Werther's suicide, like that threatened by St. Preux in *La Nouvelle Héloise;* and a good many love-suicides of men for other causes have been noted in English romantic verse. Southey has one for bereavement in "Madoc."[176] The suicide of the bard Carril, in Sayers' "Moina," at the news of the sacrifice of his mistress at her husband's funeral rites, was originally followed by a chorus in praise of the deed; but this was subsequently struck out when the author became more strictly pious, "from excessive moral scrupulosity," as his friend and editor explains, "lest the praise of heroic suicide should perhaps operate dangerously in common life, and prepare some hesitating sufferer for a rash and unhallowed act."[177]

But it is the women who most frequently lose life or reason because of the loss of a lover.[178] The obsession of the preromantic and romantic writers with this theme is perhaps the clearest indication of the shifting point of view of which we have spoken. It was right, according to the sentimental ideal, that a woman should be too delicately balanced to bear a grievous emotional shock; and it was right—even inevitable—according to social convention, that a woman should so center her whole being in devotion to a lover or husband that his loss would leave her nothing to fall back upon. And a sensitive human creature with no work to busy her, no future to look forward to, is in life as in literature an easy prey to consumption[179] or to that vague fading away which our ancestors euphemistically referred to as "a decline." The literary convention—borrowed from the ballads and *Os-*

sian—whereby perhaps half of these poetic victims die at once upon the body of the beloved is more diffi-cult of belief, and doubtless has less foundation in fact, though such things, too, have been known to occur.

In this group of poems on the death of a woman be-reaved of her lover, the ballad influence, with strong con-tributory influence from *Ossian,* is predominant. This is especially true before about 1800. The later long narrative poems are frequently after the Italians, especially Boccac-cio—whose tales, while more sophisticated, are no less violent. A not unusual situation in both these sources is that of the death of the lover at the hands of the enraged father or brother of the girl; the bereaved maiden falls upon his body and dies.[180] Part I of Joanna Baillie's "Night Scenes of Other Times" (1790) is a pleasant il-lustration of the fusion of Ossian and the true ballads in this type of tale. The girl is wandering over the all-but-inevitable bleak heath, on which she meets her murdered lover's ghost:

> The night winds bellow o'er my head,
>   Dim grows the fading light.
> Where shall I find some friendly shed
>   To screen me from the night?
>
> .   .   .   .
>
> For angry spirits of the night
>   Ride on the troubled air . . .[181]

If the lover is not murdered or killed in single combat, he is likely to fall in war. Then, if the woman is near enough to seek his body among the slain, she sometimes falls upon it and dies; otherwise she will fade away to an

early grave.[182] Mary, the Scottish peasant girl who is
heroine of a ballad by Mary Robinson, is more like the
heroines of the longer sentimental tales than most ballad-
heroines. She liked to sing "sad and plaintive" songs to
the moon; and

> Her eye was dimm'd with sorrow's tears,
>   Which from their azure fountain roll'd;
> Her throbbing heart was fraught with fears;
>   Pale was her cheek, and deadly cold!

This was due to her friendless situation. What wonder
then that when her lover was killed in battle, she wandered forth over "the thistled heath" and, lost "amidst
the frowns of night," was chilled by "the cold blast" and
died?[183] "O Love and Death!" cries Felicia Hemans,[184]

> Ye have sad meetings in this changeful earth,
> Many and sad! . . .

It may be added that of course not all these meetings are
in scenes of mutual slaughter. Accident or disease or unspecified causes of mortality may make as sad a record—
and as good a story.[185]

If the victim of grief does not die, but loses her reason,
she is almost always represented as wandering alone in
the wilderness, like Scott's Madge Wildfire,[186] often singing some wild song.[187] Her unbound hair loose on the
wind, she wanders over some desolate moor,[188] or, amidst
the midnight blasts, plays with the ivy overspreading some
ruined abbey, imagining that the night-owl's shriek is her
drowned lover's voice.[189] Or the "lovely maniac" climbs
some promontory over the "melancholy main" to bewail
his death.[190] Among the longer narratives of this group,

those by Beddoes, Procter, and Campbell, are of interest.
Beddoes' "Albert and Emily,"[191] a youthful production
(1821), tells of how Albert was struck dead by lightning
as Emily clung to him during a storm, and how all summer she haunted the scene of the tragedy, protected by
her innocent loveliness and singing a wild sad ditty, then
one chilly autumn night died kneeling on his grave. Procter retells the story of the pot of basil (1820);[192] in his
version, when Isabella perceives that her cruel brothers
have taken away her lover's heart, she flees "into the
dreary wilderness . . . a craz'd heart-broken thing," and
only after long months does she wander home to die. In
"The Girl of Provence" (1823)[193] he matches Keats's
legend of Endymion in love with the Moon, with a Medi-
terranean story of a girl driven to madness by an hallu-
cination that she has been the bride of Apollo, the Sun.
Most appealing of all, perhaps, is Campbell's somewhat
earlier story, with Irish background, concerning "O'Connor's pale and lovely child" (1809).[194] This has a haunting romantic music—

> Sad was the note, and wild its fall,
> As winds that moan at night forlorn
> Along the isles of Fion-Gall.[195]

It tells of a lady, not after all very seriously deranged, who
dwells in the wilderness beside the grave of the lover her
cruel brothers tore from her very arms one ghastly night
and slew before her eyes.[196]

Suicide as a result of the loss of a lover by death is
also somewhat more frequent among the heroines than
among the heroes of romance. Lovers' suicides, in the

pastorals, the ballads, and the tales, for whatever cause
and whatever the sex of the lover, are almost invariably
by drowning, normally by a leap off a precipice into the
water. Thus the grieving girl, sane or insane, who wanders
by a stream or haunts the characteristic romantic precipice over the water, may one day leap over it to join her
drowned lover.[197] Two examples of these love-suicides
must suffice. The first, Chatterton's "Elinore and Jura,"[198]
one of the Rowley poems, is chosen because it illustrates
the use of melancholy and even graveyard material. Jura
says to Elinore:

> Sisters in Sorrow, on this daisied bank,
> Where Melancholy broods, we will lament,

and likens herself and her friend to "leven'd oaks" and
"forletten halls of merriment" where "lethal ravens bark
and owlets wake the night." Elinore replies by saying that
she will go at night to the graveyard and relate her woes
to the "passing sprites." In the end, receiving news that
their lovers have fallen in battle, they leap together over a
cliff. The other example is from the time of the full romantic triumph—Darley's haunting if oversentimental
song of "The Enchanted Lyre."[199] It begins

> Listen to the Lyre!
> Listen to the knelling of its sweet-toned ditty!
> Shrilly now as Pain resounds the various wire,
> Now as soft as Pity!
> Soft as Pity!

The story the wind-touched lyre (an instrument much
fancied by the romanticists) sang to the Dreamer was of
a maiden "once the flower, The all-beloved lily of this

sweet, sweet valley," who had leaped after a lover drawn down by "the flood's green daughters," into the "roaring wave"—

> Where amid the billows I was shown my grave
> With a hideous laughter!
> Hideous laughter!

—and who now, finding no peace in Heaven, haunts the spot where her coffinless love is lying. See how "with this deep wail" the "very bosom-strings" of the harp, "like mine, are broken!" Here we have the marvellously mellifluous music of the romantic lyrists put at the disposal of that vague sentimental emotionalism which was both their beauty and their bane.

A large and interesting group of melancholy love-poems concern women whose suffering arises not from the absence or death of their true lovers but from the loneliness and shame of desertion. The seduced and forsaken maiden is a common theme of folk-poetry; and humanitarian and semi-feminist tendencies in the latter half of the eighteenth century also stimulated interest in her and a sympathetic attitude toward her plight. The man involved is often vigorously blamed,[200] and not infrequently dies of remorse when he realizes the havoc he has wrought.[201] The girl herself is sometimes overcome with remorse, and perhaps returns home to seek forgiveness, or half rejoices that she has no home to darken with her shame.[202] Occasionally she kills herself.[203] Sometimes, like her sisters who grieve over a lover's death, she wanders mad over the heath, perhaps to destroy herself in the end.[204] Wordsworth has a group of poems about deserted women, all

written in 1798-99[205]—an interesting fact, whether or not
it has any biographical significance. In two of these the
woman's wits are wandering. Motherwell has a rather attractive lament or "mad-song" of such a woman.[206] Oftenest of all, the deserted one dies heart-broken from grief
and shame. Her story is told in ballad, song, and poetic
tale.

> In no-one's face she look'd—her bloom
>   Was fading—and for ever . . .[207]

> No human form could she behold
>   Across the barren heath;
> Her pallid cheek grew deathly cold,—
>   She sunk inwrapp'd in Death . . .[208]

Some of this at least is legitimate poetry. Yet sometimes,
unfortunately, the blight of sentimentalism falls over this
situation too, as in such truly incomprehensible nonsense
as "Naemia; or, the Tears of Sensibility,"[209] in which a
supersensitive damsel wanders forth on her wonted "path
of Pain" one highly Gothic night when "poised on the
tempest—sat Despair!" She finds the "ruined" Naemia
distractedly weeping, and having heard her story and seen
her fall prostrate on the "rude clay that gave her birth,"
stands a moment, *The weeping spectacle of thought*
(whatever that may be), till her fine nerves give way and
"on her cheeks the lilies died." Whether either or both of
them ever recovered is not stated.

VI

All of which brings us to say a word in conclusion
about the heroes and heroines of the poetry of sentimen-

tal-romantic love melancholy. That the heroine approaches the feminine ideal of sensibility must have become evident from the plots and quotations given. The ideal might be further illuminated *ad infinitum* from this verse and that of kindred themes of family affection, love of country, and the like. The young hero is also a man of delicate feeling, chaste and loyal, brave and gentle, often with an ingrained melancholy of temperament. Shelley's heroes and heroines owe much to the sentimental conception, but are so much more essentially ideals and symbols than they are human lovers that we must not pause on them here. It may be remarked in passing, however, that his heroines, especially Cythna, represent much more fully than those of any feminine writer a conception of true equality of the sexes. Cythna, indeed, as her other name of Laone indicates, is as it were the feminine half of an ideal of which Laon is the masculine half, and the glory and the martyrdom are not more his by right of actual first hand participation than they are hers.[210]

It is interesting to observe, on the other hand, the fate of the Byronic hero-type[211] at the hands of Byron's feminine followers, the two most popular and prolific writers of narrative verse at the close of our period—Felicia Dorothea Hemans and Letitia Elizabeth Landon ("L. E. L.").

Mrs. Hemans was a very religious and very sentimental person, but she had her own gentle, if not very subtle, strength, as deeply sentimental and religious women often have. She delighted in tales of steadfast courage and loyal martyrdom to some noble cause, and, seeking such tales in the history and legends of many lands, assiduously turned them into idealizing verse. One turns her pages of narratives, therefore, expecting and finding records such as that of the faith and devotion of the last Constantine in his final battle,[212] or the story of the noble woman who all one terrible night soothed her husband's dying agonies on the wheel.[213] Yet she was fascinated by the dark-souled Byronic hero. Something of his proud and defiant suffering she transferred to certain of her heroines, notably Zayda in "The Abencerrage" (1819); yet Zayda is utterly without guilt, and in the end dies to prove her steadfast love for the man she has repudiated.[214] Something of the Byronic preoccupation with remorse she transferred to an occasional character not quite the hero of the tale: to Otho, the treacherous emperor in "The Wife of Crescentius,"[215] to the father in "A Tale of the Secret Tribunal."[216] But these men lack the defiance and lonely pride of the Byronic type, and the latter at least dies a humble and pious penitent. She came remarkably near success in Hamet, the hero of "The Abencerrage," which is a "Moorish" tale, the central situation of which is closely parallel to that in "The Siege of Corinth." Hamet, seeking vengeance on the treacherous Moorish King for the death of his kindred, turns apostate, like Byron's Alp, and leads the Spaniards to the destruction of his own people. Like Alp, he is devoured by remorse, and like him steals away by night after a battle to indulge in lonely musing. Like Alp, too, he is in love with the daughter of his enemy. He is proud and lonely and brooding:

> His was a lofty spirit, turned aside
> From its bright path by woes, and wrongs, and pride . . .[217]

But Byron would never have allowed so much spirit to the heroine, nor would he have allowed his hero to come so close in the end to humility and heart-break, or to pine away in silence until he lay beside his mistress in the tomb over which the woods and waves moaned an eternal dirge. Felicia Hemans was after all too calmly poised and religious a person to have sympathy with real and unrepentant guilt.[218]

As for Letitia Landon, her difficulty was not so much moral or religious scruples as it was sheer lack of artistic and intellectual stiffening. Her "lyre" was ever wreathed with withering roses, and she never woke it except to plaintive strains of languid sorrow in some twilit cypress grove. It is a rare thing for one of her stories to close without at least one too-fond youth's or maiden's having sunk to an early grave. Her heroes, especially in the earlier poems, are wont to be palely proud and remotely melancholy, in obvious imitation of Byron:

> But on his cold, pale cheek were caught
> The traces of some deeper thought,
> A something seen of pride and gloom
> Not like youth's hour of light and bloom:
> A brow of pride, a lip of scorn,—
>   Yet beautiful in scorn and pride . . .[219]

But one never believes in this alleged pride and scorn— the fabric is too soft. She says of another of these heroes that there is something almost of "female softness" in the "mingled gloom and flame" of his eye;[220] the softness, unfortunately, is *more* than female. Nevertheless the most interesting thing she did was to attempt the transference of the Byronic hero-type, minus the remorse and in combination with the Edwin-type of misunderstood poet, to her heroines. And even as Byron is always his own hero, so she is always her own heroine; the "withered heart"[221] of which she writes is always her own. "Erinna"[222] is her "Prelude," or rather in spirit her "Childe Harold"; she is "frought with pride, the melancholy pride of thought"; she is "lonely from my childhood hour," given to solitude, early disillusioned. Yet the Byronic echoes seem hollow and pathically futile. She understood better her own artistic character and that of a great deal of the literature of sentimental love melancholy when she wrote:

> My lyre asks but a wreath of fragile flowers.
> I have told passionate tales of bleeding hearts,
> Of young cheeks fading even before the rose;
> My songs have been the mournful history
> Of woman's tenderness and woman's tears;
> I have touch'd but the spirit's gentlest chords,—
> Surely the fittest for my maiden hand;—
> And in their truth my immortality.[223]

CHAPTER VI

THE SOUNDING CATARACT

The tender dimness of the night appeared
Darkening to deeper sorrow, and the voice
Of the far torrent from the silent hills
Flow'd, as I listen'd, like a funeral strain
Breath'd by some mourning solitary thing.
—*Wilson*

Into almost every phase of our discussion of the melancholy arising out of man's attitude toward time and death and God and human affection, has entered as background or undertone something of man's attitude toward the world of external nature. This would be almost inevitable in any but a completely urban civilization, if such a thing be possible; in a civilization so basically rural in economy and so increasingly primitivistic in thought as that of the England of our period, it is quite inevitable. But so important a part does nature play in preromantic and romantic melancholy that such incidental and implied discussion is utterly inadequate: much more is needed for an understanding of the tendencies of the transition period or the melancholy masterpieces of the great romanticists.

For our purposes, perhaps four of the possible attitudes toward nature are of especial importance. The approach may be essentially religious. Nature will then be thought of as primarily a revelation of Deity; and when melancholy occurs at all, it will be the religious solemnity of adoration or the contemplation of human sins and mortality. Or the approach may be in less or greater degree subjective or lyric. Nature may become the favored and congenial setting for pensive musing, half philosophical, half personal. From the least subjective end of this gamut the changes may be rung through all the notes of more and more intense introspection to a subjectivity in which consciousness of nature is almost absorbed in the ego. The dangers besetting this last type are sentimentality and a too loose dealing in pathetic fallacy. Again, the approach may be less individual and more social. Nature may become the arena of human tragedy, or melancholy may arise from a sorrowful contemplation of the encroachments of industrialism or human short-sightedness on nature's domains. Lastly, the approach may be metaphysical and touched with mysticism. There arises the conception of nature as the nurse and teacher of the poet—a conception not in theory necessarily melancholy, but in practise very often so. And in certain ardent spirits, the religious, the philosophical, the individual, the social, and the poetical may fuse and culminate in adoration of nature as the encircling mystic reality, and in moments of ecstatic personal identification with her. In this, the most purely romantic and lyric of all the moods, the presence or absence of melancholy will depend essentially on the temperament of the poet: Blake may be lifted to glory by contemplating the myriad of angelic presences that are the sun—or Shelley may become the mournful lyre of the autumnal wind.

Obviously, these moods and attitudes are not mutually exclusive. What moods and attitudes are? Each poet, especially in a period of ferment and experimentation, will make his own choices and combinations. But if the reader will bear with necessary doublings and approximations, such an arrangement will be found to be roughly chronological (at least so far as origins go) and reasonably convenient.

I

The attitude toward nature which sees in it primarily an argument for the existence and beneficence of God, is not of course essentially melancholy—rather the contrary. It is not surprising therefore that such of the long descriptive poems stemming from "Grongar Hill" and "The Seasons" as are essentially religious in point of view, owe any touches of melancholy they may have to other elements. This being so, they will be more conveniently grouped with other descriptive poems having a different emphasis. But in certain of the descriptive poems which are indebted to Young as well as to Thomson, and in a good many of the innumerable odes, sonnets, elegies, and other reflective pieces on the seasons, the times of day, and so forth, certain distinctively religious and at the same time melancholy motifs recur.

Thus an ode to spring may end on the melancholy reflection that when once the "spring of life" is over, it returns only if our prospect is "lengthen'd through the vale of death" to Paradise.[1] Autumn, of course even likelier to inspire melancholy moralizing, may lead an aging poet to a resolution to leave fruit behind him, like the dying year,[2] or a younger one to exhort himself or his lady to lay up virtue and honor against the coming of old age;[3] or its melancholy implications may send the poet for comfort

to his belief in immortality.[4] Fading flowers, especially in
the hands of women, have ever aroused poets with a didactic turn of mind to similar reflections; in mid-eighteenth century it was especially fashionable to admonish
"the fair" concerning these things.[5] Or an evening meditation may take a religious turn. The poet may welcome
nightfall because it brings him one day nearer heaven,[6]
or draw from it the somber moral of the relentless passage
of time toward the judgment day,[7] or compare its solemn
beauty with the greater beauty of God.[8] Religious and
philosophical meditation are of course too closely allied
to be always separable. James Hurdis has them walking
together in the melancholy woodland shades:

> Such is the haunt
> Religion loves, a meek and humble maid,
> Whose tender eye bears not the blaze of day.
> And here with Meditation hand in hand
> She walks, and feels her often-wounded heart
> Renew'd and heal'd . . .[9]

Bernard Barton, the Quaker poet, is a good example of the
essentially religious attitude toward nature persisting into
the romantic period; yet his nature poems are by no
means always melancholy.

Naturally the poems on night were a most attractive
vehicle for religious meditation. Something has already
been said of them in connection with the influence of
"Night Thoughts." But the occurrence of religious elements in these poems goes far outside the circle of the
followers of Young. Probably more than half the odes,
sonnets, and other verses to night, at least before 1800,
include some reference to Deity. Often the orthodox de-

tails of pensive description—the "sad nightingale," the "midnight owl" that steals from the "tott'ring ruins of some antient dome . . . bent on black deeds," the invocation to "sacred silence!"—will be followed by a passage of praise or prayer.[10] Or a midnight storm turns the poet's thoughts to God.[11] Sometimes the main point of the poem is an enumeration of the uses or abuses of night; such poems will be deeply moral if not actually religious. One of the most pretentious of the treatments of night, after Young's, is of this type: George Harley's long blank verse "Night" (1796), which begins with a general welcome to Night in her "shadowy car," but thereafter concerns itself almost wholly with an enumeration of the wrong ways to use the time of darkness, with the merest mention of the right ways.[12] This poet, by the way, was an actor, and is especially concerned with the state of the theater; his poem is moral rather than religious, and seems to owe little except perhaps the general conception to Young. But the abuses-of-night poems take us too far from our subject of the melancholy treatment of nature.

The religious motif most frequent in the night poems, however, might serve as a symbol for the religious attitude in its more somber aspect. This motif is the meditation on the starry heavens. Besides being in itself almost inevitable as an expression of the religious attitude toward nocturnal nature, the theme has the authority not only of Young, who has been credited with the beginning of English poetical moon-worship,[13] but also of Hervey. Hervey's *Contemplations on the Night* and *Contemplations on the Starry Heavens* (1747), much less florid and melodramatic than his *Meditations among the Tombs,* carry on his prose imitations of Young, and seem to have been only less popular than the *Meditations* themselves. Young had used the Newtonian system of astronomy as an argument for Christianity;[14] the minor verse of the next three generations echoed the idea in many a half-poetical, half-doctrinal meditation from study window or star-lit field. The theme occurs in several poems already referred to in other connections: in "The Pleasures of the Night" (1747) and "Il Meditante" (1752) (Chapter II), in Kirke White's "Time" (c. 1803) (Chapters III and IV), in Robert Montgomery's "Death" (1827) (Chapter IV). William Woty (1760), his mind turned to "solemn musing and celestial wonder" by the "dirge" of Philomel and the "pleasing melancholy air" of the owl, gazes upon the moonlit sky and decides that atheists—if such may be, in the face of the glory of the nocturnal heavens—will wake "in torments wrapt."[15] A little blank verse poem called "An Astronomical Thought" (1782)[16] is headed with the quotation from Young: "An undevout astronomer is mad." Michael Bruce (1786), sitting on the shore of Lochleven, watches the twilight fade into darkness and raises a song of praise to the "Maker of yon starry sky," who

> Pours life, and bliss, and beauty, pours Himself,
> His own essential goodness, o'er the minds
> Of happy being, thro' ten thousand worlds.[17]

Anna Barbauld, musing deep into a summer evening, feels her thoughts sweep through the universe, out beyond the stars, and wishes that in this quiet place she might "wait the appointed time, And ripen for the skies."[18] Robert Bloomfield's Farmer Boy (1798)—we might call this the meditation on the starry heavens new style—is fascinated by the wintry sky on his way to tend his snow-bound flock, and sees the stars as a great flock of sheep which "aloud proclaim Their Mighty Shepherd's everlasting Name."[19] A blank verse meditation on the night (1810), after making its bows to Milton and Collins and discussing the exile and the shipwrecked mariner, concludes with the poet's forgetting his own sorrows as he gazes on the star-strewn heavens and praises God.[20] Even Satan, in Robert Montgomery's account of him (1830), cannot forbear growing half reconciled to God under the canopy of the midnight sky.[21]

II

Most of the melancholy poems on seasons and times of day, with the exception of those on night, are, however, more philosophical or personal than religious, more beholden to "Il Penseroso," the "Elegy in a Country Churchyard," the "Ode to Evening," "The Enthusiast," and "The Pleasures of Melancholy" than to "Night Thoughts" and *Contemplations on the Starry Heavens*. The love of wandering at evening along the banks of some quiet river and listening to the mournful notes of Philomel in a mood of half-philosophical, half-sentimental melancholy, has already been illustrated again and again in the pseudo-Miltonic odes discussed in Chapter II. But the odes are only a small part of this literature, and Milton is only the earliest of many masters of the mood. Of the mid-century secondary masters—Gray, Shenstone, Collins, Joseph and Thomas Warton—something has also been said, in Chapter I and elsewhere.

There now arose, in the generation after theirs, what

was almost a school of young poets, attracted primarily by the work and personalities of the brothers Warton— who were both educators, it may be remarked, and thus in a particularly advantageous position to pass on their ideas. Thomas Russell (1762-1788) and William Lisle Bowles (1762-1850) sat under Joseph Warton at Winchester. Both went on to Oxford, where Bowles chose Trinity College because of Thomas Warton's presence as Senior Fellow there. At Trinity he was an intimate of Henry Headley (1766-1788), another of the group. John Bampfylde (1754-1796), on the other hand, was a Cambridge man, and on his part, or that of Samuel Morse Oram (1767-1793), there seems to have been no direct personal contact with the masters. It was at Cambridge also that Henry Kirke White (1785-1806), who may be counted a belated member of the group, worked himself into a fatal consumption at the beginning of the new century. But most of the poets mentioned publicly identified themselves with the Wartons and the things they stood for. At only twenty-two, Headley, inspired by Thomas Warton's antiquarian activities, published his *Select Beauties of the Ancient English Poets,* a landmark in the revival of the older poetry of which critics still speak with respect. At twenty, Russell ably defended Thomas Warton's *History of English Poetry* against the irascible Ritson.[22] Bampfylde wrote a sonnet on the appearance of the *History,* in which he declared that the old bards would weave for the author a "laureate wreathe that ne'er will die."[23] Both Bowles and White wrote poetical tributes to Thomas Warton.[24]

It was an ill-fated group. Of them all, only Bowles and Bampfylde lived beyond the age of twenty-six, and Bampfylde went hopelessly insane at twenty-two. Headley, Russell, and White died of tuberculosis, at twenty-three, twenty-five, and twenty-one respectively. Except Oram, of whose life little is known, and White, whose mistress was his insatiable thirst for knowledge, each of them suffered deeply from an unfortunate love affair, which with Headley, Bampfylde, and Russell was credited with being partly responsible for their surrender to disease. When compared with the life-stories of the greatest among the younger romantic generation, these facts make one wonder if there is after all some subtle psychological or physiological connection between romantic genius in poetry and physical suffering and disease. For some at least among these youths had a spark of the true fire, and it was fire of a quality as nearly akin to true romanticism, as distinct from mere sentimentalism, as that of anyone else in their generation.

Their verse is practically all of a melancholy cast—a fact doubtless due partly to their models and partly to the circumstances of their lives; and it is for the most part concerned with nature. Their achievement, as far as the melancholy treatment of nature is concerned, was to combine, at their best, a real and observing love for her in her gently elegiac moods with an infusion of subjectivity which yet kept clear of pathetic fallacy or sentimentality.

Bampfylde, the oldest of the group, carried on Warton's work with the sonnet, and produced, besides certain sonnets of a humanitarian cast, several really exquisite vignettes of nature in melancholy mood. He observes the sea in storm and calm;[25] he celebrates country retirement.[26] He describes the "Irksome thrall" of summer rain with touches as felicitous as those of John Clare, the highly

gifted peasant poet of the romantic triumph: in this sonnet he tells of sitting "in parlour dim" to watch

> the wistful train,
> Of dripping poultry, whom the vine's broad leaves
> Shelter no more.—Mute is the mournful plain;
> Silent the swallow sits beneath the thatch,
> And vacant hind hangs pensive o'er his hatch,
> Counting the frequent drop from reeded eaves.[27]

He is a little less original, and by that very token more
typical of the school, in "On the Evening,"[28] which smacks,
though pleasantly enough, of the Milton-Gray-Collins-
Warton composite:

> Slow sinks the glimmering beam from western sky;
> And woods and hills, obscured by Evening gray,
> Vanish from mortal sight, and fade away.
> Now with the flocks and yearlings let me hie
> To farm, or cottage lone, where, perch'd hard by,
> On mossy pole the redbreast tunes his lay,
> Soft twittering, and bids farewell to day:
> Then, whilst the watch dog barks, and ploughmen lie,
> Lull'd by the rocking winds, let me unfold
> Whate'er in rhapsody, or strain most holy,
> The hoary minstrel sang in times of old;
> For well, I ween, from them the Nine inspire
> Wisdom shall flow, and Virtue's sacred fire,
> And Peace, and Love, and heavenly Melancholy.

There is also, as there had to be, a tribute to a river.[29]
Bampfylde seems normally to find comfort in nature, although in one lyric cry of agonized love,[30] he admits that
he can no longer find pleasure even in the setting sun.

The work in the sonnet was carried forward by Russell

and Oram. The latter, most obscure of the group, wrote a series of sonnets deeply colored with personal melancholy, and almost all dealing with nature: with the "pleasing melancholy" of congenial sorrow in the song of the nightingale;[31] with the rural churchyard;[32] with the "musing melancholy" of evening and of night;[33] with the woodlark, whose hard fate in winter is like Chatterton's;[34] with the stormy sea, whose shipwrecks are no more tragic than that of the poet's soul.[35] Russell translated sonnets from the Italian, the Spanish, and even the German, and wrote excellent love sonnets of his own. His few nature poems are darkly melancholy: a misanthropic sonnet "To a Spider," which ends with the observation that its cruelty, unlike man's, at least spares its own kind;[36] an owl-sonnet, with graveyard touches, in similar spirit;[37] a sonnet on the joyless return of spring;[38] a despairing ode to Silence and her "sister Solitude."[39] Professor Havens suggests that Bowles may have learned to handle the sonnet not only from Thomas Warton, but from Bampfylde and Russell also.[40]

Headley wrote few sonnets, but his verse is pitched in similar key. His friend Bowles wrote of him as loving to wander "in tearful mood" "Far from the murmuring crowd," at "gray morn" or "meekest eve," or to lie on some cliff and listen to the "murmuring waterfall" or "winter's wind."[41] So it is not surprising to find him writing the "Invocation to Melancholy" and the poem on the "Ruins of Bromholm Priory" referred to in Chapters II and III. He also wrote fragments on the moon and the nightingale,[42] celebrated winter and mountains and rural retirement,[43] and wrote the to-be-expected "Ode to the

Memory of Chatterton."[44] His last two poems, posthumously published, are dark with approaching death: the
elegy called "Sickness"[45] is reminiscent of Gray; in "To
the River Isis"[46] he wonders, with a not inexcusable touch
of pathetic fallacy, whether the stream that has known
him so well will

> With regret miss the step of a death-stricken guest,
> And Echo list oft for the sound of his oar.

Bowles was by far the best known and most influential
of these poets. And with him we return to the sonnet
revival, for his best work was in the melancholy treatment
of nature in sonnet form. The first of his sonnets, published in 1789, were written on a tour of England, Scotland, and parts of the continent, in search of forgetfulness
after a disappointment in love. It was these poems which
aroused Coleridge's youthful enthusiasm, and prompted
his "Sonnet to the Reverend William Lisle Bowles," in
which he speaks of

> those soft strains
> Whose sadness soothes me, like the murmuring
> Of wild-bees in the sunny showers of spring!

and whose "mild and manliest melancholy" brought a
"strange mysterious pleasure" to the "wavy and tumultuous mind."[47] Bowles went to nature for comfort in his
personal sorrow, and, literary convention aside, it was not
unnatural that he should be attracted to her more mournful aspects.[48] Unexpectedly, there is in the sonnets only
casual mention of autumn, although ample amends are
made later in the blank verse "Monody, written at Mat-
lock," which is an elegiac autumn meditation.[49] Among the

sonnets, however, are two[50] of those sad spring-poems which the reader of preromantic verse learns to expect— poems in which the poet grieves the more as nature grows more glad. Evening causes Bowles to think of those friendless ones who, "by melancholy led," seek its still retreats from human woe.[51] Rivers fascinate him, whether the quiet winding streams of England, the mountain torrents of the Highlands, or the majestic Rhine. He leaves the "sequestered" Wainsbeck, that sings its "plaintive song To the dark woods above," with a hope of future joy in recollection such as Wordsworth might have felt.[52] He greets the Tweed as a sweet friend, on whose banks he will muse "at eventide."[53] He bends over the banks of the Itchin, where he has played as a Winchester schoolboy, in romantic sorrow for the lost joys of youth, yet feeling at the same time the solace of meeting with "some long-lost friend."[54] On the banks of the Cherwell he bids farewell to the lute and "that sad lay" whose music he has wooed upon his "melancholy way"; and he confides to the stream:

> Whate'er betide, yet something have I won
> Of solace, that may bear me on serene,
> Till eve's last hush shall close the silent scene.[55]

He found this melancholy solace also in wilder landscapes—in the mountains and the sea. Once again, as he departs from a remote Highland village, he hopes to carry with him a picture of its towering rocks and wild mountain torrents to sooth him as he pursues his "path in solitude."[56] The melancholy spell of mountains was still upon him a decade later when he wrote his long descriptive pieces on "St. Michael's Mount" and "Coombe-Ellen" (1798). "Hast thou in youth known sorrow!" he cries:

> Here, lapped into a sweet forgetfulness,
> Hang o'er the wreathed waterfall, and think
> Thou art alone in this dark world and wide!
>   Here Melancholy, on the pale crags laid,
> Might muse herself to sleep . . .[57]

He felt a kinship also with "the melancholy surge" of the sea, which he loved to watch "from some dark promontory,"[58] especially if the promontory were dignified by a mouldering ruin. Two of the best of the sonnets celebrate the sea. On Dover Cliffs he muses mournfully of "many a lonely wanderer" who has there said farewell to friends and country at "still eve," and cries that if such an one knew, like him, the fruitlessness of regret—

> Soon would he quell the risings of his heart,
> And brave the wild winds and unhearing tide—
> The World his country, and his God his guide.[59]

Possibly he comes the closest to that strange half-mystic sadness which seems to draw into the suffering self all the sorrows and vague regrets of humanity—the sadness which lies closest to the heart of romanticism—in the sonnet on the bells at Ostend:

>   along the white and level tide,
>   They fling their melancholy music wide;
> Bidding me many a tender thought recall
> Of summer-days, and those delightful years
>   When from an ancient tower, in life's fair prime,
>   The mournful magic of their mingling chime
> First waked my wondering childhood into tears![60]

Outside the sonnet form Bowles has only occasional felicities, and as he grew older he spent his energy more and more on rather long-winded descriptive and informative poems, so that the promise of his youth was never fulfilled, and as far as poetry was concerned, for all his eighty-eight years, he scarcely outlived his unfortunate friends Russell and Headley, who died in their early twenties.

Kirke White, born too late to have felt the personal influence of the Wartons, and yet to be counted among their followers, was perhaps the most original and promising, as he was certainly the most introspective and romantic, of them all. In fact, reading his life or his poems, one is perpetually being reminded of Keats. Of his precocious maturity and his intense preoccupation with the idea of mutability, we have already spoken. Of his obsession with the fore-vision of his own early death, and his conception of the essential unhappiness of the poetic genius, we must speak hereafter. Here it is to be noted that his attitude toward nature has close affinities with the school of the Wartons, and consists therefore in a pensive delight in nature's melancholy aspects—evening and night, autumn and winter, shady woods and sequestered streams—all to be enjoyed, of course, in solitude—and of a seeking out of these scenes as comfort in his own sore distress. This pensive spirit suffuses not only the poems on contemplation, but also the long descriptive poem "Clifton Grove," which gave its title to the only volume published in his lifetime (1803). Here, as elsewhere in White,[61] a clearly discernible Ossianic element occasionally contributes a certain eerie or wild quality like that of an Aeolian harp. So deep

and introspective was his melancholy, so indefatigable his
night-vigils with his studies, that in the more personal
shorter poems, it is the night which is oftenest celebrated,
and that most frequently from a study window, where the
poet wakes only

> to watch the sickly taper
> Which lights me to my tomb . . .[62]

In this particular poem, the poet is meditating ("while
meditate we may"), like Keats, on the impending wreck
of "many a sanguine scheme Of earthly happiness." Like
Keats, again, White was fascinated by the moon:

> Methinks thou lookest kindly on me, Moon,
>   And cheerest my lone hours with sweet regards!
> Surely like me thou'rt sad, but dost not speak
>   Thy sadness to the cold unheeding crowd;
> So mournfully composed, o'er yonder cloud
> Thou shinest, like a cresset, beaming far
> From the rude watch-tower, o'er the Atlantic wave.[63]

In another fragment,[64] he speaks of the moon's "mournful
melancholy gleam" cast through his casement, and cries

> Lowly I kneel before thy shrine on high . . .

In White we have already high tide of romantic introspection. Yet he manages for the most part, though not
always, to avoid offensive sentimentality or pathetic fallacy.

Outside the circle of more immediate discipleship, the
influence of the Wartons, compounded, as always, with
that of Gray, Collins, and Milton, and latterly with that
of Bowles, would lead us far and wide through the more

and the less fugitive verse. One more name may be mentioned, with particular reference to the sonnet. As a young man, in the 1780's, Sir Samuel Egerton Brydges wrote a series of rather attractive sonnets, many with a rural out-of-door background and in the pensive tradition. As early as Sonnet III[65] (written in July, 1782) the note is struck. This sonnet is called "On the Charms of Nature," and is full of pensive descriptive details: "Ye melancholy sighings of the breeze"—"pale Moon"—"sober, peaceful, genuine joys." Sonnet IX (1783)[66] is "To Evening," and contains an apology for attempting the subject after Collins. Autumn has a fascination for the young poet, and he celebrates it in something like six sonnets first and last. The earliest of these (1782)[67] is interesting because of the personification of autumn on which it is built: for, un-explicable as it may seem in an age of such facile personification, the personification of the seasons is unusual. Here Autumn is a "sweet dying maid forlorn," whose portrait reads like a description of Melancholy, and whom the poet prefers not only to Winter, but to "blooming Spring" and "dazzling Summer." Brydges' later sonnets, mostly from novels, show much stronger Ossianic influence, and are somewhat Gothic in spirit—full of howling blasts, and lovelorn benighted wanderers. This more hectic tone is already heard in "The Winds" (1784),[68] a storm-description which includes not only the "full Aeolian notes" of the sky, but "shrieking Spirits" that "Groan in the blast," "aerial beings sighing soft Round once-lov'd Maids," and "Spirits of Torment" that "warn the wretch who rolls in guilt, to heed!" This is not Warton.

III

Meanwhile, the ego-centric sentimentalism which some-times threatens to engulf the sonnets and other pensive na-ture verse of the poets we have been considering, was having ample triumphs elsewhere. Della Cruscanism by no means confined itself to love-epistles and laments over pet mice (which are after all a part of nature anyway), but spread over the verse consecrated to rivers and evening landscapes, to tempestuous promontories and midnight forests. Yet as a group the Della Cruscans will be met only casually here, and the important names are those of partially kindred, and yet on the whole considerably su-perior, spirits: Anna Seward, Charlotte Smith, Mary Tighe. These talented women, especially Charlotte Smith, fixed upon the sonnet in particular a tearful elegiac spirit in the presence of nature which it only with difficulty managed to shake off.

Anna Seward (1742-1809),[69] the "Swan of Lichfield," with whom we have met several times in preceding chap-ters, was the center of one of those provincial literary eddies which disputed the leadership of the capital all through our period. She was a woman of some spirit and consequence, a brilliant conversationalist and something of a beauty, who did not fear heartily to dislike her fel-low-townsman, Samuel Johnson, and was sure enough of her own powers to be willing to trust her fame to posterity. She was the admired friend of the beautiful Honora Sneyd who became Thomas Edgeworth's second wife—of the ill-fated Major André, whose indignant elegist she became[70] —of Lady Miller, patroness of the Batheaston literary coterie, who launched her on her public career as a poet—

of William Hayley, strangely the most popular poet of the 1780's—of Erasmus Darwin, whose memoir she wrote, and for whose amazing poem on *The Botanic Garden* she claimed to have written the introductory lines. Her affectionate and enthusiastic if over-sanguine personality holds, in fact, at this distance of time, more charm than her grandiose and sentimental verse.

The three volumes of this poetic output, as somewhat unwillingly edited after her death by Sir Walter Scott, offer examples on almost every page of sentimental melancholy of one sort or another, very frequently using nature at least incidentally as background. The atmosphere is established in the early elegies on the death of a sister and on the estrangement, and early death of the dearly loved Honora Sneyd. In the first poem in Volume I, we find the very young Anna wandering inconsolably through the grove, which she calls "haunt of my youth," and in which she drops her "blighted garlands" as she roves.[71] On page 11 she is already talking about the "trembling light" of "mild Sensibility."[72] On page 16 she decides that Love's "sweet enchantment" soon departs and leaves the "wounded heart" to bleed "at every vein."[73] On page 25 she is already painting one of those melancholy backdrops after Rousseau and *Ossian,* and coloring it with the pathetic fallacy which was her favorite literary pigment:

> Dreary and dark, in autumn's wane,
> The mournful evening falls,
> And hollow winds and chilling rain
> Beat fast upon the walls.[74]

She is always wandering in dim glades at twilight in tearful memory of the happier past:

> Ah! dear Honora, summer sheds again
> Music, and fragrance, light, and bloom, in vain,
> While my sick heart thy smiles no longer cheer . . .[75]

This particular poem was "written in a summer evening, from the grave of a suicide." None of these youthful tendencies was wholly outgrown, but illustrations need not be multiplied. The sentimental-Gothic landscapes of "Louisa" (1782) were referred to in Chapter V. Here a word is due to the century of sonnets which were written at various times after 1770 and published in 1799.

Miss Seward had very definite theories about the sonnet, and kept herself pretty strictly to the Petrarchan metrical scheme. The subjects are various, nearly all personal, and predominantly melancholy. Many have to do with her sorrow over Honora's marriage and estrangement (she disliked Edgeworth intensely and tried to prevent the marriage), several with her beloved father's decline and death, several with other personal sorrows or bereavements. There are three in the character of Werther. A constantly recurring theme, as in the other poems, is fond regret for childhood and the past in general. A great many of the sonnets describe wild and melancholy natural scenery with almost as "romantic" a love as that of Bowles. In Sonnet IX,[76] to be sure, she advises Lesbia to seek "the sequester'd dale" only if she can bear thither a "tranquil heart," since pain "rankles most in Solitude"; but she continued, like the other advocates of sensibility, to seek these retreats herself, and, indeed, in XCIV[77] repeats the old sentiment that

> All is not right with him, who ill sustains
> Retirement's silent hours . . .

And that she found comfort in nature is specifically stated as early as Sonnet XV (1774).[78] She wrote sonnets on the seasons,[79] finding, in autumn, her thought exalted "as the glooms efface Variety and glow." She repeats the old personal plaints that her life droops like the dying year,[80] that spring's return no longer brings her joy.[81] She finds solace in haunting the wild promontory over the "tumultuous waste" of the sea.[82] She draws peace from the stars.[83] Yet she is quite capable still of using growing things as sentimental lifeless symbols of stereotyped sentimental regrets:

> —and cypress buds we find
> Ordain'd life's blighted roses to supply,
> While but reflected shine the golden lights of joy.[84]

These sonnets contain an occasional felicity, and were well thought of in their day; but doubtless what Miss Seward herself once called the "pale florets of her pensive song"[85] do not entitle them to better than the oblivion into which they have fallen.

Even more concerned with a sentimental exploitation of nature as the background of personal woe, and even more highly praised by contemporaries, were the poems of Charlotte Turner Smith (1749-1806). An extremely early and unhappy marriage, and continuous and innumerable family and financial difficulties, furnished but too much reason for the lamentations of this "mistress of the pensive Lyre."[86] Yet, "fair mourner" that she was, "in rudest season born,"[87] she appears outside her poetry to have been a courageous, practical, and even cheerful-tempered person, who managed her large family and spendthrift husband as long as was humanly possible, and then man-

aged the family without the husband, supporting them all
by indefatigable literary labors. The first group of her
sonnets appeared in 1784, published at her own expense.
They proved very popular, and went through eleven editions in all, the latest dated 1851; after 1797 they appeared with miscellaneous other verses. Not only were
Cowper, Walpole, Sarah Siddons, and the two Wartons
subscribers to the 1797 edition, but even Wordsworth
spoke well of the sonnets, and no less an authority than
Mary Russell Mitford wrote to Elizabeth Barrett of their
author's appreciation of external nature.[88] Yet to the
modern reader the reiterated ah's and oh's, the monotony
of method, and the insistent exploitation of personal suffering, are more than likely to obscure the occasional
poetic feeling or metrical facility the poems possess.

Sonnet I establishes the point of view with a rose-simile,
somewhat more felicitous than Anna Seward's "blighted"
garland, though trite enough at that: happier they who
have never wooed the "dear, delusive" muse,

> Which while it decks the head with many a rose,
> Reserves the thorn, to fester in the heart.[89]

And though she loves nature and seeks her and observes
her moods, she can never forget—or allow the reader to
forget—the rankling of that thorn. She envies the nightingale, bird "dear to Sorrow, and to Love,"[90] because it
can "sigh, and sing at liberty."[91] She compares the glow-
worm, which becomes at dawn rayless as the dust," to
the delusive joys of the world.[92] She looks at the moon,
and, imagining it to be the habitation of suffering spirits
released by death, yearns to join them there;[93] or, on a

murky night, she addresses the moon, concealed from
"Melancholy's votaries" as it is, and tells it she prefers to
keep her vigils under red Mars—

> While thy fair beams illume another sky,
> And shine for beings less accurst than I.[94]

She dramatizes her suffering against ·a background of
rugged cliffs over a stormy sea, and in sonnet after sonnet
represents herself as wandering by the sea or over some
waste or about some ruin at midnight amid howling
blasts.[95] "Mournful, sober-suited Night" is dear to her
because, in its quiet gloom, calm and resignation may
come to the hopeless and exhausted heart.[96] No season of
the year can bring her joy. When the "chilly waves whiten
in the sharp Northeast," she can remember only that, unlike the sea, she will never again know summer's joys.[97]
Spring brings similar reflections. "Ah! why," she asks,
"has happiness—no second Spring?"[98] As it is, the blooming season has "power to cure all sadness—but despair."[99]
Even "radiant June" but brings renewal of the plaint.[100]
And though the "blasts of Autumn" are better attuned to
her "dejected mood,"[101] it is only because they are more
congenial to despair. Still it was an autumn evening on
her beloved Arun which set her musing less desperately
in the sonnet "To Melancholy":[102]

> When latest Autumn spreads her evening veil,
> And the grey mists from these dim waves arise,
> I love to listen to the hollow sighs
> Thro' the half-leafless wood that breathes the gale . . .

There we may leave her, in dream-converse with "Pity's

own Otway," who once had haunted the banks of the Arun as a child.

The sonnets of the Irish invalid, Mary Tighe, author of the pleasantly sentimental pseudo-Spenserian "Psyche" which caught the ear of the youthful Keats,[103] are very like Charlotte Smith's in spirit, although Mrs. Tighe often had to listen to the melancholy sea from her couch at home.[104] Uncounted others, from the late 1770's on, were filling the periodicals and bookstalls with sonnets and would-be sonnets. The habit, caught from Milton, of addressing a sonnet to a friend or eminent person, or dedicating one to some abstraction (perhaps delusive hope is the favorite), persisted; and of course many such sonnets are not melancholy. A good many deal with love after the model of Petrarch—even Charlotte Smith translated several of Petrarch's sonnets, and they constitute her only contribution to love melancholy. But the favorite subjects seem to have been introspective laments and melancholy landscapes, the latter usually with a personal twist.

There were never wanting those who could keep the thing within reason. Besides those already mentioned, such, for example, were the quiet sonnets of Robert Holmes (1778),[105] with their rural backgrounds in the Collins-Gray tradition. And reading through Capel Lofft's erudite *Laura* (1814), or even Richard Polwhele's *Poems Chiefly by Gentlemen of Devonshire and Cornwall*, published at the height of the furor (1792), one comes upon many pensive sonnets by obscure authors that would not altogether disgrace the Warton tradition. The sonnets by John Leyden[106] are deeply sad though not maudlin. Like Mrs. Smith, he has a sonnet on "Melancholy," which has the familiar pensive river-background:

Where its blue pallid boughs the poplar rears
    I sit, to mark the passing riv'let's chime,
    And muse whence flows the silent stream of Time;
And to what clime depart the winged years . . .[107]

It must be repeated that the line beyond which this introspective lyric use of nature becomes offensive must be left to individual taste. Certainly the line is too often passed in the effusions which filled the files of the *European* and *Gentleman's Magazines* between 1780 and 1800.[108] But surely no sufficient purpose would be served in seeking horrible examples to add to the sufficiently ample collection of such things already gathered on our way. It seemed to certain contemporaries as though some poets were determined to extract

> Poison from Nature's beauties, gloom, and dusk,
> And murky fancies from the blessed sun,
> And ill in everything.[109]

Coleridge made fun of his own early efforts no less than of those of others in the well-known Higginbottom sonnets (1797):

> Pensive at eve on the hard world I mus'd,
> And my poor heart was sad: so at the moon
> I gaz'd—and sigh'd, and sigh'd—for ah! how soon
> Eve darkens into night . . .[110]

Less familiar is Frank Sayers' sonnet "To a Weeping Willow," "in a late fashionable and highly-finished style," which is paired with one "in the present fashionable and truly simple style." The "highly-finished" sonnet begins:

> Ah me! I trace thy tendril's sombrous sweep,
>   O'er yon blue lake that streams with tinted light,

> Thy pensile [l]ocks, reflected on the steep,
>   Wave their pale umbrage to my quivering sight.

He wonders what "love-lorn Dryad" or pensive Naiad taught it to mourn, "Tho sun-bath'd Nature sweetly laughs around." And, having given us the affected Della Cruscan epithets, the alliteration, the sheer nonsense, the sentimental tears, the pathetic fallacy, he ends with the personal application:

> Alas! this woe-worn heart of misery
>   Sighs to thy sighs, and fondly weeps with thee.[111]

What need be added?

IV

A great deal has been said of sonnets in this discussion. But it is not to be forgotten that the same themes recur in ode, elegy, and miscellaneous lyric forms, and in semi-lyric passages in descriptive poems. To follow these themes in detail through the fugitive poetry would be but to add illustration to illustration of what has already been presented. A brief recapitulation must therefore suffice.

The poems on evening naturally owe a great deal to Collins' "Ode," with strong contributory influence from Gray's "Elegy." Occasionally a bold poet tempts comparison by addressing evening in Collins' own stanza. Amelia Opie's "To Twilight" (1792) is a case in point; it is written, however, in the mood of Charlotte Smith's sonnets:

> For I am Sorrow's child, and thy cold showers,
>   Thy mist-encircled forms, thy doubtful shapes,

> Wake a responsive chord
> Within my troubled soul . . .[112]

Oftener the stanza is used for spring or night or some other descriptive or sentimental subject.[113] Sometimes, too, one comes across a stanza which gives an impression of having been built on that used by Collins, although it is impossible to be sure. It is not often, however, that the peculiar pensive charm and dying fall of the stanza as Collins used it is very successfully reproduced. In mood the poems will be closer to or farther from the model according to the subject chosen and the temperament of the writer: there is an "Ode to Indolence" (1792)[114] in Collins' stanza, which is signed "Philo-Thomson," but is nevertheless a close imitation of the "Ode to Evening," with one line borrowed from Gray. Solitude, Contemplation, ruins, Philomela, and an occasional bat or owl figure largely in most of the evening poems, with more or less sensibility and egoism according to the writer. Ann Radcliffe built an evening sonnet around the flitting of the bat;[115] it represents, as do all her nature poems, the occasional triumph of the Gothic-Ossianic spirit over that of Collins and Gray. There are signs also here and there of that more objective and loving observation of nature which later helped rescue nature poetry from over-much sentimentality: such details as make Bampfylde's sonnets memorable, illumine Cowper's nature poetry, or find their way into the nevertheless pensive poem on "The Naturalist's Summer Evening Walk"[116] by Gilbert White, author of the *Natural History of Selborne*.

The poems on night are more likely than not to be religious or at least moralistic in tone. Where they are otherwise, they approach in type those on evening, except that owls, bats, and ravens appear more frequently, and ghosts are not unusual. Yet by no means regularly are they "horrific."[117] There is a large group of poems addressed to the various night birds—the raven, the owl, and above all the nightingale, who figures oftener merely as the symbol of the pensive delights of evening and night than as the bird of love. Doubtless the most interesting thing about the poetic treatment of these birds is the gradually won ability occasionally to see them not as paraphernalia but as living creatures. Sometimes this ability interferes with their use as symbols of melancholy: George Dyer actually had the temerity (1800) to publish in the *Annual Anthology* a poem hailing the nightingale not as "the bird of night" but as "the poet of the spring."[118] Sometimes it merely strengthens the symbolism by better understanding: Bernard Barton, for example, had really looked at the owl, yet he still calls upon it to be "Thy Poet's emblem."[119] An interesting point in this connection is the extreme infrequency, even among the naturalizing poets of the romantic period, of a realization of the actual war-in-nature which is the best basis in reason for making such birds of prey as the raven and the owl symbols of horror. There are a few scattered references to the matter—a very few. Grahame treats it at length and ruthlessly in his frankly didactic "Birds of Scotland."[120] There is a passage about "Mysterious Nature, prodigal of life," in George Wallace's *Prospects from Hills in Fife*,[121] with mention of the nonchalance of gorged birds in the face of "the pangs and agony The twisted worm or painted insect felt," which is startlingly similar in spirit to some of the rebellious evolution-stanzas in "In Memoriam." Keats has a memorable passage at the close of the poetic epistle to Reynolds "Written from Teignmouth."[122] in which he tells his friend that too keen insight spoils for him the singing of the nightingale, and that he sees

> Too far into the sea, where every maw
> The greater on the less feeds evermore . . .

But for the most part the romanticists, like the preromanticists, were content to ignore the harsher aspects of nature except when it suited them to paint tempests and avalanches for dramatic effect.

The most interesting thing about the treatment of the seasons is the continuing and increasing love for pensive autumn and barren or stormy winter. The moods represented are roughly analogous to those of evening and night. Yet one learns to expect more dwelling on the abstract theme of mutability in the autumn poems than in those consecrated to evening; and when winter poems are melancholy, it is oftener because of humanitarian pity for the unfortunate, beast or man,[123] than because of religious musings. To the introspective poet, autumn becomes a season of fond regrets for the past or comparisons of the dying year to his own fading joys, and winter is the congenial expression of his own passionate despair.[124] Even spring, as has been shown, to the poet obsessed with the mutability of things, will suggest only the promise it carries within itself of another fading or the sad analogy of man who has no second spring; and to the introspective poet, it will bring thoughts of the joys that come not again.

> Now spring returns: but not to me returns
> The vernal joy my better years have known

wrote the dying Michael Bruce, in an elegy (1767)[125] which has even been compared to Gray's; and in his lovely ode "To the Cuckoo"[126] he cries

> Sweet bird! Thy bow'r is ever green,
>   Thy sky is ever clear;
> Thou hast no sorrow in thy song,
>   No winter in thy year!

—but far other, alas, is the poet's fate. Summer poems are practically never melancholy; nor are there, comparatively speaking, many of them, except in series or pairs of poems descriptive of the seasons.

Three important poets may be mentioned to represent what came of all this descriptive-lyric activity in the heyday of romanticism: Keats, and John Clare, and George Darley, each representing a somewhat different emphasis in development.

Keats, perhaps more nearly than any other, was heir to the Gray-Collins-Warton tradition. His kinship with Kirke White has already been noted. It is true that in his earlier poems he had affinities with the sentimental prettiness of the Della Crusca-Leigh Hunt line,[127] and was influenced directly not only by Hunt (who does not typically project melancholy into his treatment of nature) but by Mary Tighe (who does). But the lush sensuous beauty and yearning moon-madness of "Endymion" are not always merely sentimental. And in the great sonnets and odes of his poetical maturity, as well as in the austere solemnity of "Hyperion," Keats's treatment of nature, where it is melancholy at all, rarely transgresses the bounds of legitimate subjectivity. The sea whispers eternally around "desolate shores."[128] The mountains, like human life, are hid in mist,[129] winter is bitter with the memory of the past,[130] autumn is sweeter than spring,[131] the melancholy voice of the nightingale from the dim forest is the eternal voice of the sweetness of sorrow. The great "Ode to a Nightingale"[132] may be felt to be the apotheosis of introspective sorrow yearning for communion and consolation in nature and then falling back mournfully upon itself:

> Forlorn! the very word is like a bell
>   To toll me back from thee to my sole self!

In the extreme of anguish even the melancholy comfort of nature fails.

Among the lesser romantic poets who wrote of nature without mysticism or didactic purpose, loving beyond all things her pensive moods, and seeking them for mere love, and for comfort in affliction, first place must be accorded to John Clare (1793-1864), "the Northamptonshire peasant poet," who, like Bampfylde, after a time of struggle and suffering, spent the last decades of his life in an institution for the insane. In Clare's case, the encroachments of insanity only intensified and deepened an already notable lyric gift, with the result that most of his finest poetry, largely left unpublished till long after his death,[133] was written in the asylum. However, as even the latest (and best) published volume falls beyond our period, we must confine ourselves to the earlier and less original material. It shows him already enamoured of autumn and of evening, and able to describe them both in loving and more or less objective detail. The sonnets in the early volumes, it is true, are still largely under the spell of the lacrymose egotism of the Charlotte Smith school and show little of the luminous objective beauty they later attained.[134] But if vignettes are lacking, more complete pictures of the Northamptonshire countryside are there in abundance, and almost never obscured by pathetic fallacy or falsified by personal emotion. The poet's love for evening was partly conditioned by the fact that only then was he released from labor and free to indulge his delight in solitary rambles. But the charm of autumn for him must have been rooted in his romantic temperament. He excells in catching the lyric sadness of autumnal moods:

> Come, pensive Autumn, with thy clouds, and storms,
>> And falling leaves, and pastures lost to flowers . . .[135]

> The landscape sleeps in mist from morn to noon;
>> And, if the sun looks through, 'tis with a face
>> Beamless and pale and round, as if the moon,
>> When done the journey of her nightly race,
>> Had found him sleeping, and supplied his place . . .[136]

Occasionally he allows himself to moralize a little on mutability or look forward to his own death. The personal note oftenest lending a melancholy tone to Clare's nature description, whether of autumn or anything else, is that of regret for the care-free days of childhood—a sufficiently romantic theme. It lends an emotional intensity to nearly all his musings in nooks and pleasant places which he loved as a boy.

The emotional content has risen until it almost overwhelms the descriptive details in the nature lyrics of George Darley (1795-1849). Like Beddoes, Darley was steeped in Elizabethan and Jacobean literature, but, though he once in a while achieved a beautiful love lyric in the spirit of the seventeenth century,[137] he lacked the strength and sinew of the Elizabethans, and his lyric ecstasy or sorrow is often monotonously exclamatory and shrilly sweet as the notes of a piccolo. He was moon-struck, like Keats—his first published poem was a dialogue between a Mystic and the Moon[138]—but he lacked Keats's compensating earthiness. A delicate melancholy hangs over his verse. Spring, autumn, winter, all bring him thoughts of mortality.[139] The hero of "Sylvia, or The May Queen" says:

> There is a melancholy in sun-bright fields
> Deeper to me than gloom; I am ne'er so sad
> As when I sit amid bright scenes alone.[140]

Darley writes of the Dove's loneliness in her haunts where there is "nothing sweet but melancholy,"[141] of a robin's grave,[142] of the pale lilies weeping over a maiden's tomb;[143] he begs a harebell growing by a grave to mourn for him.[144] It is the fastidious fragility of these poems which constitutes their distinguishing characteristic: sometimes lovely as a flower or a song bird may be, but without solid substance, too sweet to be strong. And they are full of ecstatic exclamation points and of an emotionalism ever trembling on the brink of sentimentality. Their fittest symbol—and that of the strain of romanticism which they represent—is the Aeolian harp, to which Darley has recourse in several poems besides the "Enchanted Lyre" quoted in Chapter V.[145]

This wind-touched instrument[146] had from the first fascinated the poets. It seems to have had for their ideal

worship of nature and mystery something of the imaginative connotation a poetic spirit in our science-worshipping
age might sense in the aerial music of the ether instrument. Its wild melancholy strains, like the legendary harp
of the Celtic minstrel or the metaphorical "lute," "harp,"
or "lyre" which romantic poets usually substituted for a
"muse," express the very essence of romantic sadness in
the presence of nature. To my ear, the most romantic
poem that Thomson ever wrote is his "Ode on Aeolus's
Harp." The wind moaning through the harp of Ossian as
it hangs on a "blasted branch" admirably symbolizes the
peculiar quality of the Ossianic landscape description.[147]
"Most musical, most melancholy" seemed the inevitable
characterization of the Aeolian music.[148] "The wild
Aeolian lyre"[149]—"the wild cadence of these trembling
strings"[150]—"Soft, wild, and mournful"[151]—"Wild Lyre,
that speakest to the heart"[151]—"Music of nature! . . .
Swelling the eye with a luxurious tear"[152]—"thy soft sighs
melancholy breathe"[153]—"your soft complaining airs":[154]
thus the poets describe its tones. One writer[155] wonders if
it can be "some fairy, tiny voice," or a plaintive nymph
like Echo, or "Ossian's passing ghost" telling Malvina "the
tale of other years." Its "Ravishing soft tones" conjure up
before Kirke White visions of Druid sages, lost pilgrims,
and a shepherd "on the lonely heath" who hears in them
portents of death.[156] It so fascinated Robert Bloomfield
that he compiled a little history of the instrument, with
poetic extracts ranging from Spenser to his own neighbors.
Darley's own stanzas on "The Aeolian Harp" begin

> I am for aye, for ever, ever sighing
>   My voice is full of woe, as my breast is of pain . . .

They stand, in the *Muses' Library* edition, appropriately at the beginning of his miscellaneous verse.

It is perhaps not necessary to give a further detailed account of how the principles of this melancholy attitude toward nature—or better these melancholy attitudes—are applied to the settings of narrative verse. Romantic heroes and heroines naturally like the same sort of landscape beloved of their creators, and get the same melancholy joy from communion with nature. This is to be said, however: the influence of the Ossianic tales and *La Nouvelle Héloise,* and later of the Gothic novels, especially those of Ann Radcliffe, is much more apparent in the narrative backgrounds than in the lyrics or descriptive poems. It would be hard, for instance, to find outside of narrative a landscape as Ossianic as that described in the opening of Hector Macneill's "The Harp" (1789):

> Still'd is the tempest's blust'ring roar;
>> Hoarse dash the billows of the sea;—
> But who on Kidda's dismal shore
>> Cries—"Have I burnt my harp for thee!"
>
> 'Tis Col, wild raving to the gale
>> That howls o'er heath, and blasted lea;
> Still as he eyes the lessening sail,
>> Cries—"Have I burnt my harp for thee!"[157]

The landscapes in the narratives tend to be wilder and more Gothic, full of deep glens and lofty pines and resounding waterfalls; the characters of the tales can be transported with perfect ease to mountains or ocean, whereas the lyrists often have to be content with rivers and woodlands. So strong is the spell of the melancholy tradition, so suffused is romanticism with a certain faint wistfulness in the presence of natural beauty, that it is sometimes hard for the reader to realize that the wild romantic scenes of Wilson's "Isle of Palms" or Peacock's *Rhododaphne* are really for the most part not melancholy at all.

V

In the longer descriptive poems, written mostly in blank verse after Milton and Thomson,[158] or in couplets more or less after Goldsmith, or in octosyllabics after Milton and Dyer, the subjective element, and indeed the element of melancholy, is much less nearly ubiquitous. Many of these poems, to be sure, notably çertain of those by Bowles, are suffused with the twilight pensiveness of the nature odes and elegies. Oftener, subjective or any other type of melancholy occurs only in scattered passages. The basic mood may be frankly didactic: Thomas Gisborne describes his "Walks in a Forest" (1794) in order "to inculcate . . . those moral truths, which the contemplation of the works of God in the natural world suggests, and that reverence and love for the great Creator which it is adapted to inspire";[159] or James Grahame meticulously describes "The Birds of Sctland" (1806) in due rank and order.[160] Very often the purpose is to present the topographical and historical features of some particular region, frequently viewed from the vantage point of a convenient hill.[161] These topographical poems[162] vary in subjectivity from such a poem as N. T. Carrington's intensely personal account (1826) of the Dartmoor wilderness, which he had loved and wandered over as a child,[163] to such a poem as David Carey's dissertation on the blessings civilization has brought to distant Craig Phadric (1811).[164] The general trend leads away from a tendency to contemplative musing in either the "L'Allegro" or the "Il Penseroso" mood, in any one of several directions: more accurately objective and less mannered description (Cowper, Clare); more preoccupation with the social aspects of the region described (Crabbe, Ebenezer Elliott); more metaphysical intensity (Wordsworth, Coleridge).

Melancholy may therefore be practically absent from these poems, or where it does occur it may be due to one or more of several causes. There is the old theme of retirement and contemplative solitude: this has been sufficiently discussed already, but the fact that it persisted and was partial source of later developments must by no means be forgotten. Not only Cowper in the period of transition, but Wordsworth in the new age, both preached and practiced each his own sort of philosophical retirement.

Then there is the habit, almost as old, of seeking ruins or twilit places to meditate on mutability. So jocund a poem as "Grongar Hill" contains an interpolation on this theme, and it continues to creep into the descriptive poems of all sorts. George Keate (1763) interpolates pensive material into his poem on *The Alps* literally in parentheses.[165] William Crowe, musing on an English hilltop (1788), describes in a memorable metaphor the "indefatigable flight" of Oblivion in pursuit of Time.[166] Peacock's "Genius of the Thames" (1810) is suffused with an elegiac spirit due to this theme.[167] When personal sorrow intrudes into the mood, it takes more and more typically the form of regret for the past, usually the childhood of the poet—as remarked in Clare and in Carrington, and further illustrated in Leyden's well-known "Scenes of Infancy" (1803).[168] Occasionally the influence of the Ossianic landscape affects these poems also, and lends an atmosphere of mist and hollow winds.[169]

Another source of melancholy as old as the descriptive type itself[170] is the sad narrative episodes so frequently introduced. These have been sufficiently illustrated from the mournful love-stories among them. But it should not be supposed that other melancholy tales—the tales are almost always melancholy—were excluded. The melancholy arising from pity is also more and more frequently excited by humanitarian digressions on hunting or war or the African slave trade: the discursive nature of the type makes these timely subjects simple enough to introduce. From this source arises, for example, most of the "divinely melancholy" tone of James Grahame's well-known poem on "The Sabbath" (1804),[171] and of such melancholy passages as occur in Langhorne's "The Country Justice," (1774-77),[172] or Bloomfield's *The Farmer's Boy* (1798).

Closely connected with this source of melancholy is the horrified contemplation of the bloody annals of history, suggested by the locality being described. "Avaunt!" cries one poet (1796) to his visions of these "barbarous times" —visions already lengthened through several sections of his poem—"My aking bowels tear not; No . . ."[173] Druid rites in particular had a horrid fascination for the romanticists from Mason's "Caractacus" (1759)—which of course is not a descriptive poem, though it contains much descriptive matter—to Felicia Hemans' prize-winning description of the landscape and history of "Dartmoor"

(1821). This sort of melancholy may, however, be more apparent than real, if like Mrs. Hemans in this poem or Richard Polwhele (in *his* poem on Dartmoor)[174] or David Carey (in "Craig Phadric"), the poet contrasts the dark past with the brighter present, and sings the praises of "bright Improvement."[175]

Perhaps the most interesting development in these poems, from our point of view, is the appearance of a source of melancholy almost directly opposed to that just mentioned—that is, the distressed contemplation of the degenerate present. With these poems, which, where they stem from anything but bitter experience, are in part the descendants of "The Deserted Village," our subject emerges from the academic groves of retirement and the shadows of obscure personal sorrows, into the glaring light of history, and stands face to face with the devastating French wars and the ruthless advance of the Industrial Revolution. In 1770, Goldsmith described in verse, for the first time so far as I have observed, the melancholy train of desolation left in rural districts in the wake of the process of enclosure. In 1783, George Crabbe, in "The Village," caught him up on the idealization of the past by which he had sought to point the contrast of the desolate present, but by no means brightened that picture of the present. Instead he painted a scene, more melancholy than Goldsmith's because more unsparingly realistic, of the village caught in the grip of poverty and the backwash of war. This outline he later filled in with a long series of incomparable thumb-nail sketches and pitiless tales,[176] the best of which are so meticulously objective that, gloomy as most of them are, it seems impossible to fit them closely into a discussion of romantic melancholy.

Meanwhile Goldsmith's plaint was taken up by others. William Halloway published (1802) "The Peasants Fate,"[177] in which, with many verbal reminiscences of "The Deserted Village," he laments the mournful changes in his childhood haunts:

> The path with grass o'ergrown,
> The mould'ring tombs, the fences broken down,
> While delving hogs, and toil-worn horses tread
> The regions of the undistinguish'd dead . . .

Only "an unhappy remnant" of the once-cheerful peasants remain—to inhabit the almshouse:

> A hopeless race, that own yon bleak abode,
> Of Grief and Care, beside the public road . . .

Matters are made worse by the war.[178] The theme of enclosures recurs constantly in Clare's earlier verse, and constitutes an indissoluble element of that regret for the past of which we have spoken:

> There once were springs, where daisies' silver studs
> Like sheets of snow on every pasture spread;
> There once were summers, when the crow-flower buds
> Like golden sunbeams brightest lustre shed;
> And trees grew once that shelter'd Lubin's head;
> There once were brooks sweet whimpering down the vale:
> The brooks no more—kingcup and daisy fled;
> Their last fallen tree the naked moors bewail,
> And scarce a bush is left to tell the mournful tale.[179]

The subject, or at least the general question of the effects of the new industrial order on nature and "nature's children," finds its way even into the determinedly optimistic pages of "The Excursion" (1814).[180] It almost completely dominates the descriptive verse of that ardent and indomitable lover of nature and man, Ebenezer Elliott, who sets it forth with spirit, poetic eloquence, and at times with salutary irony, in "The Village Patriot," "The Splendid Village," and "The Ranter," all written during the last few years of our period. Sometimes it is difficult to say whether the mournful indignation of these writers arises more from their participation in human misery or from their regret for the defilement of the beautiful face of that nature to which they have been accustomed to turn for comfort or for delight.

That several of these sources may combine in one poem to give it a distinctly melancholy cast is obvious. Three very different examples may be noted from the beginning, the middle, and the end of the romantic period. "The Deserted Village" (1770), written in heroic couplets and still palatable to the devotees of the neo-classic tradition, gains its elegiac tone not only by virtue of the social theme of enclosures, but also by virtue of that personal regret for childhood which links it with nascent romanticism, and somewhat on the other hand from the neo-classic praise of musing retirement. Hector Macneill's "Links o' Forth" (1796), written in "Burns's stanza" and in Scots, may represent the large Scottish element in the romantic revival, and the tendency among many poets to inject a lyric note into description. Its strong elegiac tone arises from a combination of meditations on mutability (with verbal reminiscences of Gray), a dwelling on the tragedies of history, and personal regret for the happy past, as the author, banished from his native land

on account of ill health, looks sadly back on his youthful
days, when along the beloved river

> He'd muse, and dream, till dark midnight,
> Then daunder hame![182]

For our last example we may take the aging Bowles's
long poem on "Banwell Hill" (1829).[183] Of the five parts
of this blank verse piece, Part I is strongly elegiac by
reason of the regret aroused by childhood memories, and
the meditations on mortality aroused by the antique bones
piled in Banwell Cave. Part II combines childhood memories by the melancholy sea (with a tribute to "Night
Thoughts"), an indignant glance at the changes wrought
by the Industrial Revolution, and an ecclesiastical tirade
which is little to our purpose. Part III consists entirely
of a tragic love story (a village legend, as is usual), in
couplets with interspersed lyrics; it tells of a deserted
girl who goes mad and drowns herself, leaving a curse
which pursues the false lover like embodied remorse until he dies. Part IV is almost straight description of the
delighted objective type. Part V, the last, contains more
childhood memories, a vision of the deluge, and a farewell
to the poet's "harp." In short, "Banwell Hill" is practically an epitome of the tradition, at that time already
vanishing.

VI

It would have been strange if so much preoccupation
with external nature, so much loving dwelling with her
and emotional projection into her moods, had not finally
bred in some ardent and poetic spirits a mystic nature-
worship, and a conviction that somehow there was com-

munion between the spirit of nature and the spirit of the poet, from which flashed forth the spark of poetic inspiration. And this, as everyone knows, is precisely what happened. Our concern is not primarily with the fact, but with the question as to how far and in what way (if at all) this attitude toward nature, in theory or in practice, involved poetic melancholy.

The earliest important study of the "growth of a poet's soul" and the part played by nature in a poet's education is James Beattie's "The Minstrel" (1770-74). This poem is written in Spenserian stanza[184] and is strongly influenced by both Gray[185] and Milton, and thus might be expected to stand in the main stream of melancholy poetry. It is also autobiographical, and its scenery is the mountainous country around Aberdeen which Beattie loved. Book I is introduced by a development of Gray's "mute inglorious Miltons" passage, followed by a passage on the charms of nature; then comes one of the pronouncements which adumbrate the Wordsworthian attitude:

These charms shall work thy soul's eternal health,
And love, and gentleness, and joy impart.[186]

Then Edwin appears, a "shepherd swain" of "Gothic days," and the rest of the book relates how in early youth his soul draws this "eternal health" from nature. He ever seeks solitude, but not to hunt—he can draw no joy from shedding innocent blood. He watches the "foaming torrents" from pine-covered precipices; he wanders on the uplands at dawn, finding a "dreadful pleasure" in viewing from some lofty cliff "the enormous waste of vapour" below him.

In truth he was a strange and wayward wight,
Fond of each gentle, and each dreadful scene.
In darkness, and in storm, he found delight:
Nor less than when on ocean-wave serene
The southern Sun diffused his dazzling sheen,
Even sad vicissitude amused his soul:
And if a sigh would sometimes intervene,
And down his cheek a tear of pity roll,
A sigh, a tear, so sweet, he wish'd not to control.[187]

Follows a lament over the fading autumn, with the familiar analogy to human life, and the consolation of immortality (which "truth sublime," indeed, was at that time "almost all the shepherd knew"). More of his generous sensibility; stanzas on the delusive rainbow, a symbol of man's hope; evening's "long-sounding curfew," with dreams of Gothic charnels and a moon hung "o'er the dark and melancholy deep"; dreams of fairies, interrupted by dawn, which brings an interpolated complaint concerning broken dreams by the author; rapturous morning in the mountains, with more interpolations by the poet as to how Nature rescued him "From Pyrrho's maze, and Epicurus' sty"; sad stories around the fire in winter—witch-legends from Shakespeare, and the ballad of the Babes in the Wood; an exhortation to Edwin (here speaks the author of the *Essay on Truth*) not to give way to rebellious "discontent and doubt," although "Dark even at noontide is our mortal sphere"; a forecast that "in riper years" Nature will give him "strength and fire, to soar On Fancy's wing above this vale of tears"; winter out-of-doors; "the lone enthusiast" musing by the sea in autumn, then straying far from the noise of rustic revelry; a concluding address by the poet to his patroness:—thus runs the remainder of Book I.

It will be seen at a glance that all this is fully in the pensive tradition we have been studying, only with a dash of Rousseauistic educational theory to give it individuality. In fact, I have held back the clearest proof of this contention, which is found just before the conclusion. Edwin retires from the rude mirth of the peasantry:

> Soothed with the soft notes warbling on the wind,
> Ah! then all jollity seem'd noise and folly,
> To the pure soul by Fancy's fire refined;
> Ah! what is mirth but turbulence unholy,
> When with the charm compared of heavenly melancholy?
>
> . . . .
>
> Is there, who ne'er those mystic transports felt
> Of solitude and melancholy born?
> He needs not woo the Muse; he is her scorn.[188]

The proposition could scarcely be put more directly. It only remains to be added that in Book II, which need not be examined in detail, Edwin learns of life, philosophy, and resignation to all the evils of the world, from the identical Hermit Sage whom we have so often met before.

There were minor efforts to tell of such a poet's progress, and they all, so far as I have observed, have a good deal to do with nature. Ann Yearsley (1785) found it natural to compare her own youth of rural poverty and delight in natural beauty to Edwin's, and her patroness's aid and instruction to the Hermit's, although it cannot be said that she stresses a melancholy attitude.[189] Even the ill-natured T. J. Mathias, author of *The Pursuits of Literature* (1794-1797), who really approves, it would seem, of nothing except the works of Pope and William Gifford, describes his ideal poet as taught by "rocks and groves, the wildness of waste," and learning from them, and other things, to bend "his weary eyes On life and all its sad realities."[190] James Montgomery (1803) has what seems to be an elegy on a young poetic friend, in which he presents Nature, Sorrow, and the Muse in close association.[191] His friend was young and poor, and

> His fervent soul, a soul of flame,
> Consumed its terrestrial frame.

He was reared by the Muse of Sorrow, and waked his lyre for her. He learned to love Nature and to sing her, and through her to see and sing her God and the "hidden majesty of Man."[192] Yet always there was in his song a "tone of uncomplaining woe,"

> So sweetly, exquisitely wild,
> It speaks the Muse of Sorrow's child.

The "fond enthusiast" who raises the "melody of woe" in Hector Macneill's "Pastoral, or Lyric Muse of Scotland" (1808) is "loved nature's child."[193] The Highland bards in Hogg's "Queen's Wake" (1813) are vividly described as living embodiments of the wild and melancholy regions from which they come. Scott has a hero unmistakably of the Edwin-type in young Wilfrid ("Rokeby," 1813), who

> loved the quiet joys that wake
> By lonely stream and silent lake,

or the "dizzy peak" of Catcastle, and who would indulge
in ecstatic dreams until

> The enthusiast could no more sustain,
> And sad he sunk to earth again.[194]

John Wilson, too, in "The Isle of Palms" (1812) describes his hero as a mountain bard, who has known the
"wailing tempest's dreariest tone," and the "mystic voice
of the lonely night"—and thus has "learn'd to wake
the lyre."[195] Clare wrote a long autobiographical poem in
Spenserian stanza,[196] obviously imitated from "The Minstrel," in which he adapts the details to his own youth
of penury and wistful solitude, and illustrates on nearly
every page how far nature poetry had travelled in the direction of simplicity and directness of observation. We
know, indeed, that many poets who did not write about
it, actually practised in youth the doctrine of seeking solitary inspiration in nature.[197]

"The Prelude" (written 1798-1805) was of course not
published until 1850, and could not directly have influenced any of these poets, with the possible exception of
Wilson, who was a friend and disciple of Wordsworth.
This is not the place for a detailed discussion of "The
Prelude," the doctrines of which are too well known to
need recapitulation. The concluding philosophy, of course,
is too strongly optimistic to be melancholy, and a man
who came to be convinced that "the inner frame is good,
And graciously composed"[198] and to think of happiness
as an actual duty, cannot be counted as on the whole a
melancholy philosopher. On the other hand, Wordsworth
was by no means a gay person, and his happiness was of

so austere a quality as to verge on that solemnity which the unphilosophical find it difficult to differentiate from sadness. By the same token "The Prelude" is a sober poem, and the nature passages in it are often of a melancholy cast. The poet dwells insistently on solitude. He speaks of the "solemn imagery"[199] of mountain scenery, and in another passage, of a great peak as the emblem of a mind

> That feeds upon infinity, that broods
> Over the dark abyss . . .[200]

He calls himself in one passage a "somewhat stern In temperament, withal a happy man"[201] and in another a "meditative, oft a suffering man."[202] Even when he had shaken off "the Poet's tender melancholy, And fond conceit of sorrow"[203] which had set his early descriptive poems in the main current of the melancholy tradition, he could not dissolve altogether the traditional association of nature and melancholy.

For the comfort which he found in nature was rooted in a deep and terrible disillusionment, and even in her solitudes there still rang in his ears the "still, sad music of humanity." Furthermore there frequently enters into his mature serenity a deep note of melancholy regret for the more passionate glories of youth, which have faded into the light of common day. This regret is felt in the apostrophe to his sister in "Tintern Abbey," in the sharp cry of fear—"Or let me die!" —at the end of "My Heart Leaps Up," most strongly perhaps in "Intimations of Immortality":

Whither is fled the visionary gleam?
Where is it now, the glory and the dream?

It has been suggested that Wordsworth no sooner achieved an exalted interpretation of his ecstatic communings with nature than the ecstasy itself began to fade.[204]

Yet the mystic communion with nature, when it could be achieved, was by no means melancholy. Still less did Coleridge's melancholy connect itself with his nature worship. He finds an exultation even more intensely religious than Wordsworth's in the imagined presence of the stupendous beauty of Mt. Blanc.[205] To him it seemed that in nature there was "nothing melancholy,"[206] and she is ever presented in his best nature poems as a comfort and a delight and a revelation of the divine. Yet the profound introspective melancholy of his temperament would not suffer him for long to receive that comfort and revelation. One of the most tragically moving poems in the language is his ode on "Dejection,"[207] written in the same year as the great "Hymn," in which the crux of his problem—of that terrible "grief without a pang, void, dark, and drear"—he gives as the slipping away of the "shaping spirit of Imagination" by which, in joy, he had *felt* that loveliness of nature which he now only *sees*. For joy or sorrow dwells within the individual soul,

And in our life alone does Nature live:
Ours is her wedding garment, ours her shroud!

Thus came to articulate metaphysical expression that egocentric melancholy in the presence of natural beauty of which we have had so much to say.

In the equally introspective and profoundly rebellious spirits of Byron and Shelley, both of whom drank deep at the wells of inspiration in solitary communion with nature, even the moments of mystic vision and identification are darkly colored by their temperamental melancholy. Byron, being the stormier and more dramatic nature, glories in tumultuous midnight high in the Alps, and feels himself a "portion of the tempest" and the night.[208] It is the magnificent and somber fastnesses of the mountains which Manfred seeks, and which in point of fact Manfred's creator had sought in similar distress, just before the writing of the poem. Shelley's gentler and more generous spirit yearns with secret kinship toward the mournful autumn wind, "tameless, and swift, and proud," and would project into these "mighty harmonies" its own "deep, autumnal" sadness and its own eager hopefulness of spring for earth and man.[209]

In Shelley, and also in Keats, there is hinted another somber mood of mystic identification with nature. It is a weary longing to be drawn into the bosom of nature by death:

> Now more than ever seems it rich to die,
> To cease upon the midnight with no pain . . .[210]

Thus Keats. And Shelley:

> Yet now despair itself is mild,
> Even as the winds and waters are;
> I could lie down like a tired child,
> And weep away the life of care
> Which I have borne and yet must bear,
> Till death like sleep might steal on me,
> And I might feel in the warm air

My cheek grow cold, and hear the sea
Breathe o'er my dying brain its last monotony.[211]

It is perhaps a spiritual paradox worth pondering that
the most profound introspective individualism seems also
at times the most capable of mystic identification of the
self with the encircling presence of external nature.

CHAPTER VII

THE SOUL OF A POET

Ay, in the very temple of Delight
Veil'd Melancholy has her sovran shrine.
                                    —*Keats*

At the beginning of Chapter I were proposed certain questions, the answers to which were to serve as guide-posts in our inquiry: how did the poets of the period look upon the mutability of things? upon the more immediate and terrible aspects of death? upon unhappy love? upon the relation of external nature to melancholy musings? upon the folly and misery of mankind and the suffering within the poet's own soul? Some answer has been attempted to all of these questions except the last, and the last is so closely bound up with the others that in the answering of them much has been said of it also. It remains for us to examine somewhat more in detail the reactions of the melancholy poet to evil and misery without and within, and to round our discussion to some sort of conclusion.

I

Johnson's "Vanity of Human Wishes" (1749), which, as we have seen, appeared in Dodsley's *Collection,* is undoubtedly the finest expression of the eighteenth-century adaptation of the classical "complaint of life."[1] Such a complaint is generalized and didactic, as is characteristic of neo-classic poetry, and as purely unemotional and impersonal as the nature of the poet will allow him to make it. It is almost never, however, strictly classic in thought—it is not so even in Johnson—but includes also Christian elements, usually in the form of apologetics or consolations. Thus the literary sources are the Latin classics and the Bible, in characteristic if not altogether natural combination. The most important perpetuators, indeed, of the neo-classic complaint were various of the long blank verse poems on Christian apologetics which continued to appear for the confutation of atheists and unbelievers. For to the poets as well as the prose-writers who attempted to justify the ways of God to man in an age of rational inquiry, might well have applied Voltaire's rebuke, *"Vous cries 'Tout est bien' d'une voix lamentable!"* The favorite method of proving personal immortality was to enlarge on the woes of life until only the assumption of otherworldly adjustment seemed left to make life bearable, and then with serene pragmatism to make that assumption in order to extricate mankind from the dilemma of meaninglessness. Young's "Night Thoughts" is the great mid-century example of the lugubrious effects of this sort of reasoning. At the latter end of our period, Coleridge's small poem called "Human Life"[2] uses the same dubious logic. Or the philosopher describes in great detail the sad state of man, and lingers over the various plagues and disasters to which he is subject, and then escapes again to his official optimism by arguing that all this is man's own fault and due to his folly and his sin. The first and second books of Foot's *Penseroso* (1771), to which reference was made in Chapter II, are an example of this technique. Book I is called "The State of Man," and in it Penseroso, the "western Job," moralizes

on man
And human life, to prove it vain intent
And full of woe

—all due to man himself, not Heaven. Book II is called "On the Disasters which happen in the World, and the Wisdom of the Divine Government," and describes the disasters in such detail as ill to prepare us for the conclusion that

The Lord of nature is supremely good.[3]

With a poem of this type may be compared the more deistic arguments of George Harley's "Leander" (1796), which approach those used two generations later by Browning—the arguments that "It is the bitter that improves the sweet" and that

Defeated Sorrow is triumphant bliss!
And vanquish'd evil the sublimest Good![4]

Both of these latter poems, it may be added, show the influence of Young.

The theme of human misery is usually combined with the theme of mutability: "Man that is born of woman is of few days, and full of trouble,"[5]—and somehow the first of these lamentable facts serves not to comfort us for the second but only to add one crowning trouble more. Yet there are a good many little poems in which that crowning trouble is not the main theme, as we found it to be in so many of the elegies. Especially in mid-century one runs across such titles as "Reflections on the Uncertainty of all Sublunary Enjoyments,"[6] "On the Vanity and Vicissitude of Human Life,"[7] "Deception, or the Vanity of Human Prospects and Possessions,"[8] "On the Vanity of Human Pursuits,"[9] "The Vanity of Human Life" (a monody).[10] One finds, too, poems entitled grandiosely "Life," and ringing the changes on the old question:

> Life! the dear precarious boon!
> Soon we lose, alas! how soon!
> Fleeting vision, falsely gay! . . .[11]

> Life! thou dear, delusive guest,
> Lovely phantom! fleeting jest!
>
> .   .   .   .
>
> In every state, do what we can,
> Life is, at best, a plague to man . . .[12]

Among other things, such poems are likely to contain a restatement of the orthodox ages of man. Rogers' long and very sentimental couplet poem on "Human Life" (1819)[13] has in it little else but an expansion of this sequence of ages; it is, however, so idealized as almost altogether to escape melancholy. Of course the notable thing about this verse is, not that the poets should have had such obvious thoughts, but that they should so often have repeated them in so obvious a manner.

Sometimes the elegies are concerned with neither death nor love nor ruins, but rather with the misery of mankind in general, and frequently of the poet in particular. The most interesting of these is Beattie's "The Triumph of Melancholy" (1760).[14] The poet begins by bidding his memory, which has tortured him by "scenes deep-stain'd with Sorrow's sable dye," to be still or show happier scenes. But the memories of innocence and youth which arise only lead him to lament the swift poison of passion. Exclaiming "How Memory pains!" he sets himself to musing comfortably by a winter fire, then to imagining the coming of the genial spring. But he immediately reflects on the impotence of the spring to bring relief to sickness, death, slavery, and disappointment—and all comfortable musing is lost in contemplation of the want and oppression which still rule the earth. When he turns for comfort to the "pictured scroll" of history, what he sees is the defeated and dying Brutus mourned over by weeping Liberty. Not even Virtue, he reflects, can "still the burst of sighs, When festers in the soul Misfortune's dart," or save man from his woeful fate. He calls on his friend Philander to come to cheer him in his retirement; but even the thought of friendship and of love leads straight to the thought of mutability, and the poem becomes for a space almost a paraphrase of Gray. Finally the poet gives up the struggle and admits that Melancholy has triumphed. The poem closes with much its finest stanza:

> The traveller thus, that o'er the midnight waste
>   Through many a lonesome path is doom'd to roam,
> Wilder'd and weary sits him down at last;
>   For long the night, and distant far his home.

This poem on examination proves to be almost as objective as "The Vanity of Human Wishes"; but the very fact that it is written in elegiac stanza instead of coup-

lets contributes to the elusive sense of half-personal emotionalism characteristic of the transition verse of mid-
century. And the closing simile has a wistfulness at least
half way to romanticism.

II

Many things were contributing during the latter half of
the eighteenth century to touch the pseudo-classic complaint of life with the shaping spirit of imagination and
deepen it into true romantic *Weltschmerz*. Since *Weltschmerz* looks both outward and inward, since it is a
"feeling in which the mystery of life and the sense of
the infinite mingle with personal weariness or satiety,"[15]
it involves not only a touch of mysticism or at least of
mystery, but also both a strong imaginative sympathy with
the suffering of others and an acute introspective awareness of suffering or frustration in the individual. In none
of these things, of course, was pure neo-classicism rich.
Its clear and rationalizing intellect, its passion for nor-
mality and willingness to overlook the trees if it might
but see the forest (even if the poet himself were one of
the trees), its distrust of emotion other than a tamed
and superficial sentimentalism—these things all are evident in its poetic treatment of the mystery of existence.
It ever tended to protect itself by paraphrasing Horace,
imitating Juvenal, or versifying Job, when it wished to
express its satiric contempt of society or its realization
of the tragedy of the life of man. What happened between 1740 and 1810 to turn poetic optimism from "The
Essay on Man" to "Prometheus Unbound," poetic pessimism from "The Vanity of Human Wishes" to "Childe

Harold's Pilgrimage"? Whence came the mystery, the imaginative sympathy, the introspection, which are implicit even in Shelley's ecstasies and are the very warp and woof of Byron's lamentations? It is a question often answered by those wiser and more erudite than I; yet it must be here answered once again from the particular angle of our inquiry.

The element of mystery is esthetic and metaphysical, and must be left for the moment in favor of more mundane considerations. Of these there are quite enough to make practically inevitable some development analogous to the element of imaginative sympathy of which we have spoken. For England, and indeed all Europe, was during the period 1740-1830 undergoing the most tremendous and intimate transformation since the Renaissance, if not since the birth of feudalism.[16] Even before the violent impact and repercussions of the French Revolution and the wars incident upon it had battered upon the thought and twisted the domestic economy of the nation, England had begun to stir with profound uneasiness in the tightening grasp of the Industrial Revolution. The easy indolence of a vestigial feudalism was over. The middle classes, with their insatiable energy turned from religion to trade, were moving toward the triumph of 1832. Meanwhile, the peasantry, crowded from its village common and herded into the fetid air of the prodigiously increasing industrial centers, or left to eat a pauper's crust and breed stunted pauper children for the slavery of the mills, were sinking into hopeless degradation or nursing the smoldering resentments which later flamed into Chartism and Socialism. The face of England was being transformed, and by no means uniformly into something more beautiful: sheep pastures are no more lovely than the tilled fields of contented peasants, and quiet villages are pleasanter to look upon than "dark Satanic mills." Increasingly as the period advanced, unutterable squalor and profound degradation on the one hand, and on the other ruthless greed and oppression, thrust themselves upon the notice of the sensitive observer, accentuated by the sense of change and restless newness in the forms they took. If the poets had been completely blind to the devastation in the path of the industrial Juggernaut, they must have lived in ivory towers indeed.

Furthermore, the pose of sympathy was already fashionable. It was only necessary for the man of sensibility to transfer the center of his interest from the sentiment or emotion itself to the object of it, in order that sentimentalism should become a true and genuine sympathy. And in sincerer spirits this was bound to happen. The result of the transfer was humanitarianism of one sort or another, and issued in private charity, reforming zeal, revolutionary ardor, or religious consolation, according to the nature of the individual concerned. Of course the victims of the Industrial Revolution were by no means the only objects of this generous enthusiasm: it also abolished the slave trade and fostered a widespread reform in the treatment of dumb animals. But it seems clear that the rise of the movement and its continuance down through the nineteenth century is closely intertwined with the history of the human aspects of modern industry.

Something of how this movement expressed itself in poetry has already been indicated. We have heard of the

prolific crop of odes to benevolence and of the glorification of charity. We have seen how a more vital appreciation of the problem, particularly of the rural laborer,
insinuates itself into descriptions of the English countryside. Cowper was not altogether insensible to the suffering of the poor,[17] and Crabbe dwelt on it till Hazlitt cried
in vexation that he had turned the world into a vast in-
firmary and Parnassus into a penitentiary.[18] But both
Cowper and Crabbe ascribe misery to the inscrutable
decrees of Providence. Blake was acutely and less re-
signedly aware of it—witness not only the famous invocation to Milton which contains the phrase about "dark
Satanic mills," but many a somber poem from *Songs of
Experience* and the Rossetti and Pickering Manuscripts.[19]
Shelley was so stirred by it that he wrote not only several
pieces of trenchant prose but a whole group of fiery
poems inspired by the Peterloo Massacre (1819), including a revolutionary song still sung among English work-
ingmen.[20] Ebenezer Elliott dedicated his muse almost
wholly to the dispossessed, in a crescendo of spirited complaints culminating in the famous *Corn Law Rhymes*,
whose date (1831) falls just outside our formal limits.
Space fails for the enumeration of fugitive verses inspired
by sympathy for the victimized poor, or for more than
passing mention of the large group of related poems
against the slave trade, concerning the horrors of war,
and in behalf of animals.[21] By no means all of this literature can by any stretch of the imagination be called melancholy: it is moralistic or indignant or rebellious or pathetic as the case may be, and impinges on our subject
only in that it voices an important element in romantic
Weltschmerz.

The revolutionary note in much of this verse connects it with the other great upheaval of the time, the French Revolution. The psychological states engendered by England's multifarious and intimate contacts with the French Revolution were nearly all of them in the final analysis conducive to melancholy in the poetic temperament. Either the sensitive and essentially conservative observer followed its course with mounting horror, as did Burke, or, to compare small things with great, Mary Robinson; or the first flush of too sanguine ecstasy faded into a gray and deadening disillusion, as with Wordsworth and to a less extent with Coleridge; or an enthusiasm sturdy enough to outlive the Terror (like Blake's) or born too late to be overwhelmed by it (like Shelley's) carried within itself the secret sense of frustration and exposed its possessor to periodic visitations of despair. At different stages of the progress of the twin revolutions the reactions even of the same sensitive observer must necessarily have been different. But at each stage there would be dubious change to deplore, destitution and brutalization to pity, ruthlessness and bigotry and materialism to recoil from in disillusioned horror.

III

But the world-sorrow of the romanticists, though it is much more often other-regarding than is sometimes realized, has its roots deep within the individual soul. It is by contemplation of his own suffering, indeed, that the romanticist has typically learned whatever he has learned of the suffering of others. Of the three elements involved in the attitude of the individual toward mankind, any one may be emphasized: the emotion itself may be the important thing, in which event, as has been said, the result is sentimentalism; mankind may be the important element, and when the emotion is pity the result will be an imaginative projection of the individual into the suffering of the race; or the individual himself may be the center of emphasis, and his own introspective melancholy may be intensified by drawing about itself like an aura the suffering of the race. The last two types are both essentially romantic, and will shortly be analyzed more fully in the persons of Shelley and Byron. Both types were got upon the nymph Sensibility by the satyr Imagination, and were nourished by Individualism.

A detailed analysis of the causes, phases, and results of that great eighteenth-century pendulum-swing from the general to the particular, from the type to the individual, with its concomitant increase of ego-centric introspection, is impossible here. Since art and life and philosophy are forever acting and reacting one upon another, an adequate discussion of the romantic *"étalage du moi"* would involve also a minute history of the currents of thought, the economic and political events, the changing social conditions of the time. Much would have to be said of the competitive independence of the increasingly important trading classes and of the birth of the theory of *laissez-faire*. Much would be said of the spread of that sentimentalism which we have met at every turn, and of its invitation to study the emotions and reactions of the individual. Much space would certainly be given to the doctrines of the French Revolution, whose origins would carry us outside of England and back of the eighteenth century, but whose progeny live on in English life and letters to this day. Something would certainly be due to the more obvious element of mere reaction to neo-classic theory, and the naturalness of applying the eye-on-the-object campaign to emotions and motives as well as flowers and mountains. It has even been suggested that the very argument used by neo-classic theologians to explain the evil of the universe was seized upon by the romanticists to justify their delight in individual deviation from the norm.[22]

However it is to be explained, we have already seen the increasing tendency to exploitation of the poet's personality in elegy, song, and sonnet. The odd thing is that the more one reads of the verse of the earlier and middle years of the eighteenth century, the more one realizes that the pronoun *I* is no new-comer with the rise of sentimentalism and romanticism. Yet the tone of the confidences is none the less altered. In fact it is possible to choose a romantic poem in which the first person singular does not occur at all and still feel in it that lyric intimacy which is characteristically absent from neo-classic verse.[23] Doubtless it is this very matter of emotional introspection which explains the paradox. The earlier writers of witty epistles, graceful compliments, and elaborately-titled funeral elegies are showing us only the smooth surfaces of their minds, or the conventionally to-be-expected griefs of their hearts. Only occasionally, as in the sudden confidences of Cowper, do we feel that we have really been given a glimpse into the depths; yet even Cowper's confidences have something of the forthrightness of intimate conversation. The romanticists, on the other hand, tell us things in their verse which they would not express to us in talk—their inner secrets and uncensored grievings, which we are sometimes supposed politely to assume are not their own at all but merely the creations of a poetic imagination. Thus they are frequently chary of actual names as their predecessors seldom were, and often mask their self-relevations under the thin disguise of some Childe Harold—not caring so very deeply perhaps that no one believes in the disguise, but for a time at least observing the fiction of personal reserve.[24] It often happens that the subtler the artistry the deeper the revelation and at the same time the more indirect the technique.

We have already seen that the man of sensibility is more easily hurt than made happy; and our own observation will probably convince us that the introverted personality is apt to be frustrated and melancholy. If the sensitive spirit hurt by the wrongs and miseries of life can lose itself in some active campaign of reform, its energy may be turned outward and its essential happiness may be preserved. This was the reaction of the great reforming spirits of our period—Howard and Wilberforce and the others whose names recur in panegyric odes as well as in the pages of history; and, on the borders of literature, of such a spirit of strong practical piety as Hannah More. A less perfect catharsis was found by the more passive religious resignation of the great mass of minor writers of the period, from such nearly-great names as Cowper and Crabbe, through popular mediocrities like Felicia Hemans and Bernard Barton, to the most obscure versifiers of the periodicals and anthologies. But the consolations of religion, however sincerely believed in, are much less productive of happiness and personal fulfillment than the consolations of action: a wistful melancholy of sentiment and unresolved questioning remains, which hovers like an atmosphere about most minor romantic and early-Victorian verse. As for the greater spirits, who sought a new way of consolation through some new philosophical synthesis, their essential melancholy was perhaps the deepest of all, for they had the profoundest sense of the unutterable mystery of the world without and the world within.[25] Thus to the richly imaginative and poetic spirit beyond all others came that weary drooping of the questing spirit which the Germans—and we after them—have called *Weltschmerz*.

Long ago Aristotle wrote that men of genius are melancholy. Cicero repeated the dictum. Rousseau, with his doctrine of *la belle âme*, gave the conception its characteristic eighteenth-century form, and Goethe crystalized it in the appealing figure of Werther. It became a commonplace of preromantic and particularly of romantic verse that the lot of the poet was even more lamentable than that of the ordinary man. The reason is of course that he is more sensitive, more aware of suffering about him and more delicately attuned to suffering in himself. His values are different from those of coarser souls. He is driven in upon himself, and finds himself misunderstood and tragically alone amid his kind. He suffers obloquy and neglect and looks forward to an early and forgotten grave. For his spirit has been consumed with a secret fire, he has known all life has to offer when other men are just beginning to live, he is old before his time.

What joy life holds lies behind him in the innocence of childhood and the earliest dawn of youth. Let death take him, and in the bosom of earth perhaps he will find at last both understanding and rest. . . . The picture is familiar enough. Change a few strokes of detail and it might do fairly well for the misunderstood young artist in our own Narcissus fiction of a few years ago. Thus baldly stated, it sounds effeminate and weakly sentimental; but though it retains a slightly adolescent coloring, it is nevertheless capable of representing no little beauty and tragic reality.

One does not have to go to the greatest writers for illustrations of the expression of this conception. The Chatterton legend embodies it perfectly, and we have already had occasion to refer to the constant stream of poetic tributes poured out to the "marvelous boy." The conception is frequently implicit in other minor verse, or even explicit, as has already been illustrated, for example by the poet in James Montgomery's "The Pillow," through whose song there flowed a "tone of uncomplaining woe," or by the passage in Robert Montgomery's "Death" about the lonely poet who sank beneath the "wear of passion and the waste of thought," or by L. E. L.'s feminine Childe Harolds, or by John Clare's misunderstood Village Minstrel.[26] The poet's harp is all too likely to be "sweet soother of my secret grief,"[27] or to find its natural resting place on the willow,[28] or to respond, like the "light Aeolian lyre," only to the notes of grief:

> I gave my Harp to Sorrow's hand,
> And she has ruled the chords so long,

They will not speak at my command;—
They warble only to *her* song.[29]

And with that veiled abandon of which we have spoken, the romantic poet reveals to us his own individual loneliness and sorrow:

O, I could weep myself into a stream,
    Making eternal fountains of mine eyes;
Would that the ancient mythologic dream,
    Were true, that peopled earth with deities,
Then might some God, compassioning my cries,
    Turn me into an ever-weeping rill,
Or bend me to a willow that with sighs
    The very region of the vale doth fill.
For I have woes too mighty for such tears,
    As these I shed, but am compelled to hide;
Their burning bitterness mine eyeballs sears,
    And I am forced to drink the scalding tide;
Lest the orbs melt to brine, and leave me more
    Desolate and darkly-fortuned than before.[30]

Better perhaps than any of the greatest of the romantic poets, for the very reason that he is less original and individualized than they, Henry Kirke White embodies in his life and his writings the romantic type of unhappy poet. Of obscure and rural origin, he passed his childhood and early adolescence in penury, uncongenial toil, and thwarted ambition. At length finding patronage, he went up to Cambridge, but only managed to complete the work begun by fevered midnight vigils with his books by working himself into a consumption and expiring at the age of twenty-one (1806). Obscurity, loneliness, adversity, and early death—these are familiar shadings in the picture. Acute sensitiveness, an almost exaggerated belief in his own powers, a precocious sense of maturity, a brooding and gloomy introspection overshadowed by the realization of an early doom—these are the inner concomitants. At fourteen White was writing that if the mistress of his dame-school had realized "all the ills by talent often brought," she would have wept for her favorite pupil. In the same early fragment we find him already talking about "this world of woe" and looking back on twilight walks with a friend now dead, as though he were already old.[31] Even in childhood, he writes to a friend, he "lived an unloved, solitary thing," learning

> to bury deep from day
> The piercing cares that wore my youth away,[32]

and to weep for the woe about him which he was unable to heal. Like Shelley's, his lonely solitude was filled with visions of a fair girl who loved him and was beloved.[33] Once he becomes almost quizzical in apostrophizing Misfortune:

> Misfortune, I am young, my chin is bare,
>   And I have wonder'd much when men have told,
> How youth was free from sorrow and from care,
>   That thou shouldst dwell with me, and leave the old.
> Sure dost not like me! . . .[34]

Examples have already been quoted (Chapter VI) of his midnight musings on his lonely grief and his approaching death. Nor is the juvenile remark about his first school-mistress the only indication of a settled theory of the essential unhappiness of poets. The belief appears in

his monody on the poet Dermody,[35] and with elaborate
explicitness in the "Ode on Genius":[36]

> But, ah! a few there be whom griefs devour,
>   And weeping Woe, and Disappointment keen,
> Repining Penury, and Sorrow sour,
>   And self-consuming Spleen.
> And these are Genius' favorites . . .
>
> . . . .
>
> Thou gav'st to him with treble force to feel
>   The sting of keen neglect, the rich man's scorn;
> And what o'er all does in his soul preside
> Predominant, and tempers him to steel,
>   His high indignant pride.
>
> . . . .
>
> Lo! where dejected pale he lies,
>   Despair depicted in his eyes,
> He feels the vital flame decrease,
>   He sees the grave wide-yawning for its prey,
> Without a friend to soothe his soul to peace,
>   And cheer the expiring ray.

It is after all cold comfort that posterity may, as has
happened with White himself, be almost more generous
to the dead poet than his genius deserves.

Thus far in the present chapter some attempt has been
made to emphasize the woes of life and avoid the subject of death, inasmuch as so much has been said of
death in previous chapters. Yet it is obviously impossible to keep the two subjects apart, as is abundantly
evident both here and in other parts of our discussion.
Certainly the neo-classic complaint of life included a complaint of death; and just as certainly romantic *Welt-*

schmerz includes oppressive awareness of both the one and the other. Indeed, part of the mystery of existence which broods over the romantic mood consists in their subtle relationships. But having presented some of the factors in the emotional deepening of the neo-classic into the romantic mood and having tried in part to describe and account for the proneness of poetic genius to suffer from it, we shall do better not to attempt summary or further theorizing until we have gathered together some impressions of romantic melancholy as it occurs in the greatest of the poets. For, as the reader was warned at the very beginning, the thing is not simple at all, but highly complex and even multifarious in its manifestations.

IV

Of Wordsworth, it is perhaps necessary to add little to what has been said in preceding chapters, particularly in Chapter VI. His earlier verse reveals traces of the melancholy pose so popular among poets of the nineties; and we know from "The Prelude" and other sources that he actually lived through a rather long period of mental confusion and bitter desolation of spirit, which marked his naturally strong and passionate personality with a quiet austerity not unreflected in his mature verse. We know also that he was sometimes visited by a romantic nostalgia for his own departed youth and its high ecstasies. Yet his nostalgia for a peaceful rural retirement he satisfied, and his nostalgia for the infinite he believed he had satisfied also; he came to be increasingly in tune with his age, and increasingly sure that all was essentially right with the world. There is little room left, therefore, for a genuine romantic melancholy.

With Coleridge, matters took a different course. His tragedy is essentially the tragedy of frustration. That sense of personal fulfilment which one attributes to the other "Lake Poets"—to Southey the extroverted and conventional, to Wordsworth the balanced and serene—is wholly lacking in Coleridge. That many of us value his marred and anguished personality, his fragmentary and incomplete genius, above even the greater of his associates, is neither here nor there. The man whose reach exceeds his grasp is not likely to find his futile exertion delightful, especially if he himself and all his friends have been certain that he could accomplish the feat if he would but make the effort.

There was never anything pessimistic in Coleridge's philosophy. Although in his radical period his faith was not orthodox and gave offense to his clergyman brother, yet the Unitarianism of the "Religious Musings" period is a distinctly optimistic doctrine; and in fact Coleridge never at any time lost faith in God or man. He suffered much less than did Wordsworth from the disillusion of his loss of faith in France. He found nothing but beauty and delight in nature. He always had the enviable ability to abstract himself intellectually from the tyranny of the particular fact and escape to the philosophical generalization. He always believed in the necessity of faith to cover the apparent marginal balance of evil, and faith he never lost, either in God's essential goodness or in man's immortality.

Not that it would be other than absurd to say that he

lived entirely inward and was untouched by public trouble and private suffering about him. Leaving his political prose out of the question, there is in the poetry abundant evidence of his early humanitarianism, his revolutionary indignations, his hatred of war. There is little to distinguish the phase of adolescent humanitarianism from the fashionable sensibility of the nineties. Coleridge wrote poems about faded flowers and pathetic old men and young jackasses and ruined girls[37] as did his contemporaries. He expressed his practice perfectly in an early poetic epistle (1792):

> Yet though the hours flew by on careless wing,
> Full heavily of Sorrow would I sing.
> Aye as the star of evening flung its beam
> In broken radiance on the wavy stream,
> My soul amid the pensive twilight gloom
> Mourned with the breeze, O Lee Boo! o'er thy tomb.
> Where'er I wandered, Pity still was near,
> Breathed from the heart and glistened in the tear:
> No knell that tolled but filled my anxious eye,
> And suffering Nature wept that *one* should die![38]

In the Pantisocracy period there is less sentimental melancholy and more indignation. To it belong the fulminations against man's inhumanity and tyranny in "Religious Musings," and the encounter of Joan of Arc with the unfortunate waggoner who has lost his whole family and is about to lose his own life as a result of the senseless depradations of an invading army.[39] As his interest drew away from social and political questions and his belief in the new social order died, he would have liked to shut out the clamorous world. But it would not be shut out:

> My God! it is a melancholy thing
> For such a man, who would full fain preserve
> His soul in calmness, yet perforce must feel
> For all his human brethren . . .[40]

During the years 1798-1801 he continued to express an interest in public affairs, although in such poems as "The Devil's Thoughts," and "Fire, Famine, and Slaughter,"[41] melancholy is swallowed up in indignant satire. In March, 1801, we find him writing to Poole of the "true heart-gnawing melancholy" induced by contemplation of "the state of my poor oppressed country," where "our pestilent commerce, our unnatural crowding together of men in cities, and our government by rich men . . . are bringing about the manifestations of offended Deity."[42] Yet by December of the same year his search for tranquility has led him pretty definitely to eschew the world:

> The feeling heart, the searching soul,
> To thee I dedicate the whole!
> And while within myself I trace
> The greatness of some future race,
> Aloof with hermit-eye I scan
> The present works of present man—
> A wild and dream-like trade of blood and guile,
> Too foolish for a tear, too wicked for a smile![43]

Whether or not the melancholy of social disillusion struck inward and remained a part of Coleridge's peculiar type of romantic melancholy, cannot be certainly told; it practically disappears from the verse. It is true, of course, that the greatest of the poetry had already been written. Yet this turning within himself when he was not yet quite thirty is surely symptomatic of what was deepest and

most characteristic in the poet's nature, though it by no
means indicates that a social consciousness was not part
of the *Weltschmerz* of his earlier days.

But why did this withdrawal—this escape to nature,
in which is "nothing melancholy," to metaphysics, in the
mazes of which one may escape from a clamorous reality
—fail to bring that tranquility so fondly sought after?
The answer is, clearly, that from Nature "we receive but
what we give," and that ideal metaphysics must be built
with infinite pains from introspective analysis[44]—and that
Coleridge, as everyone knows, found the self upon which
he was thus thrown back pain-racked, unstable, torn with
remorse and thwarted ambitions, frustrated in its yearning for joy, for love, and for achievement. He has himself told us, in the ode on "Dejection," of his need of
joy in order that he may do his best work. His greatest
poems are not melancholy. This is true not only of the
imaginative ballads and visions, but of the best of the
nature poetry in Wordsworth's manner. It cannot be said
of him that his sweetest songs all tell of saddest thought.
The alliterative languishings of the early sonnets are
largely pose. The revolutionary verse is indignant, the
later political verse satiric. It is in the infrequent lyrical
confessions—most of them written after 1801, when the
sun of his short day of happiness had set, and none of
them with the probable exception of the ode on "Dejection" in the same class poetically with the best of his
happy poems—that we must seek the expression of the
Coleridgean *Weltschmerz*.

Posterity, sitting in somewhat self-righteous judgment
on the sad disparity between promise and achievement

in Coleridge, has talked glibly of his irresolution, his lack of will-power, his sloth. The accusing finger has been pointed at the poet's own admissions of this besetting weakness, in particular to the first of his poetic self-portraits (1794), in which he calls his reason, imagination, and humanity "sloth-jaundiced all."[45]

> Frail is my soul, yes, strengthless wholly,
> Unequal, restless, melancholy,

he writes nine years later from the midst of sore bodily anguish.[46] But though his soul was certainly unequal and restless, it was hardly *wholly* strengthless—as witness the crowning victory of his final recovery from slavery to opium. I am convinced that in our haste to lay the blame on drugs and spinelessness, we underestimate the part played in the frustration of Coleridge's genius and personal happiness by sheer brute pain. To have won anything like either happiness or literary success in the face of the onslaughts of pain to which Coleridge was subjected almost constantly from his early twenties onward, would have been little less than a miracle.[47] The wonder is that he came as near succeeding as he did:

> Sickness, 'tis true,
> Whole years of weary days, besieged him close,
> Even to the gates and inlets of his life!
> But it is true, no less, that strenuous, firm,
> And with a natural gladness, he maintained
> The citadel unconquered, and in joy
> Was strong to follow the delightful Muse.[48]

Thence it comes that he seemed never to lose the zest of life, and even to the last showed no impatience to be gone. Yet meanwhile the "years of weary days" wore heavily upon him, not only with actual physical suffering but with distraction and dissipation of energy resulting in mental frustration.

Although he was by no means given to whining about his bodily infirmities, there are various references in the poems as well in the letters, to his physical sufferings. In a very early poem (about 1790) he writes that "seas of pain seem waving through each limb" and asks what "Life's gilded scenes" can then avail.[49] It was about 1796 that he began to suffer with abnormal intensity and frequency: in one letter of that year he tells of running about the house naked, "endeavouring by every means to excite sensations in different parts of my body, and so to weaken the enemy by creating division."[50] He writes to Wordsworth from Ratzeburg in experimental hexameters about the "rheumatic heats," the gnawings and throbbings, which keep him sleepless.[51] He whimsically apostrophizes the all-too-frequent rain of the Lake country, begging it this one day, for a special reason, to stay away—in return for which favor he will welcome it back, though years have slipped by

> Since body of mine, and rainy weather,
> Have lived on easy terms together.[52]

Not whimsical but truly terrible is his description of "The Pains of Sleep." "It is hard thus to be withered," he confessed to Southey in the letter enclosing these verses, "having the faculties and attainments which I have."[53] Yet so strong was the will-to-live within him that some years later, writing again of his pain-racked days and tortured nights, he averred that his "visionary hope" was for something deeper and more spiritual than mere freedom from pain—such a hope as

should give
Strength that he would bless his pains and live.[54]

Coleridge does not say very clearly what this hope is which would conquer pain and despair, but it seems to be the hope of love. In "The Pains of Sleep," he tells us that all he needs for happiness is to be beloved. And although he has less to say than some others of the loneliness of genius,[55] yet he shows a very human need of affection. Affection was showered upon him, indeed, all his life, in spite of his vagaries. Yet he was never satisfied. It grieved him that he had drifted away from his family.[56] He craved public approbation, and was troubled that his early radicalism was held against him.[57] He longed for domestic affection;[58] and, though there may be some truth in the contention[59] that he had only his own folly and irresolution to blame for the loss of Mary Evans, it cannot be contended that he found much happiness with Sarah Fricker. He leaned heavily upon the love of his friends, and was acutely sensitive to their attitude toward him. He struggled desperately against envy of Wordsworth's self-sufficient genius,[60] and resented any touch of superiority or condescension in him or others:

O worse than all! O pang all pangs above
Is Kindness counterfeiting absent Love![61]

Surely the knowledge that his friends were disappointed in him must have had a deep and paralyzing influence upon his spirit.

The latest autobiographical poems are not about pain or loneliness, but about the emptiness of departed hope:

> For Oh! big gall-drops, shook from Folly's wing,
> Have blackened the fair promise of my spring;
> And the stern Fate transpierced with viewless dart
> The last pale Hope that shivered at my heart![62]

One can still work on, but work without hope "draws nectar in a sieve."[63] And too often, in "dreary mood," when all seems to slumber but a "dull continuous ache," one may find oneself confessing how,

> bereft alike of grief and glee,
> I sate and cow'r'd o'er my own vacancy![64]

It was not altogether pious convention which moved Coleridge to say in his self-epitaph that he had "many a year with toil and breath Found death in life." Yet the phrasing is misleading. What he found was not death, but a brave, yet twarted and melancholy, struggle for fullness of life—for personal joy and completeness both in human relationships and in adjustment to the mystery of existence.

V

Coleridge had the elements of romantic *Weltschmerz* as it were disparately in his minor verse: the outward-looking in the humanitarian and polemic poems, the inward-looking in the autobiographical. In Bryon we come much nearer a fusion—with the emphasis, however, over-whelmingly on the inward-looking element. As a melancholy poet, Byron is much more complex, as well as much more important, than Coleridge, and a very long chapter might easily be written to analyze the "Byronic gloom." Some elements of this hypothetical chapter have, however, been anticipated in various connections, and all that need be attempted here is to summarize the most important elements of Byron's melancholy, leaving the reader to fill out the outline from Byron scholarship and biography in general. We have studied Coleridge as the poet of pain and frustration. Byron may be considered as the poet of world-weary disillusion, spiritual isolation, and "impenitent remorse," and above all as the apotheosis of gloomy and highly articulate introspection.

Of attempts to pluck out the heart of Byron's mystery there is no end. Since his poetry, in both its sentimental and its cynical phases, is so clearly an externalization of his ego, discussion has centered in attempts to elucidate his paradoxical and enigmatic personality, and in particular to discover the secret of his unhappiness. The truth is, of course, that there is no single secret. Certain more or less external biographical facts are of great importance: a neurotic heritage, a most unwise rearing at the hands of an irresponsible and violent mother, a club foot which interfered with normal development either physical or mental, a constitutional tendency to corpulence to be fought off only by prolonged periods of voluntary malnutrition, a precocious and abnormal sexual development, an unhappy marriage issuing in scandal and perpetual exile—none of these unfortunate circumstances may be wisely forgotten. Yet another personality might have made shift with all of them, might almost surely have prevented the last altogether.

Most seekers for a single key have looked rather among

the Byronic paradoxes, and found the main reason for the poet's unhappiness in the conflict between superficial vanity and innate nobility,[65] or between the ideal and the actual, especially in love,[66] or in a feeling of being out of place symbolized by the contrast between his physical beauty and his lameness.[67] In truth, it would be difficult to find another personality—except possibly Rousseau, whom Byron in many ways strikingly resembled[68] —quite so bafflingly paradoxical as Byron. He was sure that "we are all wrong" and the "great little Queen Anne's man" all right—yet he continued to shatter in practice all Pope's dicta. He never really believed that poetry was a fit occupation for a real man, much less for a peer of the realm, and felt that he himself was best fitted to be a man of action—yet he wrote more poetry in his thirty-six years than most fairly prolific poets produce in four score. He loved liberty, praised Washington, and died for Greek independence—yet no romanticist was less interested in the common people, and he had to stop his journal in Cephalonia because he could not help abusing the Greeks in it. He had all his life professed a hatred of or at most an indifference to his native land—yet he bitterly resented his exile, and his letters to England are full of half-suppressed homesickness.[69] He flaunted before the public his cynicism, his sins, and his heterodoxies —yet he winced and cried out in bitterness when the public took his Satanism in serious earnest. He allowed the world to curse him as an impious freethinker—yet he was willing to discuss fine points of literalist doctrine with Kennedy[70] and admitted to Moore the possibility that he might die a Catholic.[71] He was a shameless libertine, who

stopped not even at incest[72]—yet he never really believed in free love, and would have liked above all things
an impossible reconciliation with his wife and the secur-
ity of an establishment in the shadow of his ancient
name.[73]

In short, Byron was all his life a rebel against his own
convictions. Some preverse demon within him seemed forever driving him onward to his own destruction:

> There was that in my spirit ever
> Which shaped out for itself some great reverse.[74]

Or shall we say rather that he failed ever to bring to a
synthesis the warring elements of his personality—to
teach to dwell in social amity the colony of personalities
which was his spirit? He was no mystic, and so missed
a solution such as Blake's. He was hopelessly introverted,
and only in the last few months, if at all, was able to
turn his energy into stabilizing action. Always he fell
back on the multitudinous inner conflict. And that conflict he was unable to resolve. If these things be so, an
understanding of them will not indeed explain his melancholy, but may make it somewhat more comprehensible.
It is nevertheless necessary to repeat the warning against
overemphasizing any one factor or group of factors in
the analysis of a complex personality. And in regard to
his poetry, its moods and themes were partly conditioned
also, as we have seen, on the development of a series of
strong literary traditions.[75]

Thus the enormous weariness and disillusion with
which Childe Harold looks upon the world is the reflection not only of the youthful debauches at Newstead and

(in later cantos) the satiety and cynicism engendered by the years of melodrama and Don Juanism in London, but no less of the ancient aristocratic disease of ennui (practically identical with one type of spleen), long known to literature, and now complicated by the philosophizings and poetic mystery of Wertherism. Byron's letters and diaries from first to last are full of complaints of how he is perpetually "conjugating the accursed verb ennuyer."[76] In his desire to avoid ennui, he was perpetually oscillating between periods of intense activity and violent reaction; he once wrote that he thought perhaps gamblers were the happiest of men, because they lived in continual excitement.[77] Conversely, if he should die in Italy, he wished on his tomb the simple epitaph *Implora pace*.[78] Childe Harold, accordingly, before he sets out on his first pilgrimage, has tasted life and love and found them wanting:

> When all is won that all desire to woo,
> The paltry prize is hardly worth the cost . . .[79]

He has quaffed the cup of youth too quickly, and "the dregs were wormwood."[80] He and his brother heroes have all grown old before their time. For

> there is an order
> Of mortals on the earth, who do become
> Old in their youth, and die ere middle age,
> Without the violence of warlike death;
> Some perishing of pleasure—some of study—
> Some worn with toil, some of mere weariness,—
> Some of disease—and some insanity—
> And some of withered, or of broken hearts;
> For this last is a malady which slays

More than are numbered in the lists of Fate,
Taking all shapes, and bearing many names.[81]

Thus weary and disillusioned, the Byronic hero looks
back with faint nostalgia to the innocence of childhood,
and forward without hope or fear to the peace of death.
Meanwhile he nourishes his inner despair in spiritual
isolation from his kind. This element of Bryon's contribution also has its origin both in his own proud and wayward nature and in the philosophical-literary tradition
of solitude and the loneliness of genius.

I stood
Among them, but not of them . . .[82]

He stood a stranger in this breathing world,
An erring Spirit from another hurled;
A thing of dark imaginings . . .[83]

My spirit walked not with the souls of men . . .[84]

Alone, come all the world around me, I
Am now and evermore. But we will bear it . . .[85]

Think and endure,—and form an inner world
In your own bosom—when the outward fails . . .[86]

"Who would willingly possess genius?" Byron is reported
to have said to Lady Blessington. "None, I am persuaded,
who knew the misery it entails, its temperament producing continual irritation, destructive alike to health and
happiness,—and what are its advantages?—to be envied,
hated, and persecuted in life, and libelled in death."[87]
So the Byronic hero draws into himself, and frequently
seeks that solitude "where we are least alone."[88] Fleeing
from men, he sometimes makes friends of mountains and

ocean,[89] of night and storm. Thither we have already
followed him, and have seen something of how this na-
ture-worship is related to that of his predecessors and
contemporaries. But for the most part the Byronic hero
lives inward, and his lonely suffering feeds upon itself:

> There is a very life in our despair
> Vitality of poison . . .[90]

All that is left is a proud endurance. "I can bear"—"I
can endure it"—"We will bear it"—"We must bear": the
refrain recurs with almost rhythmic reiteration. It is
strange that, though the figure of Prometheus in his indomitable lonely agony moved Byron to attempt putting
it into verse, the result was only a mediocre fragment.

The Byronic hero differs from other proudly sensitive
and lonely souls in that a large part of his secret burden
is the remorseful consciousness of guilt. We have seen
how this element of remorse without penitence is related
to the Gothic tradition. That it is related also to Byron's
own temperament and story cannot be doubted. Ethel
Colburn Mayne has argued that the force which drove
Byron to disaster was a deep need of his spirit to experience remorse, and that when, in the tragic consequence of
his liaison with Augusta Leigh, he had achieved that experience, he ceased to dwell upon the theme in his poetry.
It seems to me to be only partly true that the theme vanishes, as there are traces of it in the dramas, especially
"Cain"; and a perusal of the letters and journals indicates that if remorse was achieved, it was, as in the earlier
heroes, wholly without penitence. At all events, the mys-

terious taint of guilt clinging to his essential nobility but causes the Byronic hero to gather his dark mantle about him with a jauntier defiance.

It will be seen that the Byronic *Weltschmerz* centers all things inevitably in the self. "My pang shall find a voice!" cried Manfred[91] on behalf of his creator; and in the unbelievably intimate revelations of poems frankly lyric or autobiographic, in the phantasmagoric succession of heroes in romance and drama, in the cynical openness of satiric narrative, Byron voices his pang. He may write at times—and with magnificent eloquence—of other things; but all subjects lead finally back to the central theme, as we found his meditations among the ruins ending with reflections on his own ruined fortunes. He may attempt, as recorded in "Manfred" and the third canto of "Childe Harold," to lighten the weight on his heart by losing his "own wretched identity in the majesty" of nature; but he cannot do it with much success.[92] In his later years we hear almost nothing of nature at all. As for man, we hear much more of his follies and wickedness than of his sorrows, especially as Byron's melancholy becomes increasingly self-conscious and transforms itself into satire to escape sentimentality. Life is darkly cruel, assuredly, and all men suffer; yet the only suffering of which Byron is very intensely aware is his own. How the unplumbed sadness of life draws in and centers itself in his own regret and disillusion may be illustrated, in conclusion, by those "Stanzas for Music" which Byron told Moore[93] he considered "the truest, though the most melancholy" he ever wrote. They are headed with the

familiar Latin from Gray— *"O Lachrymarum fons . . ."*
—and open with a mournful music:

There's not a joy the world can give like that it takes away. . . .

The poet speaks of the fading of youth's bloom and
youth's innocence, of the mature spirit wrecked between
unhappiness and guilt, of the deathlike lethargy settling
upon the soul which can no longer feel or weep. And suddenly we know that all the time he has been talking about
himself.

> Oh, could I feel as I have felt,—or be what I have been,
> Or weep as I could once have wept . . .

Disillusion, isolation, and remorse; and finally not even
the poor comfort of tears.

VI

Shelley was probably on the whole a happier man than
Byron, although he too was inveterately pursued by ill-
health, misfortune, and obloquy. He did not disbelieve in
the possibility of happiness, as Byron was tempted to do,
nor could any amount of private injury or public calam-
ity serve to undermine his strong faith in the essential
worth of mankind and the inevitability of the final triumph of the good. He found much more relief in action,
for contrary to the common idea, he was in many respects
a practical man—what with his detailed plans of public
reform, his private benevolences, his inveterate habit of
trying to straighten out the troubles of all his friends, and
the exigencies of his own family and financial history.
Furthermore, he never had reason to suffer more than

another the pangs of remorse, for, unlike Byron, he actually believed in the rebellions he practiced.[94] Yet his friends tell us that from his youth his temperament was melancholy. And his poetry reveals not only the touch of the sinister and the preoccupation with time and death and disillusioned love of which we have already spoken, but a diffused poison of despair, sometimes concentrating into some of the most poignantly melancholy lyrics in the language:

> Misery—O Misery,
> This world is all too wide for thee . . .[95]

> Misery! we have known each other,
> Like a sister and a brother . . .[96]

> Rarely, rarely, comest thou,
>   Spirit of Delight! . . .[97]

> O world! O life, O time!
> On whose last steps I climb
>   Trembling at that where I had stood before;
> When will return the glory of your prime?
>   No more—Oh, never more![98]

This is not the voice of a fierce Byronic gloom, but of a spirit lonely, intense, and devoured by its own generous enthusiasms.

Shelley's loneliness was no proud and misanthropic isolation, but the aloneness of ardent and thwarted love. It is true that, like most poets and mystics, he had great need of solitude. It is recorded of him that he would sometimes wander away for whole days to lose himself in nature, or forget his food in solitary communing with the great dead in books. Yet he had as imperative a need for human companionship. In particular was he haunted by the phantom of some "soul out of my soul" with whom he might know perfect union and understanding, physical, mental, and spiritual;[99] the story of this perpetually disillusioned quest is told in "Alastor" and in "Epipsychidion," and by contrast in the perfect union of Laon and Cythna.[100] But in a wider sense, Shelley was a lover of mankind, and, although it never occurred to him to gain peace by surrender or even compromise, his sensitiveness shrank before the abuse and ostracism which were his lot as a man and the scorn and neglect which were his lot as a poet.

> Alas, good friend, what profit can you see
> In hating such a hateless thing as me?

he asks a nameless reviewer.[101] Perhaps the profit accrues not to those who hounded the poet nearly into his grave, but rather to us, the heirs of his genius—if there be truth in the dictum which Shelley puts into the mouth of Maddalo:

> Most wretched men
> Are cradled into poetry by wrong,
> They learn in suffering what they teach in song.[102]

There is no doubt that Shelley suffered keenly from this isolation: he came almost perfectly to embody the conception of the lonely and misunderstood poet so familiar to us. It is his involuntary aloneness on which he dwells in the self-portrait in "Adonais"—"companionless As the last cloud of an expiring storm"—"A Love in desolation masked"—"neglected and apart; A herd-abandoned deer struck by the hunter's dart."

The extreme sensibility of the unhappy genius was his also. The intensity of his physical perceptions was such that delight, "Sick with excessive sweetness,"[103] sometimes

> denies itself again,
> And, too intense, is turned to pain . . .[104]

There was the same intensity in his spiritual perceptions, and the same excess of pain. Of his constant wistful eying of the stream of time we have already spoken, and of how his perception of mutability was at once a more abstract and a more personal and intimate thing than the orthodox meditation among ruins. "We look before and after," in his own famous phrase; and surely no poet has more frequently and memorably written of that homesickness for the past (the poet's own past) so characteristic of romanticism,[105] or dwelt with more nostalgic yearning on the future. In the present we dwell with misery, and the poet bows beneath the "heavy weight of hours." He too is old before his time, "his scattered hair Sered by the autumn of strange suffering."[106]

But with Shelley sorrow does not, as with Byron, lie inert within the individual soul, or burrow deeper and deeper, dragging the sorrowful mystery of life after it. Rather the subjectivity is an active principle, which flows outward, seeking to understand and identify itself with all of life. It has been remarked that this active quality differentiates Shelley's moments of mystic absorption in nature from the passivity of Wordsworth's.[107] More fully it effects an identification between the poet and his fellow men, so that their pain becomes his pain, their martyrdom his own:

> *Me*—who am as a nerve o'er which do creep
> The else unfelt oppressions of this earth . . .[108]

Shelley's heroes, who are as autobiographical as Byron's, all suffer (except him who perished through the evil genius of solitude) from a *Weltschmerz* which is truly *world*-sorrow. Laon, Lionel, Athanase, the madman in "Julian and Maddalo"—they pass before us, hunted and destroyed by their love of man. Only Prometheus, being not a man but a symbol, is delivered this side of death. But before the deliverance, come "the weary years From which there is no refuge," the

> sleep-unsheltered hours,
> And moments aye divided by keen pangs
> Till they seemed years, torture and solitude,
> Scorn and despair . . .

And when the Furies strive to move the great rebel by added agonies, they do it by forcing him to look upon images of the suffering world, and to hear how

> The good want power, but to weep barren tears.
> The powerful goodness want: worse need for them.
> The wise want love; and those who love want wisdom;
> And all best things are thus confused to ill.[109]

The Titan, from the depth of his anguish, pities those whom such things torture not. Shelley's Prometheus has no less fortitude than Byron's; but it is his character as symbol of pitying love and steadfast martyrdom in the cause of humanity which endears him to the poet.

> To love and bear; to hope till Hope creates
> From its own wreck the thing it contemplates . . .[110]

Prometheus, like the earlier heroes, is an idealized projection of Shelley's own self, here magnified to Titanic proportions.

This Shelleyan philosophy of love and hope and final deliverance, which grew more and more mystical as the poet's maturing mind and imagination drew away from William Godwin and closer to Plato and his followers, was not indeed in itself all ecstasy. The thinnest of veils (to use one of Shelley's favorite symbols) separates good and evil; evil (to use another of them) is a strong poison which interpenetrates the good. Only by some strange and mystic conversion of all things animate and inanimate may we hope that the evil will some day be at least partially sloughed off.[111] Meanwhile, he who sees with such intensity the glory of beauty and light will see with equal intensity the horror of darkness and decay: hence that strong element of the sinister in Shelley's verse, to which reference was made in the fourth chapter.[112] Nor can Hope be forever recreating the vision from the wreck: there will be moments of weariness and reaction—the "Shelleyan fall," as at the close of the "Ode to Liberty" and of "Hellas." Hope and despair will shake the mind with conflict or dwell together in unstable truce. Perhaps something like this is the meaning of that strange figure used to describe the secret gnawing sorrow of Prince Athanase:

> For all who knew and loved him then perceived
> That there was drawn an adamantine veil
>
> Between his heart and mind,—both unrelieved
> Wrought in his brain and bosom separate strife.[113]

Shelley says of the hero of "Alastor," that "insatiate hope" had "stung His brain even like despair."[114] Even if we could lift the "painted veil" of life, behind it would still be Hope and Fear, "twin destinies."[115]

This, then, is the second type of true romantic *Weltschmerz*—the type which sorrows not only for self but for all mankind, which seeks to embrace within itself the whole sorrowful mystery of life and death.[116] "The great secret of morals," wrote Shelley, "is love; or a going out of our own nature, and an identification of ourselves with the beautiful which exists in thought, action, or person, not our own"; "to be greatly good," he goes on, a man must feel within himself the pains and pleasures of his species.[117] Unfortunately, one who aspires thus to partake of the great soul of Prometheus, is too often doomed to share some portion of his tragic fate.

VII

By a deliberate oversimplification which may have some illuminative value, Keats may be considered as the poet of the sorrowful mystery of life, in contrast to Byron as exploiter of the suffering ego, and Shelley as tortured dreamer of the eventual deliverance of mankind. Although his years of maturity were even fewer than those of the other two, it is probable that before his flame was extinguished in disease he had experienced life more fully and seen deeper into its mystery than either of the others, though what he found there at the last it was not written that he should live long enough to bring to full expression. In Keats, with the possible exception of one or two love poems not published in his life-time, there is none of that deliberate and circumstantial exposure of intimate agonies which sometimes in Byron affects the reader with guilty uneasiness as of a very personal letter opened by mistake. Nor is there, on the other hand, as sometimes in Shelley, direct lament over specific wrongs and sorrows in the world. We know that his theory of art rejected both the "egotistical sublime" and the doctrinaire. His best work is clearly illustrative of the paradox set forth some pages back: that a romantic poem is often most poignantly self-revealing when in it is made no specific allusion to the poet who wrote it. And while there is very little in Keats's poetry about the suffering of any particular class of created beings, it is interpenetrated with the sorrows and gropings of the individual man. Its melancholy arises from an agonized introspection which seeks to plumb the secret of all life through the strife and aspiration of the poet's own soul.

As compared with the others, there is little loneliness in Keats's melancholy. He was not abnormally isolated, but lived in close sympathy with his nearest kin and surrounded by devoted and intellectually congenial friends. No poet ever had a richer humanity: "Above his grave the double aureole of poetry and friendship shines immortally."[118] His own early doctrine that men of genius have no individuality[119] and his ambition to be a great dramatist are doubtless connected with his acute aware-

ness of other identities.[120] Whatever suffering this intensity of sympathy brought him would not be in the nature
of loneliness. His need of women was almost wholly physical, and he seems not to have been teased with longing
for a love which would understand and complete his personality as well as satisfy his passion; so that the anguish
which love brought him was scarcely that of isolation of
spirit. Yet there is within every individual an island of
loneliness, and the stronger the spirit the wider the seas
will probably be about its island. Certainly the intense
activity of senses and brain which Keats knew between
his periods of apathy must have given him a feeling of
rich inward life.

It was through the very intensity of this life that suffering came. Love of nature was not enough, and passion
was his undoing. The ability to enter vicariously into the
identities of all creatures from the dying Tom to the spar-
row picking about the gravel under his window[121] reacted
in an acute awareness of evil, ugliness, and suffering. His
own misfortunes were the harder to bear no less because
of appreciation of the joy that was lost than because
of sensitiveness to the present pain. Keats was no spine-
less coward, and he bore the onslaughts of an adverse
fortune—bereavement and separation and public ridicule
and desperate financial straits and baulked desire and insidious disease—with a fine determination not to give
in. Before the time when passion and disease had beaten
down his courage into a sort of numb despair, he had
ceased to write. The great poetry belongs to the time of
strongest battlings; and, as we shall see, the battle was
not only for hope and fortitude but for understanding.

The rich sensuousness of Keats's poetry, which so attracted the Pre-Raphaelites and which remains its most obvious characteristic, is the basis of certain phases of its melancholy. This sensuousness, of course, was by no means altogether erotic. The swooning ache of desire comes to the poet in the presence of nature—

> My heart aches, and a drowsy numbness pains
> My sense, as though of hemlock I had drunk . . .

—or of art—

> My spirit is too weak; mortality
> Weighs heavily on me like unwilling sleep . . .

—as well as of love.[122] The gentle sorrow of vague love-longing, with its delicate pathetic fallacy, finds haunting expression in the roundelay to Sorrow in "Endymion."[123] There is a suggestion of the lassitude of satiety in the conclusion of this lyric—the return to Sorrow after the rout of Bacchus. But not Swinburne himself has described the weary emptiness of sensuous apathy more perfectly than has Keats, in the passage on the Cave of Quietude in "Endymion"—that "dark Paradise" where

> anguish does not sting; nor pleasure pall:
> Woe-hurricanes beat ever at the gate,
> Yet all is still within and desolate . . .[124]

In an earlier book of "Endymion," Keats had powerfully described the inextricable confusion of joy and pain in the very midst of passion.[125] It would be by no means easy to find a more perfect expression of the eternal beauty and transience of passionate youth than Keats's masterpiece in the depiction of the sensuous, "The Eve of St. Agnes,"

with its recurrent contrasts between the warm youth of
the lovers and the chilly age of the Beadsman and "An-
gela the old," and its incomparable closing stanza—

> And they are gone: ay, ages long ago
> Those lovers fled away into the storm . . .

But although there is often over-lushness, there is seldom
decadence in Keats (even in the earlier poems) in the
sense of delight in decay or in perversion. The nearest
approach to the first is "Isabella"; but Keats was too
much in love with bright beauty to do very well with the
macabre, and "Isabella" is merely sentimental. There is
a suggestion of sadism in certain lines of the "Ode on
Melancholy"—

> Or if thy mistress some rich anger shows,
> Emprison her soft hand, and let her rave . . .

But on the whole, there is little of this sort of thing. Nor
is there that fierce half-masochistic insistence on details
of horror or that search for hidden beauty in ugliness
which we have noted in Shelley. Keats did not seek to
find beauty in ugliness; rather he wept to find ugliness
in beauty.

But the ugliness forced itself upon him. Thought was
too active within him, sensibility too acute, to leave him
long in peace.

> Pleasure is oft a visitant, but pain
> Clings cruelly to us, like the gnawing sloth
> On the deer's tender haunches . . .[126]

We have seen how often too keen a perception of the war
in nature spoiled for him the singing of the nightingale.

His surgeon's apprenticeship as well as his attendance upon his dying brother Tom had given him but too much vicarious experience of human suffering: he wrote to Bailey once that if it were in his choice he would reject "a petrarchal coronation—on account of my dying day, and because women have Cancers."[127] His own misfortunes came so thickly that he lost the faculty of hoping, and near the end uttered the desperate cry, "O, that something fortunate had ever happened to me or my brothers! —then I might hope,—but despair is forced upon me as a habit."[128] The joys of sense were not enough. Like Apollo in the published version of "Hyperion," he set himself to satisfy his "aching ignorance."[129]

Sensation without knowledge had come to seem to him like falling into an abyss and being blown upward again without steadying wings. But knowledge, as he says in the same letter (May, 1818),[180] is Sorrow; and Sorrow is Wisdom. The secret, however, is involved in mist.[131]

> Why did I laugh to-night? No voice will tell:
>   No God, no Demon of severe response,
> Deigns to reply from Heaven or from Hell.
>   Then to my human heart I turn at once.
> Heart! Thou and I are here, sad and alone;
>   I say, why did I laugh? O mortal pain!
> O Darkness! Darkness! ever must I moan,
>   To question Heaven and Hell and Heart in vain.
> Why did I laugh? I know this Being's lease,
>   My fancy to its utmost blisses spreads;
> Yet would I on this very midnight cease,
>   And the world's gaudy ensigns see in shreds;
> Verse, Fame, and Beauty are intense indeed,
> But Death intenser—Death is Life's high meed.[132]

In sending this sonnet to his brother and sister-in-law (March, 1819), Keats told them that "it was written with no Agony but that of ignorance; with no thirst of anything but Knowledge when pushed to the point though the first steps to it were through my human passions— they went away, and I wrote with my Mind—and perhaps I must confess a little bit of my heart."[133] As to the closing lines of the sonnet: an intensity of life issuing in paradoxical love of death was not unknown to the Elizabethans; among the romanticists it is fairly common. Yet few other poets as full of life as Keats have been at the same time so "in love with death."[134]

But though there is longing to escape—to the quietness of death, to mere apathy ("Ode to Indolence"), to the romantic past, to the contemplation of the eternal ideal in nature ("Ode to a Nightingale") or in art ("Ode on a Grecian Urn"), both letters and poetry tell us that the search for understanding went on.[135] In "Endymion" this search is confused and futile; in the first version of "Hyperion" either the solution was still dark to the poet's mind or he found the austere objectivity of the style he had chosen unsuitable to his allegory. In the magnificent fragment of a revision, the poem usually called "The Fall of Hyperion" (written July-September, 1819), Keats most nearly expressed in poetry the nobly mournful faith of his brief maturity.[136] If the altar with the overturned image of Saturn be raised to that beauty which is also truth, and the pavement be mere sensuous fact, then the anguished struggle to reach the lowest of the encircling steps represents the poet's rescue from spiritual death by his wrestling for truth. "None can usurp this height," the Priestess tells him,

> But those to whom the miseries of the world
> Are misery, and will not let them rest.

The poet's misery, then, looks definitely outward as well as inward. Nor do the active lovers of mankind, the Priestess explains, have need of refuge at that altar: they are "no dreamers weak," and

> Only the dreamer venoms all his days,
> Bearing more woe than all his sins deserve.

Thus from the lips of the veiled Prophetess we hear again of the misery of imaginative genius. She herself is Moneta, the Shade of Memory, and in her awful face when it has been unveiled, the poet sees the deathless sorrow of the ages:

> Then saw I a wan face,
> Not pined by human sorrows, but bright-blanch'd
> By an immortal sickness which kills not;
> It works a constant change, which happy death
> Can put no end to; deathward progressing
> To no death was that visage; it had past
> The lily and the snow; and beyond these
> I must not think now, though I saw that face.

He would have fled, but was held back by those "planetary eyes," whose "blank splendour" shone upon him with the impersonal benignity of the moon. It is through the eyes of this all-seeing all-suffering Memory that he is to behold the fall of the primitive forces of nature before the gods of man's philosophy:

> whereon there grew
> A power within me of enormous ken
> To see as a god sees, and take the depth
> Of things as nimbly as the outward eye
> Can size and shape pervade.

Not much of the story itself was written. But the changes made in the little we have, notably in the character of Saturn, who is made less admirable, and of Moneta, who becomes here infinitely more full of wisdom than her predecessor Mnemosyne, indicates that the poet wished to show more clearly what he had come to believe—that the beauty which is truth has more to do with suffering humanity (the world under Jove) than with nature (the realm of the Titans), more to do with human art and philosophy (Apollo) than with sense (Hyperion). From our point of view, the truth which emerges is that in Keats the romantic *Weltschmerz* is neither didactically philanthropic nor morbidly egotistical, but rather from the vantage point of an introspective individualism which is yet acutely aware of all other individual identities, looks deeply and sorrowfully into the heart of the mystery.

As for the "Ode on Melancholy" (written, like the "Ode to a Nightingale" and the "Ode on a Grecian Urn," in May, 1819), it represents rather a somewhat morbid mood in the poet's development than his maturest philosophy. It nevertheless is of great significance for us, standing as it does toward the close of a long line of such odes, and embodying also most of the elements of Keats's habitual melancholy. As remarked in an earlier chapter,

it owes very little directly to the tradition—the idea of
writing such an ode, perhaps, the repudiation of the night-
shade and yew and "downy owl," the image of a veiled
figure, even the immemorial "Beauty that must die." As
Amy Lowell observed: "Keats did not find his paradox
in Burton, Fletcher, or any other of his forerunners, but
in the amazed and disgusted perusal of his own heart."[137]
That his heart was very much concerned and that the
poem grew out of his passion for Fanny Brawne rather
than out of those more august meditations through which
we have been striving to follow him, is suggested by the
lines already quoted concerning the "rich anger" of one's
mistress. Certainly the poem is drenched with the half-
morbid sensuousness out of which at the time of writing
Keats was slowly climbing: its atmosphere is heavy and
swooning like that of parts of "Endymion." Yet that it
is expressed in sensuous imagery does not invalidate the
paradox. It does not even mean that the paradox may not
stand also for melancholy more all-embracing than that of
"aching Pleasure."

Ay, in the very temple of Delight
  Veil'd Melancholy has her sovran shrine,
      Though seen of none save him whose strenuous tongue
Can burst Joy's grape against his palate fine . . .

Had he not indeed found it so? Joy is in beauty, and
beauty is truth. But if we find truth only through knowledge, and if knowledge be sorrow? Keats's soul, at least,
was "among her cloudy trophies hung."

VIII

This profoundly imaginative conviction of the inextricability of joy and pain is perhaps the deepest thing in romantic melancholy. We have found it everywhere: in Ossian's "joy of grief," in Shelley's joy which "too intense, is turned to pain," in Darley's melancholy of the "sun-bright fields," in the conclusion of Hood's ode to "Melancholy," in many other sayings of Keats besides this in his "Ode." But it is much oftener implicit than explicit. Something very like it must be an unconscious part of the vague wistful melancholy which hangs over so much minor romantic verse like a delicate atmosphere of sorrow. A philosophical realization of it conditions Shelley's theorizings concerning the thinness of the veil between good and evil. The pendulum having swung from generalizations to particulars, every generalization becomes hedged about with so many modifications that nothing remains in a separate category. There are no longer clean lines between good and evil, joy and pain. Even our own emotions, beneath intense introspective scrutiny, prove to be fluid, contradictory, chaotic. We find joy in a sorrowful tale or even in quiet nursing of an individual grief, we are struck in the midst of passionate pleasure with a thought of sorrow. All things are involved one in another, all are parts of a multifarious whole. The only thing clear is that nothing is clear: that all life is touched with the primeval mystery.

Mystery envelopes also the evil and suffering which are too certainly *not* joy, but the roots of which seem nevertheless to be tangled with the roots of finer things. So there is pain without, and pain within, and everywhere there is mystery.

That romantic nostalgia of which so much has been written, is in its simpler manifestations a desire to turn from the immediate contemplation of this mystery in the present and find refuge somewhere from weariness and bewilderment. We have seen how the poets often sought such refuge: in memories of childhood innocence, in a world of fanciful dreams, in nature, in idealized reconstructions of the Middle Ages or of ancient Greece, in imagined Utopias, in the stillness of death. In its higher manifestations romantic nostalgia is a yearning for the infinite, a passion for truth and understanding, an indefatigable search for the one beyond the many, for some sort of comprehension of the mystery.[138]

Now the shaping elements in all this are emotion, introspection, and imagination, the trio of romantic elements which we have watched gradually taking possession of melancholy verse: emotion to soften and sometimes to destroy the rationalizing generalizations of the eighteenth century, introspection to probe and analyze the bewildered suffering within, and imagination to realize that without and to build philosophical or mystic syntheses. When the emotion is shallow, or the artistic fire too weak to fuse it into shapes of the creative imagination, we have not true *Weltschmerz* but sentimentalism. This happened habitually in the later decades of the eighteenth century, and all too frequently among the minor writers of the great period. In its purest forms, *Weltschmerz*, which I take to be synonymous with true romantic melancholy, is, as we began by premising, a mood of weariness and sorrow conditioned both upon personal suffering or satiety and upon a brooding consciousness of the mystery of existence.

Yet this definition fits but loosely upon much romantic verse, and even within itself is subject, as we have seen in the analysis of its four leading exemplars, to such modification and variety of emphasis that it can be made to sound rather absurd. Must it be stretched also to include Beddoes' intoxication with the wine of death, Darley's delicate sighings in the flowered meadows, the autumnal moods of Clare, the pious grievings of Felicia Hemans, the pseudo-Byronic languishings of Letitia Landon, the melodious sentimentalities of Barry Cornwall and Thomas Moore? Yet all these must, one supposes, be also part of romantic melancholy. And if we turn back to the last two decades of the eighteenth century, now usually included in the romantic period, other types appear: the half-artificial pose of sentimental-philosophical melancholy as seen in the odes and elegies, the morbidity of the Gothic school, the sentimental swoonings of the Della Cruscans, the pensive yearnings of Bowles toward comfort in nature, the sentimental egotism of Charlotte Smith. It may very well be that a less useful purpose is served by attempted synthesis, a task frequently undertaken before, than by definition and discrimination, all too often ignored. For, after all, the stream of a literary tendency never flows straight and isolated like a canal, but is ever being modified and increased by innumerable tributaries up to and beyond the point where it spreads into a wide meandering delta at its mouth. Too many critics, perhaps, have tried to dredge a channel through the delta and have thus falsified the natural aspect of the landscape.

We may immediately simplify the situation by differentiating between romantic and preromantic—or early romantic, if you prefer—types of melancholy, and including in the latter those in the ascendency shortly before the appearance of *Lyrical Ballads*. Here, at least three distinct types emerge: the sentimental-philosophical, the Gothic, and the sentimental. Each merges easily with the others, but can often enough be detected in a relatively pure state. In the romantic period proper, probably the division already suggested is as useful as any: into the egotistical, the philanthropic, the philosophical, and the sentimental (though the last alone has but doubtful credentials). This is, however, much too neat. Byron, for example, was both egotistical and sentimental, Shelley both philanthropic and philosophical, and neither Clare nor Beddoes fits in at all. I should like, therefore, to serve up abundant salt with my own generalizations. And if we must have a thesis, let it be this: that except in the sense that all the arms of a delta are after all parts of the same river and flow into the same sea, there is no exact type of romantic melancholy, but only romantic melancholies which alike betray the influence of the *Zeitgeist*.

That they do reflect the time-spirit, and are in fact a potent element in it, is clear from the immense popularity of the less esoteric types—the egotistic Byronic gloom and the semi-genuine sentimental melancholy represented by Moore and Procter. The time-spirit having given rise to genuine melancholy, that melancholy reacted on the times. Life and thought and literature being ever in intermingled ebb and flow, not only will the great men of the day be different beings from what they would have been in any other age, but the little people will ape their betters and consciously or unconsciously take on the characteristic attitudes of the time. Therefore much of the melancholy of the romantic period is nearly as artificial as that of the nineties—nearly, but not quite, for the time-spirit has had time to strike deeper. To some contemporaries even before the days when Carlyle lifted up his voice and exhorted England to close its Byron and open its Goethe (*not* the Goethe of *Werthers Leiden*), the net result was almost as distasteful as it is in our own day to Professor Irving Babbitt. Peacock, quite cured of his early "philosophy of melancholy," called Byronism "the black bile of the nineteenth century," poked fun even at his good friend Shelley, and cried in amused derision, "Come, let us all be unhappy together!" Whoever would know romantic melancholy should read not only *Manfred* and *English Songs,* but also *Nightmare Abbey.* The very setting side by side, it may be added, of the two representative books of verse just mentioned, will serve as a reminder of that wide divergence of type within even the more popular forms of romantic melancholy, to which we have been drawing attention.

The real business of this inquiry has been to follow the manner in which these romantic types developed, changing with the changing time-spirit, from the types known in the days of Young and Gray. And since this book is essentially a history, it is right to put the reader in mind of certain of the facts and tendencies which have seemed to emerge from the welter of detail. These then are some of the contentions for which evidence has been presented:

—That a pseudo-Miltonic tradition of melancholy at least partly philosophical persists into the nineteenth century.

—That the influence of Gray's "Elegy," aside from its minor contributions to humanitarianism and nature poetry, developed in two chief directions: combining with *Ossian* in one to influence the ruin- and mutability-literature, and with Young, Blair, and Hervey, in the other, to influence meditations on death.

—That the religious meditations on death and judgment persist, though with diminished force, to the end of the romantic period.

—That there is a psychological and historical connection between the wane of religious terrorism and the rise of terror-romanticism.

—That, given the status of women in the period under consideration, it was inevitable that they should be an influence toward the over-sentimentalizing of melancholy.

—That from the first there were two tendencies in the melancholy treatment of nature: a disposition to seek nature for comfort and a disposition to exploit nature in the interests of sentimental egotism.

—That the outward-looking aspect of romantic *Weltschmerz* is different in kind from the sensibility and the sentimental humanitarianism out of which it grew, in that it involves an imaginative realization in the self of the suffering contemplated.

—That the melancholy verse of the great romantic poets is deep-rooted in traditional modes of thought and expression, by which each poet in varying degree was directly influenced: Coleridge most in his youth, Byron most in the whole body of his work, Shelley but little, Keats scarcely at all.

—That the great romantic poets and many of those of second rank, had each his own sort of *Weltschmerz,* so that, while the influence of the time-spirit makes these various 'melancholies each recognizably romantic, it is dangerous to speak without qualification of *the* romantic *Weltschmerz.*

It is hoped that the following of these particular meanderings will make the contours of the romantic delta somewhat more familiar.

Yet it is impossible to close without one more attempt, in spite of admitted danger, to see the main direction of the course of our river. Melancholy of one sort or another has always been present in English poetry. A complete history of its varying modes of expression would involve a pretty thorough analysis of the course of English letters—not to mention English society and English thought. Its presence does not, I think, necessarily imply any more than normal failure of current philosophy. For is it not to adopt a philosophy of one's own to assume that a current philosophy should not be melancholy? But the particular form which poetic melancholy takes in an age does certainly reflect the qualities of its current philosophy, and is therefore an index of certain aspects of its best thought. Thus we come closer to an understanding of men's outlook on life in the middle decades of the eighteenth century by the study of "Night Thoughts," the "Elegy in a Country Churchyard," and "The Vanity of

Human Wishes," than by the reading of much factual history: for these masterpieces tell us what the best minds of the age outside of formal philosophy thought of life and death and the possible beyond. The same illumination comes from a reading of "The Prelude," "Childe Harold's Pilgrimage," "Prometheus Unbound," and "The Fall of Hyperion." Men thought of these things more intimately and with more imaginative daring in the later period. They leaned less upon dogma (literary, philosophical, or theological) and more upon what they found within themselves and imagined in their fellows. They were therefore incapable of arriving at the one except through intense scrutiny of the many. And because it is so difficult, if it be possible, to win through the multiplicity and contrariety of the many to any satisfying concept of the one, they often dwelt sorrowfully with the many, or carried with them into their faith in unity the clinging pain of contradictions. Their melancholy was therefore deeper and more passionate than that of their predecessors, having within itself that nostalgia for the infinite of which we have spoken. But to say whether this be more nearly a failure than any other way of thinking and feeling would be to turn philosopher and pass judgment on the whole romantic *Weltanschauung*.

NOTES

CHAPTER I

COMPOUNDED OF MANY SIMPLES

1. In Dodsley's edition of his *Works*, 2 vols., London, 1764. Dodsley does not say when the elegies were written, but remarks that the introductory essay was composed nearly twenty years before. Shenstone writes in this essay as though he had already written at least a good number of the 26 elegies which follow. Three of the elegies are dated, one each 1743, 1745, 1746.

2. *Pamela*, 1740; *Clarissa*, 1748; *Sir Charles Grandison*, 1753-54.

3. For an illuminating analysis of this anthology in comparison with the Dryden-Tonson *Miscellanies* (1684-1727), as well as information as to its popularity and representative character, see R. D. Havens: "Changing Taste in the Eighteenth Century," *Publications of the Modern Language Association*, XLIV (1929), 501-36.

4. "Postscript," VI, 333. My quotations are from the 1778 edition, but contents and pagination are identical with the 1758 ed., called the 5th.

5. Dr. Havens (*op. cit.*, p. 528 and note), with necessary warning of inevitable inaccuracy, counts "between 12 and 15" elegies and 15 other pieces predominantly melancholy. I have counted elegies only when they seemed to me really mournful in tone, but have doubtless been more liberal in my interpretation of the melancholy mood, as I have included poems suffused with the vague Miltonic pensiveness considered melancholy at the time. See *post*.

6. "Ode to Fancy," Dodsley, III, 111.

7. Quotations from the 2d ed., London, 1755-56.

8. "Why Hammond or other writers have thought the quatrain of ten syllables elegiac, it is difficult to tell."—"Life of Hammond," in *Lives of the Poets*.

9. Dodsley, II, 52 ff. Dated 1729-30.

10. *Ibid.*, IV, 73 ff. All Hammond's elegies after Ovid are in couplets, his much more numerous elegies after Tibullus in "elegiac stanza."

11. "A Prefatory Essay on Elegy," in *Works*, 2 vols., London, 1765 (2d ed.), I, 20 ff.

12. Dodsley, IV, 511-18.

13. *Op. cit.*, pp. 16 ff.

14. *Op. cit.*, p. 18.

15. V, 90 ff. The poem is signed J.G.

16. "Part of an Elegy of Tibullus Translated" [by Lord Lyttelton], II, 52 ff; "Elegy to Miss D-w-d. In the Manner of Ovid," by James Hammond, IV, 73 ff; "Elegy," V, 314 ff; "An Elegy Written on Valentine's Morning," VI, 217 ff; "Cynthia, An Elegiac Poem," by T. P[er]cy, V, 234 ff. The first two are in couplets, the last three in elegiac stanza.

17. "An Elegy Written in an Empty Assembly Room," by Richard Owen Cambridge, VI, 302 ff.

18. VI, 41 ff.

19. Letter to West, May 27, 1742, *Correspondence of Gray, Walpole, West, and Ashton* (ed. by Toynbee), Oxford Univ. Press, 1915, II, 42.

20. "Ruins of Rome," Dodsley, I, 233.

21. Columbia Univ. Press, 1924.

22. See especially pp. 38 ff.

23. Dodsley, I, 221.

24. *Ibid.*, p. 233.

25. *Ibid.*, p. 217.

26. Harvard Univ. Press, 1922.

27. Page 472. See also his article "The Literature of Melancholy," *Modern Language Notes*, XXIV (1909), 226-27.

28. *Op. cit.*, pp. 18-22, 249-50, and *passim*.

29. "Pre-Existence," Dodsley, I, 158 ff. Quotation, p. 166. The poem is dated by Havens, 1714.

30. *Ibid.*, IV, 50 ff. Quotations, pp. 51, 52, 53, 59, 60, 60 respectively. The poem is dated by Havens, 1750.

31. *Ibid.*, III, 215 ff. Dated by Havens, 1746.

32. *Ibid.*, VI, 97 ff. Quotation beginning of the poem.

33. Quotations respectively from Gray's "Elegy," Dodsley, IV, 1; Collins' "Ode to Evening," *ibid.*, I, 325-26; Joseph Warton's "The Enthusiast," *ibid.*, III, 106 and 107; Thomas Warton's "The Pleasures of Melancholy," *ibid.*, IV, 210-11. It is interesting to note that all these poems owe a good deal to Milton.

34. "Blenheim," *ibid.*, II, 22 ff.

35. "To Mr. Fox, written at Florence." Significantly "In Imitation of Horace," *ibid*, III, 187 f.

36. "Elegy XIII." Hammond's elegies may be found in the Chiswick *British Poets,* Vol. LXIII. Johnson's comment is in his "Life" prefixed. Lyttelton has a translation of part of the same elegy of Tibullus in Dodsley (dated 1729-30), II, 52 ff.

37. *Ibid.,* III, 2.

38. "Of Active and Retired Life," *ibid.,* I, 203 ff. Quoted phrases, pp. 211-13.

39. "The Trophy, being Six Cantatas to the Honour of his Royal Highness William Duke of Cumberland . . ." By Benj. Hoadly. Set to Music by Dr. Greene. 1746, *ibid.,* III, 255 ff.

40. "To Mr. Mason," *ibid.,* VI, 312 ff.

41. *Ibid.,* II, 272 ff; IV, 7 ff.

42. *Ibid.,* I, 168 ff. Cf. also Thomas Denton's "Immortality; or the Consolation of Human Life," a very lugubrious monody, V, 226 ff.

43. *Ibid.,* I, 186 ff; IV, 152 ff. Quotations, pp. 158, 162, 162, 165 respectively.

44. *Ibid.,* IV, 195. Quoted entire.

45. A neat illustration of the psychological connection of these apparently opposed moods, whether or not they both have their origin in a disordered spleen, is to be found in Fletcher's *The Nice Valour* (1647), which contains the famous song to Melancholy beginning "Hence all you vain delights." The melancholy fit of the mad lord, we are told, was ever followed by his angry one—and Act III illustrates the process. Cf. "Melancholy is the nurse of frenzy"—*Taming of the Shrew,* Induction, Scene 2, 1.135.

46. Some authorities thought that the complaint in women had its seat in the womb, in men in the spleen. It was also argued that women were naturally more sprightly than men and took the spleen to ape the men. On the whole matter of spleen see the entertaining dissertation by Florine Kalkühler, *Die Natur des Spleens bei den englischen Schriftstellern in der ersten Hafte des 18. Jahrhunderts,* Leipzig, 1920, on which my paragraph is partly based.

47. In *The Rape of the Lock, A Tale of a Tub, Spectator* #115, *Spectator* #53 respectively. I owe these references to Kalkühler, *op. cit., passim.*

48. Boswell's *Life of Johnson,* p. 300 in the *Modern Student's Library* edition.

49. It is found in Dodsley, I, 116-46. The quotations are on pp. 117, 119, 121, 133, 144 respectively.

50. "Elegy," V, 314 ff; "An Elegy written on Valentine's Morning" [Horace Walpole], VI, 217 ff; "Cynthia, an Elegiac Poem," by T.

P[er]cy, VI, 234 ff. The pastoral one is the first; the one with more of the breath of the outdoors in it is not Bishop Percy's, but Walpole's.

51. *Ibid.*, II, 198 ff. There is also a poem by Richard Graves, Shenstone's friend, on "The Parting," which rings true, *ibid.*, IV, 329 ff.

52. *Ibid.*, I, 26 ff.

53. *Ibid.*, I, 41 ff.

54. *Ibid.*, IV, 78 ff. By Lord Hervey.

55. *Ibid.*, I, 114 f.

56. "Upon an Alcove, now at Parson's Green," *ibid.*, V, 296 f.

57. See John Draper: *The Funeral Elegy and the Rise of English Romanticism*, New York Univ. Press, 1929, and the companion volume, *A Century of Broadside Elegies*, London, 1928.

58. The best summary I have found of the personal background of "The Complaint" is in Paul Van Tieghem's *La Poésie de la Nuit et des Tombleaux en Europe au XVIIIe Siècle*, in *Memoires de l'Academie Belgique, Classe des Lettres et des Sciences Morales et Politiques*, Bruxelles, 1922, 2e sér., 15 ff. All parties suppose the Lucia of the poem to be Young's wife, who died in January 1739/40. The older view, not very well borne out by the facts, identified Narcissa with her daughter by a former marriage, and Philander with the daughter's husband. Young's chief biographer, W. Thomas, has an interesting theory that Philander is the poet Tickell, and Narcissa a carefully concealed natural daughter. See *Le Poète Edw. Young: Étude sur sa Vie et ses Œuvres*, Paris, 1901, pp. 144-69.

59. "Night I," in *Poetical Works*, Little, Brown & Co., 1854, I, 18, from which my quotations are taken.

60. "Night VII," *ibid.*, 166.

61. Cf. Van Tieghem: *op. cit.*, p. 27.

62. Cf. for example, H. H. Clarke: "A Study of Melancholy in Edward Young," Part II, *Modern Language Notes*, XXXIX (1924), 202: "And there lies a deep significance in the fact that, after the neo-classic artificiality, the return of 'I' to literature,—the subjective, introspective tone—should be inseparably linked to the return of melancholy." But surely, granting for the moment the return of the I, we should still exaggerate, in the light of recent researches, to speak of the *return* of melancholy.

63. Cf. Reed: *op. cit.*, 194-97.

64. There are innumerable editions and anthologies wherein one may read "The Grave." My quotations are from *The Poetical Works of Beat-*

tie, Blair, and Falconer (edited by Gilfillan), Edinburgh, 1854, where the poem occupies pp. 133-56.

65. R. D. Havens points out that Blair is one of the very few eighteenth-century authors whose non-dramatic blank verse is definitely Shakespearean rather than Miltonic. See *Influence of Milton*, p. 384.

66. See Draper: *The Funeral Elegy, passim*.

67. "A Poem on Death" (1729), in *Poems on Several Occasions*, 2d ed., London, 1739. On this whole literature see also Reed: *op. cit., passim*.

68. George Gilfillan says in the "Life" prefixed to his edition of Blair that Blair seems to have been nearly an ideal country minister, and that, far from being a "morose and melancholy *solitaire*—musing amid midnight churchyards—stumbling over bones," he was much more likely to be found botanizing on his way home from pastoral visits. *Op. cit.*, p. 122.

69. There could have been no influence from Young. "The Grave" was completed before the "Night Thoughts" began to appear, and published before any beyond the fourth book of Young's poem. It is probable, on the other hand, that Blair's work influenced the later books of Young's. See Carl Müller: *Robert Blair's "Grave" und die Grabes- und Nacht-dictung*, Weimar, 1909, pp. 59 ff.

70. Dodsley, II, 274 ff and III, 303 ff respectively. Mason's youthful opus is avowedly in imitation of "Lycidas." West's "Monody," as well as Lyttelton's, mentioned later, is clearly Miltonic. Dr. Havens remarks that the word monody seems to have come into use through Milton's use of it. See *Influence of Milton*, pp. 549 ff.

71. Dodsley, VI, 284 ff.

72. "To the Right Honourable the Earl of Warwick &c on the Death of Mr. Addison," *ibid.*, I, 22 ff; "To the Memory of the Same Lady. A Monody," *ibid.*, II, 67 ff.

73. *Ibid.*, V, 138 ff.

74. *Ibid.*, V, 202 ff.

75. *Ibid.*, V, 177 ff.

76. "Immortality; or, the Consolation of Human Life. A Monody," *ibid.*, V, 226 ff.

77. *Ibid.*, III, 111.

78. "The Pleasures of Melancholy," *ibid.*, IV, 210-21. Quotations, pp. 211, 211, 217, respectively.

79. See [Young, John]: *A Criticism of the Elegy Written in a Country Churchyard*, London, 1783, p. 10: "Who is there that says, or would be endured to say, 'I will take me pen, ink and paper, and get me out into a

churchyard, and there write me an elegy; for *I do well to be melancholy?"* A review of this book (*Gentleman's Magazine,* May, 1784) says, however, that it is thought to be a burlesque of Johnson's strictures on Gray in the *Lives of the Poets.* The possibility of burlesque is enhanced by the subtitle: "Being a continuation of Dr. Johnson's Criticism on the Poems of Gray."

CHAPTER II

INVOCATION TO MELANCHOLY

1. "The Rosciad," Chalmer's *English Poets,* XIV, 276.
2. See *ante* Chapter I, p. 15 and notes 31, 32. Cf. Mason's "Il Pacifico," and "Il Bellicoso," Chiswick *British Poets* LXXVII, 177 ff; Greville's "The Man of Sorrow" and "The Man of Pleasure," Bell's *Classical Arrangement of Fugitive Poetry,* London, 1789-1800, XIII, 79 ff; also Kirke White's "Thanatos" and "Athanatos," *Poetical Works of Henry Kirke White and James Grahame* (Gilfillan, ed.), Edinburgh, 1856, pp. 105 ff.
3. Text from Globe Edition of the *Poetical Works,* Macmillan, 1917, p. 504.
4. "The Passions. An Ode for Music," *Poetical Works of Gray and Collins,* Oxford edition, 1917, pp. 284-85.
5. "Ode to Fancy," Chalmers, XVIII, 164.
6. "Song" from *The Nice Valour, or the Passionate Madman, Works of Beaumont and Fletcher,* Edinburgh, 1812, IV, 319.
7. Chalmers, XV, 42.
8. "The Fields of Melancholy and Chearfulness," *Poems upon Several Occasions,* London, 1748, pp. 148-49.
9. Henry Headley: "An Invocation to Melancholy. A Fragment," Chiswick *British Poets,* LXXIII, 95. One would not need to know that Headley was a follower of the Wartons to suspect the origin of this variant on Joseph Warton's "goddess of the tearful eye."
10. John Whitehouse: "Ode to Melancholy," *Poems: Consisting Chiefly of Original Pieces,* London, 1787, p. 48.
11. T. R. Shepherd: "Ode to Melancholy," *Gentleman's Magazine,* July, 1796, p. 600.
12. George Dyer: "Ode to Melancholy," *Poems,* London, 1801, p. 5.
13. Hole: "Ode to Melancholy," *Poems, Chiefly by Gentlemen of Devonshire and Cornwall,* [Polwhele, ed.], Bath, 1792, I, 87.

14. "Ode to Melancholy. To the Memory of a Lady who Died of a Cancer in the Breast," Nichols' *Select Collection of Poems*, London, 1782, VIII, 62.

15. "Nerva": "Invocation to Melancholy," *European Magazine*, XI, 452 (June, 1787).

16. W. H--e: "On Melancholy," *Scots Magazine*, LXVI, 219 (Mar., 1804).

17. John Whitehouse: "Elegy, written near the Ruins of a Nunnery," *Poems etc.*, p. 3.

18. "Melancholy. A Fragment" (1794?), Globe Edition of *Poetical Works*, Macmillan, 1924, p. 34. Bowles too describes "desponding Melancholy" as in rags:

> The wind and rain her naked breast had beat,
> Sunk was her eye, and sallow was her hue . . .

("Hope, an Allegorical Sketch," *Poetical Works*, Gilfillan, Edinburgh, 1855, I, 85. The poem was written about 1798.) This seems a rather romantically humanitarian conception.

19. "C": "A Picture of Melancholy," *European Magazine*, XLIX, 374 (May, 1806).

20. Neither is in Havens' bibliography.

21. In "The Pleasures of Melancholy," *Poetical Works* (Mant, ed.), Oxford, 1802, p. 72.

22. An exception is Ann Radcliffe's ode, quoted *post*, pp. 52-53.

23. There are 17 odes, hymns, and invocations to melancholy in Havens' bibliography of poems influenced by the octosyllabics, but only one of them (William Broome's) is dated before 1750, and only one (Motherwell's) after 1805. Neither Hood's poem nor Keats's is included.

24. "Ode to Melancholy," *Scots Magazine*, XVIII, 75 (Feb., 1756).

25. Elizabeth Carter: "Ode to Melancholy," *Poems on Several Occasions*, 2d ed. London, 1766, p. 79.

26. Hole: "Ode to Melancholy," *Poems Chiefly by Gentlemen of Devonshire and Cornwall*, p. 87.

27. Ann Radcliffe: "Ode to Melancholy," *Mysteries of Udolpho*, London, 1824 [first published 1794], p. 325.

28. E. F. Smith: "Ode to Melancholy," *European Magazine*, XLIX, 444 (June, 1806; written, 1796).

29. 3d ed. London, 1759, pp. 77 ff. Both poems have hints also of familiarity with Blair, or more probably with Hervey, of whom Ogilvie was a friend and admirer.

30. In *Poems, etc.*, pp. 79-83.

31. John Whitehouse: "Ode to Melancholy," in *Poems, etc.*, pp. 47-51.

32. Mary Darby Robinson: "Ode to Melancholy," *Poetical Works,* London, 1806, I, 114-16.

33. "Ode to Melancholy," *Poems Chiefly by Gentlemen of Devonshire and Cornwall,* I, 86-94.

34. In the Palmyra passage is one phrase which sounds Ossianic—
        Or call'd to arms, and shook the threat'ning spear—
amid much reminiscent of Gray and possibly of Volney's *Ruins of Empire.*

35. Text from *The Mysteries of Udolpho,* London, 1824, p. 325. The poem is here called simply "To Melancholy," but it was published in *European Magazine,* XXX, 117 f (Aug., 1796) as an "Ode to Melancholy."

36. Emelius Felix Smith: "Ode to Melancholy," quoted in a review of Smith's *Fugitive Pieces in Verse* (Calcutta, 1804), *European Magazine,* XLIX, 444-45 (June, 1806).

37. "Ode to Melancholy," *Poems,* pp. 5-8. The sensibility takes on a definitely humanitarian coloring in another ode of this decade—"The Genius of Melancholy, an Ode," *European Magazine* XXVII, 125 (Feb., 1795), by Wm. Ashburnham Jun. In this poem the youth of Gray's "Elegy" appears as it were in person: he
            Loves to live and die alone,
        For Melancholy mark'd him for her own.
This Enthusiast invokes "Melancholy, heav'nly maid," and with her would do the customary things in the customary places—but would also go about doing good to various unhappy people and thus "Catch a melancholy joy." The mixture of Milton and Gray here is interestingly obvious.

38. "Alphonso": "Melancholy," IV, 211 f.

39. G-e D-n-l: "Ode—To Melancholy," III, 167 ff.

40. Text from *Poetical Works,* 2 vols., Boston, 1857, I, 212-16.

41. Respectively: "Contemplation. An Ode," *Poetical Calendar,* London, 1763, VI, 7; H. Lemoine: "Ode to Contemplation," *London Magazine,* XLVII, 569 (Dec., 1778); Robert Southey: "To Contemplation," *Poetical Works,* New York, 1850, p. 125; Henry Kirke White: "To Contemplation," *Poems, Letters and Prose Fragments (Muses' Library),* p. 70.

42. Henry Green: "To Content. An Ode," *London Magazine,* XLII, 459 (Sept., 1773).

43. Mary Darby Robinson: "Ode to Meditation" (1791), *Poetical Works,* I, 143.

44. Tho. Cole: "Ode to Silence," to be found among other places in Dodsley's *Collection;* see ante Chapter I, p. 15 and note 32.

45. Joseph Warton: "Ode to Solitude," Chalmers, XVIII, 168-69.

46. "Ode to Solitude," *Poetical Calendar*, VIII, 19 (written, 1761).

47. J. C.: "Ode to Solitude," Pearch's *Collection of the Most Esteemed Pieces of Poetry*, 2d ed. London, 1770, III, 277.

48. William Woty: "To Solitude," *Blossoms of Helicon*, London, 1763, p. 82. This is clearly a variant of the opening lines of Thomas Warton's "Pleasures of Melancholy": "Mother of Musings, Contemplation Sage."

49. T. T. R.: "On Solitude," *Gentleman's Magazine*, Feb., 1788, p. 159.

50. Mary Darby Robinson: "Ode to Solitude," *Poetical Works*, I, 37.

51. "Contemplation. An Ode," *Poetical Calendar, op. cit.*

52. H. Lemoine: "Ode to Contemplation," *op. cit.*, pp. 560-70.

53. Southey: "To Contemplation," *op. cit.*, pp. 127-28.

54. Kirke White: "To Contemplation," *Poems, Letters, etc.*, pp. 127-28.

55. J. M.: "Ode to Content," *London Magazine*, XXXV, 431 (Aug., 1766). The first of these phrases is a favorite: cf. for instance Henry Green: "To Content," *op. cit.*

56. J. W.: "Peace of Mind," *European Magazine*, XLIV, 136 (Aug., 1803). This seems to be an unacknowledged reprint of a poem published anonymously in *Gentleman's Magazine*, July, 1758—a curious testimony as to how little the tradition changed in forty-five years.

57. Tho. Adney: "Ode to Health," *European Magazine*, XX, 143-45 (Aug., 1791).

58. Robert Merry: "Ode to Indolence," *Florence Miscellany*, Florence, 1785, pp. 51-52.

59. "Ode to Solitude," *op. cit.*

60. "Fantom": "Solitude," *Scots Magazine*, XIV, 500 (Oct., 1752).

61. William Woty: "To Solitude," *op. cit.*

62. "Ode to Solitude," *London Magazine*, XXXIX, 589 (Nov., 1770).

63. T. T. R.: "On Solitude," *op. cit.* (note 49).

64. Mary Darby Robinson: "Solitude," *op. cit.* (note 50), pp. 37-42.

65. It is interesting to see all the conventional paraphernalia of an ode to solitude vivified by the close and loving observation of a true lover of nature in a late example of this species, John Clare's "Solitude," in *The Village Minstrel*, London, 1820, II, 200 ff.

66. "To the Moon," Chalmers, XV, 149.

67. "Address to Meditation," *London Magazine*, Enl., I, 130 (Aug., 1783). This poem has a reference to druids and is semi-romantic.

68. "On Solitude," *London Magazine*, XLVII, 377 (Aug., 1778). The poem is in elegiac stanza.

69. "Ode to Taste," Bell, XIII, 45.

70. "To Contemplation," *op. cit.*, p. 128.

71. Robert Merry: "Ode to Indolence," *op. cit.*, p. 52.

72. Kirke White: "To Contemplation," *op. cit.*, p. 72. That the tradition was pretty fully established even before the time of "The Enthusiast" and "The Pleasures of Melancholy" may be illustrated by the fact that a long octosyllabic poem called "Contemplation," by William Hamilton of Bangour (written about 1739), appeared serially, unsigned, in the *London Magazine*, XXI, 188, 233-34 (Apr., May, June, 1752), and gives hint of archaism only in the introduction of a love-motif. The poem appears in Havens' bibliography under both dates.

73. *Anatomy of Melancholy*, Pt. I, Sect. II, Mem. II, Subs. VI. Text from Bohn's Library ed., London, 1926, I, 283.

74. Robert Dodsley still prescribes herbs for it; the scarlet poppy of "somniferous head" will bring sleep—

Lo, from thy baum's exhilarating leaf,
    The moping fiend, black Melancholy, flies . . . ("Agriculture" [1754], Chalmers, XV, 361).

75. [Wm. Woty]: *Scots Magazine*, XXII, 425 (Aug., 1760).

76. *Poetical Works*, I, 114-16.

77. "The Progress of Melancholy, a Fragment," *ibid.*, p. 43-48.

78. "The Progress of Melancholy. A Vision. To a Friend," in *Poems and Plays*, a new ed., 2 vols. in 1, Edinburgh, 1805, I, 168 ff. This volume contains also a Miltonic "Address to Meditation" (pp. 11 ff) and Miltonic hymns "to Solitude" (pp. 52 ff) and "to Melancholy" (pp. 79 ff).

79. "Ode addressed to H. Fuseli, Esq., R. A.," *Poems, Letters, etc.*, p. 126.

80. As in Joseph Warton's "Ode against Despair" (Chalmers, XVIII, 166), wherein the poet has a rendezvous with Despair at a Gothic ruin, but is met and strengthened by Patience; and in the "Ode to Despair" by "Horatio" (*European Magazine*, XXVI, 437-38, Dec., 1794), wherein the poet is saved from suicide by Religion.

81. *Poetical Works*, p. 127 (1791). Similar in type is Nathaniel Howard's "To Horror," *Bickleigh Vale, with Other Poems*, York, 1804, pp. 110 ff.

82. *Poetical Works, etc.*, p. 249. Cf. Andrew Erskine: "Shakespeare alone thy ghastly charms enjoy'd"—"Ode to Fear," *Scots Magazine*, XXV, 219 (Apr., 1763).

83. In the ode by "Horatio" mentioned in note 80, and in Mary Robinson's "Ode to Despair," *Poetical Works*, I, 117.

84. James Scott: "Ode on Despair," *Odes on Several Subjects,* Cambridge, 1761, pp. 37-42.

85. "Ode to Superstition" (from the *Speculator,* Vol. I), *Universal Magazine,* LXXXIX, 305-06 (Oct., 1791). The passage seems to owe something to *Macbeth.* The poet later invokes the milder type of superstition which deals in fairies and fancies.

86. Both these common expressions occur in Joseph Warton's "Ode to Superstition," Chalmers, XVIII, 165.

87. "Ode VII," Chalmers, XVII, 350-51 (written, c. 1758). In Dodsley's *Collection* the poem is entitled "Ode to Melancholy." See *ante* Ch. I, p. 8.

88. "On Poetic Melancholy," June, 1791, p. 567.

89. January, 1794, pp. 66-68.

90. Bryan Waller Procter: "Melancholy," *Marcian Colonna,* London, 1820, pp. 171-72.

91. Cf. Anna Laetitia Barbauld's wish in "To a Friend":

> May never more of pensive melancholy
> Within thy heart, beneath thy roof appear,
> Than just to break the charm of idle folly,
> And prompt for others' woes the melting tear . . .
> —*Works* (Aiken, ed.) London, 1825, I, 303.

92. *Poetical Calendar,* London, 1763, V, 111. Lines 3-8 are doubtless levelled at the early Spenserians and the Gothic revival in general, with which we have little to do.

93. Pages 313-15. Signed and dated from Christ-Church, Apr. 11, 1751, Chimaericus Oxoniensis. For the evidence of authorship, see A. S. P. Woodhouse: "Thomas Warton and the 'Ode to Horror,'" *Times* [London] *Literary Supplement,* Jan. 24, 1929.

94. This poem itself offers something of the same confusion. See *post,* pp. 79-81.

95. *Gentleman's Magazine,* May, 1788.

96. John Whitehouse: "Inscription near a Natural Fall of Water," *Poems,* p. 93 (1787).

97. XII, 1-6. The odes are by Sir James Marriot (for retirement) and R. Shephard (against retirement).

98. *Works,* 18 vols., London, 1818, Vol. XVI, Chapters 14 and 15; pp. 1-48. Quotation, p. 30.

99. William Hayley's phrase, in "Epistle to a Friend, on the Death of John Thornton Esq.," *Works,* Dublin, 178-, I, 78.

100. "A Garden-Seat at Home," *Poetical Works*, I, 94.

101. "The Hermit's Vision," Chiswick *British Poets*, LXIII, 220-23. The poem shows strong influence of Gray's "Elegy."

102. "Soliloquy of the Hermit of Lansdowne," *Miscellaneous Works*, Dublin, 1789, p. 31.

103. *Gentleman's Magazine*, Jan., 1788. Cf. also Beattie's early poem "The Hermit," *Poems of Beattie, Blair, and Falconer* (Gilfillan, ed.) Edinburgh, 1854, pp. 86-88; and George Keate's "The Contented Philosopher," Pearch's *Collection*, III, 82-86, in which the philosophical recluse dispenses wisdom in a decidedly elegiac strain.

104. "The Hermitage," *The Isle of Palms and Other Poems*, New York, 1812, pp. 171 ff.

105. Bell, XVII, 75.

106. *Poetical Works of Henry Kirke White and James Grahame*, pp. 37 ff.

107. *Poetical Works with Autobiography*, 2 vols., London, Edinburgh, and Dublin, 1850, II, 234.

108. *Poetical Works*, pp. 81-82.

109. John Miller: "The Wish," April, 1746, p. 216: "Verses occasioned by the Wish," May, 1746, p. 266; "Y": "On Wishing. Occasioned by the Wish in your last," *ibid.*, p. 266.

110. Cf. for example "Content. A Fable" (from the *Cornucopia*), *Gentleman's Magazine*, Mar., 1766, wherein we are told that Content can find a home neither in courts nor in the mountain fastnesses where dwells despairing Poverty, but does find one in Arcadia, with Simplicity.

111. Cf. the very bad "Ode to Content" by William Woty, *Shrubs of Parnassus*, London, 1760, pp. 44-45, in which the "Angelic Seraphim" is told that she can "harmonize despair." Other poems stressing the connection with affliction are "Sacred Contentment. Dedicated to the Afflicted Mind," *London Magazine*, XXI, 379-80 (Aug., 1752) and "A Hymn to Contentment. In Imitation of Gray's Hymn to Adversity," "by a youth not yet nineteen," *Scots Magazine*, XV, 518 (Oct., 1753).

112. "Contentment," *Scots Magazine*, XXXIV, 38 (Jan., 1772).

113. Joseph Holden Pott: "On Content," Elegy II in *Elegies, with Selmane, a Tragedy*, London, 1782, p. 16.

114. *European Magazine*, XI, 108 (Feb., 1787).

115. *Poetical Works*, p. 84.

116. Reviewed in *Gentleman's Magazine*, May, 1782, p. 236. I have not seen the poem.

117. From *A Fortnight's Ramble to the Lakes in Westmoreland, Lan-*

cashire, and Cumberland, by a Rambler. Reviewed with long extracts in *Gentleman's Magazine,* Jan., 1796, pp. 134 f. The places frequented by Retirement include mountains, vales, "a rivulet's pellucid side," and a pagan ruin.

118. "On Retirement," *European Magazine,* XI, 368.

119. *Poems,* 4th ed., London, 1807, pp. 193-207.

120. "Philosophical Retirement. A Poem," *London Magazine,* XLVII, 472-74.

121. [Cowper, Wm.]: *Il Penseroso. An Evening's Contemplation in St. John's Church-yard, Chester. A Rhapsody, Written More Than Twenty Years ago; and Now (First) Published. Illustrated with Notes, Historical and Explanatory,* London, 1767.

122. *Penseroso, or the Pensive Philosopher in His Solitudes, a Poem in Six Books,* London, 1771.

123. *London Magazine,* XXI, 84-85 (Feb., 1752).

124. *European Magazine,* XLIV, 300-1 (Oct., 1803). Signed "Sabinus." Note the hermit-motif.

125. Strictly speaking, the first book of Akenside's work preceded Warton's; and Addison's series of prose essays on "The Pleasures of the Imagination," in the *Spectator,* from which Akenside professed to have taken his title, preceded them all. But Warton's is the first of the melancholy series.

126. *Poetical Works,* I, 68 ff. Warton's admirer, Henry Kirke White, sets forth the argument for the "refined" pleasures of melancholy solitude in the first of a series of prose essays called *Melancholy Hours* (*Remains,* London, 1819, II, 220 ff). In the third essay of the series he presents melancholy as brought to trial as a pernicious idler by an empty-headed worldling, and triumphantly vindicated and set by the side of enthroned Wisdom.

127. *London Magazine,* 239-40 (May, 1747). The poem is about two columns long.

128. *Gentleman's Magazine,* June, 1758.

129. Pearch's *Collection,* III, 120-23. By Miss Whately.

130. B. F.: "The Poet's Pleasures," *Gentleman's Magazine,* Feb., 1767.

131. I. I.: "The Pleasures of Solitude," and "Fantom": "Solitude," *Gentleman's Magazine,* Sept., 1752, p. 428. Francis Fawkes has "Pleasures of Solitude," from the *Fragments of Menander* in the same periodical for July, 1761. There is also a poem signed I. S. in the number for June, 1800, called "The Genius of Solitude. A Vision"; it is a variant on the hermit-motif.

132. In *Poems,* London, 1796, pp. 95-114.

133. For this theme, see *post,* Chapter IV.

134. Compare the fact that "Thanatopsis," the masterpiece of the melancholy genre in the United States, was written by a youth of seventeen. It may be added that there is a blank verse poem called "The Pleasures of Solitude" in *The Poetical Magazine,* II, 335 ff, as late as 1810. It is somewhat religious in tone.

135. Text from *The Pleasures of Memory with Other Poems,* London, 1802. It is interesting to note that Robert Merry ("Della Crusca" in his lighter moments), an acquaintance of Rogers, could not find in memory even the melancholy pleasure which Rogers describes. He wrote a reply called "The Pains of Memory," in the same measure, which is bound with some editions of Rogers' poem—e.g. *The Pleasures of Memory, and Other Poems, by Samuel Rogers, Esq. to Which Is added The Pains of Memory, by Robert Merry, A. M.,* New York, 1820. Merry's poem occupies pp. 123-42. Bernard Barton also wrote a fragmentary reply ("The Pains of Memory. A Fragment," *Metrical Effusions,* Woodbridge, 1812, pp. 3-24), the main burden of which is the pains of remembered guilt.

136. This passage is introduced by a couplet strongly reminiscent of the opening lines of Johnson's "Vanity of Human Wishes":

> Survey the globe, each ruder realm explore;
> From Reason's faintest ray to Newton soar . . . p. 21

137. Page 49.

138. Page 52.

139. Page 55.

140. Page 61.

141. Text from *Poetical Works with a Memoir by Professor W. E. Aytoun,* Boston, 1857, pp. 17-54. George Darley's "Sorrows of Hope" (*Poetical Works, Muses' Library,* pp. 499-520) is a love story, and seems to owe nothing to Campbell except possibly the title.

142. London, 1927. The poem occupies pp. 189-248 (including 24 pages of notes) in Volume VI, *Poems.* Text from this edition.

143. The motto for Part II is from one of Gray's Latin poems: *O Lacrymarum fons, tenero sacros* etc.

144. *Ibid.,* p. 190.

145. Page 191.

146. Page 193.

147. Page 209.

148. He had met Jane Gryffydh, it will be recalled, in his youthful wanderings in Wales. Eight years passed, during which the two did not

once see or communicate with each other. Then suddenly Peacock proposed marriage—by letter—and was immediately accepted. The marriage, which seems to have been completely successful, was, as Shelley remarked, like the conclusion of one of Peacock's own novels. Its date is subsequent to that of this poem.

149. Page 212.
150. Page 223.

CHAPTER III

SIC TRANSIT GLORIA MUNDI

1. *A Bibliography of Thomas Gray,* Yale Univ. Press, 1917.
2. A reviewer in the *Gentleman's Magazine* for Nov., 1788, reproaches John Whitehouse for not writing his "Elegy Written Near the Ruins of a Nunnery," in "the English elegiac measure, introduced by Gray."
3. "Grenville and Julia," by Anna Seward, pp. 12 ff; "Stanzas," p. 35; "The Robin Red-Breast," by Mrs. Witlen, pp. 113 f; "The Fond Wife, to Her Husband at Sea," by Mrs. le Noir, pp. 353 f; "Epitaph in a Downtown Church-Yard. On a Young Lady, Who Died in a Consumption in 1796," p. 401.
4. Anna Seward, by the way, wrote a good many elegies published elsewhere, but did not use Gray's stanza in them.
5. "Elegy," by Adeline, dated from Edinburgh, December 19, 1804, pp. 86 f; "Propertius, Elegies, I, II, III," by W. Preston, pp. 102 ff; "Love Elegy. The Thoughts from Petrarch," by J. K., pp. 109 f; "Elegy on the Death of a Poor Idiot," pp. 300 ff; "Elegiac Ode," by P. H. F., pp. 426 f.
6. Of the 106 items on Northup's list dated between 1751 and 1830, I have seen, entire or (in half a dozen cases) in representative extract, all but 19; of these 19 I have seen a stanza or two or a press notice of 6. One of the press notices (Review of "A Parody of Gray's Elegy" by an Oxonian, *Monthly Review,* Apr., 1776) is an exposure of plagiarism. Several other instances of plagiarism, as well as some which may be merely reprintings, are revealed by an examination of the material. William Woty's "The Long Vacation," a partial parody (*Shrubs of Parnassus,* 1760) was reprinted in *The Mirror* (Apr. 19, 1823) as by W. R. An Anonymous "Elegy Written among the Tombs of Westminster Abbey" (1762) reappears in Roach's *Beauties of the Poets of Great Britain* (1793) under the title of "Evening Reflections written in Westminster Abbey," credited to G. W. Considering the vogue of initials, pseudonyms, and anonymity

in the eighteenth century, these might conceivably be altered reprints. But there is clear plagiarism involved in the transformation of the anonymous "Elegy Written in Westminster Hall during the Long Vacation" (1777) into J. B. Fisher's only slightly different "Pettifogger, written in Westminster Hall during the Long Vacation of 1812, and addressed to a Little Attorney." Both these parodies, oddly enough, are printed by Walter Hamilton, *Parodies of the Works of English and American Authors,* London, 1888, V, 9 f and 25, with no notice taken of the close correspondence between them. More amusing is the change that has come over "An Elegy, Written in St. Stephen's Chapel" between 1798 and 1816, in order to admit the castigation of the unpopular Castlereagh (*European Magazine,* XXX, 189, Mar. 1798, and *New Tory Guide,* London, 1819—poem dated 1816). The "Elegy in a London Church-yard" printed in Southey's *Annual Anthology* for 1800 seems also to be an inexact reprint or a plagiarism of the parody of the same reprinted by Hamilton (*op. cit.,* pp. 18-19) from the *Morning Post and Gazetter* for Nov. 28, 1799.

7. Specifically: "An Evening Contemplation in a College" (1753), by John Duncombe, quoted from the *Poetical Calender,* VII, 34; "The Nunnery. An Elegy. In Imitation of the Elegy in a Church-yard" (1764) [by Edward Jerningham], Hamilton *op. cit.,* p. 5; "Elegy on the Death of *The Guardian Outwitted*" (1764), *ibid.,* p. 6; "An Elegy Written in Westminster Hall during the Long Vacation" (1777), *ibid.,* p. 9; "An Elegy Written in St. Stephen's" (1784), *ibid.,* p. 10; "An Elegy in a London Church-yard" (1799), *ibid.,* p. 18; "Elegy, Written in Poet's Corner, Westminster Abbey" (1802), *The Spirit of the Public Journals,* VI, 131; "Elegy, Written at a Christmas Feast in the Country" (1803), by David Carey, Hamilton, *op. cit.,* p. 13; "Elegiac Stanzas, on returning at Daybreak, through an Alley in London, from a Ball at Lady Dash's" (1814), by Horace Twiss, *ibid.,* p. 14; "The Camp. A Parody on Gray's Elegy in a Country Churchyard" (1814), by Sir Wm. Young, *Notes and Queries,* 3d Ser., I (May 31, 1862), 432; "An Elegy, Written in the King's Bench Prison" (1821), Hamilton, *op. cit.,* p. 16.

8. "Parody of Gray's Elegy in a Country Churchyard" (1765), *Poetical Register* for 1804, p. 471; "An Elegy Written in a London Church-yard. Parody," *Annual Anthology* for 1800; "Elegy Written in Drury-Lane Theatre" (1818), Hamilton, *op. cit.,* p. 12; "Elegy in St. Stephen's Chapel" (1816) *New Tory Guide,* 1818, p. 83; "An Elegy, Written in the King's Bench Prison" (1821), Hamilton, *op. cit.,* p. 16.

9. "Elegy, Written in a Grub Street Garret" (1788), Hamilton, *op. cit.,* p. 10.

10. "Elegy on the Death of *The Guardian Outwitted*" (1764), *ibid.,* p. 6.

11. The first line of this elegy is the second quoted above.

12. "An Elegy. In Imitation of Gray. Written in the King's Bench Prison. By a Minor" (1790), Hamilton, *op. cit.,* p. 17.

13. Phrase from "Nocturnal Contemplations in Barham Downs Camp" (1795), Hamilton, *op. cit.,* p. 20. The other camp elegy is "The Camp. A Parody of Gray's Elegy in a Country Churchyard" (1814), by Sir Wm. Young, "sometime Governor of the Island of Tabago," the opening line of which is the next to last quoted above.

14. Compare Reed: *Background of Gray's Elegy,* the final sentence, p. 250: "Milton had presented Melancholy as enlightened and noble: Gray pictures it as lovely and humane." I have called a poem a parody when it follows, in whole or in part, the structure of the model and even adapts its phrases; an imitation is a poem inspired by the model, but not following it in structure, or, except incidentally, in phraseology.

15. See "An Elegy, written on a Poor, Honest Man, who lived and died an Honour to his Species in the most enviable Obscurity," *Gentleman's Magazine,* July, 1775, p. 339; "Verses written after the Funeral of Billy Twigger, of Hadleigh," *Suffolk Garland* (1818), pp. 300 ff, which celebrates a harmless idiot; "The Grave of the Convict," reviewed in the *Literary Gazette,* Oct. 25, 1817, with a seven-stanza quotation; "A Paraphrase of Gray's Elegy, written on the Unfortunate Catastrophe of the late Mr. Henry Weston, who was executed for Forgery, July, 1796," reviewed in *Monthly Review,* Aug., 1796, as an example of "misplaced compassion for criminals"; J. H. Moore's "The Chelsea Pensioner," Chiswick *British Poets,* LXXIII, 52. All these are on Northup's list except the last.

16. The nature poems on Northup's list seem to me rather doubtful as imitations. See Abraham Portal's "Morning Elegy" and "Evening Elegy," *Poetical Calendar,* XII, 65 ff; John Scott's four "Elegies," which follow the seasons, Chiswick *British Poets,* LXX, 136 ff. The Spring elegy from this group, by the way, proves to be identical with the "Elegy Written at the Approach of Spring" listed as by J. S., *Poetical Calendar,* III, 5 ff.

17. For these themes in connection with melancholy see *post,* Chapters VII and VI.

18. *The Poetical Works of Gray and Collins,* Oxford, 1917, pp. 91 ff.

19. *Poetical Works* (Globe Edition), Macmillan, 1924, p. 487. The poem was first published with "Alastor" in 1816.

20. No. 26, March 30, 1711. The adoption of this prose piece into the

fraternity of poetic meditations on death is illustrated by the fact that Roach reprints a passage from it in his *Beauties of the Poets of Great Britain* (1793) along with "The Grave," the "Elegy in a Country Church-yard," and various verses imitative of Gray, Young, and the rest.

21. "An Elegy Written in St. Bride's Churchyard," reviewed as a "very indifferent imitation" in *Gentleman's Magazine*, Mar., 1769, p. 157—I have not seen the poem; "Meditations, Written in a Churchyard," by J. B., *ibid.*, May, 1791, p. 661; and the two elegies in a London Churchyard referred to *ante*, note 6.

22. "Woodstock" (1761), attributed to Hugh Dalrymple, reprinted in Bell's *Fugitive Poetry*, IX, 9 ff; "An Elegy on a Family-Tomb," by J. J. B—, *European Magazine*, Jan., 1786, p. 49; "Elegy, on the Tomb of some Sailors shipwrecked on the Coast of Cornwall," *Universal Magazine*, Apr., 1797, pp. 287 f; "The Grave of the Convict" reviewed in the *Literary Gazette*, Oct. 25, 1817.

23. "Written among the Tombs of Westminster Abbey" (1762), altered to "Evening Reflections written in Westminster Abbey" (1793)—see *ante*, note 6; "Elegy, written in Westminster Abbey," by P. Courtier, *Universal Magazine*, Feb., 1796, pp. 136 f; "Elegy, written in Poets' Corner, Westminster Abbey," *Spirit of the Public Journals*, 1802.

24. "Written in a Churchyard, on Seeing a Number of Cattle Grazing in It," *Poetical Works* (Henry Lonsdale, ed.) Edinburgh, 1842, pp. 164 ff. The poem is dated, 1766.

25. "The Church-Yard," in *Poems Pastoral, Satirical, Tragic, and Comic*, Edinburgh, 1791, pp. 252 ff. There are even stronger reminiscences of Gray in Learmont's "Address of Death to the Proud Man," *ibid.*, pp. 150 ff.

26. "Elegy, composed among the Tombs," *Poetical Magazine*, II, 179 ff. The poem is in elegiac stanza and the first part frequently paraphrases Gray. Then there is a series of meditations on the possible inhabitants of individual tombs, somewhat after the manner of Hervey, and a long death-bed scene which probably owes something to Young.

27. Pages 99 ff; quotation from first stanza.

28. *Complete Poetical Works, Muses' Library*, pp. 450 ff. A version of this poem appeared in *The Amulet; or, Christian and Literary Remembrancer* for 1828, pp. 105 ff. Bowles also has a poem, of uncertain date, in elegiac stanza, "On a Sun-Dial, in the Churchyard of Bremhill," *Poetical Works*, I, 292.

29. Chiswick *British Poets*, LXVI, 35 ff. Mickle has also a funeral

elegy in Gray's stanza wherein he represents himself as meditating at night by the tomb of the departed: "Pollio" (1765), *ibid.*, p. 39.

30. *The Poetical Works of Henry Kirke White and James Grahame,* p. 115. White's dates are 1785-1806.

31. *Minor Poems,* London, 1824, pp. 140 ff.

32. *Memoirs, Letters, and Poems of Bernard Barton,* edited by his Daughter, Philadelphia, 1850, pp. 196 f.

33. "Lines written beneath an Elm in the Churchyard of Harrow," *Complete Poetical Works* (Globe ed.), Macmillan, 1907, p. 71. The poem was written in 1807 and published in 1808.

34. "A Summer Evening Churchyard, Lechlade, Gloucestershire," *Works,* pp. 487 f. The poem seems to have been written in 1815.

35. *Poems,* p. 41. The sonnet is from a novel, and dated 1798.

36. "The Author," Chalmers, XIV, 333. He is less respectful in "The Candidate," where he writes that

some rhyming guest
Roams through the church-yard whilst his dinner's dress'd.
—ibid., p. 357.

37. Edward Moore: "An Elegy, Written among the Ruins of a Nobleman's Seat in Cornwall (1760), *Poetical Calendar,* VIII, 88 ff; John Cunningham: "Elegy on a Pile of Ruins" (1761), Chalmers, XIV, 443 ff; Edward Jerningham: "An Elegy written among the Ruins of an Abbey" (1765), Pearch's *Collection,* II, 117 ff; George Keate: *Netley Abbey. An Elegy,* London, 1764; Thomas Warton: "Written at Vale-Royal Abbey in Cheshire" (1777), *Poetical Works,* I, 139; Edward Hamley: "Reflections in Netley Abbey" (1796), reviewed with long extract in *Monthly Review,* Aug., 1796, p. 47.

38. "An Elegy written at a Carthusian Monastery in the Austrian Netherlands" (1775), reviewed with long extract in *Gentleman's Magazine,* Dec., 1775, pp. 580 f.

39. "Written among the Ruins of Pontefract Castle" (1756), Chiswick *British Poets,* LXV, 169. This poem is not on Northup's list, but it seems to me to be clearly an imitation as many of the others. Cf. also "Lines, Written at Midnight, amongst the Ruins of Ludlow Castle," by "Mr. Hodges, an attorney," *Gentleman's Magazine,* Sept., 1795.

40. "Reflections in Netley Abbey," *op. cit.,* note 37.

41. *Op. cit.,* note 37.

42. "Elegy," *Poetical Works* (Skeat, ed.), London, 1891, I, 58 f. Northup does not mention this poem, but Skeat gives it as "Elegy [after Gray]."

43. "Elegy on Newstead Abbey," *Poetical Works*, p. 38. Published 1807.

44. "The Sequestered Bard. An Elegy. Occasioned by the Death of Mr. Shenstone, Esq." (signed Philander, Worchestershire), Feb., 1763, p. 90.

45. "Elegy on the Death of R. Burns, the Ayreshire Plowman" (signed Ninfield), Aug., 1796, pp. 183 f.

46. "Elegy," by Bryan Edwards, Apr., 1764.

47. "To Miss Whately on her Poems," by B. F., Apr., 1766.

48. "Elegiac Stanzas on the Rev. Mr. Eccles (lost trying to save a boy from drowning in Avon)," Sept., 1777.

49. "On the Approach of Winter. An Elegy," by J--n W--e, Nov., 1778.

50. "Elegy," by W. J., Sept., 1783.

51. "Lines Written Impromptu on the Tolling of a Bell," by D. Rivers, Aug., 1798. No wonder he could write them impromptu, with so much help from Young and Gray! These extracts are all from the 19 poems mentioned as not on Northup's list.

52. "Philanthus: A Monody" (1752), Chalmers, XVIII, 200.

53. "Sickness" (published posthumously, 1790; probably written about 1788), Chiswick *British Poets,* LXXIII, 125.

54. Quotations respectively from "Written . . . in the Cloisters of Christ Church, Oxford" (1762), Chiswick *British Poets,* LXIII, 203; "Elegy on Leaving the River of Plate" (1763), *ibid.,* p. 206; "The Hermit's Vision, *ibid.,* p. 223. The first is clearly a conscious imitation, practically a parody.

55. "A Day in Autumn," *Poetic Vigils,* London, 1824, p. 169.

56. *Fragments of Ancient Poetry, collected in the Highlands of Scotland,* 1760; *Fingal, an Ancient Epic,* 1761; *Temora,* 1763. In 1773 Macpherson published a definitive edition called the *Poems of Ossian.* A convenient statement of the history of the Ossianic controversy and of what appear to be the real facts of the case may be found in J. S. Smart's *James Macpherson, an Episode in Literature,* London, 1905, or in the "Introduction" to P. Van Tieghem's *Ossian en France,* Paris, 1917.

57. The phrase is J. S. Smart's, *op. cit.,* p. v.

58. See *post,* Chapters V and VI.

59. "Fingal," Book VI, *The Poems of Ossian* (Wm. Sharp, ed), Edinburgh, 1926, p. 99.

60. "Lathmon," *ibid.,* p. 123.

61. "The Battle of Lora," *ibid.,* p. 144. Note the ability of the pagan Ossian to quote the Bible.

62. "Carthon," *ibid.*, p. 175.

63. "Carthon," *ibid.*, p. 184. The quotation is from the famous hymn to the sun with which the poem ends.

64. "Berrathon," *ibid.*, p. 405.

65. See "Cath-Loda," Duan I, *ibid.*, p. 3, and "Carthon," *ibid.*, p. 172.

66. See "Fingal," III, *ibid.*, pp. 69, 95; "Carthon," *ibid.*, p. 172; "Sul-Malla of Lumon," *ibid.*, p. 378.

67. See "The Death of Cuthullin," *ibid.*, p. 107.

68. See "Oina-Moral," *ibid.*, p. 187.

69. See "Temora," VI, *ibid.*, p. 301, "Songs of Selma," *ibid.*, p. 416.

70. See "Cath-Loda," Duan III, *ibid.*, p. 16; "Temora," VI, p. 299, and VII, *ibid.*, p. 313; "Cathlin of Clutha," *ibid.*, p. 335; "Songs of Selma," *ibid.*, p. 417.

71. See "Carric-Thura," *ibid.*, p. 154; "Croma," p. 202; "Temora," VII, p. 313; "Dar-Thula," p. 353.

72. James Montgomery used it as the title and burden of a poem.

73. Book VII, *ibid.*, p. 313.

74. "Fingal," I, *ibid.*, p. 35.

75. "Fingal," III, *ibid.*, p. 71.

76. "Battle of Lora," *ibid.*, p. 148.

77. "Fingal," II, *ibid.*, p. 53.

78. "Battle of Lora," *ibid.*, p. 149.

79. See *ibid.*, pp. 91, 137, 221; 160; 213.

80. See *ibid.*, pp. 274, 295; 61, 91; 42; 164; 265, 313, 335, 417.

81. See *ibid.*, pp. 42, 46, 48, 60, 85, 98, 148, 161.

82. *Ibid.*, pp. 3-10. The notes and argument take up at least half the space in these pages.

83. See *ibid.*, pp. 8, 236; 10; 35, 47, 81; 49; 50; 81; 87; 89, 177; 158; 183; 184; 247; 256; 76; 301.

84. See *ibid.*, pp. 38, 49, 54, 100, 149, 150, 381.

85. See *ibid.*, pp. 2, 56, 68, 146, 196, 323, 361.

86. See *ibid.*, pp. 5, 56, 289; 16, 43, 136, 197, 294, 308, 321.

87. See *ibid.*, pp. 76, 82, 148, 258.

88. See *ibid.*, pp. 249, 365, 401.

89. See *ibid.*, pp. 373, 253.

90. See *ibid.*, pp. 9, 252, 299, 319, 373.

91. See *ibid.*, pp. 5, 13, 54, 177, 127; 286, 323; 252, 276, 189, 276, 313; 17, 174, 349, 352, 388; 285, 290; 310; 321; 136, 197; 250.

92. "Fingal," III, *ibid.*, p. 71; "Cath-Loda," I, *ibid.*, p. 9. The various references given above are merely illustrative and by no means exhaustive.

370 NOTES: CHAPTER III

93. "Ossian in der Schönen Litteratur Englands bis 1832, mit Ausschluss der sogenannten Englischen Romantikers," *Englische Stüdien,* XXIII, Leipsig, 1897, 31-70 and 366-401.

94. Schnabel lays this grouping to the initial interest in the appearance of the "translations" and the revival of interest at the time of the report of the Highland Society.

95. Couplet: Ewen Cameron: *The Fingal of Ossian . . . rendered into Heroic Verse,* Warrington, 1776; George Hervey: *Ossian's Fingal . . . rendered into English Verse,* London, 1814. Blank verse: Anthony Davidson: *The Poems of Ossian . . . turned into blank verse,* Salisbury, 1810 (?); John Shackleton: *The Poems of Ossian . . . attempted in English Verse,* Birmingham, 1817.

96. This is particularly true of Davidson. In his "Temora," also, he is more faithful than the others. For instance, the word *dark* or its derivatives occurs 45 times in his version of Book I, as against 31 times in Thomas Burke's couplet version (*Temora: an Epic Poem . . .* Perth, 1818) and 35 times in Shackleton's very Miltonic blank verse.

97. *Monthly Review,* XXIX, 210 (Sept., 1760).

98. Another anonymous version of the same fragment in elegiac stanza appeared, along with an heroic couplet rendering of Fragment XII, in *Scots Magazine,* XXII, 360 ff (July, 1760); the elegiac version is called "a piece in the taste of the celebrated Mr. Gray." Edward Lovibond has a fairly successful version of the same story in a twelve-line stanza (Chalmers, XVI, 292 f). Richard Polwhele's "Ossian Departing to his Fathers" (1780) (*Poems Chiefly by Gentlemen of Devonshire and Cornwall,* I, 148 ff) is in elegiac stanza.

99. Jenyns: passage from "Carthon," Chalmers, XVII, 619; Logan: "Ossian's Hymn to the Sun," *ibid.,* XVIII, 55; Seward: "Crugal's Ghost," "The Ghost of Cuthullin," *Poetical Works,* III, 15 ff; Byron: the hymn to the sun from "Carthon," *Poetical Works,* p. 78.

100. "Imitated from Ossian" and "The Complaint of Ninathoma" (1793), *Poetical Works,* p. 20 f.

101. *The Works of the Caledonian Bards,* Edinburgh, 1778.

102. Edinburgh, 1780.

103. See *Ossian en France,* I, 39 ff.

104. Edmund, Freiherr von Harold: *Poems of Ossian Lately Discovered,* Dusseldorf, 1787.

105. Cf. the attempt of an anonymous American to furnish Christian coloring for Gray's "Elegy" by inserting a stanza about the piety of the poor and the eventual "trump divine." See Hamilton, *op. cit.,* p. 42.

106. "Ethelgar," "Kenrick," "Cerdick," "Godred Croven," "The Hirlas" (two versions), "Gorthmund," in *Works* (Southey and Cottle, editors), London, 1803, III, 5 ff, 231 ff. Schnabel examines these "poems" in detail to indicate borrowings, etc., *op. cit.*, pp. 46 ff. "Gorthmund" alone is somewhat "dark" in spirit.

107. *Poems,* pp. 87 ff; quotation, p. 95. Brydges says this is versified from a note to "Croma."

108. "Anna and Harland," *Poetical Works,* p. 11.

109. II, 90 ff. By Wm. Case, Jr.

110. *Collective Works,* Norwich, 1823, I, 37 ff. Sayers has also a "War-Song of Fingal," pp. 236 ff, in the style of Macpherson, though in verse. All Sayers' rather numerous Celtic pieces show Macpherson's influence. Yet Schnabel omits Sayers from his bibliography.

111. "Eclogue in the Manner of Ossian," *Poetical Works,* Paisley, 1895, pp. 195 ff. This imitation is for some reason not listed by Schnabel. Nor does he mention Peacock's two imitations, "Clonar and Tlamin" and "Foldath," *Poems,* pp. 76 ff. These, like Brydges', are "imitated from a little poem in Macpherson's notes on Ossian." They are in stanzaic form. Anna Barbauld, also, has an imitation not in Schnabel's bibliography: "Seláma; an Imitation of Ossian," *Works,* II, 176 ff. It is in Ossianic prose.

112. "The Death of Colmar and Orla," *Poetical Works,* pp. 60 ff.

113. Sir John Hawkins and others: *Probationary Odes for the Laureateship,* London, 1787, pp. 22 ff.

114. See Van Tieghem: *Ossian en France,* and Rudolph Tombo: *Ossian in Germany* (New York, 1901). Tombo points out how thoroughly the German romanticists fell under the spell of Macpherson's vague melancholy. Scarcely a writer of note escaped. Even Goethe in youth translated the "Songs of Selma" and sent them back to England with immensely increased authority in *Werthers Leiden.*

115. Detailed discussion of the debt of all the writers mentioned to *Ossian* may be found in Schnabel, *op. cit., passim.* A much fuller account of the very large influence on Byron's early verse is given in Friedrich Wilmsen's *Ossians Einfluss auf Byrons Jugendgedichte,* Jena, 1903.

116. See the descriptive poems in *Poetry, Chiefly in the Scottish Language,* 2 vols., Inverness, 1804, *passim,* for Ossianic influence; for the conversations referred to see "Kinraka," pp. 149 ff, and "Glenfiddich," pp. 161 ff.

117. See *Zingis* (1769) and *Sethona* (1774). Both, especially *Zingis,* are full of Ossianic imagery.

118. "On Leaving Newstead Abbey" (1803, motto added in 1807), *Poetical Works*, p. 1.

119. Hector Macneill: "The Pastoral, or Lyric Muse of Scotland" (1808), Walsh's *British Poets*, XXXIX, 239.

120. Hole: "Ode prefixed to a Version of Fingal," *Poems Chiefly by Gentlemen of Devonshire and Cornwall*, I, 82.

121. Robert Lloyd: "The Poetry Professor," *North Briton*, No. 22, Sat., Oct. 30, 1762.

122. George Dyer: "Ode XVI," *Poems*, p. 88. There are amusing glimpses of this young poetic radical in some of Lamb's early letters. See especially the account of the argument between the two youthful poets concerning the appropriateness of the epithet "dark" in the next to last line quoted—To Robt. Southey, Nov. 28, 1798, *The Letters of Elia* (*Everyman's Library*), Dutton, n.d., I, 107 f.

123. "Lochleven," *Poetical Works*, pp. 91-92.

124. "Lines Written on Visiting a Scene in Argyleshire," *Poems*, pp. 113-14.

125. "A Poetical Fragment on a Deserted Mansion," *Poems*, pp. 153 ff.

126. *Ante*, Chapter II, p. 45. The poem opens the volume of *Poems, consisting Chiefly of Original Pieces*.

127. III, 124 ff.

128. "The New Style; or, Lord B--'s Gardener," *Gentleman's Magazine*, Oct., 1757, p. 471.

129. "English Garden," I, Chalmers, XVIII, 382.

130. Cf. Edw. Lovibond: "On Rebuilding Combe Neville," Chiswick *British Poets*, LXIII, 128; E. W--g: "Elegy, on Leaving the Neighborhood of Southampton, July, 1809," *Poetical Magazine*, II, 29 f.

131. The *Poetical Magazine* (1809-11) has poems on the ruins of Tintern, Kirkstal, Dover, Denbeigh, and Netley Abbeys, of Harleich Castle, and of "St. B-- Priory."

132. See Sneyd Davies: "Describing a Voyage to Tintern Abbey," Bell, IV, 35 ff.

133. Chiswick *British Poets*, LXXIII, 116 f. The poem has echoes of Gray and Thomas Warton.

134. Robertson, Eric S. (ed.) : *English Poetesses*, London, 1883, pp. 72 f.

135. *Poems*, pp. 424-25.

136. "Written at Ocriculum, Italy," *Gentleman's Magazine*, Aug., 1773.

137. *Florence Miscellany*, p. 87.

138. "Italy: Rome," *Poetical Works* (Bell, ed.) London, 1892, p. 292.

139. Cf. Darley: "Nepenthe," *Poems*, pp. 66-67; Bryan Waller Procter: "Babylon," *English Songs*, Boston, 1844, p. 85.

140. *Scots Magazine*, XXII, 316 (June, 1760). An extended account in elegiac quatrain in Hole's "Ode to Melancholy" has already been referred to.

141. *Poems*, pp. 7 ff and 169 ff.

142. *Oxford Prize Poems*, 8th ed., Oxford, 1834.

143. "Ode to Time, Occasioned by Seeing the Ruins of an Old Castle," *Day of Judgment and Other Poems*, pp. 91 ff.

144. *Poems*, 2 vols., London, 1864, I, 296-97.

145. "Fuimus," *ibid.*, p. 319.

146. E.g. Elizabeth Carter's two poems on a watch (1766) (*Poems on Several Occasions*, pp. 29 f, 56) and James Montgomery's "The Time Piece" (1816) (*Poetical Works*, 4 vols., London, 1841, III, 111 ff).

147. "Time," *Poems, Letters, etc.*, pp. 105 ff; *The Course of Time*, in 10 books (1827), Philadelphia, 1864.

148. Wilmsen (*op. cit.*) says that before 1803 there is evidence of the influence of Gray's "Elegy," but not of Ossian. Between 1803 and 1807 there are Ossianic phrases and the heroic couplet "Hymn to the Sun." Then there is a sudden abundance of material and evidence of a deeper understanding. Wilmsen had access to Byron's *Ossian* (an 1806 edition) with its abundant marginal annotations; one of these refers to "that melancholy which distinguishes every great genius and which seems so remarkably to have distinguished the character of Ossian." Wilmsen thinks the influence of Ossian on Byron waned rather suddenly after 1807; but he finds Ossianic phraseology here and there in "Childe Harold" and the eastern tales. The most lasting influence he takes to be an awakening of Byron's interest in nature.

149. "The Gaiour," *Poetical Works*, p. 316. Here it is a wild-dog, to be sure, not the usual village mastiff.

150. "Childe Harold," IV, stanza 107, *ibid.*, p. 272.

151. "Childe Harold," II, 4, *ibid.*, p. 192; III, 51, p. 228; IV, 107, p. 272; IV, 182, p. 288; "Churchill's Grave," *ibid.*, p. 470.

152. "Siege of Corinth," stanza 18, *ibid.*, p. 438.

153. "Don Juan," IV, 101, *ibid.*, p. 1068. Cf. the prophetic imaginings of London or Britain in ruins in Anna Barbauld's "Eighteen Hundred and Eleven" (*Works*, I, 232 ff), in Kirke White's "Time" (*Poems, Letters, etc.*, p. 112), at the close of Peacock's "Genius of the Thames" (*Poems*, pp. 154-55), and in Ebenezer Elliott's "Love" (*Poetical Works*, 2 vols., London, 1876, I, 74).

154. "Childe Harold," III, 18, *Poetical Works*, p. 222.

155. *Ibid.*, IV, 25, p. 255.

156. *Ibid.*, IV, 131, p. 278.

157. *Ibid.*, IV, 78, p. 266.

158. Byron has a poem "To Time," but it turns out to be only an expression of personal suffering and defiance at the time of his flight from England, *ibid.*, p. 308.

159. *Poetical Works*, pp. 487, 503, 558, 662, 664.

160. *Ibid.*, pp. 487, 571.

161. *Ibid.*, p. 569.

162. "Ozymandias," *ibid.*, p. 506. The sonnet written by Horace Smith on the same theme in one of the famous sonnet contests at Hampstead is not a contemptible poem either.

163. "Prometheus Unbound," close of Act III, *ibid.*, p. 283. Cf. "Hellas," in which we are told that

> The future and the past are idle shadows
> Of thought's eternal flight . . .

and that Thought, Will, Passion, Reason and Imagination "cannot die," but are

> The stuff whence mutability can weave
> All that it hath dominion o'er . . .
>
> —*ibid.*, pp. 446-47.

164. Last lines of "Hellas," *ibid.*, p. 452.

CHAPTER IV

KING DEATH

1. See *post*, Chapter VII.

2. See *Blackwood's Magazine*, XXXIII, 280-81 (1833). The author remarks that "modern taste" shrinks from Young's "epigrammatic labour of expression, and clouded though daring fancy."

3. Cf. Van Tieghem: *La Poésie de la Nuit et des Tombeaux*, pp. 15 ff. Both Van Tieghem and Thomas (*Le Poète Edward Young*, Chapters VIII and IX) discuss the influence of "Night Thoughts" at home and abroad. Thomas notes that after considerable vogue in England, the poem was comparatively unpopular during the first half of the nineteenth century, and that a nascent revival in the 1850's was nipped partly by the attacks of George Eliot in the *Westminster Review*. They both emphasize the vast influence of the poem in Germany—on Ebert, whose transla-

tion is sometimes thought to improve on the original; on Klopstock, who is reported to have been in the habit of preparing himself for work on his *Messiah* by reading Young; on Herder, who all his life counted "Night Thoughts" among his favorite books; and even fleetingly (like Ossian) on Goethe, Richter, Novalis, the Schlegels, and Tieck. In France, as was to be expected from the national temperament, the influence was less; furthermore, it was exercised largely through the highly inaccurate and misrepresentative "translation" of Le Tourneur, who tried, among other innovations, to make the poem deistic instead of Christian. In Spain, on the other hand, its Protestant elements had to be expurgated to escape the Inquisition.

4. Van Tieghem says (*La Poésie, etc.,* Chapter IV) that, with the help of Professor Crane of Chicago, he has found 25 indubitable imitations of "Night Thoughts" in English periodicals for the latter half of the eighteenth century. Unfortunately he does not give references, and I have by no means located them all. He considers that the crest of the wave of English sepulchral verse occurred about 1758-59.

5. Chalmers, XVIII, 27.

6. "The Contemplatist, A Night Piece," Chalmers, XIV, 432 f.

7. Bethune, Geo. W. (ed.): *The British Female Poets,* Philadelphia, 1858, pp. 432 f. The lines appear without title in her *Poems on Several Occasions,* pp. 31 ff.

8. XVIII, 441 (Sept., 1756). Among the other imitations, cf. these from the *Gentleman's Magazine:* "A Midnight Piece, after the Manner of Dr. Young" (Jan., 1755); "Soliloquy of a Repentant Fellow of a College"— which sounds like a parody (Apr., 1759); "Thoughts on Death, Hope, and Trust Occasioned by a Recent Loss" (signed A. H., Oct., 1797); "An Autumnal Thought. In Imitation of Dr. Young" (March, 1799).

9. "More Night Thoughts," *Poetical Calendar,* XII, 102 f (1763). The poem is signed "Mr. W-," and is doubtless identical with the parody by William Whitehead referred to by Thomas (*op cit.,* p. 493), although it does not occur in any edition of Whitehead's works which I have seen. Thomas mentions also a parody by J. Kidgell.

10. For a statement of the literary influences on Blair, and of his own literary influence on others, see Müller, *op. cit., passim.*

11. No one seems ever to have made a study of Hervey's influence, unless we except the incidental material in Van Tieghem, Müller, and Thomas. The edition of the *Meditations* published in Edinburgh in 1797 contains nine encomiums in verse, and an editorial opinion that "There are few books in the English language, which, in so short a time, have

ever passed through such numerous and very large editions." "How many," the editor goes on, "have they [the *Meditations*] transportingly entertained in their retirement and lonely walks!"

12. "Sickness," Book V, Chalmers, XV, 52. He calls Young, among other things, "the friend of virtue and of man."

13. He finds the influence in Cotton's "Night Piece," Thompson's "Sickness," Joseph Warton's odes to "Fancy," "Superstition," and "Despair," Thomas Warton's "Pleasures of Melancholy" and "Ode Written at Vale Royal Abbey," Collins' odes "to Fear" and "on the Superstitions of the Scottish Highlands," Gray's "Elegy," Cunningham's "Elegy on a Pile of Ruins," Beattie's "Triumph of Melancholy" and "The Minstrel," Burns's "Song of Death," and Pollok's *Course of Time*. Practically all of these poems either have figured or will figure in our discussion.

14. Beilby Porteus: "Death," in *Musae Seatonianae: A Complete Collection of the Cambridge Prize Poems, from the first Institution of that Premium by the Reverend Thomas Seaton, in 1750, to the Year 1806. To which are added, Three Poems, Likewise Written for the Prize, by Mr. Bally, Mr. Scott, and Mr. Wrangham*, 2 vols., Cambridge, 1808. This series begins with Smart's five prize-winning poems, and includes, besides "Death," two poems on the Last Judgment, and poems on miscellaneous other religious subjects.

15. XVII, 518 f (Nov., 1748). Signed T. S.

16. Chalmers, XVIII, 28 ff.

17. "Death. A Poem," *Poetical Calendar*, XII, 9 ff.

18. "Thoughts on Sudden Death. To a Lady," *Gentleman's Magazine*, July, 1765.

19. XXIV, 256 (May, 1772).

20. Stanza 10, *Poetical Works*, p. 637.

21. "Thoughts on the Author's Own Death. Written when very Young," *Poems on Several Occasions*, 3d ed., London, 1785, pp. 14 ff. She has also a very melancholy blank verse piece on "Night" written in the shadow of bereavement, *ibid.*, pp. 1 ff.

22. *European Magazine*, XI, 109 (Feb., 1787). It immediately follows the other verses referred to. Has she also been reading *Twelfth Night?*

23. See *ante,* Chapter III, note 6.

24. By Van Tieghem, for instance, *La Poésie etc.*, Chapter IV.

25. *Poetical Works*, I, 55 ff.

26. Text from *A Universal Prayer; Death; A Vision of Heaven; and A Vision of Hell etc.*, etc., from the 2d London ed., Boston, 1829, pp. 25-63.

27. For the theme of the meditation on the starry heavens, see *post*, Chapter VI.

28. Page 42.

29. For discussion of these poems, see Reed, *op. cit., passim.*

30. Glynn's poem occupies pp. 71-82, Bally's pp. 299-320.

31. Text from 3d ed., London, 1759.

32. "The Last Day," *Poetical Works,* pp. 96 ff.

33. *Poetical Works,* pp. 1 f.

34. H. S.: "The Last Day. An Ode," *Town and County Magazine,* VII, 493 f. (Sept., 1775).

35. "Judgment and Eternity," *Flowers from Sharon; or Original Poems on Divine Subjects,* London, 1794, p. 93. Lee has another Last Day poem called "The Second Advent," *ibid.,* pp. 148 ff.

36. *Poems, Letters, etc.,* p. 124.

37. *Poetical Magazine,* II, 316-23. This poet has in the same periodical also a "Hymn on the Day of Judgment," and "Lines, written in a Church, while waiting to Bury a Corpse," as well as "On the Stings of Conscience," which ends with fear of hell.—*ibid.,* III, 93 f; III, 279 f; and II, 276.

38. John Clare: "The Dream," *Shepherd's Calendar,* London, 1827, pp. 200-18.

39. "Memoir" in *The Course of Time,* p. xx.

40. "A Vision of Hell," in *A Universal Prayer, etc.,* pp. 84 ff. Montgomery said, of course, that he was describing types, not individuals; and in truth I am assuming from the "type" that it was Byron and not another he was accused of describing in this particular passage. Montgomery has also a long poem (London, 1830) on *Satan.* This strange composition takes the form of a monologue by the Fiend in which the author cannot refrain from allowing him to talk suspiciously like a Christian minister.

41. Our sage hermit, it would seem, has penetrated even into Heaven.

42. Book I, *op. cit.,* p. 37.

43. Book VII, *op. cit.,* p. 201.

44. *English Thought in the Eighteenth Century,* London, 1902, I, 15.

45. Book III, *op. cit.,* p. 579.

46. *Charles Wesley Seen in His Finer and Less Familiar Poems* (Frederick M. Bird, ed.), New York, 1878, pp. 186 ff.

47. "Perseverence," *ibid.,* pp. 198 ff. It is only fair to add that predestination is not stressed, nor, I think, even mentioned, by the writers of the Last Day whom we have been discussing, though some of them were Calvinists.

48. Hymns illustrative of the conviction of sin and the tortures of doubt are "Jesu, the sinner's Friend, to Thee" (1739), "For One Fallen from Grace" (1749), "Father, I have Sinned" (1740), "For One Convinced of Unbelief" (1749), "For One in Doubt" (1749), "The Tempest" (1749)—*ibid.*, pp. 3 ff, 312 ff, 316 ff, 308 ff, 311 f, 345 ff. There are many others. An interesting group approaching erotic mysticism includes "Groaning for the Spirit of Adoption" (1740), "For Love" (1767), "Another" (on the same) (1767), "Desiring to Love" (1742), "Another" (on the same) (1749), and the deservedy famous "Wrestling Jacob" (1742)—*ibid.*, pp. 321 ff and 334 ff.

49. Journal for Tuesday, Oct. 23, 1739, *The Heart of John Wesley's Journal* (Percy L. Parker, ed.), New York, [1903], p. 65. This is of course only one of his stories of the effects of religious excitement.

50. "Religious Melancholy. An Emblematical Elegy," Chambers, XVI, 400 ff.

51. The field is rather barren also after 1800, although doubtless an examination of the hymns and sacred verse of the dissenters, if the material were available, would reveal traces of religious melancholy. Thomas Gisborne has a little poem "Written for the Use of a Decidedly Pious Young Person Oppressed by Religious Melancholy" (*Walks in a Forest, and Other Poems,* 8th ed., London, 1813), in which he attempts reassurance of his young friend's fears. There is an occasional trace of religious melancholy in Kirke White, and, as has been said, in John Clare. Joseph Swain, the author of *Redemption* (1st American from 5th Edinburgh ed., New York, 1827), to judge by the Memoir prefixed to the poem, certainly experienced it at the time of his conversion (which reminds one somewhat of Cowper's) and occasionally afterwards in intervals of ecstasy; but it has no place in the long doctrinal poem named, although there may be traces of it in his numerous hymns, of which I have seen only one.

52. "A Caution against Despair," Chalmers, XV, 260.

53. Cowper's latest biographer, David Cecil (*The Stricken Deer; or, the Life of Cowper,* London, 1930) is convinced that Calvinistic religion, far from being the cause of Cowper's insanity, gave him the only period of real happiness he ever knew. It is true that Newton's circle found happiness in their assurance of salvation. But, even discounting the harm Newton did to Cowper's shrinking personality by insisting on public prayer and testimony, was not the very intensity of Cowper's delight in salvation fertile soil for the madness which overtook him when he became doubtful of the basis of that delight? Even the Evangelical Dr. Cotton, under whose care Cowper recovered from the 1763 attack, seems to have been rather

dismayed at the almost unbalanced avidity with which his pupil-patient devoured the new belief.

54. *Memoir of the Early Life of William Cowper, Esq., written by Himself,* 3d ed., London, 1817; quotation, p. 71.

55. Aug. 21, 1781, *Correspondence of William Cowper* (T. Wright, ed.), New York, 1904, I, 343.

56. Aug. 16, 1781, *ibid.,* I, 342.

57. "Lines written under the Influence of Delirium," *Poetical Works* (Globe ed.), Macmillan, 1921, p. 23. The descriptive phrase is the editor's.

58. "To the Rev. Mr. Newman," *ibid.,* p. 328, and toward the close of "On Receipt of my Mother's Picture," *ibid.,* p. 322.

59. *Ibid.,* p. 400.

60. Lines 707-14, *ibid.,* p. 143.

61. Lines 325 ff, *ibid.,* p. 153.

62. Book III, 11.108 ff, *ibid.,* p. 217.

63. Apr. 23, 1781, *Correspondence,* I, 292.

64. Lines 515 ff, *Poetical Works,* p. 86.

65. Nov. 5, 1781, *Correspondence,* I, 373.

66. "The Melancholy Evening," Chiswick *British Poets,* LXX, 124.

67. "Vision of Judgment," stanzas 13-15, *Poetical Works,* pp. 637-38. He of course was not alone; interesting poetic evidence of which assertion is Charles Lamb's blank verse meditation "Written at Midnight" (*Poems, Plays and Miscellaneous Essays,* New York, 1893, pp. 22 f), in which he rejoices that God's judgments "are not fix'd By man's erroneous standard."

68. Remembering that David Hume advised a young sceptic to go into the Church for the sake of the "learned leisure" there to be enjoyed, we must not take this fact too seriously.

69. Much more must be said about sensibility and sentimentalism in the following chapters.

70. "The Ghost," Book II (1762), Chalmers, XIV, 304.

71. "Epistle to Miss Honora Sneyd" (1770), *Poetical Works,* I, 80.

72. Chiswick *British Poets,* LXXIII, 98. He will see her "supplicating martyr'd form . . . Bent on the fragments of a broken cross."

73. "Theagenes to Sylvia," Chalmers, XV, 518.

74. Book II, *ibid.,* p. 524.

75. For the development of these types see Eino Railo: *The Haunted Castle. A Study in the Elements of English Romanticism,* London, 1927.

76. "The Minstrel," Book I, *Poetical Works,* p. 11.

77. *Poetical Works, with Memoir by Thomas Brown,* London, 1875, pp. 134 ff.

78. *Complete Works,* pp. 86 ff.

79. Beckford's masterpiece, especially the description of the Hall of Eblis, seems frequently to have furnished suggestions to the Gothic poets. There is an heroic couplet version of the last part of the book in the *Gentleman's Magazine,* Jan., 1790, and following months.

80. James Hogg (1814) also has a heroine who wanders among the stars in a vision. He conceives of each soul as assigned to the star of being to which it is fitted, but ever learning and striving, until all reach perfection. There are, he explains, "prisons in the deep below, Where wickedness sustains proportioned woe." But he does not dwell on them.—"The Pilgrims of thè Sun;" *Works of the Ettrick Shepherd,* London, 1866, II, 125 ff; quotation, p. 138.

81. Chiswick *British Poets,* LXVI, 89.

82. See *The Road to Xanadu, a Study in the Ways of the Imagination,* Houghton Mifflin, 1927.

83. *Complete Poetical Works* (Cambridge Ed.), Houghton Mifflin, 1900, pp. 11 ff. This ballad has also a few touches reminiscent of Scott's early enjoyment of *Ossian.*

84. *Ibid.,* pp. 14 ff.

85. *Ibid.,* pp. 23 ff.

86. *Ibid.,* pp. 26 ff.

87. *Poetical Works,* pp. 111 ff. Amusing stories are told of how the youthful scholar secured for himself the undisturbed use of the rural church as a study during the week. On one occasion he raised the Devil (in the person of a complying brother) to scare away an impertinent neighbor. On another, he caught an old sow whose habit it was to root among the graves in the churchyard, and covered her with some phosphorescent material—to the alarm and amazement of the country people, who were sure that the Devil himself had entered into her.

88. As in the hilarious tale of "The Witch of Fife" in "The Queen's Wake," *Works,* II, 13 ff.

89. *Ibid.,* pp. 32 ff.

90. *Ibid.,* pp. 52 ff.

91. *Ibid.,* pp. 27 ff; the introduction containing the account of the bard begins p. 25. Cf. Wm. Ashburnham: "Sir Archibald, or, the Bark of Hell," which the author says is founded on Scottish tradition. It is not the same story, but a more horrific one, in which the body of Sir Archibald is stolen from his coffin by the impatient fiend.—*Poetical Register* for 1803, pp. 144 ff.

92. "Sir David Graeme," *ibid.,* pp. 62 ff.

93. "The Pedlar," *ibid.*, pp. 64 ff.

94. "Mess John," *ibid.*, pp. 74 ff.

95. "Willie Wilkin," *ibid.*, pp. 80 ff.

96. "Superstition," *ibid.*, pp. 392 f.

97. Respectively: "Lord Archibald," *Poetical Works*, Boston, 1863, pp. 191 ff; 'The Ettin o' Sillarwood," *ibid.*, p. 241 ff; "The Fause Ladye," *ibid.*, pp. 258 ff. Motherwell's poems were published in 1832.

98. Besides the ballads on native themes mentioned, Scott contributed "The Fire King," a lurid tale of an apostate Crusader (*Poetical Works*, pp. 19 ff), and "Frederick and Alice," imitated from "a fragment introduced into Goethe's *Claudina von Villa Bella*" (*ibid.*, pp. 25 ff).

99. There is an hilarious parody of Lewis' style by Horace Smith in *Rejected Addresses* (1812), which purported to be dedicatory poems rejected for the contest held at the time of the rebuilding of Drury Lane Theater after the fire which destroyed it in 1809. The parody is called "Fire and Ale," and relates how the Fire King carried off Miss Drury the first, and the Ale King (alias Samuel Whitebread, President of the committee for the rebuilding of the theater and a noted brewer) magically produced in her stead Miss Drury the second—*Rejected Addresses and Other Poems* by James and Horace Smith (Epes Sergent, ed.), New York, 1860, pp. 348 ff. Cf. also the take-off of the paraphernalia of tempest, midnight, and ghosts, in James Brown's "Sonnet—Being (it is presumed) a very fair specimen of the Pathos, or *Modern Sublime,* and likewise a striking illustration of the *Bathos,* or *Art of Sinking.* Respectfully inscribed to Monk Lewis, Walter Scott, Robert Southey, and William Wordsworth [who seems in strange company here], Esqrs. the most celebrated Masters of these Arts in the Present Day."—*Poetical Magazine*, I, 91 (1809).

100. *The Castle Spectre*, 8th ed., London, 1799, "Prologue," pp. iii ff.

101. Cf. for example: Robert Merry: "Sir Roland," *Florence Miscellany*, pp. 37 f: T. L.: "Leonora, or The Castle of Alvarez," *European Magazine* XXXIV, 332 f. (Oct., 1798); John Learmont: "The Gothic Tale," *Poems etc.*, pp. 11 ff; Hannah Cowley: "A Tale for Jealousy," *Poetry of Anna Matilda*, London, 1788, pp. 82 ff; William Junius Mickle: "The Sorceress," Chiswick *British Poets*, LXVI, 78 ff; Mary Robinson: "The Lady of the Black Tower," *Poetical Works*, II, 80 ff, and "Golfre. A Gothic Swiss Tale," *ibid.*, III, 189 ff; Kirke White: "Gondoline" (which also shows the influence of *Macbeth*), *Poems, Letters, etc.*, pp. 23 ff; Robert Southey: "Donica," *Poems*, Oxford Ed., 1909, pp. 611 f, "Rudiger," *ibid.*, pp. 612 ff, and "Bishop Bruno," *ibid.*, pp. 632 f; Joanna Baillie: "Malcolm's Heir," "The Elden Tree," and "The Ghost of Fadon," in "Metri-

cal Tales," *Dramatic and Poetical Works,* 2d ed., London, 1853, pp. 710 ff; Thomas Moore: "The Ring," *Poetical Works,* Oxford Ed., 1924, pp. 61 ff; Thomas Lovell Beddoes: "Rodolph," *Poems, Muses' Library,* pp. 406 ff, and "Leopold," *ibid.,* pp. 421 ff.

102. (1810) *Complete Works* (Julian Ed.), Scribner's, 1927, I, 5 ff. The plagiarized poem was "The Black Canon of Elmham; or, Saint Edmond's Eve." Cf., also the poem Shelley wrote with Medwin about "The Wandering Jew," *ibid.,* IV, App., pp. 347 ff.

103. Burns has a fragment, for example ("Remorse," *Poetical Works,* Cambridge Ed., Houghton Mifflin, 1897, p. 181) stating that thesis; Anna Barbauld states it in an "Ode to Remorse" (*Works,* I, 251). Byron expressed himself explicitly on this point in conversation with Lady Blessington (See *Conversations of Lord Byron with the Countess of Blessington,* Philadelphia, 1836, p. 106).

104. For example, see "The Story of the Unfortunate Miss M. W. who lately died at Cotton, in Suffolk," *Sentimental Magazine,* July, 1774; Julius Jones: "An Ode to the Memory of Lord Andover," *Gentleman's Magazine,* May, 1800; S. B. Frome: "Forgery; or, The Reflections of a Culprit During the Morning of his Execution," *Poetical Magazine,* I, 128 ff (1809).

105. Phrases from "Childe Harold," III, st. 59, *Poetical Works,* p. 230, and "The Corsair," II, st. 10, *ibid.,* p. 369.

106. Kehama, of course, is a villain, but he is hardly represented as anything else.

107. Railo (*op. cit.*) shows that Southey's Orientalism is little more than a veneer on the Gothic.

108. The incidents referred to occur in "Thalaba," Books II, VIII, and XII, and in "Kehama," Books II, XVI, and XX-XXIV. But selection is difficult.

109. In "Madoc" (1805), Southey made use of the bloody rites of the Aztecs as a source of horror, and here, as the hero and his followers are Christians, the religious tone is even more pronounced.

110. *Poetical Works,* pp. 343 ff; quotation, p. 351.

111. "Melpomene, or the Regions of Terror and Pity: An Ode," Chalmers, XV, 348.

112. Chiswick *British Poets,* LXXIII, 95. Several references have already been made to this poem.

113. Many references have been made to the Spenserian grostesques, which are of course Elizabethan, although non-dramatic.

114. *Poetical Works* (Oxford Ed.), Oxford, 1914, p. 151. God is addressing Jesus :

> Awake, arise to spiritual strife,
> And Thy revenge abroad display
> In terrors at the last Judgement Day . . .

It is interesting to note, too, that Blake illustrated the *Inferno*.

115. "Fair Elenor," *ibid.*, pp. 6 ff.

116. *Ibid.*, p. 12.

117. "The Poison Tree," from "Songs of Experience" (1794), *ibid.*, p. 94.

118. "I Saw a Chapel all of Gold," from the Rossetti MS (written about 1793), *ibid.*, p. 110.

119. *Ibid.*, pp. 241 ff (1789).

120. Cf. Archibald Strong: "The Sinister in Shelley," in his *Three Studies in Shelley and an Essay on Nature in Wordworth and Meredith*, Oxford, 1921. The description in Byron's "Darkness" (1816) is strikingly similar in spirit to certain passages in "The Revolt of Islam."

121. The details of his death are still obscure. It is certain that he attempted suicide at least once. See Royal Snow: *Thomas Lovell Beddoes, Eccentric and Poet*, Covici-Friede, 1928, pp. 90 ff.

122. This fact has been thought sufficient to justify its inclusion here. Certainly Beddoes belongs in spirit rather to the late romantics than to the Victorians.

123. "The Phantom-Wooer," *Poems*, pp. 351 f. Among Beddoes' minor poems, by the way, is a fragment on "Doomsday," *ibid.*, pp. 382 ff. It has Beddoes' inimitable freshness of treatment and eerie lyricism. It begins :

> If I can raise one ghost, why I will raise
> And call up doomsday from behind the East . . .

There is much in the fragment about awakening ghosts and "doomsday's morning star," but nothing of God, or Heaven, or hell.

124. Act IV, sc. 2, *ibid.*, p. 87.

125. Act III, sc. 3, *ibid.*, pp. 67 f (1829) ; Act IV, sc. 4, *ibid.*, pp. 105 ff. (This ballad is first recited, to be sure, in the ducal palace, but it is afterwards referred to and added to in the churchyard) ; Act V, sc. 4, *ibid.*, p. 121 (1824).

126. Act IV, sc. 4, *ibid.*, p. 109.

127. Act II, sc. 2, *ibid.*, pp. 37-38.

128. Act V, sc. 4, *ibid.*, pp. 118 and 128.

129. "Grim, King of the Ghosts; or, The Dance of Death. A Churchyard Tale," *Tales of Terror and Wonder*, London, 1887, pp. 54 ff.

130. "Song from Fragment of an Eccentric Drama," *Poems, Letters, etc.*, pp. 49 ff.

131. *Poetical Works,* pp. 421 f.

132. *The English Dance of Death, by the Author of Dr. Syntax. With 38 Coloured Plates by T. Rowlandson,* 2 vols., London, 1903 ("founded on the original edition published . . . in the year 1815"). There is a foreword also, called "Time and Death."

133. *Ibid.,* I, 188 ff.

134. *Ibid.,* II, 213 ff.

CHAPTER V

BLIGHTED ROSES

1. There are twelve love elegies in *The Poetical Calendar,* an average of one a month, although they are not so distributed, besides one "pastoral elegy" dealing with unhappy love. The editors (Francis Fawkes and William Woty) surprisingly print only one funeral elegy; but there are ten other elegies on various subjects, not all melancholy.

2. There are exceptions. Pratt's elegy called "Tenderness," in *Poetical Amusements at a Villa near Bath* (IV, 195 ff, London, 1781), is in an irregular meter like an ode or a monody. Usually, however, such exceptions as occur are in the "pastoral elegies."

3. "Damon and Sylvia," Bell, VIII, 146 ff.

4. [Francis Noel Clarke Mundy]: "Absence" (1764), *Poems,* Oxford, 1768, pp. 61 ff.

5. "Elegy," *Gentleman's Magazine,* Oct., 1788.

6. Tho. Percy: "Cynthia, an Elegiac Poem," Dodsley, VI, 234 ff; reprinted, Bell, VIII, 141 ff.

7. "Two Love Elegies" (II), *Poetical Calendar,* V, 81 ff; reprinted, Bell, VIII, 162 ff.

8. John Whitehouse: "Elegy. To Delia," *Poems, etc.,* p. 26.

9. "In Answer to the Foregoing" (advice from a friend under title of "To Damon"), *Poetical Calendar,* V, 67 ff; reprinted, Bell, VIII, 151 ff.

10. Tho. Blacklock: "The Wish. To Urania," Bell, VIII, 122 ff; quotation, p. 125.

11. B. H.: "A Pastoral Elegy," *Town and Country Magazine,* VII, Aug., 1775.

12. "Patricius": "The Dying Shepherd," second of "Two Pastoral Elegies," *Gentleman's Magazine,* Aug., 1766.

13. "An Elegy written on Valentine's Morning," Dodsley, VI, 217 ff; reprinted, Bell, VIII, 113 ff.

14. "Elegy," (1770), *Poetical Works*, pp. 190 ff.

15. "Two Love Elegies" (I), *Poetical Calendar*, V, 76 ff; reprinted, Bell, VIII, 157 ff.

16. "Love Elegies" (I), *Poetical Magazine*, III, 86 ff.

17. "Elegy," Chiswick *British Poets*, LXXI, 255.

18. "Elegy," *ibid.*, p. 252.

19. "Elegy Written Near the Ruins of Cuthally Castle," *ibid.*, p. 238. It is interesting to note that Graeme has also a "Nightpiece," blank verse fairly bristling with "horrendous" paraphernalia; a few lines of it cry aloud to be quoted:

> the melancholy bird
> Portentious and obscene, the hooting owl
> Of formal phiz, in grave discordance hails
> The full orb'd moon . . .
> . . . the sullen ghost
> In sheeted grandeur through the churchyard stalks
> Horrendous, muttering to the sickening moon . . .
> —*ibid.*, p. 261.

20. This statement is true also of some few of the other love elegies, as those of Mundy, one of which was quoted above.

21. Bell, VIII, 137 ff.

22. "The Disinterested Lover," I, 73.

23. I, 218 ff.

24. Bell publishes one ("Il Latte," pp. 132 ff) by Edw. Jerningham ("the Bard") among his "Amatory" elegies—though why is hard to see, as it is a plea to mothers to nurse their own children! It is effusively sentimental. "Arley" has a very lugubrious love "Elegy" in *The British Album* (2d ed., London, 1790, II, 50 ff). The only other example of the form in this Della Cruscan treasury ("Della Crusca to Anna Matilda," I, 29 ff) is not called an elegy, though it is written in elegiac quatrian and in decidedly elegiac mood; but since, on account of the vagaries of the form, I have not ventured to call anything an elegy which does not bear the word in its title or subtitle, this poem is ruled out. "Edwin," one of the later followers of Della Crusca, published several love elegies in the *European Magazine* (Aug., Oct., Dec., 1795); the Nov. number contains a reply from an anonymous lady.

25. J. Lilly: "The Shepherd's Complaint: A Pastoral, in Imitation of Shenstone," *Poetical Magazine*, II, 142 ff.

26. E.g., "The Complaint. A Pastoral Elegy" (*Poetical Calendar*, III, 86 ff) is a complaint against rural poverty which sounds strangely genuine; and "November. A Pastoral Elegy" (*ibid.*, XI, 3 f) consists of a dialogue between the poet and a shepherd, in which the latter mourns the death of a considerate lord of the manor.

27. The extent to which Shenstone was identified with the rise of sensibility is suggested by the address to him in his friend Grainger's "The Sugar Cane" (Book II, Chalmers, XIV, 491):

> Yes, thou wilt weep; for Pity chose thy breast,
> With Taste and Science, for their soft abode:
> Yes, thou wilt weep: thine own distress thou bear'st
> Undaunted; but another's melts thy soul.

What Shenstone is supposed to weep over is the distresses of West India planters with cane diseases and pests!

28. On the whole subject of the development of the eclogue during the eighteenth century, see Marion Bragg: *The Formal Eclogue in Eighteenth Century England*, Oronto, Me., 1926. It is of interest to note that the author credits Thomas Warton's war eclogues with introducing a melancholy note often heard thereafter in the eighteenth-century examples of this type of pastoral. These "Five Pastoral Eclogues" (Chalmers, XVIII, 136-41), which carry the explanatory subtitle "The scenes of which are supposed to lie among the shepherds, oppressed with the war in Germany" are particularly interesting also as steps in the humanizing process referred to, which was preparing the way for Crabbe.

29. One poetical tribute, from Dodsley's *Collection*, has already been quoted. There are "Verses to Mr. Richardson, on his History of Sir Charles Grandison," by Anna Williams, in *Gentleman's Magazine*, Jan., 1754.

30. The number for January, 1774, contains an anonymous life of Sterne, ending with an epitaph in heroic couplet, lauding him as the true man of feeling. The complete title of this magazine, by the way, is worth quoting: *The Sentimental Magazine; or, General Assemblage of Science, Taste, and Entertainment. Calculated to Amuse the Mind, To Improve the Understanding, and to Amend the Heart.* The emphasis is decidedly on the last-named objective.

31. Bell, V, 76 ff; quotation, p. 78.

32. See "Preface" to "Louisa, a Poetical Novel, in Four Epistles," *Poetical Works*, II, 222 ff.

33. Canto V, *Works*, I, 313 f.

34. "To Mrs. B-- Reading Julia with Tears, during a Hard Frost,"
Chalmers, XVI, 298.

35. *The Sorrows of Werter* [*sic*]; *a German Story*, 4th ed., 2 vols.,
London, 1783. This version was a translation not directly from the German
but from a French translation. At that time, of course, scarcely anyone
in England knew German: it is said that only Klopstock's *Messiah* and
Gessner's *Death of Abel* had previously been translated. See Johann Wilhelm Appell: *Werther und seine Zeit*, Oldenburg, 1882. Eugene Oswald
says, however (*Goethe in England and America: Bibliography*, 2d ed.,
revised and enlarged by L. and E. Oswald, *Publication of the English
Goethe Society*, No. 11, London, 1909) that the British Museum Catalogue mentions French as the intermediary only with reference to a later
publication, that of 1789. The copy I have seen is catalogued as of 1783;
the Preface contains a definite statement that a French translation was
used.

36. *Eleanora. From the Sorrows of Werter. A Tale* (2d ed. 1785). I
have not seen this book. My knowledge of its contents is from Appell (*op.
cit.*) and the quoted critical phrases are from a review in the *Gentleman's
Magazine*, Oct., 1785.

37. *Werter; a Tragedy, in Three Acts*, London, 1802. First produced in
1786.

38. *The Sorrows of Werter. A Poem*, London, 1788. This poem em-
phasizes the elegiac tone of the original, but is not at all discreditable as
such things go.

39. Smith: Sonnets XXI-XXV inc., *Elegiac Sonnets, and Other Poems*,
9th ed., 2 vols. in 1, London, 1800, pp. 21 ff; Seward: Sonnets LXXXVIII-
XC, inc., *Poetical Works*, III, 209 ff. Thomson's I have not seen, but cite
from Appell and Oswald, neither of whom, by the way, mentions Miss
Seward's. The quoted phrase is from one of the many reproaches heaped
upon the popular Charlotte Smith for her interest in Goethe's unorthodox hero.—*Gentleman's Magazine*, Apr., 1786, p. 334. There is an interesting verse argument concerning the dangerous tendencies of *Werther* in
James Hurdis' "Adriano, or the First of June" (*The Village Curate, and
Other Poems*, London, 1810, pp. 178 ff).

40. "Written in the Blank Page of *The Sorrows of Werter*," *Poetical
Works*, II, 131.

41. Strange eyelids—but so it is written.

42. "Elegy to the Memory of Werter. Written in Germany, in the year
1786," *Poetical Works*, I, 252. I reproduce the capitals here as a sample of

"Laura Maria's" highly Della Cruscan style. The reader will please imagine them as frequently as suits him in other selections from this author. His imagination is not likely to exceed the reality.

43. "The Sorrows of Charlotte at the Tomb of Werter," *Gentleman's Magazine,* Apr., 1785.

44. Mrs. Hughes: "A Description of the Tomb of Werter," *ibid.,* May, 1785.

45. "Amelia": "Supposed to have been addressed by Werter to the breast-bow Charlotte had on the first time he saw her, and which she had given him on his birth-day, and which he always wore in his bosom," *ibid.,* March, 1786.

46. Robert Merry: "Elegy, written after having read *The Sorrows of Werther," British Album,* pp. 13 ff.

47. See *Universal Magazine,* LXXVI, 329 (June, 1785). Of the items mentioned in this paragraph Appell and Oswald list those by Amelia Pichering, Charlotte Smith, Thomson, and Merry; they mention several others which I have been unable to examine.

48. Gifford reprints a priceless elegy on this last subject ("Baviad," in *The Baviad and the Maeviad,* London, 1799, note on pp. 56-57). It is by "Edwin" (T. Vaughan, according to Gifford, though the victim denied the identification). Edwin's Prologue reads: "On a tame mouse, which belonged to a lady who saved its life, constantly fed it, and even wept, poor lady! at its approaching death. The mouse's eyes actually dropped out of its head, poor mouse! the DAY BEFORE IT DIED." The versified comment on this unhappy circumstance is to the effect that the "feeling mouse" had wept his eyes away in gratitude for his mistress's pity, and then when "The grateful tear no more could flow," it "liked it not, and died."

49. E.g., "A Negro Love-Elegy," *Gentleman's Magazine,* July, 1792.

50. "An Elegy," *ibid.,* March, 1769.

51. Mr. Pratt: "Elegy of a Nightingale," *ibid.,* May, 1785.

52. J. H.: "On the Death of a Favourite Goldfinch," *Sentimental Magazine,* II, 127 f (Mar., 1774). At least birds may not only have heroic impulses but express them heroically—hear this feathered Barbara Frietchie, Mr. Pratt's mother partridge at the opening of the hunting season:

> Strike, strike, the leaden vengeance thro' the heart,
> Spare, spare my babes, and I the death embrace.

This is from "The Partridges: An Elegy Written on the last day of August," *Scots Magazine,* XXXIV, 442, Aug., 1772. Cf. the anonymous "Elegy on the First of September; when partridges are allowed to be killed by act of parliament," *ibid.,* XXV, 556 (Oct., 1763).

53. E.g., *Universal Magazine,* XCI, 212 (July, 1792); "Claudius": in *Gentleman's Magazine,* Aug., 1799.

54. *Universal Magazine,* XCVI, 51 (Jan., 1795). This poem is apparently by Sir Grey Cooper, as what reads like a revised version of it appears under his name in the *Poetical Register* for 1801 (pp. 3 ff).

55. Mrs. Lovett: "Ode to the Willow," *Poetical Register* for 1803, pp. 32 ff; cf. Mrs. Hughes: "To the Willow in the Character of Sterne's Maria," *Gentleman's Magazine,* Sept., 1785.

56. Mary Robinson: "The Tear," *Poetical Works,* III, 120.

57. M. A. M.: "Sonnet to a Sigh. In Imitation of Mrs. Robinson's Sonnet to a Tear," *Poetical Magazine,* I, 41.

58. "Alphonse": "To a Rose, seen in Blossom very Late in the Season," *ibid.,* IV, 64 f. The poet finally snatches its "op'ning charms" from the inclement weather, for all the world like Thomas Moore in "The Last Rose of Summer." Roses had a great fascination for sentimentalists—then as now.

59. Campbell's *Specimens of the British Poets,* London, 1819, VI, 453 ff.

60. *Poems on Various Subjects,* London, 1787, pp. 49 ff.

61. Mrs. King: "A Prize Poem, 'Whether Sensibility be Conducive to Happiness,' " *Gentleman's Magazine,* June, 1798.

62. "Psyche," part of Cantos V and VI, *Psyche, with Other Poems, by the late Mrs. Henry Tighe,* 3d ed., London, 1811, pp. 169 ff.

63. "Addressed to Miss Macartney, afterwards Mrs. Greville, on Reading her 'Prayer for Indifference,' " *Poetical Works,* pp. 20 f.

64. "Ode to Sensibility," *Poetical Calendar,* XI, 95 f.

65. *London Magazine,* XL, 167 (March, 1771).

66. "On Reading some Lines in Praise of Indifference," *Poems,* Egham and Chertsey, 1803, I, 21.

67. E.g., "Camisis": "An Ode to Indifference," *European Magazine,* XIV, 68 (July, 1788); "Ode to Apathy," *Universal Magazine,* XCVI, 51 (Jan., 1795).

68. E.g., "Sensibility and Indifference. A Dialogue," *Poetical Magazine,* III (1810), 157 ff.

69. "Sensibility. An Epistle to the Hon. Mrs. Boscawen," *Works,* I, 167-87.

70. She had referred in early lines of the poem to Mrs. Boscawen's recent loss of a son, asking if she would rather lack the sensibility to suffer.

71. A notable exception (late) is James Smith's "Ode to Sentiment," published in the *Poetical Register* for 1808-09, pp. 417 f. It begins "Daugh-

ter of dulness! canting dame!" and has especial reference to the sentimental comedy of Hugh Kelly and others.

72. *Gentleman's Magazine,* Apr., 1795. Quoted entire.

73. *Craig Phadric, Visions of Sensibility, with Legendary Tales, and Occasional Pieces,* Inverness, Elgin, Edinburgh, and London, 1811, pp. 119-71.

74. Page 120. This last is by no means the only Ossianic touch.

75. Page 121.

76. See next chapter.

77. Page 124.

78. The phrase is from the Argument.

79. Part II, p. 156.

80. *Vindication of the Rights of Women,* London, 1792, pp. 65-66.

81. Richard Polwhele: *The Unsex'd Females; a Poem, addressed to the Author of The Pursuits of Literature,* New York, 1800 (Republished by Wm. Cobbett), *passim.* The phrase in the title is borrowed from T. J. Mathias, to whom the poem is addressed. Cobbett himself, who even in his radical phase agreed with Rousseau about women, is responsible for the "fearful example." The Reverend Mr. Polwhele, it may be remarked, in the notes to his satire, tells the tragic story of Mary Wollstonecraft's desertion by Imlay and her attempts at suicide as though she were little better than a street walker.

82. See especially *op. cit.,* p. 138.

83. *Ibid.,* p. 123. Cf. the conditions of domestic hurry and responsibility under which many of the best women writers of that age and the Victorian worked: Jane Austen, for example, and Charlotte Brontë. Cf. also the remarks on this subject in John Stuart Mill's *Defense of Women,* and, to come down to our own generation, in Virginia Woolf's *A Room of One's Own.*

84. "Verses occasioned by a little Miss's bursting into Tears upon reading the Ballad of the Babes in the Wood," *Gentleman's Magazine,* Oct., 1755.

85. "Sympatheticus": "The Beggar-Woman," *ibid.,* Mar., 1786.

86. Wm. Hayley: "Triumphs of Temper," *Works,* I, 243.

87. T. C.: "Song," *Gentleman's Magazine,* Sept., 1789.

88. J. T.: "The Tear. To Miss Geddes," *Poetical Register* for 1803, p. 58.

89. David Carey: "The Nursling Care," *Craig Phadric, etc.,* p. 184.

90. "Address to Woman, from the Italian," *Poetical Works,* II, 176. So this, too, was probably first said by a man.

91. *Works,* Vols. VII and VIII, especially Chapters II and VIII (Vol. VII) and Chapter XVI (Vol. VIII). In the last-named chapter she counsels moderation in the development of sensibility. "But let it be remembered likewise, that as there is no quality in the female character which more raises its tone, so there is none which will be so likely to endanger the peace, and to expose the virtue of the possessor; none which requires to have its luxuriance more carefully watched, and its shoots more closely looped." (p. 109).

92. "Angelina, or, L'Amie Inconnue," in *Moral Tales,* Philadelphia, 1849.

93. W. Preston: "Ethic Epistles. II Sentiment. To a Lady," *Poetical Register* for 1803, pp. 3 ff.

94. Not even her artistic talent. Fame, said Felicia Hemans, "can only afford *reflected* delight to a woman." (Quoted in "Memoir" affixed to her *Poetical Works,* Edinburgh and London, Gall and Inglis, n.d.). She has a small lyric presenting a similar idea (*ibid.,* pp. 574-75). Unhappy as she was in her marriage she would have been glad to lay her literary trophies at Captain Hemans' feet, if he had cared to have them.

95. E.g., "Sapho": untitled stanzas, *Gentleman's Magazine,* Feb. 1752; "Maria": "Verses by a Lady," *ibid.,* Mar., 1759; "A Lady": "A Midnight Ode," *Poetical Calendar,* VII, 68 ff; "Hymn to Resignation," by the same, *ibid.,* pp. 74 f; A. W. S.: "Sonnet by a young Lady, who, at the same time that her Parent Died, Received an Account that her Lover was Married," *Gentleman's Magazine,* Aug., 1791. There is likely to be a note of religious resignation in love lyrics by women, as in those in the *Poetical Calendar.* Philosophy and passion for the men—religion and sentiment for the women.

96. A clear narrative of the known facts about the Della Cruscans may be found in Roy Benjamin Clark's *William Gifford: Tory Satirist, Critic, and Editor,* Columbia Univ. Press, 1930, Chapter II.

97. Gifford says he was not aware of its existence when he wrote "The Baviad."

98. Most of these pseudonymous writers have been identified: Della Crusca is Robert Merry, Anna Matilda is Hannah Cowley (the dramatist), Laura Maria and Julia are Mary Robinson (actress and author), Reuben is Bertie Greatheed, Arley is Miles Peter Andrews, Edwin (according to Gifford) is T. Vaughan, Yenda is Thomas Adney (an acrostic), the Bard is Edward Jerningham, Cesario (according to Mrs. Robinson—see note in *Poetical Works,* II, 244) is Miss M. Vaughan. Of these only Merry and

Greatheed had been in the original Florence coterie. Mrs. Piozzi's connection with the group was mostly that of early patroness, though the magazine verse signed "Adelaide" may be hers.

99. The name arose from the circumstance that Merry, who was a leading member of the Florence salon, had been elected to the Della Cruscan Academy, an international institute of the arts seated in Florence.

100. Introduction to "The Baviad," p. xix. He adds in a note: "This is a trifle. Heaven itself, if we believe Mrs. Robinson, took part in the general infatuation"—and he quotes from one of Laura's panegyrics of Della Crusca to prove it.

101. "To Anna Matilda," *British Album,* I, 5 ff (July 31, 1787).

102. She had tried to warn him—but his poetic ardor overrode all such mundane suggestions. See correspondence from the *World,* Aug. 4, 1787, and Aug. 21, 1787, *ibid.,* p. 8 f and 10 ff.

103. Space fails us to speak at length of the somewhat analogous coterie that had gathered about Lady Miller at Batheaston in the late seventies. Lady Miller, like Mrs. Piozzi in Florence, aspired to set up a salon. She had brought an antique vase from near the site of Cicero's estate at Tusculum, and the guests who drove from Bath during the season, deposited anonymous poetic efforts—of much the same quality as the Della Cruscan output—in this vase. The verses were then drawn out and judged, and the winner crowned with laurel. Anna Seward was "discovered" by Lady Miller. Contributors to the Batheaston anthologies—*Poetical Amusements,* 4 vols. (1775, 1776, 1777, 1781)—included Jane Bowdler, Jerningham (the Bard), Richard Graves (Shenstone's friend), Thomas Whalley (whom Lady Miller addressed as Edwy from the hero of his *Edwy and Edilda*—see *post*), Christopher Anstey (author of *The New Bath Guide*), Hayley (at the instigation of his wife) and even Garrick. See R .A. Hesselgrave: *Lady Miller and the Batheaston Literary Circle,* Yale Univ. Press, 1927.

104. "Stanzas on Reading Petrarch's Sonnets on the Death of Laura," *Florence Miscellany,* pp. 75 f.

105. "Serenade," *ibid.,* p. 32.

106. See "Ode to Indifference," *British Album,* I, 74 ff. The rest of this phase of the correspondence is in the four following epistles.

107. See the three-cornered correspondence *ibid.,* II, 137-62.

108. "To Anna Matilda" (Dec. 5, 1787) *ibid.,* I, 29 ff.

109. "Ode to Death," *ibid.,* I, 41 ff.

110. "To Anna Matilda," *ibid.,* p. 100.

111. "To Anna Matilda" (Mar. 16, 1789), *ibid.,* II, 153 ff.

112. Ibid., II, 137 ff. Reprinted in Poetical Works, II, 218 ff.

113. "Laura to Anna Matilda," ibid., II, 150. This is a little difficult to construe, but that is part of the manner.

114. These sonnets are in II, 91-97; quotations pp. 94, 92. There are also two or three poems by Arley called sonnets, but wrongly.

115. See R. D. Havens: The Influence of Milton, Chapter XIX.

116. In Keats's love poetry, as in his actual passion, a characteristic ingredient is fierce jealousy: cf. the sonnet "I cry you mercy—pity—love! —ay love!" (Poetical Works, Globe Ed., p. 344) and the stanzas "To Fanny" (ibid., pp. 326 f). Other love sonnets are "Time's sea hath been five years at its low ebb" (ibid., p. 340), "As Hermes once took to his feathers light" (ibid., p. 343), and "Bright star! would I were constant as thou art" (ibid., p. 345). They were all published posthumously.

117. I have noted only one such lyric in Moore: "O Say, thou Best and Brightest" (Poetical Works, p. 252). Shelley's "Indian Serenade," with its purposeful assumption of Oriental extravagance, is another example.

118. "To—" [Emelia Viviani], Poetical Works, p. 574.

119. Ibid., p. 594.

NOTES: CHAPTER V393

112. *Ibid.,* II, 137 ff. Reprinted in *Poetical Works,* II, 218 ff.

113. "Laura to Anna Matilda," *ibid.,* II, 150. This is a little difficult to construe, but that is part of the manner.

114. These sonnets are in II, 91-97; quotations pp. 94, 92. There are also two or three poems by Arley called sonnets, but wrongly.

115. See R. D. Havens: *The Influence of Milton,* Chapter XIX.

116. In Keats's love poetry, as in his actual passion, a characteristic ingredient is fierce jealousy: cf. the sonnet "I cry you mercy—pity—love! —ay love!" (*Poetical Works,* Globe Ed., p. 344) and the stanzas "To Fanny" (*ibid.,* pp. 326 f). Other love sonnets are "Time's sea hath been five years at its low ebb" (*ibid.,* p. 340), "As Hermes once took to his feathers light" (*ibid.,* p. 343), and "Bright star! would I were constant as thou art" (*ibid.,* p. 345). They were all published posthumously.

117. I have noted only one such lyric in Moore: "O Say, thou Best and Brightest" (*Poetical Works,* p. 252). Shelley's "Indian Serenade," with its purposeful assumption of Oriental extravagance, is another example.

118. "To—" [Emelia Viviani], *Poetical Works,* p. 574.

119. *Ibid.,* p. 594.

120. Almost all of Beddoes' and Motherwell's, most of Procter's, and many of Darley's love lyrics give the impression of being rather the interpretation of someone else's mood than the searching of the poet's own heart. This is true also of a goodly number of Moore's, but not of most of those of the major writers. These poems in a measure take over the function of the old pastorals, which were usually dramatic.

121. E.g. "How Lang and Dreary is the Night," *Poetical Works,* p. 211; "Highland Harry," p. 216; "Ay Waukin, O," p. 217; "The Bonnie Lad That's Far Awa," p. 234; "Wae is My Heart," p. 260; "Jockie's Ta'en a Parting Kiss," p. 268; "Wandering Willie," p. 270; "Thou Hast Left Me Ever, Jamie," p. 287; "How Can my Poor Heart," p. 293. Burns's love poetry is not, however, predominantly melancholy.

122. James Hogg: "Row on, Row on," *Works,* II, 428.

123. Robert Tannahill: "The Braes o' Gleniffer" (1806), *Poems and Songs Chiefly in the Scottish Dialect,* New York, 1819. Cf. the songs beginning "Langsyne, beside the woodland burn," and "Our bonny Scots lads," *ibid.,* pp. 138 f and 147 f, and "The Dear Highland Laddie, O," *ibid.,* pp. 165 f.

124. William Motherwell: "O, Wae be to the Orders," *Poetical Works,* pp. 151 f.

125. E.g. Hogg: "The Soldier's Widow," *Works,* II, 264; "Mary at Her Lover's Grave," *ibid.,* p. 265; "The Soldier's Widow," *ibid.,* pp. 407 f;

"I'll Bid my Heart be Still," *ibid.,* p. 438. Tannahill: "Wi' Waefu' Heart," *Poems and Songs,* pp. 203 f.

126. Wm. Motherwell: "My Heid is Like to Rend, Willie," *Poetical Works,* p. 79.

127. George Darley: "Love's Devotion," *Poems,* pp. 429 f.

128. James Hogg: "The Broken Heart," *Works,* II, 430. Hogg says that this poem refers to the plight of a young relative, who was jilted, but that, fortunately, the girl recovered in the end.

129. Besides the poem quoted, see "He is Gone! He is Gone," *Poetical Works,* pp. 160 f; "Away! Away! O, do not Say," *ibid.,* p. 167.

130. E.g. "The Night is Closing Round, Mother," *English Songs,* p. 40; "Perdita," *ibid.,* p. 66; "Sister, I Cannot Read To-Day," *ibid.,* p. 187.

131. *Poetical Works,* p. 353.

132. *Ibid.,* pp. 354 f. "Death's Jest Book" contains two lyrics addressed to a bride, in which the rejected lover anticipates his own death as imminent. (Act IV, sc. 3, *ibid.,* p. 98). The second is referred to by the singer as "Thy bridal song and my own dirge as well."

133. *English Songs, and Other Small Poems, Boston,* 1844 (first ed. 1832), p. 100.

134. *Poetical Works,* I, 217.

135. *Poetical Works,* p. 432.

136. *Poetical Works,* pp. 353, 354, 354-55, 370, 371.

137. E.g. *English Songs,* pp. 40, 41, 146, 181. Brydges has a "Dirge" for a man dead for love (*Poems,* p. 103).

138. "Ding! dong!," *Poetical Works,* p. 188.

139. Of course desertion is in a way unrequited love; but the phrase is used of love never requited.

140. Explanatory heading of untitled and unsigned poem in *Gentleman's Magazine,* Oct., 1771. Even so much of the phrasing as I have quoted betrays the comparatively early date.

141. William Motherwell: "True Love's Dirge," *Poetical Works,* p. 95. This poem is an excellent example of the brief narrative written in lyric style.

142. E.g., S. D.: "A True Story," *Gentleman's Magazine,* Dec., 1780; L. E. Landon: "The Neglected One," *Poetical Works* (Wm. B. Scott, ed.), London, n.d., pp. 320 ff; "The Rose," *ibid.,* pp. 169 ff (1826); Felicia Hemans: "Properzia Rosa," *Poetical Works,"* pp. 326 ff; "The Peasant Girl of the Rhone," *ibid.,* pp. 341 ff. The stories by Mrs. Hemans are founded on fact, and occur in "Records of Women" (1828). Letitia Landon has also an historical tale of a peasant girl who drowned herself for love

of Henry IV (*op. cit.*, pp. 299 ff). Hogg has an elegy ("St. Mary of the Lowes," *Works*, II, 391 f), the main point of which is a rather sentimental sigh over the grave of a girl who has died of disappointed love.

143. *Poetical Works*, II, 222-94.

144. Tho. Sedgwick Whalley: *Edwy and Edilda, a Tale, in Five Parts. Embellished with Six Fine Engravings, from Original Designs, by a Young Lady.* London printed: Albany: Reprinted by Loring Andrews, 1800. The poem dates from the days of the Batheaston salon.

145. "Sebastian. A Spanish Tale," *Poetical Works*, London, 1830, II, 187-253.

146. *Ibid.*, pp. 207, 213, 237 respectively.

147. *Poetical Works*, pp. 189-91.

148. *Poetical Works*, pp. 499-520. The title, reminiscent of Campbell's "Pleasures of Hope," has reference to the repeated disappointments of the hero, who himself tells the story, in his search for his lost love.

149. A popular theme elsewhere also: Scott uses it in "Marmion" and "The Lord of the Isles," Byron in "Lara," Southey in "Madoc," Hemans in "Theresa's Song" (*Poetical Works*, p. 582). Both in *Ossian* and elsewhere, these feminine pages usually have a hard time of it, and frequently the ending is tragic.

150. *Poetical Works of Beattie, Blair, and Falconer*, pp. 175 ff, especially pp. 186-89 and 260-67; the quoted phrase is from the "Occasional Elegy" affixed at the end.

151. "November," *London Magazine*, XXXIX, 589 ff (Nov., 1770).

152. Chalmers, XIV, 44. This ballad has funereal paraphernalia, including "the churchyard path" and "the dark owl."

153. *Jessy; or, the Forced Vow. A Poem*, London, 1785. This poem is better done than most fugitive verse.

154. E. W.: "The Convent, a Ballad," *European Magazine*, XVII, 468 f (June, 1790).

155. "Vaudracour and Julia," *Poetical Works* (Globe Ed.), Macmillan, 1924, pp. 221 ff.

156. *Poetical Works*, p. 131-60.

157. "Anselmo, the Hermit of the Alps," *Poetical Works*, II, 30 ff.

158. "The Brave Roland," *Poetical Works*, p. 176 f. Cf. Motherwell's "Serenade," "Isabelle" (*Poetical Works*, p. 234 f), in which the lover, whose lady is about to take the veil, prophesies his own death. Campbell's own "domestic tragedy" of "Theodoric" (*op. cit.*, pp. 55-74) is a longer story of separated lovers.

159. "Roland's Tower. A Legend of the Rhine," *Poetical Works*, pp.

279 ff. A rather unusual variant of this theme is L. E. L.'s "The Guerilla Chief," (*ibid.*, pp. 280 ff) wherein the hero, Leandro, who has evidently spent a wicked youth, goes away penitent, followed by Bianca's tears, and returns years later to find her dying in a ruined garden after a raid. Cf. also the main story in her "Improvisatrice," *ibid.*, pp. 1-33.

160. *Poetical Works,* p. 184.

161. Canto II, st. 112 to Canto IV, st. 73, *Poetical Works,* pp. 1018-64. Cf. also the fate of the woman in "The Seige of Corinth," "The Corsair," and "The Bride of Abydos."

162. *Ibid.,* III, st. 2, p. 1034.

163. There is a sort of apotheosis of the drowned lovers so popular in romantic verse in Keats's "Endymion" (Book III, *Poetical Works,* pp. 141 ff), when Glaucus and Endymion raise from death the great host of them laid in long rows by Glaucus during the course of a thousand years.

164. *Craig Phadric, etc.,* p. 137.

165. *Poetical Works,* pp. 108 f. Other examples of double death by drowning are W. H. H.: "Orsino and Zephilinda. An Elegiac Tale," *Sentimental Magazine,* Nov., 1774; Letitia Landon: "A Moorish Romance" (in "The Improvisatrice"), *Poetical Works,* p. 6 ff.

166. "The Lover's Rock," *Poetical Works* (Oxford Ed.), pp. 629 f. This too is a "Moorish" tale. There is double suicide also in Jerningham's *Faldoni and Teresa* (London, 1773) and in Chatterton's "Narva and Mored" (*Poetical Works,* I, 179 ff).

167. Occasionally in the periodicals one runs across a funeral elegy for some youth who has died of grief or disappointed love. E.g. J. D. Cotton: "Epitaph on a young Gentleman who died for Love," *Gentleman's Magazine,* Sept., 1750; I. H. C.: "An Elegy on the Death of a Poetical Friend" (for whose death Laura's coquetry is blamed), *ibid.,* Dec., 1786.

168. *The Alps. A Poem,* London, 1763. The story occurs on pp. 21-25.

169. Book II, Chalmers, XIV, 495 ff; quotation, p. 496. Cf. the episode of Levina (sometimes attributed to Logan) in Michael Bruce's "Lochleven," wherein the heroine is drowned and the hero pines away and dies of heart-break—Chalmers, XVIII, 70 f.

170. E. S. J.: "Volsan and Oray. A Tale," *European Magazine,* XXXIV, 261 (Oct., 1798). Cf. "St. Andrew's Eve. A Village Legend," *Poetical Register* for 1803, pp. 17 ff; Mary Robinson: "The Murdered Maid" (another hermit-tale), *Poetical Works,* II, 162 ff.

171. "Henry and Sophy," *Gentleman's Magazine,* Mar., 1770. There is a moral tag: "True joy exists not here below." Nor is this the only instance of the fatal consequences of that ability to refine joy to agony ascribed

by Mrs. Greville to sensibility. The same catastrophe turns a joyful re-union to a scene of mourning in the episode of Alcander and Nervia at the close of Mason's "English Garden" (Book IV, Chalmers, XVIII, 392 ff). Alcander, who was not the favored lover anyway, dedicated his life to melancholy and the building of a mournful shrine in a gloomy glade, where he might indulge his "solemn luxury of grief."

172. "Lines supposed to be spoken by a Lover at the Grave of his Mistress. Occasioned by a situation in a Romance," *Poetical Works of H. K. White and James Grahame*, 63 ff. Was the romance an Ossianic one? White's poem is properly a dramatic lyric; it is cited here for the sake of the Ossianic echoes.

173. "The Despairing Lover," *Poetry, etc.*, pp. 189 ff.

174. R. M.: "Madness," II, 285. Other instances are Mary Robinson: "Jasper," *Poetical Works*, III, 215 ff; C. Z.: "Crazy Luke," *Gentleman's Magazine*, Mar., 1798; Margaret Langley: "The Unfortunate Maniac at Coniston Priory, in Westmoreland," *ibid.*, Jan., 1799.

175. *Marcian Colonna. An Italian Tale with Three Dramatic Scenes and Other Poems*, by Barry Cornwall, London, 1820.

176. "Madoc in Aztlan," Section 22, *Poetical Works* (Oxford), p. 588 ff.

177. *Collective Works*, I, xliv. There are no moral strictures, oddly enough, in "Madoc," and none in a little ballad-like "Elegy," signed I. W. M., which records another lover's suicide (*Gentleman's Magazine*, Oct., 1797).

178. To illustrate the popularity of the theme: Amelia Opie's volume of *Poems* (London, 1802) has a frontispiece by her husband, the well-known artist, illustrating a song about a woman dying of grief for her dead lover.

179. Cf. Maunde: "On a Lady Dying of a Consumption," *Poetical Register* for 1802, pp. 28 f. This lady is really dying for love, although she will not admit it.

180. E.g.—ballad type: "Edwin and Ethelinda. A Ballad," *Gentleman's Magazine*, July, 1767; "Edwin and Emily" (an almost identical story) *ibid.*, Feb., 1782; Wm. Julius Mickle: "Hengist and Mey," Chiswick *British Poets*, LXVI, 66 ff; John Learmont: "Helen, an Ode" (but why an ode?), *Poems Pastoral, etc.*, pp. 34 ff (although here it is a villain who kills the lover, not a relative). Interesting variants on this theme of the lover killed by the beloved's brother are George Bruce: "Roslin, a Ballad" (*Poems, Ballads, and Songs on Various Occasions*, Edinburgh, 1813, pp. 51 ff), in which it is the lover who kills the brother—in a mistaken fit of jealousy—and, when the girl dies of heart-break, becomes an ascetic re-

morse-gnawn recluse; and Bernard Barton: "Jane Ashford, A Tale of Humble Life" (*Metrical Effusions,* pp. 65 ff), in which the bride's reprobate brother heads a press gang which seizes and in the struggle kills the bridegroom at the very door of the church, leaving the bride to die of a broken heart. Cf. the episode of Monimia in Carey's "Visions of Sensibility" (*Craig Phadric etc.,* p. 157 ff), and Keats's treatment of the Italian legend of the pot of basil. In both these last the girl fades away slowly. With the ballad-Ossianic type may also be compared Chatterton's pseudomedieval "Aella" (*Poetical Works,* II, 29-90), the catastrophe of which consists in Aella's killing himself from a mistaken notion that his wife has been untrue to him, and her falling dead on his body in good Ossianic style; Jane West's "Alleyn and Ella, a Legendary Tale" (*Miscellaneous Poetry,* London, 1786, pp. 19 ff); J. T.'s "Henry and Lucy. A Ballad" (*European Magazine,* XXII, 147 f, Aug., 1792); Tannahill's "Connell and Flora" (*Poems and Songs, etc.,* pp. 81 ff).

181. *Dramatic and Poetic Works,* pp. 778 ff. This wandering maiden dies on the heath when she learns of her lover's death.

182. Examples of the first type: Mary Sewell: "Horatio and Amanda" (said to be founded on fact) (1805), *Poems,* I, 55 ff; Felicia Hemans: "Edith," *Poetical Works,* pp. 332 ff. In the latter, however, Edith proves to have merely swooned, only to die away later as soon as she has converted her Indian rescuers to Christianity. Examples of the second type: "A Lady": "Julia. A Ballad," *Gentleman's Magazine,* Jan., 1788; Scott: "The Maid of Toro" (1806), *Poetical Works,* p. 400.

183. "Donald and Mary," *Poetical Works,* II, 18 ff.

184. "Edith," *Poetical Works,* p. 333.

185. E.g., the lover in Grainger's "Byran and Pereene" (said to be founded on fact—Chalmers, XIV, 477) is killed by a shark as he swims to shore from an incoming boat in his impatience to reach his mistress; she dies of a broken heart. In "Edwin and Amelia," a blank verse poem more like a pastoral than a ballad (signed H. I.—*Poetical Register* for 1808-9, pp. 92 ff) the lover is drowned trying to save a lamb belonging to his mistress; she dies on his body. In L. E. L.'s "Gladesmuir" (*Poetical Works,* pp. 295 ff), the lover has returned home to die of some unspecified malady; she soon follows him to the grave. It is interesting to note that in the first version of Leigh Hunt's "Story of Rimini" (1816), when Paolo is forced to fight a duel with his brother and purposely runs on his opponent's sword, Francesca dies of a broken heart on hearing the news.

186. *Heart of Midlothian,* 1818. The most famous of Madge's songs is "Proud Maisie," reprinted, with the others, in *Poetical Works,* pp. 441-43.

187. E.g., Amelia Opie: "A Mad-Song," *Poems,* pp. 107 ff.

188. Cf. Mary Robinson: "Poor Marguerite," *Poetical Works,* III, 160 ff.

189. Cf. Wm. Case, Jr.: "The Poor Village Maid," *Poetical Register* for 1802, pp. 339 ff, and S. B.: "Ellen, or, the Shipwreck," *Poetical Magazine,* I (1809), pp. 191 ff. The details of the ivy and the owl are from the former, that of the howling blast from the latter.

190. "Edwin and Lucy," *Scots Magazine,* LXVI, 535 ff (July, 1804). Cf. Robert Tannahill: "The Maniac's Song," *Poems,* pp. 205 f. There are various poems also in which women stand on promontories and watch the ships bearing their lovers go down in tempest. E.g. Miss Locke: sonnet, *Gentleman's Magazine,* Mar., 1796; Mary Robinson: "Lines Written on the Sea-Coast," *Poetical Works,* II, 205.

191. *Poetical Works,* pp. 391 ff; one of the tales in "The Improvisatore."

192. "A Sicilian Story, with Other Poems," in *Spirit of Contemporary Poetry,* Boston, 1827.

193. *The Flood in Thessaly, The Girl of Provence, and Other Poems,* by Barry Cornwall, London, 1823.

194. "O'Connor's Child," *Poetical Works,* pp. 83 ff.

195. *Ibid.,* p. 83.

196. A more horrific variant on this theme is Mrs. Henry Woodcock's *Laura, a Tale* (London, 1820), in which the deserted woman, whose newborn child has been strangled by its inhuman father, wanders forth mad and finds her way to the cottage of the midwife who has been forced to witness the crime. Here she dies, and the man, seeking her in disguise but his identity discovered, commits suicide at her bier.

197. As in Logan's famous "Braes of Yarrow," Chalmers, XVIII, 53 f; Mary Robinson's "Lines Written on the Sea-Coast," *Poetical Works,* II, 205; Leigh Hunt's version of the story of "Hero and Leander," *Poetical Works,* 2 vols., Boston, 1865, pp. 199 ff. One of the insane heroines referred to above ("The Poor Village Maid") perishes by being washed off a cliff by a huge wave. In all these examples, the cause is bereavement; but, as said above, the method is characteristic without reference to cause.

198. *Poetical Works,* II, 208 ff.

199. *Poetical Works,* pp. 422 ff.

200. E.g., "Verses written near the Grave of an Unfortunate Fair One, who fell a Sacrifice to Perfidy," *Universal Magazine,* XCV, 373 f (Nov., 1794); P. Courtier: episode in "The Pleasures of Solitude," *Poems,* pp. 104 ff; "Arion": "The Suicide," *Poetical Register* for 1808-9, pp. 209 f.

201. E.g., "Ballad. Founded on Fact" (Arley), *British Album*, II, 40 ff;
J. U.: "Edgar and Anna," *Poetical Magazine*, I (1809), 376 ff; Letitia
Landon: "The Mountain Grave," *Poetical Works*, pp. 342 ff. Cf. "Will
the Ferryman, a Water-Eclogue," *Gentleman's Magazine*, June, 1758, an
early example, in which the culprit sees the dead girl's ghost and is
drowned in his terror. A really interesting psychological study has been
built on this theme in Ebenezer Elliott's "Withered Wild Flowers" (*Poetical
Works*, I, 127 ff). Elliott's early narrative verse was evidently influenced
by Byron, and harps continually on the theme of remorse.

202. Cf. Amelia Opie: "The Dying Daughter to her Mother," *Poems*,
pp. 3 ff; Laura Sophia Temple: "The Ruined Orphan," *Poetical Register*
for 1806-7, pp. 315 ff; T. L. Peacock: "Maria's Return to her Native
Cottage" (wherein the girl dies in the snow at her father's door), *Poems*,
pp. 43 ff; Letitia Landon: "Rosalie," *Poetical Works*, pp. 270 ff. Cf. the
ballad situation in which she strives in vain for admission to the house
of her perjured lover: e.g., Burns: "Lord Gregory," *Poetical Works*, p. 274;
Allan Cunningham: "Lord Randall," *Sir Marmaduke Maxwell, etc.*, London, 1822, pp. 198 f. Two early "elegiac ballads" presenting a woman's
remorse for an illicit love appear in the same issue (Sept.) of the *Gentleman's Magazine* for 1764.

203. E.g., Henry Headley: "Rosalind's Dying Complaint to her Sleeping
Child," Chiswick *British Poets*, LXXIII, 113 ff; Suzanna Blamire: "When
Night's Dark Mantle," *Works*, pp. 251 f; J. U.: "Edgar and Anna," *Poetical Magazine*, I, 376 ff. The Orphan in Sophia Temple's poem named in
note 202 decides against suicide on religious grounds, as does the woman
in Mrs. Opie's "The Wanderer. A Sentimental Ballad" (*Poems*, pp. 160
ff), who decides to live to help others. In Tannahill's "Ellen More" (*Poems
and Songs*, pp. 156 f) Ellen leaps over the cataract of Yarrow because her
lover has falsely believed her to be untrue.

204. As in C. S. B.: "The Maniac," *Poetical Magazine*, IV, 220 f.

205. "The Thorn," *Poetical Works*, pp. 76 ff; "Her Eyes were Wild,"
ibid., p. 81; "The Complaint of a Forsaken Indian Woman," *ibid.*, pp.
85 f; "Ruth," *ibid.*, pp. 121 ff.

206. "Spirits of Light! Spirits of Shade!," *Poetical Works*, pp. 180 ff.
Sometimes the specific cause of the wanderer's love-madness is not indicated by the poet. E.g., "Rosa. Love and Madness," *Poetical Register* for
1803, pp. 409 f; C. S. B.: "The Maniac," *Poetical Magazine*, IV, 220 f.

207. Allan Cunningham: "The Broken Heart of Annie," *Sir Marmaduke Maxwell, etc.*, pp. 187 ff.

208. W. B. C.: "Laura," *Poetical Magazine*, I, 202 f.

209. "Written by a Lady in Copenhagen"—*Scots Magazine*, LXVI, 455 f (June, 1804).

210. An interesting psycho-analytical essay on Shelley presents the theory that his interest in the incest-motif, especially in this poem, and his use of the hermaphrodite (in "The Witch of Atlas") points to the essentially bi-sexual nature of his ideal.—See Edward Carpenter and George Barnefield: *The Psychology of the Poet Shelley*, Dutton, 1925, especially Barnefield's essay.

211. Byron's heroines have little to distinguish them from those of other romantic writers. Perhaps Byron was not interested enough in women—as human beings—to trouble himself to depart from convention in depicting them.

212. "The Last Constantine," *Poetical Works*, pp. 180-200.

213. "Gertrude; or Fidelity till Death," *ibid.*, pp. 329-30. This is one of the "Records of Women."

214. The poem occupies pp. 64-94 in *Poetical Works;* the catastrophe pp. 92-94.

215. *Ibid.*, pp. 94-106.

216. *Ibid.*, pp. 131-60.

217. Canto III, p. 86.

218. "The Abencerrage" shows also a startlingly strong influence from *Ossian;* it begins with an elegy reminiscent of the opening of "Carthon," ends with a dirge after the manner of the Ossianic bards, and is punctuated in between with Ossianic phrases like "thou art passed away, Without thy fame" (p. 73), "Ebro's dark sons" (p. 74), "Lonely, and lost in thoughts of other days" (p. 75), "thy dark soul" (p. 78), "Wild on the gale his silvery tresses flow" (p. 81), "joy in grief" (p. 91), "Each dark remembrance" (p. 91).

219. "The Troubadour" (1825), *Poetical Works*, p. 36.

220. "The Improvisatrice" (1824), *ibid.*, p. 10.

221. *Ibid.*, p. 21.

222. (c. 1829) *Ibid.*, pp. 214-22; quotation, p. 221.

223. *Ibid.*, p. 221. She had in truth a pathetic history of futile groping for art, which was beyond her, and for life, which eluded her; after a romantic and desperate matrimonial adventure which took her to the wild coast of Africa, she is thought to have committed suicide.—See D. E. Enfield: *L. E. L.: A Mystery of the Thirties*, Hogarth Press, 1928.

CHAPTER VI

THE SOUNDING CATARACT

1. Elizabeth Carter: "Ode on the Arrival of Spring. Addressed to a Lady in London," Bell, XIV, 25 ff. Cf. the exactly similar sentiment expressed by Miss Ferrer in the ode preceding this one.

2. "Autumn," *Gentleman's Magazine,* Oct., 1753.

3. E.g., "Ode to Celia," *ibid.,* Nov., 1765; J-H-: "Autumn. An Ode," *ibid.,* Oct., 1767. Cf. Mansell: "To Autumn," *Poetical Amusements, etc.,* II, 169 ff.

4. E.g., W. O.: "An Autumnal Reflection," *Gentleman's Magazine,* Feb., 1770; Woolston: "Autumnal Elegy," *ibid.,* Nov., 1790.

5. E.g., "The instability of human perfections, extracted from Mr. Hervey's Meditation in the flower garden," *London Magazine,* XVII, 425 f (Sept., 1748—Note the influence from Hervey); D. R.: "An Ode Addressed to a Lady," *ibid.,* XX, 423 (Sept., 1751); "On Flowers in a Young Lady's Hand. A Moral Thought," *Gentleman's Magazine,* Sept., 1755; "Knowsley," *ibid.,* May, 1760 (This is a descriptive poem and the moral for the ladies is incidental, p. 242).

6. E.g., W. Richards: "The Welcome Evening," *ibid.,* Mar., 1751.

7. E.g., Wm. Woty: "An Ode to Evening," *Scots Magazine,* XXIII, 204 f. (Apr., 1761); "Ode to Evening," *Poetical Calendar,* VI, 13 f.

8. J. S.: "An Evening Elegy," *Scots Magazine,* XXXIV, 157 f (Mar., 1772).

9. *The Village Curate,* p. 45. Written, 1788.

10. The phrases are from "Evening and Night" (blank verse), *Gentleman's Magazine,* Dec., 1760. Other examples: "Midnight: a Poem" (elegiac stanza), *Scots Magazine,* XXIII, 507 (Nov., 1761); "Ode to Darkness," *European Magazine,* XI, 286 (Apr., 1787); P. Courtier: "To Night" (another pseudo-Miltonic ode), *Poems,* pp. 56 ff.

11. E.g., Hester Chapone: "Ode. Written during a violent Storm at Midnight," *Gentleman's Magazine,* Jan., 1777; G-e D-n-l: "Ode—Night," *Poetical Magazine,* III, 273 ff. The latter contains Contemplation, a mournful shepherd, Ossianic ghosts, fairies, and a personal welcome to Death, as well the specifically religious material—a sort of hodge-podge of romanticism.

12. [Geo. Davies Harley]: "Night, a Poem," *Poems,* London, 1796, pp. 26-107. Other examples of poems on the uses and abuses of night: "Spinsteria": "Midnight Reflections," *Poetical Magazine,* IV, 113 f; James Montgomery: "Night," *Poetical Works,* III, 205 ff.

13. Cf. P. Van Tieghem: *La Poésie de la Nuit, etc.,* pp. 21 ff. Van Tieghem notes that never before had the moon been invoked as a necessity of poetic description as it is toward the end of Night III; yet that when it comes to the stars, Young rather uses them as arguments than feels them poetically. It is precisely this half-poetic, half-argumentative attitude which is found also in Hervey, and in the imitators with whom we have here to do.

14. It is suggested by Van Tieghem in the passage just cited that Young may have been the first to do this; but I understand that researches are in progress at the University of Chicago which will show the earlier occurrence of the theme.

15. "The Moonlight Night," *Shrubs of Parnassus,* pp. 59 ff.

16. *Gentleman's Magazine,* Sept., 1782.

17. "Lochleven," *Poetical Works,* p. 90.

18. "A Summer Evening's Meditation," *Poetical Works,* pp. 122 ff.

19. *The Farmer's Boy. A Rural Poem,* 4th ed., London, 1801, p. 92.

20. W.C-e: "Midnight," *Poetical Magazine,* III, 226 ff.

21. *Satan. A Poem,* end of Book I. Other examples: "Orlando": "Ode to Reflection," *Gentleman's Magazine,* Dec., 1786; H. K. White: "Lines Written on a Survey of the Heavens," *Poems, Letters, etc.,* pp. 34 ff; J. G.: "Sonnet Written at Midnight," *Poetical Magazine,* III, 21; John Clare: "A Look at the Heavens," *Village Minstrel,* London, 1821, II, 176.

22. In the *Gentleman's Magazine,* Dec., 1782, pp. 574 f, and Feb., 1783, pp. 123 f; essays signed A. S.

23. Chiswick *British Poets,* LXXIII, 198.

24. Bowles: "Monody on the Death of Dr. Warton," *Poetical Works,* I, 135 ff; White: "Lines on Reading the Poems of Warton," *Poems, Letters, etc.,* pp. 53 f. White has also a prose essay ("Remarks on the English Poets: Warton," *Remains,* II, 207 ff) expressing great admiration, qualified by a realization of Warton's too heavy debt to older poets.

25. "On a Stormy Sea Prospect," "On a Calm Sea Prospect," Chiswick *British Poets,* LXXIII, 188 f.

26. "Written in Country Retirement," *ibid.,* p. 191.

27. "On a Wet Summer," *ibid.,* p. 194.

28. *Ibid.,* p. 187.

29. "Ode to the River Teign," *ibid.,* p. 195.

30. "Stanzas to a Lady," *ibid.,* pp. 195 f.

31. "To the Nightingale," *ibid.,* p. 167.

32. "Sonnet written in St. John's Churchyard, Shaftesbury," *ibid.,* pp. 167 f.

33. "Evening," *ibid.*, p. 169; "Night," *ibid.*, pp. 169 f; quotation from the latter. There is also a sonnet on "Morning," *ibid.*, p. 168.

34. "To the Woodlark," *ibid.*, p. 171.

35. "Despair," *ibid.*, p. 172.

36. "Sonnet XIV," *ibid.*, p. 141. He had doubtless never heard of the cannibalistic habits of some female spiders!

37. "Sonnet XV," *ibid.*, pp. 141 f.

38. "Sonnet XVI," *ibid.*, p. 142. Partly after Petrarch.

39. "To Silence," *ibid.*, pp. 156 f.

40. *The Influence of Milton,* p. 510.

41. "On the Death of Mr. Headley," Chiswick *British Poets,* LXXIII, 36 f.

42. "To Cynthia. A Fragment," *ibid.*, p. 101; "Philomel. A Fragment," *ibid.*, p. 102.

43. "Verses written on a Winter's Night," *ibid.*, pp. 102 f; "To Myra," *ibid.*, pp. 120 ff; "On a Fragment of some Verses written by a Lady in Solitude," *ibid.*, pp. 123 f.

44. *Ibid.*, pp. 115 f.

45. *Ibid.*, p. 125.

46. *Ibid.*, p. 124.

47. 2d version, 1796. *Poetical Works,* p. 41.

48. Cf. Myra Reynolds: *The Treatment of Nature in English Poetry between Pope and Wordsworth,* Univ. of Chicago Press, 1909, pp. 200 f. Dr. Reynolds has interesting things to say about a great many of the poets treated in this chapter.

49. *Poetical Works,* I, 61-67.

50. "Absence," *ibid.*, pp. 17 f; "Approach of Spring," *ibid.*, pp. 22 f.

51. "Evening," *ibid.*, p. 10.

52. "The River Wainsbeck," *ibid.*, pp. 8 f.

53. "The Tweed Visited," *ibid.*, p. 9.

54. "To the River Itchin," *ibid.*, p. 11.

55. "The River Cherwell," *ibid.*, p. 15.

56. "On Leaving a Village in Scotland," *ibid.*, pp. 3 f.

57. "Coombe-Ellen," *ibid.*, p. 116. Coleridge was delighted to find this reminiscence of his own fragment on "Melancholy" in verse by his early favorite.

58. Phrases (not idea) from "The Spirit of Navigation," *ibid.*, p. 128.

59. *Ibid.*, p. 12. Later (1805) he wrote a long descriptive-historical poem in five books (blank verse), called "The Spirit of Discovery." It is full of the melancholy fascination of the sea, as "The Missionary" (1813)

is of the melancholy fascination of mountains, in this case the Andes. The usual date given for the publication of "The Missionary," by the way, is 1815; but Hoxie Neale Fairchild has shown that it was first published anonymously in 1813—See *The Noble Savage*, Columbia Univ. Press, 1928, p. 274.

60. "The Bells, Ostend" (1787), *ibid.*, p. 13.

61. This is frequently true of Bowles also.

62. "Written in the Prospect of Death," *Poetical Works of Henry Kirke White and James Grahame*, pp. 71 ff. Cf. "To Midnight," *ibid.*, pp. 136 f; "To the Wind, at Midnight," *ibid.*, pp. 146 f; "To a Taper" (sonnet), *Poems, Letters, etc.*, pp. 87.

63. "Fragment II," *ibid.*, p. 103.

64. "Ode to the Moon" (fragment), *ibid.*, pp. 130 ff. There is also a sonnet "To the Moon. Written in November," *Poetical Works, etc.*, p. 164.

65. *Poems*, p. 5. Cf. Sonnet XV (1784), wherein he calls on these "melancholy scenes" to calm and comfort a mind distracted and disgusted with the world.

66. *Ibid.*, p. 11. Cf. XXII, "An Evening in May," p. 25.

67. Sonnet VI, "To Autumn, near her Departure," *ibid.*, p. 8. Other sonnets on autumn: X, "Written on the Approach of the Cold Weather," Oct. 9, 1783, *ibid.*, p. 12; XV, "Written at Wootton, in Kent" (1784), p. 18; XXIII, Oct., 1784, p. 26; XXIV, p. 27; XLII, p. 45.

68. Sonnet XX, *ibid.*, p. 23.

69. The date of her birth given in the *Dictionary of National Biography* is 1747; but the evidence of two parish church registers has recently been cited to prove the earlier date. See Margaret Ashmun: *The Singing Swan, an Account of Anna Seward*, Yale Univ. Press, 1931. Miss Ashmun's book, by the way, gives a vivid and human picture of this "female celebrity" and her circle.

70. After the peace, Washington sent a special messenger to her with papers to prove that she had slandered him in this popular poem, and she handsomely recanted. Her sympathies were normally with the colonists in the war.

71. "The Vision. An Elegy," *Poetical Works*, I, 1 ff.

72. "Knowledge: a Poem in the Manner of Spencer" [*sic*], *ibid.*, p. 11.

73. "Elegy. Addressed to Cornet V—in the Autumn of 1765," *ibid.*, p. 16.

74. From one of the love elegies between "Evander and Emilia," *ibid.*, p. 25. This series is said to shadow forth an early engagement of her own, broken off on account of parental opposition. One gathers from Miss

Ashmun's account *(op. cit.)* that the gentleman never quite recovered from this adventure, but that the lady found little difficulty in forgetting. In middle life she became, however, passionately attached to John Saville, her musical fellow-townsman, who was already married. Their friendship aroused much gossip, but seems to have been quite Platonic, if somewhat unconventional.

75. "Epistle to Miss Honora Sneyd" (May, 1772), *ibid.,* p. 85.

76. *Ibid.,* III, 130.

77. *Ibid.,* p. 215.

78. *Ibid.,* p. 136.

79. XXXV-XXXVIII (1782), *ibid.,* pp. 156 ff.

80. LXXXIV, *ibid.,* p. 205.

81. XCI, *ibid.,* p. 212.

82. XCV, *ibid.,* p. 216.

83. XCIII, *ibid.,* p. 214.

84. XXVI, *ibid.,* p. 147. Note the final Alexandrine, as well as the characteristic eighteenth-century rime of *-ply* and *joy.*

85. "Independent Industry True Virtue," *ibid.,* II, 329.

86. Dunster: "Sonnet to the South Downs," *Laura, or, an Anthology of Sonnets (on the Petrarchan Model,) and Elegiac Quatorzains . . .* (Capel Lofft, ed.), London 1813-14, Vol. III, Sonnet CCLXXII. The poet is saying that he wishes to celebrate the Downs because she has given them to fame (by her sonnet to them, number V). The sonnets and other tributes in prose and verse to both Anna Seward and Charlotte Smith in the periodicals and elsewhere are innumerable.

87. Anon.: "Sonnet V," *Gentleman's Magazine,* Sept., 1789.

88. Facts from *Dictionary of National Biography,* article by Elizabeth Lee.

89. *Elegiac Sonnets, and Other Poems,* 9th ed., 2 vols. in 1, London, 1800, I, 1. Cf. VI, "To Hope"—"Lo!—the flowers fade, but all the thorns remain," *ibid.,* I, 6. Poetry is more felicitously compared to roses in XXXVI, "Should the lone Wanderer" (I, 36), a sonnet liked by Wordsworth.

90. VII, "The Departure of the Nightingale," *ibid.,* I, 7.

91. III, "To a Nightingale," *ibid.,* I, 3.

92. LVIII, "The Glow Worm," *ibid.,* I, 58.

93. IV, "To the Moon," *ibid.,* I, 4.

94. LXXX, "To the Invisible Moon," *ibid.,* II, 21. Mrs. Smith habitually uses not the Italian but the Elizabethan rime scheme, ending, as here, with a couplet.

95. E.g., XII, "Written on the Sea Shore" (Oct., 1784), *ibid.*, I, 12; LII, "The Pilgrim," *ibid.*, I, 52; LXVI, "Written in a Tempestuous Night on the Coast of Sussex," *ibid.*, II, 7; LXVII, "On Passing over a Dreary Tract of Country, and near the Ruins of a Deserted Chapel, during a Tempest," *ibid.*, II, 8; LXX, "On Being Cautioned against Walking on a Headland overlooking the Sea, because it was Frequented by a Lunatic," *ibid.*, II, 11. The last is illustrated by a highly romantic cut representing the unfortunate lunatic, wild eyed, with flying hair and dramatically folded arms, poised over the abyss, while his garment, consisting of the conventional sketchy cloak vaguely like a Roman toga in disarray, streams outward in the blast.

96. XXXIX, "To Night" (from *Emmeline, or the Orphan of the Castle*), *ibid.*, I, 39.

97. LXXI, "Written at Weymouth in Winter," *ibid.*, II, 12.

98. II, "Written at the Close of Spring," *ibid.*, I, 2.

99. VIII, "To Spring," *ibid.*, I, 8. An admirer expostulates with her in verse on this sentiment, saying that God loves man more than He does nature, and will bring at last a "happier spring." ("Julius": "Lines to Mrs. Smith on Sonnet VIII," *Gentleman's Magazine*, July, 1790). But Mrs. Smith has very little to say of the "religious consolations." Other melancholy spring poems: XXXI, "Written on Farm Wood, South Downs, in May, 1784," *Elegiac Sonnets*, I, 31; LIV, "The Sleeping Woodman. Written in April 1790," *ibid.*, I, 54; LV, "The Return of the Nightingale. Written in May 1791," *ibid.*, I, 55; and the poem (not a sonnet) "April," *ibid.*, II, 90 ff.

100. LXVIII, "Written at Exmouth, Midsummer, 1795," *ibid.*, II, 9.

101. LXXXVII, "Written in October," *ibid.*, II, 28. Cf. XLII, "Composed, during a Walk on the Downs, in November 1787," *ibid.*, I, 42.

102. XXXII, "To Melancholy, Written on the Banks of the Arun. October, 1789," *ibid.*, I, 32. Other sonnets to the Arun are XXVI, XXX, and XLV, all of which refer directly or indirectly to Otway. In the second he appears in company with Collins—and Hayley.

103. Cf. Earle Vonard Weller: "Keats and Mary Tighe," *Publications of the Modern Language Association*, XLII, 963-85 (1927).

104. "Poem Written at Scarborough," (Aug., 1799), *Psyche, etc.*, p. 220.

105. *Alfred. An Ode, with Six Sonnets*, London, 1778.

106. *Poetical Works*, pp. 223-29.

107. *Ibid.*, p. 222. Dated, 1798.

108. Havens says that these two magazines between them published nearly 600 sonnets in these two decades (*Influence of Milton*, p. 499). I

do not know whether or not he counted the very considerable number of poems labelled sonnets with no shadow of excuse.

109. Peter Bayley, Jun: "An Evening in the Vale of Festiniog," *Poems,* Philadelphia, 1804, p. 64. This poem, by the way, is in considerable passages little more (or I should say less) than a paraphrase of "Tintern Abbey"—though the same volume contains a parody of Wordsworth's "simple" style of peasant poetry.

110. *Poetical Works,* p. 110. It is from Coleridge's remarks in *Biographia Literaria* concerning the "doleful egotism" parodied in this sonnet that the suggestion for the title of this book was drawn.

111. *Collective Works,* I, 294. Dated, 1803.

112. *Poems,* p. 173. Another example: J. G.: "Ode, in the Manner of Collins' Ode to Evening," *Poetical Magazine,* III 129 f, which is in part so close a paraphrase that it merely changes a word here and there—with lamentable effect. Cf. the variant of the stanza (third line pentameter instead of trimeter) used in another avowed imitation, Thomas Enort's "Ode to Evening," *European Magazine,* XXXIV, 403 f (Dec., 1798).

113. E.g., "On Seeing an Old Man," *Gentleman's Magazine,* Jan., 1786; "Sympatheticus": "The Beggar Woman," *ibid.,* Mar., 1786; Anna Barbauld: "Ode to Spring," *Works,* I, 102 ff; "G": "Ode to Fancy" (in a mood similar to Collins'), *Poems Chiefly by Gentlemen of Devonshire and Cornwall,* I, 71 ff; Robert Merry: "Ode to Summer" and "Ode to Winter," *Florence Miscellany,* pp. 112 ff; John Whitehouse: "Ode to Morning," *Poems, etc.,* pp. 43 ff; Frank Sayers: "Ode to Night," *Collective Works,* I, 225 ff (This too catches something of Collins' mood); Kirke White: "To an Early Primrose," *Poems, Letters, etc.,* p. 44; Dr. Perfect: "Ode to a Temperate Morning in January," *European Magazine,* XXVI, 213 (Sept., 1794). There are several poems in Collins' stanza in Nathaniel Howard's *Bichleigh Vale.* Other examples are listed in an article by A. S. P. Woodhouse: "Imitations of the 'Ode to Evening,' " *Times* [London] *Literary Supplement,* May 30, 1929. Of course experimenters with this stanza may sometimes have gone directly to Collins' metrical model, Milton's "Translation from Horace."—See Havens: *Influence of Milton,* Bibliography III D, pp. 682 ff. But this is, after all, not particularly germane to our particular enquiry.

114. *Gentleman's Magazine,* July, 1792. The line from Gray is "Scap'd from the busy world's tumultuous din."

115. *Mysteries of Udolpho,* p. 47.

116. Bell, IV, pp. 66 ff. The poem is in couplets and is addressed, like the famous letters, to Thomas Pennant. It has phrases like "a soothing melancholy joy" and "a pleasing kind of pain."

117. An incredibly hectic "Ode to my Lyre" (J. G.: *Poetical Magazine*, II, 39-42, 59-61, 175-79) may be mentioned as an indication of the popularity of evening and night as a time of poetic and pseudo-poetic inspiration. The rhapsody covers three whole nights, but it is necessary during the banale daylight to hang the lyre ("by a wreath of flowers") in "some cavern wild" while the poet catches a little sleep.

118. II, 217.

119. "To the Owl," *Poetic Vigils* (1824), p. 266. The example is purposely late.

120. *Poetical Works of Henry Kirke White and James Grahame*, pp. 249-95 (1806).

121. Edinburgh, 1796. Prospect VI, pp. 25-26.

122. *Poetical Works*, p. 285. I recall also one sonnet on the quarrels of autumn birds (Richard Polwhele: "Sonnet V," *Poems Chiefly by Gentlemen of Devonshire and Cornwall*, II, 197). Russell's sonnet about the spider may be compared.

123. Thomson's unfortunate winter traveller appears again and again. Among the lower animals, the forlorn redbreast is doubtless the favorite.

124. E.g., Francis Hoyland: "On Rural Happiness," Chiswick *British Poets*, LXXIII, 12; David Mallet: "A Winter's Day," Chalmers, XIV, 46. (This is very Gothic, with "Black Melancholy" and ghosts that "stalk around and mix their yells with mine"); Robert Merry: "Ode to Winter," *Florence Miscellany*, pp. 113 ff (This is the ode in Collins' stanza mentioned above; the somewhat horrific material does not fit the meter very well.)

125. "Elegy: to Spring," *Poetical Works*, p. 123.

126. *Ibid.*, p. 120. This poem was claimed by Bruce's literary executor, John Logan. For a convincing argument in favor of Bruce's authorship, see Memoir affixed to the edition of Bruce cited (p. 35), also Appendix A and Notes to the poem.

127. Cf. Havens: *Influence of Milton*, Chapter XIX, p. 540.

128. "On the Sea" (sonnet), *Poetical Works*, p. 335.

129. "Ben Nevis" (sonnet), *ibid.*, p. 339.

130. "Song: In a drear-nighted December," *ibid.*, p. 299.

131. Yet the famous ode "To Autumn" (*ibid.*, pp. 248 f) is surprisingly cheerful and objective in tone.

132. *Ibid.*, pp. 232 ff.

133. See J. L. Cherry: *Life and Remains of John Clare*, London, 1873; Norman Gale: *Poems by John Clare*, Rugby, 1901; Arthur Symons: *Poems by John Clare*, London, 1908; Edmund Blunden and Alan Porter: *Poems Chiefly from MS*, London, 1920; Edmund Blunden: *Madrigals and Chronicles*, London, 1924. The only volume published during the

poet's lifetime which falls outside our limits is *The Rural Muse,* London, 1835. Clare was committed to an asylum in 1837.

134. These sonnets are to be found in *Poems Descriptive of Rural Life,* London, 1820, pp. 187 ff, and in *The Village Minstrel* (1821), II, 149 ff.

135. "To Autumn," *Village Minstrel,* II, 208.

136. "November," *The Shepherd's Calendar* (1827), p. 88.

137. E.g., "It is not Beauty I Demand" (*Poetical Works,* pp. 487 f), which Palgrave took for an original.

138. "The Errors of Ecstasie" (1822), *ibid.,* pp. 1 ff.

139. Cf. "Monet Annus" (spring), *ibid.,* pp. 448 f; "Compassion" (autumn), p. 446; "Winter," p. 467.

140. Act II, sc. 2, *ibid.,* p. 108.

141. "The Dove's Loneliness," *ibid.,* p. 416.

142. "Robin's Cross," *ibid.,* pp. 417 f.

143. "The Maiden's Grave," *ibid.,* p. 432.

144. "Prayer at Burial," *ibid.,* p. 443.

145. See "The Aeolian Harp," *ibid.,* p. 415; "My Bower," *ibid.,* pp. 419 ff; "The Magic Music," *ibid.,* p. 421.

146. The Aeolian harp was the theme of much discussion in prose and verse during the eighteenth century. According to Robert Bloomfield's account ("Nature's Music . . . in Honour of the Harp of Aeolus," *Remains of Robert Bloomfield,* 2 vols., London, 1824, I, 93 ff), although a similar instrument was known in the seventeenth century, the type used in the eighteenth was invented by a Mr. Oswald, who acted on a hint from Pope arising out of his Greek studies in connection with the *Homer.* Bloomfield speaks of having himself made many Aeolian harps. They were usually affixed to the sashes of windows.

147. Quotation from "Berrathon," *Poems of Ossian,* p. 404.

148. It is so characterized at least twice in Bloomfield's compilation.

149. John Ogilvie: "An Aeolian Ode," *Poems on Several Subjects,* 2 vols. in 1, London, 1769, p. 278.

150. Amelia Opie: "Stanzas written under Aeolus's Harp," *Poems,* p. 133.

151. Peter Bayley: "Sonnet. On Hearing an Eolian Harp," *Poems,* p. 96; and "Sonnet. To the Eolian Harp," *ibid.,* p. 97.

152. Anon. sonnet quoted in Robert Bloomfield's "Nature's Music," p. 126.

153. Goodwin: untitled lines, *ibid.,* p. 135.

154. Mr. C-: "On Hearing an Eolian Harp at Midnight," *ibid.,* p. 141.

155. In the poem just quoted.

156. "On Hearing the Sound of an Aeolian Harp" (sonnet), *Poems, Letters, etc.*, p. 46.

157. *The Works of the British Poets* (Robert Walsh, Jr., ed.), Philadelphia, 1822, XXXIX, 269. The landscapes in Scott's tales and in Southey's, in Felica Hemans' and Byron's, sometimes betray the influence of Ossian.

158. After the publication of *The Task* (1785), one sometimes suspects Cowper's influence on meter as well as content—e.g., in Crowe's *Lewesdon Hill* (1788) or Hurdis' *The Village Curate* (1788) and *The Favorite Village* (1800). Still later, the movement of Wordsworth's blank verse is echoed by an occasional imitator—e.g., by Peter Bayley in "An Evening in the Vale of Festiniog" (1802). One descriptive poem noted reminded me strongly of Shakespeare in the type of blank verse—Bryan Waller's "Heysham," *European Magazine*, XXVII, 275 f (Apr., 1795). For these matters, see Havens: *Influence of Milton*, Part II, *passim*.

159. *Walks in a Forest, and Other Poems*, Preface. Cf. similar sentiment in preface to Francis Webb's *Somerset. A Poem*, London, 1811.

160. *Poetical Works, etc.*, pp. 249-95.

161. A reviewer of Crowe's *Lewesdon Hill* (1788) remarks that "the title is not very alluring to those who have been used to see the Muse labouring up so many hills since Cooper's and Grongar; and some gentle Bard reclining on almost every mole-hill."—*Gentleman's Magazine*, Feb., 1788, p. 151. But the bards did not stop climbing hills for a good many years thereafter.

162. For an account of them see Havens: *Influence of Milton*, Chapter XII, pp. 236 ff. He finds that the type pretty well died out after about 1810.

163. *Dartmoor*, London (1826). This pleasing poem was written for a Royal Society prize, but was not submitted in time. Mrs. Hemans' somewhat academic dissertation won the award.

164. *Craig Phadric, Visions of Sensibility, etc.*, pp. 9-115.

165. *The Alps. A Poem*, pp. 6 and 8. This poem is not on the whole melancholy.

166. *Lewesdon Hill. A Poem*, Oxford (1788), p. 26. This poem is nearly all in melancholy mood.

167. *Poems*, pp. 99 ff.

168. *Poetical Works*, pp. 1-69. This is of course a favored theme in the odes, elegies, and sonnets. An early example is Langhorne's ode "To the River Eden" (1759)—Chiswick *British Poets*, LXV, 98 ff.

169. E.g., Anna Seward: "Alpine Scenery. A Poem" (1785), *Poetical Works* II, 352 ff; the descriptive poems in Robert Couper's *Poetry etc.* (1804); the landscapes in David Carey's "Visions of Sensibility" (1811).

170. For the original characteristics of this type as developed in the first half of the eighteenth century, see Reed: *Background of Gray's Elegy,* Ch. IV.

171. *Poetical Works, etc.,* pp. 215-43. The descriptive phrase is from John Wilson's monody on Grahame (*The Isle of Palms and Other Poems,* p. 320), from which the lines at the head of this chapter are also quoted.

172. Chiswick *British Poets,* LXV, 113-37.

173. George Wallace: *Prospects from Hills in Fife,* Prospect XII, p. 49.

174. *Reminiscences in Prose and Verse, etc.,* London, 1836, III, 63-84. This poem also was written for the Royal Society of Literature prize.

175. The phrase is Carey's, *Craig Phadric, etc.,* p. 88.

176. See *The Parish Register* (1807), *The Borough* (1810), *Tales in Verse* (1812), *Tales of the Hall* (1819), and *Posthumous Tales* (1832).

177. *The Peasants Fate: A Rural Poem, with Miscellaneous Poems,* Boston, 1802; quotations pp. 16 and 19.

178. The suffering caused by the wars supplies the melancholy material of that bleakest of Wordsworth's descriptive-narrative poems, "Guilt and Sorrow" (1793-4), as well as the episode of the ruined cottage later incorporated into "The Excursion" (Book I), and many other poetic sketches by various hands. But here we are concerned primarily with straight description.

179. "The Village Minstrel," st. XCI, *The Village Minstrel, etc.,* I, 48. This is only part of a long passage. Cf. also "Helpaton Green," *ibid.,* II, 48 ff, and "Helpaton," *Poems Descriptive of Rural Life,* pp. 1 ff. Nathaniel Bloomfield, brother to Robert, has "An Elegy on the Enclosure of Honington Green" in *The Suffolk Garland,* pp. 33-37.

180. Book VIII and part of Book IX, *Poetical Works,* pp. 512 ff.

181. *Poetical Works,* I, 194-314, 314-42, 362-78

182. Walsh's *British Poets,* XXXIX, 303 ff; quotation p. 313.

183. *Poetical Works,* II, 1-76.

184. Which Beattie thought "from its Gothic structure and original, to bear some relation to the subject and spirit of the poem"—Preface. The poem occupies pp. 1-38 in *Poetical Works of Beattie, Blair, and Falconer.*

185. One criticism of Beattie's earlier poems had been that they were too much after Gray.

186. Book I, st. 10, p. 4.

187. Book I, st. 22, p. 8.

188. Book I, stanzas 55 and 56, p. 18.

189. "On Mrs. Montague," *Poems on Several Occasions*, pp. 78 ff.

190. *The Pursuits of Literature. A Satirical Poem in Four Dialogues. With Notes*, London, 1799, pp. 296 ff; quotations pp. 299 and 301.

191. "The Pillow," *Poetical Works*, I, 83 ff.

192. Is this an echo of Wordsworth's theory that the nobility of man is best seen through nature, or an independent development?

193. Marsh's *British Poets*, XXXIX, 243, 245. Macneill hints in several poems that he himself was a sort of Edwin. Cf. "The Links o' Forth," *ibid.*, pp. 297 ff, and "The Scottish Muse," *ibid.*, pp. 389 ff.

194. Quotations from Canto I, st. XXV, *Poetical Works*, p. 237.

195. Canto I, pp. 24-25.

196. "The Village Minstrel," *The Village Minstrel and Other Poems*, I, 1-62.

197. This is true of Mickle and of Ebenezer Elliott, to take an example from near each chronological end of our period. Each of these two seems to have embodied something of his experience in a juvenile poem now very hard to come at. It was true to a certain extent also of Shelley; and that brings me to mention "Alastor," which on first thought seems to have affinities with the poems here enumerated. The vain search of the hero of "Alastor," however, is for an ideal of human love and companionship, and the word *Alastor,* identified by the subtitle with "the Spirit of Solitude," means an evil spirit. Peacock, who suggested the title, uses the word as a common noun with its proper meaning in *Rhododaphne* (London, 1818, p. 31):

> Or what Alastor bade thee wear
> That laurel rose, to Love profane . . .

Shelley was ever torn between a natural love of solitude and an intense craving for human affection.

198. "Prelude," Book XIII, *Poetical Works*, p. 327. Most of the other poets, too, as a matter of fact, were Christian believers, and hence presumably held the theory that all was for the best in the end.

199. Book V, *ibid.*, p. 268.

200. Book XIV, *ibid.*, p. 330.

201. Book XI, *ibid.*, p. 317.

202. Book XIV, *ibid.*, p. 331.

203. Book VI, *ibid.*, p. 275.

204. This suggestion is made by Professor H. N. Fairchild in *The Romantic Quest* (Columbia Univ. Press, 1931), Chapter XI. I owe to him also the suggestion that there is an important element of melancholy in Wordsworth arising from the fading of his early ecstasies.

205. "Hymn before Sun-rise, in the Vale of Chamouni," *Poetical Works*,

pp. 165 ff. The germ of this poem was borrowed without acknowledgment from an obscure German writer, but the emotion is certainly genuine enough.

206. "The Nightingale, a Conversation Poem" (1798), *ibid.*, p. 131.

207. *Ibid.*, pp. 159 ff.

208. "Childe Harold," III (1816), st. 93, *Poetical Works*, p. 235. Cf. *ibid.*, stanzas 72 and 75, p. 232.

209. "Ode to the West Wind" (1819), *Poetical Works*, pp. 526 f.

210. "Ode to a Nightingale," *Poetical Works*, p. 233.

211. "Stanzas written in Dejection, near Naples," *Poetical Works*, p. 515. Cf. the death of the hero of "Alastor," *ibid.*, pp. 92-93.

CHAPTER VII

THE SOUL OF A POET

1. For this theme in the first half of the century, see Reed: *The Background of Gray's Elegy, passim.*

2. *Poetical Works*, p. 186.

3. Quotations from *Penseroso, etc.*, p. 12, p. 93.

4. *Poems*, pp. 208, 218.

5. James Montgomery has a poetic paraphrase of the chapter of *Job* which opens with these words (the 14th)—*Poetical Works*, III, 118.

6. *London Magazine*, XX, 423 f. (Sept., 1751).

7. *Gentleman's Magazine*, Sept., 1753. This poem reappeared in *Scots Magazine* the following month: the latter periodical apparently had a habit of reprinting what caught its fancy from its southern contemporaries.

8. *Gentleman's Magazine*, Jan., 1781. This has the further subtitle of "A Serious Ode."

9. *Scots Magazine*, XLII, 494 (Sept., 1780). Subtitle: "Said to be the first attempt of Lady M- W-d-ve, on her late Matrimonial Disappointment."

10. Bell, IX, 128 ff. By James Scott. Subtitle: "Sacred to the Memory of the Most Hon. Francis Russel, Marquis of Tavistock." For a late example (1821), cf. John Clare: "Man's Mortality. Partly from the Scriptures. Written in Sickness"—*Village Minstrel*, II, 126 ff.

11. [John Hawkesworth, d. 1773]: "Life," *Universal Magazine*,

LXXIX, 362 (Supplement, 1786). Reprinted with variants in Bell, XII, 128.

12. Thomas Adney: "Thoughts on Life," *European Magazine,* XXVI, 212 (Sept., 1794).

13. *Poetical Works,* pp. 108-46.

14. *Poetical Works,* pp. 71-79.

15. S. H. Butcher: "The Melancholy of the Greeks," in *Some Aspects of Greek Genius,* 3d ed., Macmillan, 1916, p. 173.

16. An excellent account of the relation between the Industrial Revolution and English romanticism may be found in G. F. Richardson: *A Neglected Aspect of the English Romantic Revolt, University of California Publications in Modern Philology,* Vol. III, no. 3 (1915).

17. Cf. "The Task," Book IV, 1.333 ff, and 1.659 ff, *Poetical Works,* p. 238, pp. 244 f. Cowper fulminates with more conviction against war, slavery, and cruelty to animals.

18. *Spirit of the Age,* 4th ed., London, 1906, p. 309.

19. E.g., "The Little Vagabond," *Poetical Works,* p. 92; "Holy Thursday," p. 93; "London," p. 102; "The Chimney Sweeper," p. 104; "A Divine Image," p. 106; Why Should I Care for the Men of Thames," p. 117; "The Gray Monk," pp. 169 f. From this last comes the phrase "A tear is an intellectual thing."

20. "Song to the Men of England," *Poetical Works,* p. 521. The other poems in the group include "Lines Written during the Castlereagh Administration," *ibid.,* pp. 520 f; "Sonnet: England in 1819," p. 524; "An Ode: To the Assertors of Liberty," pp. 524 f; "The Mask of Anarchy," pp. 347 ff. This is to omit for the present Shelley's more generalized doctrinal verse. In all his verse of this type, Shelley illustrates the fusing of the influences of the two revolutions.

21. For the treatment of animals in the eighteenth century see Dix Harwood: *Love for Animals, and How it Developed in Great Britain.* New York, 1928.

22. Arthur O. Lovejoy: "Romantic Optimism," *Publications of the Modern Language Association,* XLII, 921 ff (1927). The argument referred to is that of plentitude. It occurs, for example, in John Ogilvie's apologetic poem "Providence" (*Poems on Several Subjects,* pp. 17-190), toward the end of Book I, pp. 65 ff.

23. An example is Shelley's lyric beginning "When the lamp is shattered."

24. Even the fiction of personal reserve continually breaks down in Byron, to be sure; but then Byron is not the whole of romanticism.

25. I have found no evidence whatever in this period of the melancholy of religious disillusion such as darkens Arnold's "Dover Beach" and parts of Tennyson's "In Memoriam." Keats's "aching ignorance" (see *post*) is the nearest to it and constitutes one of his claims to be called a "transition poet." But the only specifically Christian doctrine he longed to retain was a belief in personal immortality—a belief held, as a matter of fact, by most of the heterodox also at that time. The romanticists, for the most part, threw off the Christian doctrines they did not like, and retained those they did like.

26. The sport of all the village he has been,
Who with his simple looks oft jested free;
And gossips, gabbling o'er their cake and tea,
Some after time did prophecies repeat,
How half a ninny he was like to be . . .
—*Village Minstrel*, I, 19

27. Mary Tighe: "Address to My Harp," *Psyche, etc.*, p. 238.

28. [John] Thelwall: "The Harp on the Willow," *Poems, Chiefly Written in Retirement,* Hereford, 1801, p. 164.

29. James Montgomery: "The Harp of Sorrow," *Poetical Works*, I, 183 (1807).

30. George Darley: "Tears," *Poetical Works*, p. 481. Entire. There is something in the calculated extravagance of this rather fine little poem which reminds one that Darley was a student of the seventeenth-century poets.

31. "Childhood: A Poem," *Poetical Works, etc.*, pp. 39 ff.

32. "To a Friend in Distress," *ibid.*, p. 76.

33. "Solitude," *ibid.*, pp. 84 f. The poem begins:
It is not that my lot is low,
That bids this silent tear to flow;
It is not grief that bids me moan;
It is that I am all alone.

34. "To Misfortune," *ibid.*, p. 165.

35. "On the Death of Dermody the Poet," *ibid.*, pp. 155 ff.

36. "Genius," *Poems, Letters, etc.*, pp. 79 ff. This is a comparatively late poem, having been written after the publication of the *Clifton Grove* volume in 1803.

37. Cf. "The Faded Flower," *Poetical Works*, pp. 31 f; "Charity," p. 45; "To a Young Ass," pp. 35 f; "An Unfortunate," p. 32; "To an Unfortunate Woman at the Theatre," p. 32; "To an Unfortunate Woman," pp. 32 f.

38. "To a Young Lady, with a Poem on the French Revolution," *ibid.*, pp. 6 f. The poems cited in note 37 were all written after the passage quoted and are of slightly better quality than the schoolboy effusions to which it refers.

39. See "Religious Musings" (1796), 1.135 ff and 1.260 ff, *ibid.*, pp. 55 f, p. 58; and "The Destiny of Nations" (1796), 1.172 ff, *ibid.*, pp. 73 f.

40. "Fears in Solitude" (1798), 1.29 ff, *ibid.*, p. 128. Cf. "Lines to W. Linley, Esq." (1800), *ibid.*, p. 155:

> While my young cheek retains its healthful hues,
> And I have many friends who hold me dear,
> Lindley, methinks, I would not often hear
> Such melodies as thine, lest I should lose
> All memory of the wrongs and sore distress
> For which my miserable brethren weep!

41. *Ibid.*, pp. 147 f and 111 f. The former of these poems, being mostly Southey's, is to be found in a much fuller version in Southey's works. The latter is subtitled "A War Eclogue," and is an astonishingly vitriolic attack on Pitt. Later (about 1809), Coleridge described himself as one who

> hated to excess,
> With an unquiet and intolerant scorn,
> The hollow puppets of an hollow age,
> Ever idolatrous, and changing ever
> Its worthless idols! Learning, power, and time,
> (Too much of all) thus wasting in vain war
> Of fervid colloquy . . .—"A Tombless Epitaph," *ibid.*, p. 180.

42. *Letters of Samuel Taylor Coleridge* (Ernest Hartley Coleridge, ed.), Houghton Mifflin, 1895, 2 vols., I, 353.

43. "Ode to Tranquillity," *Poetical Works,* p. 159.

44. Perhaps the hopelessness of complete success in these high searchings has its reaction of despair:

> You will see Coleridge—he who sits obscure
> In the exceeding lustre, and the pure
> Intense irradiation of a mind,
> Which, with its own internal lightning blind,
> Flags wearily through darkness and despair . . .
> —Shelley: "Letter to Maria Gisborne."

45. "Lines on a Friend who Died of a Frenzy Fever induced by Calumnious Reports," *ibid.*, p. 35. Cf. the still earlier confession in "Quae Nocent Docent" (1789), *ibid.*, p. 4.

46. From the first draft of "The Pains of Sleep," in a letter to Southey, *Letters,* I, 437.

47. "Our quaint metaphysical opinions, in an hour of anguish, are like playthings by the bedside of a child deadly sick."—*Anima Poetae, from the Unpublished Note-Books of Samuel Taylor Coleridge,* London, 1895, p. 3.

48. "A Tombless Epitaph," *Poetical Works,* p. 180-81.

49. "Pain" (1790?), *ibid.,* p. 12.

50. To Thomas Poole, Nov. 5, 1796, *Letters,* I, 173.

51. "Hexameters" (1799), *Poetical Works,* p. 138.

52. "An Ode to the Rain" (1802), *ibid.,* p. 168.

53. *Letters,* I, 437. The final version of "The Pains of Sleep" is to be found in *Poetical Works,* pp. 170 f.

54. "The Visionary Hope," *ibid.,* p. 171.

55. In one place he calls genius a disease, how seriously is a question— Letter to Southey, Christmas Day, 1802, *Letters,* I, 416; in another, he shows that he realized the melancholy tendency of solitary musings— Letter to W. Sotheby, July 13, 1802, *ibid.,* p. 370.

56.   Yet at times
   My soul is sad, that I have roamed through life
   Still most a stranger, most with naked heart
   At mine own home and birth-place . . .
         —"To the Rev. George Coleridge" (1797),
               Poetical Works, p. 82.

57.   Ah! silly Bard, unfed, untended,
   His lamp but glimmer'd in its socket;
   He lived unhonour'd and unfriended
   With scarce a penny in his pocket;—
   Nay—tho' he hid it from the many—
   With scarce a pocket for his penny!
         —"A Character" (1825), *ibid.,* p. 196.

58. "Heaven knows that many and many a time I have regarded my talents and requirements as a porter's burthen, imposing on me the capital duty of going on to the end of the journey, when I would gladly lie down by the side of the road, and become the country for a mighty nation of maggots. For what is life, gangrened, as it is with me, in its very vitals, domestic tranquillity?"—Letter to Southey, Dec. 31, 1801, *Letters,* I, 366. Cf. "Farewell to Love" (1805?), *Poetical Works,* p. 173.

59. Set forth by John Carpentier, in *Coleridge, the Sublime Somnambulist,* London, 1929.

60. Wordsworth has been reading "The Prelude" to him, and Coleridge

has fallen into a vein of regret and self-accusation, which he interrupts
to cry

> That way no more! and ill beseems it me,
> Who came a welcomer in herald's guise,
> Singing of glory, and futurity,
> To wander back on such unhealthful road,
> Plucking the poisons of self-harm! And ill
> Such intertwine beseems triumphal wreaths
> Strew'd before *thy* advancing!

—"To a Gentleman, composed on the Night after
his Recitation of a Poem on the Growth of an
Individual Mind," *Poetical Works*, p. 177.

61. "The Pang More Sharp than All" (1807-1819), *ibid.*, p. 183. He
tried in old age to take a more Stoical attitude, and told himself that Duty
was the only sure friend of declining life—"Duty Surviving Self-Love,"
1826, *ibid.*, p. 197.

62. "Monody on the Death of Chatterton" (last version, completed
1829), *ibid.*, p. 63.

63. "Work without Hope" (1827), *ibid.*, p. 203.

64. "The Garden of Boccaccio" (1828), *ibid.*, p. 204.

65. Cf. John Drinkwater: *The Pilgrim of Eternity*, Doran, 1925.

66. Cf. Felix Rabbe: *Les Maîtresses Authentiques de Lord Byron*, Paris,
1890.

67. Cf. Otto Schmidt: *Rousseau und Byron*, Leipzig, 1890.

68. Cf. Schmidt's analysis, *ibid.*

69. One may see the warring elements of his reaction to exile separated
and become articulate in "The Two Foscari": the younger Foscari, whose
love for Venice torments him in exile, draws him back to torture and imprisonment, and finally, at the prospect of leaving again his beloved city,
breaks his heart, is the voice of Byron's suppressed sentimental love for a
land which he felt had wronged him; Marina voices his fiery denuncia-
tions of the senseless cruelty and injustice of that land; the elder Foscari
shows us the proud silent suffering of the typical Byronic hero.

70. Cf. James Kennedy: *Conversations on Religion with Lord Byron
and Others*, Philadelphia, 1833. Lady Byron thought that the Calvinism
of his youth lingered and was a main cause of his unhappiness: "The worst
of it is that I *do* believe!"

71. To Moore, March 4, 1822, *Letters and Journals of Lord Byron*
(R. E. Prothero, Lord Ernle, ed.), 6 vols., London and New York, 1906,
VI, 32.

72. In view of John Drinkwater's vehement argument (in *The Pilgrim of Eternity*) that the fact is not proved, one ought not, possibly, to make this statement so dogmatically. Yet after a perusal of Lord Lovelace's *Astarte* and Ethel Colburn Mayne's lives of Lord and Lady Byron, it is practically impossible to remain unconvinced. It is probable that Mr. Drinkwater exaggerates the importance of the verdict. The events passing as effects of the fact—which have authenticity in their own right—are probably, from the point of view of either literary achievement or human happiness, of more importance than the fact itself. Even from the point of view of an unnecessary moral judgment, it is a large question whether the calculated cruelty of Byron's treatment of his young wife is not more reprehensible than anything which may have passed between him and the willing Augusta.

73. He repeatedly called Lady Byron "my moral Clytemnestra" and expressed more than once his bitter resentment at the overthrow of his "household gods."—See letter to Moore, Sept. 19, 1818, *Letters and Journals*, IV, 262, and "Marino Faliero," Act III, sc. 2, *Poetical Works*, p. 602.

74. "Marino Faliero," Act. V, sc. 2, *Poetical Works*, p. 627. Cf. "Epistle to Augusta," *ibid.*, p. 473:

> I have been cunning in mine overthrow,
> The careful pilot of my proper woe.

75. As it is well known that life copies literature, it may not be impertinent to ask whether the literary as well as the social tradition may not have had a good deal to do with the flamboyant sins and sorrows of Byron's actual career. I have seen it stated as fact that the publication of *Werther* actually raised the suicide rate in its generation.

76. This particular phrase occurs in a letter to Hodgson, Oct. 13, 1811, *Letters and Journals*, II, 55. Byron did not fail to note the paradoxical fact that while ennui is in itself characteristically British—its prevalence was perhaps the cardinal item in his indictment of his native land—we have had to borrow the *word* from the French:

> For ennui is a growth of English root
> Though nameless in our language:—we retort
> The fact for word: and let the French translate
> That awful yawn which sleep cannot abate.
>
> —"Don Juan," XIII, st. 101, *Poetical Works*,
> p. 1223.

77. "Detached Thoughts" (1821-22), *Letters and Journals*, V, 425.

78. To Hoppner, June 6, 1819, *ibid.*, IV, 310; to Murray, June 7, 1819, *ibid.*, p. 314.

79. "Childe Harold," II, st. 35, *Poetical Works,* p. 197.
80. *Ibid.,* III, st. 9, p. 220.
81. "Manfred" (1816), Act III, sc. 1, *ibid.,* p. 497. Cf. "To the Earl of Clare" (1807), p. 68.
>The measure of our youth is full,
>Life's evening dream is dark and dull . . .

Byron was nineteen when he wrote that. He was twenty-eight when he wrote:
>He, who grown aged in this world of woe,
>In deeds, not years, piercing the depths of life,
>So that no wonder waits him . . .
>>—"Childe Harold," III, st. 5, *ibid.,* p. 219.

At thirty-six, he wrote:
>My days are in the yellow leaf . . .
>—"On This Day I Complete my Thirty-sixth Year,
>>*ibid.,* p. 1306.

82. "Childe Harold," III, st. 113, *ibid.,* p. 239.
83. "Lara," I, st. 18, *ibid.,* p. 395.
84. "Manfred," Act II, sc. 2, *ibid.,* p. 487.
85. "The Two Foscari," Act V, sc. 1, *ibid.,* p. 761.
86. "Cain," Act II, sc. 2, *ibid.,* p. 791.
87. *Conversations, etc.,* p. 34.
88. "Childe Harold," III, st. 90, *ibid.,* p. 235. Cf. *ibid.,* II, sts. 25-26, pp. 195-96.
89. Where rose the mountains, there to him were friends,
Where rolled the Ocean, thereon was his home.
>—"Childe Harold," III, 13, *ibid.,* p. 221.

Cf. "The Dream," st. 8, *ibid.,* p. 467.
90. "Childe Harold," III, st. 34, *ibid.,* p. 225.
91. Act II, sc. 2, *ibid.,* p. 487. It need hardly be remarked how far Byron was, in himself, from realizing the ideal of proud *silent* suffering set forth in his typical hero. Here at least he was justified in his contention that he and his heroes were not the same.
92. See "Journal to Augusta," Sept. 29, 1816, *Letters and Journals,* III, 264.
93. Letter to Moore, March 8, 1816, *ibid.,* III, 274. The poem is on p. 426 in *Poetical Works.*
94. If I have erred, there was no joy in error
>But pain and insult and unrest and terror;
>I have not as some do, bought penitence

With pleasure, and a dark yet sweet offence . . .
—"Julian and Maddalo," *Poetical Works*, p. 239 (1818).

Not his the look of any secret crime,
For nought of ill his heart could understand,
But pity and wild sorrow for the same . . .
—"Prince Athanase," *ibid.*, p. 209 (1817).

95. "On Fanny Godwin," *ibid.*, p. 503 (1817).

96. "To Misery," *ibid.*, p. 513. (1818).

97. "Song," *ibid.*, p. 571 (1821).

98. "A Lament," *ibid.*, p. 573 (1821).

99. Interesting evidence of the influence of such an ideal in the Shelley circle is Horace Smith's only considerable essay at serious verse, *Amarynthus, the Nympholept* (London, 1821).

100. There are two pathetic fragments addressed to Mary Shelley at the time when they were drawing apart in Italy after the death of little William (1819)—*ibid.*, p. 529.

101. "Lines to a Reviewer," *ibid.*, p. 561 (1820). Cf. "Lines to a Critic," p. 505. Shelley could write a most convincing curse, for all that: see Prometheus' curse on Jove (Act I, sc. 1, *ibid.*, pp. 252 f); Cenci's on Beatrice (Act IV, sc. 1, *ibid.*, pp. 325 f); and Shelley's own on the Lord Chancellor who had denied him the care of his children (*ibid.*, pp. 500 ff).

102. "Julian and Maddalo," *ibid.*, p. 243.

103. "Revolt of Islam," V, st. 23, *ibid.*, p. 142. Cf. letter to Godwin, Dec. 7, 1817 (Julian Shelley, IX, 258) and the story of his fainting in a valley of lovely and fragrant flowers.

104. "With a Guitar, to Jane," *Poetical Works*, p. 596. Here the sense affected is hearing, not, as in the other quotation, sight.

105. Cf. "Lines: That time is dead forever, child," *ibid.*, p. 503; "Death," *ibid.*, p. 503; "The Past," p. 508; "Time Long Past," p. 566; "Remembrance," p. 573. The related theme of delusive hope, with personal application, occurs in "To-Morrow," p. 588; and in "Fragment: Alas! this is not what I thought life was," p. 566.

106. "Alastor," *ibid.*, p. 86. Cf. the opening lines of "Prince Athanase," *ibid.*, p. 209, and the description of Leon, "Revolt of Islam," *ibid.*, p. 137. The first phrase quoted in the text is of course from the "Ode to the West Wind."

107. Leslie Holdsworth Allen: *Die Persönlichkeit Percy Bysshe Shelleys*, Leipzig, 1907, pp. 71 ff. It is interesting to remember that the half-mystic

projection of self into the west wind in the great "Ode" is not wholly
personal, but social also; the poet would become one with the wind that
he may hasten the long-delayed spring of man's deliverance.

108. "Julian and Maddalo," *Poetical Works*, p. 241.

109. These quotations are from Act I, sc. 1, *ibid.*, p. 254, p. 248, p. 259.

110. Act IV, closing passage, *ibid.*, p. 293.

111. See "Prometheus Unbound," Act III, sc. 3.

112. "He had a vision of glory withheld from his fellows, and, when
this was eclipsed, he at times moved dizzily amid a night of tombs and
terrors . . . And even when he came forth into the daylight and caught its
beauty, his song had constantly something in it of the night's mystery
and terror."—Strong: *Three Studies in Shelley, etc.*, pp. 146-47.

113. "Prince Athanase," *Poetical Works*, p. 211.

114. "Alastor," *ibid.*, p. 85. Cf. this phrase a few pages later (p. 92)
in the same poem: "Hope and despair, the torturers, slept."

115. Sonnet ("Lift not the painted veil which those who live"), *ibid.*,
p. 520 (1818).

116. "Byron was, as none had ever been before, the poet of personality,
and as such was excessively egotistic . . . Shelley, perfectly free from
vanity and egotism, was absorbed in his ideas, he expanded his ego until
it embraced the Universe."—George Brandes: *Naturalism in England*,
Macmillan, 1905, p. 248.

117. "Defense of Poetry," Julian Shelley, VII, 118.

118. Sidney Colvin: *Keats*, Macmillan, 1921, p. 220.

119. Cf. letter to Benj. Bailey, postmarked Nov. 22, 1817, *Letters of
John Keats* (Maurice Buxton Forman, ed.), 2 vols., Oxford Univ. Press,
1930, I, 72. A similar idea is expressed in a letter to Richard Woodhouse,
postmarked Oct. 27, 1818, *ibid.*, I, 245.

120. He told Dilke that the identity of his sick brother Tom "presses
upon me so all day that I am obliged to go out—and although I intended to have given some time to study alone I am obliged to write,
and plunge into abstract images to ease myself of his countenance his
voice and feebleness."—*Letters*, I, 236. To Woodhouse he wrote that in
a roomful of people the alien identities pressed in upon him and annihilated
him.—*Ibid.*, I, 245. Twice he wrote to America of how the identity of
his sister-in-law pressed upon him.—*ibid.*, I, 248, 267. At another time
he wrote to the absent brother and sister-in-law a complaint of how in
company "unpleasant human identities" pressed upon him just enough
to spoil indolence without arousing interest.—*ibid.*, II, 337-38. Edward

Thomas makes a good deal of this power of passive receptivity in explaining what he speaks of as the strain of morbidity in Keats.—*Keats,* London, [1916], Chapter VI.

121. See letter to Bailey, postmarked Nov. 22, 1817, *Letters,* II, 74.

122. The first quotation is of course the opening lines of "The Ode to a Nightingale"; the other is from the sonnet "On Seeing the Elgin Marbles" (*Poetical Works,* p. 333). Examples of the love poetry were cited in Chapter V.

123. Book IV, *ibid.,* pp. 155 ff.

124. Book IV, *ibid.,* p. 166. Surely there is some symbolism also of the hollowness of desire in "La Bella Dame Sans Merci."

125. Book II, *ibid.,* p. 116. The passage, which describes the visit of Cynthia to Endymion after he has undergone his adventures under earth, is followed by the poet's comment:

> Ye who have yearn'd
> With too much passion, will here stay and pity
> For the mere sake of truth . . .

126. "Endymion," Book I, *ibid.,* p. 91.

127. June 10, 1818, *Letters,* I, 164. Cf. the letter to the same, Jan. 23, 1818, *ibid.,* p. 89-90. Both Thomas (*op. cit.*) and C. D. Thorpe (*The Mind of John Keats,* Oxford Univ. Press, 1926, Chapter V) speak at some length of the humanitarian sympathies of Keats.

128. To C. A. Brown, from Naples, Nov. 1, 1820, *Letters,* II, 569.

129. Book III, 1.107, *Poetical Works,* p. 276.

130. To Reynolds, May 3, 1818, *Letters,* I, 152, 154.

131. Sonnet on "Ben Nevis" (written Aug., 1818), *Poetical Works,* p. 339.

132. *Ibid.,* p. 342.

133. *Letters,* II, 342-43.

134. Cf. "Endymion," Book II, *Poetical Works,* p. 98:

> the subtle food,
> To make us feel existence, and to show
> How quiet death is;

the sonnet "After dark vapours" (p. 332), which names among the "calmest thoughts" a poet's death; the passage beginning "Darkling I listen" in the "Ode to a Nightingale" (p. 233); the closing couplet of the sonnet "When I have fears that I may cease to be" (p. 336); and the closing couplet of the "Bright star" sonnet (p. 345).

135. The letters to Reynolds and to George and Georgiana Keats set forth this pilgrim's progress. The most explicit expression of Keats's ma-

ture philosophy is in the "vale of soul-making" letter to America, *Letters,*
II, 361 ff.

136. "The Fall of Hyperion" occupies pp. 312-25 in the Globe Edition,
where it is called "Hyperion: A Vision," and erroneously subtitled "The
First Version of the Poem." My quotations will be found on pp. 316,
316, 318, 319 respectively. I have adopted substantially the interpretation
of the poem presented in Hugh I'Anson Fausset's *Keats: A Study in
Development,* London, 1922.

137. *John Keats,* 2 vols., Houghton Mifflin, 1925, II, 246. The "Ode"
is on pp. 250-51 in the Globe Edition.

138. It is partly the indecorous abandon of this longing and partly
its basis in the sensibility and introspective individualism of Rousseau's
"belle âme" which makes it so distasteful to Professor Irving Babbitt.
For his discussion see *Rousseau and Romanticism,* Houghton Mifflin,
1919, Chapter IX.

WORKS CITED

I. SECONDARY SOURCES: BIBLIOGRAPHICAL, BIOGRAPHICAL, CRITICAL, AND SATIRICAL

Allen, Leslie Holdsworth: Die Persönlichkeit Percy Bysshe Shelleys. Leipzig, 1907.

Appell, Johann Wilhelm: Werther und seine Zeit. Zur Goethe-Literatur. Oldenberg, 1882.

Ashmun, Margaret: The Singing Swan, an Account of Anna Seward. Yale University Press, 1931.

Babbitt, Irving: Rousseau and Romanticism. Houghton Mifflin, 1919.

Barnefield, George: see Carpenter, Edward.

Blackwood's Magazine, Vol. XXX. Edinburgh, 1833.

Blessington, Countess of: Conversations of Lord Byron with. Philadelphia, 1836.

Boswell, James: Life of Johnson. Modern Student's Library. Scribner's, 1917.

Bragg, Marion K.: The Formal Eclogue in Eighteenth Century England. University of Maine Studies, 2d series, no. 6. University of Maine Press, 1926.

Brandes, George: Naturalism in England. Vol. IV of Main Currents in Nineteenth Century Literature. Macmillan, 1905.

Butcher, S. H.: The Melancholy of the Greeks, in Some Aspects of Greek Genius. 3d ed., Macmillan, 1916.

Carpenter, Edward, and Barnefield, George: The Psychology of the Poet Shelley. Dutton, 1925.

Carpentier, John: Coleridge, the Sublime Somnambulist. London, 1929.

Cecil, David: The Stricken Deer; or, the Life of Cowper. London, [1930].

Clark, Roy Benjamin: William Gifford: Tory Satirist, Critic, and Editor. Columbia University Press, 1930.

Clark, H. H.: A Study of Melancholy in Edward Young. Modern Language Notes, XXXIX, 129 ff and 193 ff (1924).

Colvin, Sir Sidney: Keats. English Men of Letters. Macmillan, 1921.

Dictionary of National Biography. Sir Leslie Stephen, ed., 63 vols. London, 1885-1900.

Draper, John: The Funeral Elegy and the Rise of English Romanticism. New York University Press, 1929.

——— (ed.) A Century of Broadside Elegies. London, 1928.

Drinkwater, John: The Pilgrim of Eternity: Byron—a Conflict. Doran, 1925.

Edgeworth, Maria: Angelina; or, L'Amie Inconnue, in Moral Tales. Philadelphia, 1849.

Enfield, D. E.: L. E. L.: a Mystery of the Thirties. Hogarth Press, 1928.

Fairchild, Hoxie Neale: The Noble Savage: a Study in Romantic Naturalism. Columbia University Press, 1928.

——— The Romantic Quest. Columbia University Press, 1931.

Fausset, Hugh I'Anson: Keats: a Study in Development. London, 1922.

Harwood, Dix: Love for Animals and How It Developed in Great Britain. New York, 1928.

Havens, Raymond D.: The Influence of Milton on English Poetry. Harvard University Press, 1922.

——— The Literature of Melancholy. Modern Language Notes, XXIV, 226-27 (1909).

——— Changing Taste in the Eighteenth Century. Publications of the Modern Language Association, XLIV, 501-36 (1929).

Hazlitt, William: The Spirit of the Age, 4th ed. London, 1906.

Hesselgrave, Ruth Avaline: Lady Miller and the Batheaston Literary Circle. Yale University Press, 1927.

Johnson, Samuel: Dictionary of the English Language, 2d ed. 2 vols. London, 1755-56.

Kalkühler, Florine: Die Natur des Spleens bei den englischen Schriftstellen in der ersten Hälfte des 18. Jahrhunderts. Leipzig, 1920.

Kennedy, James: Conversations on Religion with Lord Byron and Others. Philadelphia, 1833.

Lovejoy, Arthur O.: Romantic Optimism. Publications of the Modern Language Association, XLII, 921 ff (1927).

Lovelace, Ralph Milbanke, Earl of: Astarte: A Fragment of Truth concerning George Gordon, Sixth Lord Byron. London, 1921.

Lowell, Amy: John Keats, 2 vols. Houghton Mifflin, 1925.

Lowes, John Livingston: The Road to Xanadu: a Study in the Ways of the Imagination. Houghton Mifflin, 1927.

Mayne, Ethel Colburn: Byron. 2 vols. London, 1913.

—— Life and Letters of Anne Isabella, Lady Noel Byron . . . Scribner's, 1929.

More, Hannah: Christian Morals, in *Works,* 18 vols. London, 1818. Vols. XV-XVI.

—— Strictures on the Modern System of Female Education, in *ibid.,* Vols. VII, VIII.

Müller, Carl: Robert Blair's "Grave" und die Grabes- und Nachtdictung. Weimar, 1909.

Northup, Clark Sutherland: A Bibliography of Thomas Gray. Yale University Press, 1917.

Oswald, Eugene: Goethe in England and America: Bibliography, 2d ed. revised and enlarged by L. and E. Oswald. Publications of the English Goethe Society, no. 11. London, 1909.

Peacock, Thomas Love: Nightmare Abbey, in *Works,* Halliford Edition, Vol. III. London and New York, 1924.

Rabbe, Félix: Les Maîtresses authentiques de Lord Byron. Paris, 1890.

Railo, Eino: The Haunted Castle: a Study of the Elements of English Romanticism. London, 1927.

Reed, Amy: The Background of Gray's "Elegy." Columbia University Press, 1924.

Reynolds, Myra: The Treatment of Nature in English Poetry between Pope and Wordsworth. University of Chicago Press, 1909.

Richardson, G. F.: A Neglected Aspect of the English Romantic Revolt. University of California Publications in Modern Philology, Vol. III, no. 3 (1915).

Schmidt, Otto: Rousseau und Byron. Leipzig, 1890.

Schnabel, Bruno: Ossian in der schönen Litteratur England's bis 1832. Mit Ausschluss der sogenannten Englischen Romantikers. Englische Studien XXIII. Leipzig, 1897.

Smart, J. S.: James Macpherson, an Episode in Literature. London, 1905.

Snow, Royall H.: Thomas Lovell Beddoes, Eccentric and Poet. Covici-Friede, 1928.

Stephen, Sir Leslie: English Thought in the Eighteenth Century. 2 vols. London, 1902.

Strong, Archibald T.: Three Studies in Shelley and an Essay on Nature in Wordsworth and Meredith. Oxford University Press, 1921.

Thomas, Edward: Keats. London, 1916.

Thomas, W.: Le Poète Edward Young: Étude sur sa vie et ses oeuvres. Paris, 1901.

Thorpe, C. D.: The Mind of John Keats. Oxford University Press, 1926.

Tombo, Rudolf: Ossian in Germany. Columbia University Press, 1901.

Van Tieghem, P.: La Poésie de la nuit et des tombeaux en Europe au XVIIIe Siècle, in Memoires de l'Academie Belgique—Classe des Lettres et des Sciences morales et politiques—Deuxième série, tome XVI. Bruxelles, 1922.

——— Ossian en France. 2 vols., Vol. I. Paris, 1927.

Weller, Earle Vonard: Keats and Mary Tighe. Publications of the Modern Language Association, XLII, 963 ff (1927).

Wesley, John: The Heart of John Wesley's Journal. Percy S. Parker, ed. New York, Chicago, Toronto, London, and Edinburgh, [n.d.]

Wilmsen, Friedrich: Ossian's Einfluss auf Byron's Jugendgedichte. Jena, 1903.

Wollstonecraft, Mary: Vindication of the Rights of Women. London, 1792.

Woodhouse, A. S. P.: Imitations of the "Ode to Evening," Times [London] Literary Supplement, May 30, 1929.

——— Thomas Warton and the "Ode to Horror," ibid., January 24, 1929.

Woolf, Virginia: A Room of One's Own. Harcourt, Brace & Co., 1929.

[Young, John]: A Criticism on the Elegy Written in a Country Churchyard, Being a Continuation of Dr. J-n's Criticism on the Poems of Gray. London, 1783.

II. PRIMARY SOURCES: ANTHOLOGIES AND PERIODICALS

Amulet, The; or, Christian and Literary Remembrancer. London, 1828.

Annual Anthology. Robert Southey, ed. Bristol, 1799-1800.

Bell's Classical Arrangement of Fugitive Poetry. 18 vols. in 9. London, 1789-1800.

Bethune, George W.: The British Female Poets with Biographical and Critical Notices. Philadelphia, 1858.

British Album, The. Containing Poems of Della Crusca, Anna Matilda, Arley, Benedict, the Bard, etc., etc., which were Originally Published under the Title of the Poetry of the World. Revised and Corrected by their Respective Authors. Also, a Poem, never before Printed, called The Interview, by Della Crusca. And Other Considerable Additions, 2d ed. 2 vols. in 1. London, 1790.

British Poets, The. Including Translations, 100 vols. Chiswick, 1822.

Campbell, Thomas: Specimens of the British Poets, with Biographical and Critical Notices, and an Essay on English Poetry, 7 vols. London, 1819.

Chalmers, Alexander: The Works of the English Poets, from Chaucer to Cowper; Including the Series Edited, with Prefaces, Biographical and Critical, by Dr. Samuel Johnson: and the Most Approved Translations. The Additional Lives by Alexander Chalmers, F. S. A., 21 vols. London, 1810.

[Dodsley, Robert]: A Collection of Poems in Six Volumes, by Several Hands. London, 1778.

European Magazine, or London Review. London.

Florence Miscellany, The. Florence, 1785.

Gentleman's Magazine, and Historical Chronicle, by Sylvanus Urban, Gent. London.

Hamilton, Walter: Parodies of the Works of English and American Authors. London, 1888.

Hawkins, Sir John (and others): Probationary Odes for the Laureateship. London, 1787.

Literary Gazette. New York.

Lofft, Capel: Laura: or An Anthology of Sonnets, (on the Petrarchan Model,) and Elegiac Quatorzains: English, Italian, Spanish, Portugese, French, and German, Original and Translated, Great Part never before published, 5 vols. London, 1813-14.

London Magazine; or, Gentleman's Monthly Intelligencer. London.

Mirror of Literature, Amusement, and Instruction. London.

Monthly Review; or, Literary Journal. London.

Musae Seatonianae: A Complete Collection of the Cambridge Prize Poems, from the First Institution of that Premium by the Reverend Thomas Seaton, in 1750, to the Year 1806. To which are Added, Three Poems, Likewise Written for the Prize, by Mr. Bally, Mr. Scott, and Mr. Wrangham, 2 vols. Cambridge, 1808.

New Tory Guide, The. London.

Nichols, J.: Select Collection of Poems, 8 vols. London, 1782.

North Briton, The. [John Wilkes, ed.] Nos. 1-45 inc. Corrected and revised by a Friend to Civil and Religious Liberty. [London, 1763?].

Notes and Queries, 3d series, Vol. I. London.

Oxford Prize Poems, 8th ed. Oxford, 1834.

Pearch's Collection of the Most Esteemed Pieces of Poetry, 2d ed. London, 1770.

Poems, Chiefly by Gentlemen of Devonshire and Cornwall [Richard Polwhele, ed.], 2 vols. Bath, 1792.

Poetical Amusements at a Villa near Bath [Lady Miller, ed.], 4 vols. London, 1775, 1776, 1777, 1781.

Poetical Calendar, The. Containing a Collection of Scarce and Valuable Pieces of Poetry; with Variety of Originals and Translations, by the Most Eminent Hands. Intended as a Supplement to Mr. Dodsley's Collection. Written and Selected by Francis Fawkes, M.A., and William Woty, 12 vols. in 6. London, 1763.

Poetical Magazine; Dedicated to the Lovers of the Muse, by the Agent of the Goddess, R. Ackermann, 4 vols. London, 1809-11.

Poetical Register, and Repository of Fugitive Poetry,

        for 1801, 3d ed. London, 1815.

        for 1802, 2d ed. London, 1803.

        for 1803, 2d ed. London, 1805.

        for 1804, 2d ed. London, 1806.

        for 1805, 2d ed. London, 1807.

        for 1806-7.   London, 1811.

        for 1808-9.   London, 1812.

Roach's Beauties of the Modern Poets of Great Britain carefully Selected and Arranged, 24 nos. in 6 vols. London, 1793.

Robertson, Eric S.: English Poetesses. London, 1883.

Scots Magazine. Edinburgh.

Sentimental Magazine; or, General Assemblage of Science, Taste, and Entertainment. Calculated to Amuse the Mind, to Improve the Understanding, and to Amend the Heart, Vol. II. London, 1774.

Spirit of the Public Journals. Being an Impartial Selection of the Most Exquisite Essays and Jeux d'esprits, Principally Prose, that Appear in the Newspapers and Other Publications. London.

Student, or, the Oxford and Cambridge Monthly Miscellany. [T. Warton and Christopher Smart, editors], 2 vols. Oxford and London, 1750-51.

Suffolk Garland, The. Ipswick, 1818.

Town and Country Magazine; or Universal Repository of Knowledge, Instruction, and Entertainment. London.

Universal Magazine of Knowledge and Pleasure. London.

Walsh, Robt.: The Works of the British Poets, with Lives of the Authors. Philadelphia, 1822.

III. PRIMARY SOURCES: PUBLICATIONS BY INDIVIDUAL AUTHORS. MOSTLY VERSE

Baillie, Joanna: Dramatic and Poetical Works, 2d ed. London, 1853.

Barbauld, Anna Laetitia [née Aiken]: Works. With a Memoir by Lucy Aiken. 2 vols. London, 1825.

Barton, Bernard: Metrical Effusions. Woodbridge, 1812.

———— Memoir, Letters, and Poems. Lucy Barton, ed. Philadelphia, 1850.

———— Minor Poems. London, 1824.

———— Poetic Vigils. London, 1824.

Bayley, Peter, Jun.: Poems. Philadelphia, 1804.

Beattie, James: Poetical Works of Beattie, Blair, and Falconer. George Gilfillan, ed. Edinburgh, 1854.

Beddoes, Thomas Lovell: Poems. Ramsay Colles, ed. Muses' Library. London and New York, [n.d.].

———— See also Snow.

Blair, Robert: Works of Beattie, Blair, and Falconer [see Beattie].

———— See also Müller.

Blake, William: Poetical Works. John Sampson, ed. Oxford Edition. 1914.

Blamire, Suzanna: Poetical Works. Henry Lonsdale, ed. Edinburgh, 1842.

Bloomfield, Robert: The Farmer's Boy. A Rural Poem, 4th ed. London, 1801.

———— Remains. 2 vols. London, 1824.

Bowles, William Lisle: Poetical Works. George Gilfillan, ed. 2 vols. Edinburgh, 1855.

Broome, William: Poems on Several Occasions, 2d ed. London, 1739.

Bruce, George: Poems, Ballads, and Songs on Various Occasions. Edinburgh, 1813.

Bruce, Michael: Poetical Works. William Stephen, ed. Paisley, 1895.

Brydges, [Sir] Samuel Egerton: Poems, 4th ed. with many additions. London, 1807.

Burke, Thomas Travers: Temora: an Epic Poem. In 8 cantos. Versified from Macpherson's Prose Translation of the Poems of Ossian. Perth, 1818.

Burns, Robert: Complete Poetical Works. Drawn from Henley and Henderson. Cambridge Edition. 1897.

Burton, Richard: Anatomy of Melancholy. Bohn's Library. 3 vols. London, 1926.

Byron, George Gordon, Sixth Lord: Complete Poetical Works. Sir Leslie Stephen, ed. Globe Edition. Macmillan, 1907.

———— Letters and Journals. R. E. Prothero, Lord Ernle, ed. 6 vols. London and New York, 1906.

———— See also Blessington, Drinkwater, Kennedy, Lovelace, Mayne, Rabbe, Schmidt, Wilmsen.

Cameron, Ewen: The Fingal of Ossian, an Ancient Epic Poem in 6 books. Translated from the Original Galic Language by Mr. James Macpherson, and now Rendered into Heroic Verse. Warrington, 1776.

Campbell, Thomas: Poetical Works with a Memoir by W. E. Aytoun. Boston, 1857.

Carey, David: Craig Phadric, Visions of Sensibility, with Legendary Tales, and Occasional Pieces. Inverness, Elgin, Edinburgh, and London, 1811.

Carrington, N. T.: Dartmoor. London, [1826].

Carter, Elizabeth: Poems on Several Occasions, 2d ed. London, 1766.

Chatterton, Thomas: Poetical Works. Skeat, ed. Aldine Edition, 2 vols. London, 1891.

———— Works, Southey and Cottle, editors, 3 vols. London, 1803.

Clare, John: Life and Remains of John Clare. J. L. Cherry, ed. London, 1873.

———— Madrigals and Chronicles. Edmund Blunden, ed. London, 1924.

———— Poems by John Clare. Norman Gale, ed. Rugby, 1901.

———— Poems by John Clare. Arthur Symon, ed. London, 1908.

———— Poems Chiefly from MS. Edmund Blunden and Alan Porter, editors. London, 1920.

———— Poems Descriptive of Rural Life and Scenery. London, 1820.

———— The Rural Muse. London, 1835.

———— The Shepherd's Calendar: with Village Stories, and Other Poems. London, 1827.

———— The Village Minstrel and Other Poems, 2 vols. London, 1821.

[Clark, John]: The Works of the Caledonian Bards. Translated from the Galic, Vol. I [all published]. Edinburgh, 1778.

Coleridge, Samuel Taylor: Anima Poetae, from the Unpublished Notebooks of Samuel Taylor Coleridge. Ernest Hartley Coleridge, ed. London, 1895.

―――― Complete Poetical Works. J. D. Campbell, ed. Globe Edition. Macmillan, 1924.

―――― Letters. Ernest Hartley Coleridge, ed., 2 vols. Houghton Mifflin, 1895.

―――― See also Carpentier, Lowes.

Collins, William: Poetical Works of Gray and Collins. A. L. Poole, ed., Oxford Edition. 1917.

[Combe, William]: The English Dance of Death. With 38 Coloured Plates by T. Rowlandson, 2 vols. London, 1903.

Couper, Robert: Poetry, Chiefly in the Scottish Language, 2 vols. Inverness, 1804.

Courtier, P.: Poems. London, 1796.

[Cowley, Hannah]: The Poetry of Anna Matilda. London, 1788.

Cowper, William: Correspondence. F. Wright. ed., 4 vols. Dodd, 1904.

―――― Memoir of the Early Life of William Cowper, Esq., written by himself, 3d ed. London, 1817.

―――― Poetical Works. William Benham, ed., Globe Edition. Macmillan, 1921.

[Cowper, William, M. D., of Chester]: Il Penseroso. An Evening's Contemplation in St. John's Churchyard, Chester. A Rhapsody, Written more than Twenty Years Ago; and Now (First) Published. London, 1767.

Crabbe, George: Poetical Works. A. J. Carlyle and R. M. Carlyle, editors. Oxford Edition. 1914.

Croly, George: Poetical Works, 2 vols. London, 1830.

[Crowe, William]: Lewesdon Hill. A Poem. Oxford [1788].

Cunningham, Allan: Sir Marmaduke Maxwell and Other Poems. London, 1822.

Darley, George: Complete Poetical Works. Ramsay Colles, ed., Muses' Library. London and New York [n.d.].

Darwin, Erasmus: The Botanic Garden. A Poem, in Two Parts, 2d American ed. New York, 1807.

Davidson, Anthony: The Poems of Ossian, Translated from the Galic Language by James Macpherson, Esq., and Turned into Blank Verse . . . Salisbury, [1810?].

[Dow, Alexander]: Sethona. A Tragedy. London, 1774.

———— Zingis. A Tragedy. London, 1769.

Dyer, George: Poems. London, 1801.

Dyer, John: The Poetical Works of Armstrong, Dyer, and Green. Charles Cowden Clarke, ed. Edinburgh, 1868.

Elliott, Ebenezer: Poetical Works. Edwin Elliott, ed., 2 vols. London, 1876.

Falconer, William: Poems of Beattie, Blair, and Falconer [see Beattie].

Fletcher, John: The Nice Valour, or the Passionate Madman. In *Works of Beaumont and Fletcher,* 14 vols. Edinburgh, 1812, Vol. IV.

Foot, James: Penseroso, or the Pensive Philosopher in his Solitudes, a Poem in Six Books. London, 1771.

Gifford, William: The Baviad and The Maviad. London, 1799.

———— See also R. B. Clark.

Gisborne, Thomas: Walks in a Forest, and Other Poems, 8th ed. London, 1813.

[Goethe, Johann Wolfgang von; translator anon.]: The Sorrows of Werter; a German Story, 4th ed., 2 vols. London, 1783.

———— See also Appell, Oswald.

Goldsmith, Oliver: The Poems and Plays of. Everyman's Library. Dutton, [n.d.].

Grahame, James: Poetical Works of Henry Kirke White and James Grahame. George Gilfillan, ed. Edinburgh, 1856.

Gray, Thomas: Correspondence of Gray, Walpole, West, and Ashton. Toynbee, ed. Oxford University Press, 1915, Vol. II.

———— Poetical Works of Gray and Collins [see Collins].

Halloway, William: The Peasants Fate: a Rural Poem. With Miscellaneous Poems. Boston, 1802.

[Harley, George Davies]: Poems. London, 1796.

Harold, Edmond, Baron de: Poems of Ossian Lately Discovered. Dusseldorf, 1787.

Harvey, George: Ossian's Fingal; an Ancient Epic Poem, in Six Books, Rendered into English Verse. London, 1814.

Hayley, William: Poetical Works. 3 vols. Dublin, 178-.

Hemans, Mrs. Felicia [Dorothea; née Browne]: Poetical Works. London and Edinburgh, Gall and Inglis, [n.d.].

Hervey, James: Meditations and Contemplations, 2 vols. in 1. Edinburgh, 1797.

Holmes, Robert: Alfred. An Ode. With Six Sonnets. London, 1778.

Hogg, James: Poems, in *The Works of the Ettrick Shepherd*. Thomas Thomson, ed. London, 1866, Vol. II.

Hood, Thomas: Poetical Works, 2 vols. Little, Brown, 1857.

Howard, Nathaniel: Bickleigh Vale, with Other Poems. York, 1804.

Hunt, James Henry Leigh: Poetical Works. S. Adams Lee, ed., 2 vols. Boston, 1865.

Hurdis, James: The Favorite Village, with an Additional Poem (Now First Published) and a Tragedy. London, 1810.

────── The Village Curate, and Other Poems; Including Some Pieces Now First Published. London, 1810.

Jerningham, Edward: Faldoni and Teresa. London, 1773.

Keate, George: The Alps. A Poem. London, 1763.

Keats, John: Letters. Maurice Buxton Forman, ed., 2 vols. Oxford University Press, 1930.

────── Poetical Works. William T. Arnold, ed., Globe Edition. Macmillan, 1919.

────── See also Colvin, Fausset, Lowell, Edward Thomas, Thorpe, Weller.

Lamb, Charles: Letters, 2 vols. Everyman's Library. Dutton [n.d.].

────── Poems, Plays, and Miscellaneous Essays. Alfred Ainger, ed. New York, 1893.

Landon, Letitia Elizabeth ["L. E. L."]: Poetical Works. William B. Scott, ed. London [n.d.].

────── See also Enfield.

Laurence, Thomas Dawson: Miscellaneous Works. Dublin, 1789.

Leapor, Mary: Poems upon Several Occasions. London, 1748.

Learmont, John: Poems Pastoral, Satirical, Tragic, and Comic. Edinburgh, 1791.

Lee, Richard: Flowers from Sharon; or Original Poems on Divine Subjects. London, 1794.

Lewis, Matthew Gregory: Adelgitha; or, the Fruits of a Single Error. A Tragedy in 5 Acts. London, 1806.

────── The Castle Spectre, 8th ed. London, 1799.

────── Tales of Terror and of Wonder. Introduction by Henry Morley. London, 1887.

Leyden, John: Poetical Works, with Memoir by Thomas Brown. Edinburgh, 1875.

M'Donald, Archibald: Some of Ossian's Lesser Poems, Rendered into Verse; with a Preliminary Discourse, in Answer to Mr. Laing's Critical and Historical Dissertation on the Antiquity of Ossian's Poems. Liverpool, 1805.

Macpherson, James: The Poems of Ossian Translated by James Macpherson, with Notes, and with an Introduction by William Sharp. Edinburgh, 1926.

──── See also Burke, Cameron, John Clark, Davidson, Harold, Harvey, M'Donald, Schnabel, Shackleton, John Smith, Tombo, Van Tieghem, Wilmsen.

[Mathias, T. J.]: The Pursuits of Literature. A Satirical Poem in Four Dialogues. With Notes. London, 1799.

Maturin, Charles Robert: Bertram; or, The Castle of St. Adobrand; a tragedy in 5 Acts. London, 1816.

Merry, Robert: The Pleasures of Memory, and Other Poems, by Samuel Rogers, Esq., to Which is Added The Pains of Memory, by Robert Merry, A.M. New York, 1820.

Milton, John: Poetical Works. David Masson, ed., Globe Edition. Macmillan, 1917.

──── See also Havens.

Montgomery, James: Poetical Works. Collected by himself, 4 vols. London, 1841.

Montgomery, Robert: Satan. A Poem. London, 1830.

──── A Universal Prayer; Death; A Vision of Heaven; and A Vision of Hell, etc. etc. From the 2d London ed. Boston, 1829.

Moore, Thomas: Poetical Works. A. D. Godley, ed., Oxford Edition. 1924.

More, Hannah: Poems, in *Works op. cit.* Vol. I.

Motherwell, William: Poetical Works, 4th ed., greatly enlarged. Boston, 1863.

[Mundy, Francis Noel Clarke]: Poems. Oxford, 1768.

Ogilvie, John: The Day of Judgment. A Poem in two Books, 3d ed. London, 1759.

──── Poems on Several Subjects, 2 vols. in 1. London, 1769.

Opie, Mrs. [Amelia]: Poems. London, 1802.

Parnell, Thomas: Poetical Works. Aldine Edition. London, 1852.

Peacock, Thomas Love: Poems, in *Works*, Halliford Edition. London and New York, 1927, Vol. VI.

──── Rhododaphne; or The Thessalian Spell. London, 1818.

Percy, Thomas: Reliques of Ancient English Poetry. J. V. Prichard, ed., 2 vols. in 1. New York [n.d.].

Pickering, Amelia: The Sorrows of Werter. A Poem. London, 1788.

Pollok, Robert: The Course of Time. A Poem. With an Enlarged Index, a Memoir of the Author, an Introductory Notice, and An Analysis Prefixed to Each Book. Philadelphia, 1864.

Polwhele, Richard: Reminiscences, in Prose and Verse, with the Epistolary Correspondence of Many Distinguished Characters, and Notes and Illustrations, 3 vols. London, 1836.

—— The Unsex'd Females: a Poem, addressed to the Author of The Pursuits of Literature . . . New York, Re-published by William Cobbett, 1800.

Pott, Joseph Holden: Elegies: with Selmane, a Tragedy. London, 1782.

Praed, Winthrop Mackworth: Poems. Derwent Coleridge, ed., 2 vols. London, 1864.

Procter, Bryan Waller ["Barry Cornwall"]: English Songs, and Other Small Poems. Boston, 1844.

—— The Flood in Thessaly, The Girl of Provence, and Other Poems. London, 1823.

—— Marcian Colonna. An Italian Tale with Three Dramatic Scenes and Other Poems. London, 1820.

—— A Sicilian Story, with Other Poems, in The Spirit of Contemporary Poetry. Boston, 1827.

Radcliffe, Ann: The Mysteries of Udolpho. London, 1824.

Reynolds, Frederick: Werter; a Tragedy, in Three Acts. London, 1802.

Richardson, William: Poems and Plays, a New Edition, 2 vols. in 1. Edinburgh, 1805.

Robinson, Mary [Darby]: Poetical Works, Including many Pieces Never before Published, 3 vols. London, 1806.

Robinson, T. P.: Jessy; or, the Forced Vow. A Poem. London, 1785.

Rogers, Samuel: The Pleasures of Memory, with Other Poems. A New Edition. London, 1802.

—— Poetical Works, with Memoir by Edward Bell. Revised ed. London, 1892.

Sayers, Frank: Poems in *Collective Works*. William Taylor of Norwich, ed. Norwich, 1823, Vol. I.

Scott, James: Odes on Several Subjects. Cambridge, 1761.

Scott, Sir Walter: Complete Poetical Works. Horace E. Scudder, ed., Cambridge Edition. Houghton Mifflin, 1900.

Seward, Anna: Poetical Works. Walter Scott, ed. 3 vols. Edinburgh, 1810.

—— See also Ashmun.

Sewell, [Mary]: Poems by Mrs. G. Sewell . . . 3 vols. Egham and Chertsey, 1803.

Shackleton, John: The Poems of Ossian, Originally Translated by James Macpherson, Esq., Attempted in English Verse, 2 vols. in 1. Birmingham, 1817.

Shelley, Percy Bysshe: Complete Works. Ingpen and Peck, editors, Julian Edition, 10 vols. Scribner's, 1927.

———— Poetical Works, Edward Dowden, ed., Globe Edition. Macmillan, 1924.

———— See also Allen, Carpenter, Strong.

Shenstone, William: Poems in *Works,* 2d ed., [Dodsley, ed.] London, 1765, Vol. I.

Smith, Charlotte [Turner]: Elegiac Sonnets, and Other Poems, 2 vols. in 1, 9th ed. London, 1800.

Smith, James and Horace: Rejected Addresses and Other Poems. E. Sargent, ed. New York, 1860.

Smith, Horace: Amarynthus, the Nympholept. London, 1821.

Smith, John: Galic Antiquities: Consisting of a History of the Druids, particularly of those of Calidonia; a Dissertation on the Authenticity of the Poems of Ossian; and a Collection of Ancient Poems, translated from the Galic of Ullin, Ossian Orran, etc., Edinburgh, 1780.

Southey, Robert: Complete Poetical Works. Collected by himself. New York, 1850.

———— Poems. Maurice H. Fitzgerald, ed. Oxford Edition. 1909.

Struthers, John: Poetical Works with Autobiography. 2 vols. London, Edinburgh, and Dublin, 1850.

Swain, Joseph: Redemption. A Poem, in Eight Books. With Memoirs of the Author's Life, 1st American from 5th Edinburgh ed. New York, 1827.

Tannahill, Robert: Poems and Songs, Chiefly in the Scottish Dialect. New York, 1819.

Thelwell, [John]: Poems, Chiefly Written in Retirement. Hereford, 1801.

Tighe, [Mary]: Psyche, with Other Poems. By the Late Mrs. Henry Tighe, 3d ed. London, 1811.

Wallace, George: Prospects from Hills in Fife. Edinburgh, 1796.

Walpole, Horace [4th Earl of Orford]: The Mysterious Mother, a Tragedy. London, 1791.

Warton, Thomas: Poetical Works. Richard Mant, ed., 2 vols. Oxford, 1802.

Webb, F[rancis]: Somerset. A Poem. London, 1811.

Wesley, Charles: Charles Wesley seen in his Finer and Less Familiar Poems. Frederick M. Bird, ed. New York, 1878.

West, Mrs. [Jane]: Miscellaneous Poetry. London, 1786.

Whalley, Thomas Sedgwick: Edwy and Edilda, a Tale, in Five Parts. London Printed: Albany: Reprinted, 1800.

White, Henry Kirke: Remains. Robert Southey, ed., 2 vols. London, 1819.

———— Poems, Letters and Prose Fragments. John Drinkwater, ed. Muses' Library. London and New York [n.d.].

———— Poetical Works of Henry Kirke White and James Grahame [See Grahame].

Whitehouse, John: Poems: Consisting Chiefly of Original Pieces. London, 1787.

Wilson, John ["Christopher North"]: The Isle of Palms, and Other Poems. New York, 1812.

Woodcock, Mrs. Henry: Laura, a Tale. London, 1820.

Wordsworth, William: Complete Poetical Works. With an Introduction by John Morley, Globe Edition. Macmillan, 1924.

Woty, William: Blossoms of Helicon. London, 1763.

[Woty, William]: The Shrubs of Parnassus. Consisting of a Variety of Poetical Essays, Moral and Comic, by J. Copywell, of Lincoln's Inn, Esq. London, 1760.

Yearsley, Ann: Poems on Several Occasions, 3d ed. London, 1785.

———— Poems on Various Subjects. London, 1787.

Young, Edward: Poetical Works, 2 vols., British Poets Series. Little, Brown 1854.

———— See also H. H. Clark, W. Thomas, P. Van Tieghem.

INDEX

Anonymous poems and poems signed with initials or fanciful names are listed by title; otherwise the listing is by author only. Where an author or poem has been quoted or paraphrased without being named, the reference has been enclosed in parentheses. All numbers above 347 refer to the notes.